R.J. HENDERSON

Dr. W.F.T. HAULTAIN

F. A. WRIGHT

B. R. TOD
CAPTAIN

J. A. WRIGHT

G. P. S. MACPHERSON

R. K. CUTHBERTSON
Secretary.

The Accies

THE
ACCIES

THE CRADLE OF
SCOTTISH RUGBY

DAVID BARNES

BIRLINN

First published in 2008 by
Birlinn Limited
West Newington House
10 Newington Road
Edinburgh
EH9 1QS

www.birlinn.co.uk

Trade Edition ISBN13: 978 1 84158 771 4
Limited Edition ISBN13: 1 84158 772 1

British Library Cataloguing-in-Publication Data
A catalogue record for this book is available from the British Library.

Typeset by Iolaire Typesetting, Newtonmore
Printed and bound in Slovenia by arrangement with Associated Agencies, Oxford

1857

ACKNOWLEDGMENTS

THE ACADEMICAL FOOTBALL CLUB, to use its original name, is the oldest rugby club in Britain and the second oldest in the world, behind Trinity College in Dublin. Over the years a handful of other clubs have claimed seniority on these shores, but none have been able to convincingly back this up.

Perhaps the most worthy rival for this distinction is Liverpool Football Club (now Liverpool St Helens FC after merging with another club in 1919). J.R.A. Daglish, who wrote a history of the club on the occasion of its 125 anniversary in 1982, says that the club's first game was on 19 December 1857, which was a week before the Academicals played their first match against an Edinburgh University side. However, the game in Liverpool was between boys from Rugby School and anyone else who had turned up, so to state that 'the Liverpool Football Club was there and then formed' seems to be quite a leap of faith. There is no record of a club captain until 1862, and no record of fixtures and results until 1867. The claim is based on letters written by several men involved in that first game more than 50 years after the event.

There are no such gaps in the long and distinguished history of the Academical Football Club, and I am extremely grateful to the authors of the *Centenary History* (published in 1958) which was particularly valuable when trying to piece together these early years.

When Ralph Lutton first asked me if I was interested in writing a new EAFC history as part of the club's 150th anniversary celebrations it seemed like a fun project which would keep me busy on those rare days when there is no news to report in Scottish rugby. I soon discovered that I was taking on far more than I had anticipated.

I would say it has been an interesting, surprisingly time-consuming, but ultimately rewarding experience. My family would say it has been a disaster, which has turned our home lives into a shambles and our social lives into a distant memory. The truth is probably somewhere in the middle.

I have gone way over the required word count, way past several deadlines, and pushed to the limit the patience of those who have helped me pull this book together. And I have no-one to blame but myself – I became too embroiled in the subject matter.

Having said that, it was hard not to be sucked in – this is such an appealing story filled with such fascinating characters. If you have an interest in the history of Scottish rugby, then you need to know the story of this great club. It has been involved in all the major moments.

I have had a lot of help from a lot of different people, but four individuals in particular deserve a special note of thanks:

Ralph Lutton has backed me all the way, even on those frequent occasions when it must have looked as if his faith was misplaced.

Peter Burns has bent over backwards to accommodate me, but is far too polite and professional to have ever let his frustrations get the better of him. He has done a lot of work in organising the logistics and technicalities of turning a couple hundred odd pages of rambling text into something coherent (I hope!) and presentable.

Ian Barnes was a bit miffed that Jim Renwick's biography (written by his son about his best friend) only mentioned him in passing a handful of times. I have tried to give him a fairer representation this time, but have probably still underestimated his contribution to the club during the last six years. He has spent a lot of time reading through this text and pointing out, in his own inimitable way, exactly where I have gone wrong.

Johanne Simpson has, with the exception of one particularly spectacular wobbly, been very patient and supportive.

Others who have kindly imparted wit, wisdom and/or some fascinating memorabilia include: Rodger Arneil, Rob Blair, B.J. Boyd, Martin Burns, Simon Burns, Finlay Calder, Greg Campbell, Rob Cowie, George Flint, Alan Fyfe, Brian Hay-Smith, Elgar Hopkins, Charlie Jackson, Graham Law, Tony Hamilton, Euan Macfie, Finlay McPherson, Malcolm McVie, Duncan Mennie, Billy Menzies, George Menzies, Ollie Miller, Vincent O'Donoghue, David Parker, Jason Parrott, John Paterson, Keith Paterson-Brown, Stuart Paterson, Jeremy Richardson, Rowan Shepherd, Ronnie Sloan, David Sole, Frank Spratt, Dan Teague, Stuart Thyne, John White, John Wright, Jake Young, Des from The Rockville Hotel and the staff at the SRU library.

My thanks go to you all – and to anyone else I might have overlooked.

I have tried to avoid making this book a narrative of the trials and tribulations of the club's 1st XVs – this club has always been about much more than that – however, the vastness of the subject makes it inevitable that certain moments and certain themes will be overlooked. I apologise in advance for those gaps in this book deserving of a mention. All I can say is that I have tried to be as comprehensive as possible.

This book is dedicated to all those who have pulled on an Academicals jersey during the last 150 years. Regardless of whether they represented the 1st XV or the 7th XV, they have each contributed in their own small way to the fabric of a great club.

Here's to the next 150 years . . .

David Barnes
September 2008

THERE IS SOMETHING ABOUT Raeburn Place and the blue and white of the Academy and the Accies that runs deep in the Blair blood.

There is a bench that sits outside the changing rooms that bears my grandfather's name (a former player from the school), gifted to the club by my father, also a former pupil, who captained Accies during the 1970s. My brothers and I all played for the school and three of us have gone on to play for Accies.

I was at the Edinburgh Academy for 13 years (15 if you count the two years I spent at the nursery) and the very foundations of my rugby career were laid on the wide expanses of Newfield and Raeburn Place. The guidance that I received there from school and club coaches, particularly Gary Bowe, have remained with me ever since.

In the early years I played for the school on Saturdays and the club minis on Sundays until committing myself to playing exclusively for the school when I was in my teens. One of my first rugby memories, however, is of being a ball-boy down

at Raeburn Place for the title-deciding match between Accies and Melrose in 1993. Both sides were filled with Scotland internationalists and I can still recall with utmost clarity the electrifying atmosphere, with the crowd 9 or 10 deep all the way around the pitch – very similar in size to the crowd at the Barbarians game at Raeburn Place in April 2008. While Accies lost the match at the death, the most fevered part of the afternoon (for me) was when two balls were kicked over the wall onto North Park Terrace in quick succession. I remember being boosted over the wall and then running around in a panic trying to retrieve the first ball from under a car and the second from a garden while the crowd and the players brayed for me to hurry up – which, I suppose in retrospect, was good practice for dealing with crowd abuse later in my career!

Upon leaving school I headed to Durham University where I was fortunate enough to have my lectures finish for the week on a Thursday afternoon. Having learned of this timetabling there was never any doubt about where I would play my rugby. Every Thursday I would leave the lecture theatre with my bag of kit and hop on a train to Edinburgh, making it up to Raeburn Place just in time for the start of the training session, staying over at my parents' house for the weekend and turning out for the club on the Saturday.

I remember the late Colin Mackay with great fondness during these years at Accies. He was always very understanding about the commitments that I had both to my degree and to the Scottish Institute of Sport, and he took the time after each match to write down the things that I did well and the things that he thought I needed to work on – an act that I appreciated hugely at the time and which I have never forgotten.

While I only played at Accies for two seasons, the club still holds a very dear place in my heart and I come down to watch as often as I can to catch up with family and friends and to keep a careful eye on the progress of my younger brothers. There is something about the place that draws you back, a familiarity and warmth that epitomises everything that is great about the club game in Scotland. I am sure that when the new clubhouse is finished it is going to be a spectacular venue and will make Raeburn Place an even greater attraction for players and spectators. Having said this, however, I will always hold the memory of the old pavilion and the Ben Tod Lounge with great affection. In particular I remember the after-match beers following my debut game. The floodlights were turned on and, shorn of all clothing save for a tackle-suit (no pun intended), I had to run lengths of the pitch hitting rucking shields and downing pints while roars of encouragement echoed from the BTL windows. It was some introduction to the club, but it is also a testament to the fun that always went with playing for Accies.

The club has always been full of characters who love their rugby, love the camaraderie of the team game, and who love to have fun. While striking a balance between all-out enjoyment and playing the game seriously has sometimes been a fine one that has cost the club strong league positions from time to time, it is something that epitomises my memories of playing there. One archetypal story which always springs to mind is of our trip to the Madrid Sevens in 2000. Accies took a fairly strong team out to Madrid that year to a tournament with a real mixed-bag of quality and we soon realised that we had quite a strong chance of doing well in it. Arriving late on the Friday afternoon we began to hit a few bars and at around 10 o'clock Jason Parrott (the self-nominated captain) got us all together and told us to 'screw the nut' – that we had a big tournament starting early the next day and that we had to be on form. So, a few more beers were drunk and then the party began to make its way back to the hotel in dribs and drabs.

The following morning, everyone got up for breakfast before the first tie and just before we were about to leave for the ground we realised that someone was missing – *El Capitano* Squawker. As one of the youngest players on tour, I was sent to retrieve a key from reception to check if he was in his room. A few minutes later I was standing over Jason who was passed out on his bed, still in his kilt and tour polo! Rousing him out of his slumber, I was given a croaked explanation that he had been out, in true 'continental style', until 7 a.m. with the tournament organiser and would follow us onto the ground shortly. A couple of games into the tournament, Jason rocked up looking more than a little jaded but somehow managed to muster enough energy to help contribute to the team's push to the semi-final, where we were eventually knocked out of the competition.

This trip was just one of the many highlights I enjoyed, and still enjoy, with the Accies. Others include winning against our local rivals Stewart's-Melville FP to secure promotion to Premier Two in 2000 and winning the BT Shield Final at Murrayfield in 2001. Seeing so many friends involved in the Cup Final at the same venue in 2007 (albeit on the losing side) and in achieving promotion back to Premier One that year has been fantastic, and I have been enormously proud to see both my younger brothers, David and Alex, follow my father and me in pulling on the 1st team shirt in recent seasons. This is our club and I am honoured to be part of such a magnificent rugby legacy – one that is sure to continue for many years to come.

Mike Blair
September 2008

I FEEL INCREDIBLY fortunate that when I came back north from Bath during the summer of 1987 I chose to play my club rugby with the Edinburgh Academicals. From the moment I walked through the gate at Raeburn Place for my first pre-season training session, I knew that it was a place where I could be very happy.

The big things for me were: the sense of family, the openness, the warmth, and the hand of friendship which was extended by everyone at the club. Jane and I were made to feel like we had come home, even though we had no previous connections with either the club or the school. It was clear from the start that the Academicals had a strong grip of the values which make this game of rugby football great. I'm not saying this was unique to Raeburn Place, but it was certainly something which we really appreciated.

During my time at school at Glenalmond I had played alongside and against several great characters who were now strut-

ting their stuff in Stockbridge – people like Rod Mitchell, Jamie Paton, Johnnie Sutton, Phil Heaney – and that was probably the main reason why I joined. I soon made many, many more friends at the club, including exceptional individuals such as George Menzies, who I will always a remember sweeping out the changing rooms when he should have been upstairs in the bar entertaining the opposition committee. I still can't imagine the president of any other club doing this. He's a lovely guy, and still pitches in around Raeburn Place.

It was a great time to be playing rugby in

Scotland. The national team were going well, interest in the game was sky high, and at Raeburn Place we managed to strike a balance between enjoying ourselves in the way that amateur players are entitled to whilst also being deadly serious about becoming the best team we could possibly be.

I will always have particularly fond memories of social events such as the Caribbean Nights and the Christmas Balls. They were phenomenal evenings with everyone from all the other clubs in Edinburgh there.

But we also worked hard. I think we did get far more professional and develop a far more competitive mentality as time progressed. When I came to Raeburn Place they were just holding onto their place in the first division by the skin of their teeth, but I could see that in guys like the Richardson brothers there was a hardcore of players at the club with a winning mentality, and by the time I had finished we were one of the top teams in Scotland. It was quite satisfying that I had been a part of that transformation in the team.

Of course it is a regret that we didn't quite achieve the holy grail of a league championship trophy. While it doesn't keep me awake at night I do feel we probably deserved to win it some stage. We had some truly exceptional players in the squad during this period.

Dave McIvor was as mad as a hatter but a great servant to the club, and I was delighted when he was eventually capped for Scotland because he was a real grafter who you could always count on to give 110 per cent. Jeremy Richardson should also have got a lot more caps than he did such was his commitment to the cause and willingness to do the 'hard yards' and unsung work. John Allan gave two years of sterling service and with people like Rob Wainwright, Andy Adamson, Dave Leckie and Rod Mitchell also there or thereabouts, I always felt we had a pack of forwards who could dominate any team they came up against.

We also had a pretty handy back division. Rowan Shepherd, Brian Hay-Smith, Simon Burns and Chris Simmers were all very talented – if mercurial – players and Alec Moore was a fantastic finisher: as he proved against John Kirwan in New Zealand in 1990, he was capable of beating anyone in the world in a one-on-one situation.

Perhaps our major short-coming was that we struggled for strength in depth. At Bath we had a system whereby they only ran three teams, with the 3rd XV more of a social side, and if changes to the top two teams needed to be made the coaches would phone up one of the junior cubs we were linked with and get a player from there. All the clubs supported the set-up so it worked really well, and it is interesting to see that this is the way that Accies is moving with its associations with Trinity Academicals, Broughton and Edinburgh University.

As an adopted Accie it is great to see the club back where it belongs, in the top flight of Scottish club rugby. I don't get down to Raeburn Place too much these days, but the first result I always look for in the Sunday papers is the Accies score. It still means a lot to me, and it always will. It is that sort of club, once you have caught the bug you are infected for life.

The Accies has been written to celebrate the 150th anniversary of a great Scottish, and indeed global, sporting institution. Over the years the club has played a crucial role in shaping the wonderful game of rugby football, and its membership has included many of the most remarkable characters from modern Scottish history. This promises to be a fascinating and entertaining read, and a worthy addition to any true rugby fan's library. Enjoy.

David Sole
September 2008

CHAPTER ONE

*Something to try the muscles of men's bodies and the endurance of their hearts
and make them rejoice in their strength.*

Thomas Hughes in *Tom Brown's Schooldays*, 1857

THE ROOTS OF THE GAME now known as rugby can be traced at least as far back as the days of the Roman Empire, when soldiers played a sport called *harpastum*, derived from the Greek word for 'snatch'. This involved two teams on a rectangular pitch trying to force a small hard ball over their opponents' end line. Running with the ball, passing or throwing the ball and forms of tackling were all allowed, meaning that the basic elements of the game as we understand it today were already in place back then.

Theories vary as to when this embryonic form of rugby was introduced to Britain. Henri Garcia, in his comprehensive work *La Fabuleuse Histoire du Rugby*, argues that *harpastum* was the basis of the Brittany-Norman game of *La Soule*, and he argues that since none of the earlier European invaders left any records of ball games being played in Britain, it must have been introduced to this country after the Norman Conquest in 1066.

But Sandy Thorburn, in *The History of Scottish Rugby*, proposes an alternative theory. He points out that Garcia has ignored the 400 or so years from around 42AD to around 410AD in which Britain was under Roman occupation, and argues that there is a significant correlation between towns which are known to have a tradition of playing ball games and their close proximity to Roman garrisons, settlements and transport routes. The major sticking point in Thorburn's theory is the lack of any first-hand accounts of ball games being played during the Roman occupation, or the 600 years which followed for that matter. However, Thorburn suggests that the tumultuous nature of this period, during which time Britain endured a succession of invasions from Europe, might go some way to explaining this anomaly. Contemporary chroniclers would surely have considered such sport a triviality during these troubled times, he reasons.

Either way, the first written record of football being played in Britain comes from 1175, when William Fitzstephen, a London-born monk of Canterbury, wrote a history of London in which he talks about the youths of the town celebrating Shrove Tuesday by taking part in games with a ball and the older men of the town coming on horseback to watch these matches.

> The morning was spent in cock-fighting and other boyish pastimes. Then, after dinner, all the youth of the city proceeded to a level piece of ground just outside the town for the famous game of ball. The students of every different branch of study had their own ball as did the various tradesmen. The older men, the fathers and the men of property, arrived on horseback to watch the contests and, in their own way, shared the sport of the young men. These elders were filled with excitement at seeing so much vigorous exercise and participated, vicariously, in the pleasures of unrestrained youth.

La *soule*, en Basse-Normandie.
D'après un croquis de M. J. L. de Condé.

La *soule*, en Basse-Normandie. D'après un croquis de M. J. L. de Condé.

From then on there is a fairly regular chain of documentary evidence relating to ball games being played throughout the country – and at various times meeting with the disapproval of either the crown, the church or the local civic authorities, and sometimes all three at the same time. Among the reasons for these groups objecting to ball games include the damage to property (which often occurred when the games were played along narrow town streets), the desecration of the Sabbath by the players (particularly in Calvinist Scotland) and the fact that it interfered with the practising of archery and other more worthwhile warlike crafts.

Ball games were often played on what we would now call holidays but might more accurately be described as festival or fair days, such as Candlemas or Shrove Tuesday. Sandy Thorburn relates an amusing and enlightening story about one of these 'Fair Day' matches, which took place in the Scottish Borders.

It appears that the Ettrick and Yarrow shepherds occupied that day [Candlemas] with games which included a football match. One well-recorded game took place in 1815 outside Selkirk at Carterhaugh on the Duke of Buccleuch's estate at Bowhill. Here the two sets of shepherds combined to play against townsmen from the whole Border region, and one estimate reckons that about 750 played before a great crowd which included most of the local noblemen and gentry. The moving spirit seems to have been Sir Walter Scott with the support of the Duke of Buccleuch and the Earl of Home. The Hawick players, who included 'Wemyss, the best thrower of a stone or ball in the Borders', walked over early and on reaching Selkirk were treated to a dram each . . . a gesture which cost the Burgh of Selkirk about 2 gallons of whisky costing £1.11s.4d. The proceedings were begun by Sir Walter's son who, suitably attired and mounted, carried the ancient Buccleuch standard [still to be seen in Bowhill] round the field whereafter the Duke started play by throwing the ball into the centre of the field. The ball was small, leather-skinned and packed with wool so the game was more handball than football.

This game is very well recorded in several papers contributed to the transactions of the Hawick Archaeological Society and here we note an incident which confirms that handling and passing of the ball was permitted. During the first session a shepherd, Walter Laidlaw, lifted the ball and threw it wide of the mass of players to William Riddell, a noted runner who was ready and tripped. He would have hailed the ba' had he not been ridden down by a mounted spectator whose actions proved so unacceptable that he found it prudent to gallop from the scene.

Great fun, but by this point it seems the popularity of these sorts of ball games throughout Britain was on the wane – with the exception of a few 'Fair Day' matches, some of which have survived in something close to their traditional form to the current day (for example at Ancrum, Denholm, Duns, Hobkirk and Jedburgh in the Scottish Borders, as well as in such diverse settings as Orkney to the north of Scotland and St Ives in Cornwall). The chief factor behind this decline in popularity of ball games must surely have been the industrial revolution, which left the working classes with neither the time nor energy to spare for fun and games.

As Thorburn points out:

Indeed the game might well have disappeared had it not been for many years an accepted recreation in schools and universities. In particular the schools during the next century not only kept the game alive but developed it, codified it and eventually through their former pupils saw it established as a robust exercise acceptable to men of their professional and social status.

He adds:

This last point is worth noting for it was during the 1800s that the public schools and universities produced a new class of men who, well endowed and well educated, moved as a matter of course into the higher circles of their professions and . . . it was men of such background and authority who were to govern the game during its early years.

The Edinburgh Academy, and particularly the Academicals club it spawned, would play a crucial role in the game's early development.

CHAPTER TWO

Edinburgh is one of the most beautiful of the world's cities, a place of splendour whose craggy skyline brings together two entirely different worlds. To the south of its main thoroughfare, Princes Street, the Castle with the towering medieval tenements and spires of the old town within its protection; to the north, the cool elegance of Georgian architecture blessed by the Smile of Reason: it is a city of bewildering contrasts.

Trevor Royle in *Precipitous City*, 1980

FOR THOSE FROM THE RIGHT background, early nineteenth-century Edinburgh was a city of endless possibilities.

A decade spent fighting shoulder to shoulder against Napoleon's France had slowly engendered a degree of mutual respect between the Scots and the English and finally expunged the fractious memories of the 1707 Union of the Parliaments. The conciliatory process was much abetted by King George IV's visit to Edinburgh in the summer of 1822. This first visit to Scotland by a reigning monarch in nearly 200 years was orchestrated by Sir Walter Scott who in 1815 had been the force behind the great Candlemas match between the Ettrick and Yarrow shepherds at Bowhill and who would later be one of the founding fathers of the Edinburgh Academy. The visit was awash with mock Highland pageantry and biscuit-tin nationalism, but it was also emblematic of an evolving appreciation of the Union on both sides of Hadrian's Wall. With the industrial revolution in full flow, many Scots began moving into influential positions in government, the armed forces and in the services of the Honourable East India Company; and Edinburgh came to be known as the 'Athens of the North', reflecting not only the architectural qualities but also the emergence of a social and economic elite which provided the backbone to the city's status as a centre of literary, medical and legal excellence.

However, there was another, less appealing, side to Edinburgh's growth during this period, with chronic overcrowding becoming a major problem. The city had become a magnet for the hard-pressed rural masses, and the narrow confines of the Royal Mile became swamped by too many people with not enough money.

While the wealthier elements of Scotland's other cities had adapted to this process of urbanisation by building outwards – with the merchants of Glasgow erecting their luxurious mansions in the West End, the middle-class Aberdonians building their fine villas beyond the Den Burn, and the prosperous Dundee families decamping to Newport on the south bank of the Firth of Tay – it was impossible for Edinburgh to follow suit. The city was perched precariously atop its rocky ridge between the Castle at one end and the Palace of Holyroodhouse at the other, and the thought of breaching the Nor Loch, where Princes Street Gardens now lie, was beyond the imagination of the town council at that time. So Edinburgh built upwards instead. Towering tenements grew and grew, with citizens of all class and type piled one on top of another. The poor would occupy the cellars and the attics, with noblemen, lawyers, ministers and doctors living in the floors between.

It was a crazy situation, and the inevitable could not be put off forever. Eventually the civic authorities were persuaded that it was safe to build a bridge connecting the Old Town with the lands to the north of the water-filled valley which had provided Edinburgh with centuries of protection. The North Bridge was completed in 1772, and almost immediately the town's wealthier citizens began building grand houses behind the line of what is now Princes Street. Within 30 years the Nor' Loch had been drained, with another link between the Old Town and the rapidly expanding New Town being created when the rubble left over from the multifarious building works going on in the city at that time was used to create the Mound.

Magnus Magnusson, in *The Clacken and the Slate: The Story of Edinburgh Academy*, discusses the impact of this long-overdue expansion of the city.

By 1823 the elegant lines of the New Town had spread from Queen Street down to Great King Street. By 1831 the population of the New Town had risen to 40,000 out of a total Edinburgh and Leith population of 162,000. The Old Town residences had been abandoned to the poorer folk, and in 1823 there were still around 50,000 people crowded into the old cellars and attics and the deserted flats of the noblemen. The overcrowding and filth were now worse than ever, but the judges and lawyers and merchants who now enjoyed more gracious living in the Georgian terraces of the New Town were far from being insulated from the discomforts they had left behind in the Old Town. The Old Town was still the heart of Edinburgh. The courts, the High Kirk, the university, the offices and the markets were all still there. Every day the occupants of New Town and Old met in one great noisy throng, now made all the more hazardous by the increased traffic of coaches and carriages hurrying across the bridges that linked the two sections of the city.

Into this disagreeable melee the New Town dwellers had to send their children to be educated at the High School on the far side of the High Street, beyond Cowgate, at the bottom of Infirmary Street. These youngsters had to dodge the carriages, rub shoulders with the destitute, breathe the fetid air of the close-mouths, and make their way homewards on winter evenings through darkened wynds where foot-pads and other perils might lurk. No wonder that Cockburn and Horner [the driving forces behind the foundation of the Edinburgh Academy] wanted a new school on their own side of the tracks . . .

However, that hazardous trip was not the main reason for the push towards building a new school in the New Town. Concerns about the quality of education provided by the High School, specifically in regard to Scotland's role within Britain's rapidly spreading empire, was an even bigger issue.

As Magnusson explains:

They [Edinburgh's New Town dwellers] were well aware of the changes that were taking place in many Scottish schools to meet the demands of the Industrial Revolution, but they were afraid that the new trend would confine Scots to a second-class position in British affairs. They knew that the average Scot was better educated than the average Englishman, and that a far higher proportion of Scots than English attended University. This was all very well for turning out droves of advocates, village dominies, doctors, and unheard-of poets and philosophers; but for those wanting to make a real mark in British scholarship, there was an undoubted advantage in having taken a degree at Oxford or Cambridge, where Latin and Greek were compulsory as entrance qualifications. This meant competing with the only people who aspired to that standard of education in England, the products of six elite Public Schools – Eton, Harrow, Charterhouse, Winchester, Westminster or Rugby, where boys were put through an intensive process of specialisation in Latin and Greek until the age of eighteen or nineteen; whereas Scottish boys were attending university at Edinburgh, Glasgow, St Andrews or Aberdeen at the age of fourteen or fifteen, or even as young as twelve.

Founded in 1578, the High School of Edinburgh provided its pupils with a classical education, but it was felt that greater provision was needed for the teaching of Greek, to compete with England's top public schools. Furthermore, by 1820 the school was hopelessly overcrowded, despite having moved into a new building in 1777. The roll had reached 890, which made it probably the largest school in Britain at that time. These pupils were divided among four masters and a rector, whose class in 1823 reached an all-time record of 257. Clearly this was an environment ill-suited to getting the best out of Edinburgh's next generation of high-achievers. Wealthy Scotsmen were already sending their sons to English boarding schools or to be tutored by English dons. Other children were being enrolled at private seminaries such as Mr Langhorne's small private preparatory school at Stoney Hill in Musselburgh, which was expanding at such a rate that it had to move to Loretto House in 1827.

This was the situation which Henry Cockburn and Leonard Horner were pondering during a walk on the Pentland Hills in late spring 1822, when they made the decision to found the Edinburgh Academy. Keen to arrest the movement away from the city by Edinburgh's finest youngsters, they came up with a plan to build a school situated in the New Town, with smaller classes than the High School and a greater emphasis on the teaching of Latin and, particularly, Greek.

They recruited the Tory John Russell – to offset resistance to a scheme which was being proposed by two members of the opposition Whig party – and set about persuading more leading members of Edinburgh society as to the merits of their scheme. Sir Walter Scott, another staunch Tory, 'eagerly' promised his support, as did 25 other eminent men who were prepared to become immediate contributors to the new school.

Within two months a plan had been produced which required £12,000 to be raised by the issue of 240 shares at £50 each. However, protracted negotiations

with the Town Council, who wanted to build the school themselves but had neither the resources nor the vision to do so successfully, delayed the school's opening until October 1824.

Inside the Foundation Stone of the Academy there are three bottles filled with various contemporary documents, maps and plans. There is also a lead casket with the names of the first directors of the school and its architect, Mr William Burn, incised on one side. On the other side of the casket is a Latin inscription, which translated into English reads:

> To meet the needs of the ever-growing number of parents in the city of Edinburgh who have long been clamouring for an ampler place than was previously available, where the rising generation could receive a liberal education, certain citizens, having contributed the necessary money, made arrangements for the construction of this building dedicated to the teaching of the young . . .

There had been plenty of opposition to this ambitious venture, principally related to the view that this represented a move away from the democratic traditions of the Scottish education system. Opponents of the new school argued that it would create a two-tier system whereby the city's wealthiest families sent their children to the Edinburgh Academy, leaving the High School to accommodate the rest. Some critics even went so far as to suggest that snobbery was the driving force behind the creation of the new school, with one letter to *The Scotsman* newspaper stating that:

> . . . it derives a very powerful support from the aristocratic feelings of many of the papas and mamas whose hearts sicken at the thought of Master Tommy being obliged to trudge through dirty streets jostled by all sorts of low and crude people, triumphed over in school by the son of the shoemaker and beaten when out of it by the son of the butcher, and associating with vulgar companions.

However, the school's founders were insistent that educational standards were the sole motivation behind the creation of the new school. They did not object to their sons sitting side by side with the sons of shoemakers, but pointed out that the High School was catering for so many needs that the standard of classical education was being compromised.

The reality was probably somewhere in between. Certainly, *The Edinburgh Academy Register 1824–1914* indicates that a large proportion of the school's initial intake came from the upper and professional classes; however, that was not a hard and fast rule, for the Dux of the Academy in 1853, was George R. Luke, who was the son of a Stockbridge master baker.

Whatever the merits were of the arguments for and against the building of this new school, it is clear that the foundation of the Edinburgh Academy allowed both the environment and the mechanism through which Scotland's oldest rugby club was to germinate. It also played a central role in the development of the game we now call rugby from a disorganised rammy with only a vague set of recognised rules, into a fully codified sport with governing bodies and properly established teams.

Previously, the game had been regarded as a worthy pursuit for Edinburgh schoolboys who needed some kind of diversion from their studies, but not the sort of activity which adults should be involved in. Now a new breed of young men was being honed in the city – brought up to question such old-fashioned conventions, they also tended to have the spare time and money needed for the participation in such idle pursuits as chasing a pig's bladder around a field.

CHAPTER THREE

So far as I know, Rugby football was introduced into Scotland in 1855 by a small knot of men connected with the Edinburgh Academy. Mr Alexander Crombie, of Thornton Castle, may fairly be said to be the father of the game in Scotland, for he was the chairman and organiser of the club. The hon. Secretary was William Blackwood, the well known publisher. The former learnt to play at Durham Grammar School.

Hely Hutchison Almond,
quoted in *Football: The Rugby Union Game* by Rev. F. Marshall
1892

ANY EFFORT TO CHART the development of the game of rugby will inevitably feature William Webb Ellis, who is often credited with inventing the game at Rugby School in 1823.

However, it has been argued that this story was apocryphal. The only source is Matthew Bloxham, a local antiquarian and former pupil of Rugby, whose brothers also attended the school and were probably contemporaries of Webb Ellis. In 1876, Bloxham wrote in the *Meteor*, the Rugby School magazine, that until he left the school in 1821, football and not handball was the pupils' game of choice and that the switch from a kicking to handling game had taken place in the second half of 1823, when Webb Ellis first picked up the ball and ran. This was written four years after Webb Ellis' death, which meant the man at the centre of the controversy was never able to confirm or deny the story.

In December of 1880, in another letter to the *Meteor*, Bloxham elaborated on his version of events:

A boy of the name Ellis – William Webb Ellis – a town boy and a foundationer . . . whilst playing Bigside at football in that half-year [1823], caught the ball in his arms. This being so, according to the then rules, he ought to have retired back as far as he pleased, without parting with the ball, for the combatants on the opposite side could only advance to the spot where he had caught the ball, and were unable to rush forward till he had either punted it or had placed it for some one else to kick, for it was by means of these placed kicks that most of the goals were in those days kicked, but the moment the ball touched the ground the opposite side might rush on. Ellis, for the first time, disregarded this rule, and on catching the ball, instead of retiring backwards, rushed forwards with the ball in his hands towards the opposite goal, with what result as to the game I know not, neither do I know how this infringement of a well-known rule was followed up, or when it became, as it is now, a standing rule.

The lack of supporting evidence to Bloxham's story soon gave rise to scepticism over Webb Ellis's role in the game's inception. By the mid 1890s the controversy over the origins of the handling game at Rugby School had reached such a level that it was decided that a group of Old Rugbeians should conduct an inquiry into the matter, and in 1897 this committee, having gathered evidence from a number of former pupils, produced a pamphlet stating the case as they saw it.

That at some date between 1820 and 1830 the innovation was introduced of running with the ball and that was, in all probability, done in the latter half of 1823 by Mr. W. Webb Ellis. To this we would add that the innovation was regarded as of doubtful legality for some time, and only gradually became accepted as part of the game but obtained customary status between 1830 and 1840 and was duly legalized first in 1841–42.

Jennifer Macrory, in her 1991 book *Running with the Ball: The Birth of Rugby Football*, says that it had never been the intention of the Old Rugbeian Society to lionise Ellis – on the contrary, he was more of an anti-hero than anything else. According to Macrory, the main purpose of their work had been to correct the suggestion that the Rugby game was the lone example of 'primitive' football surviving in a school, and once this objective had been achieved they set about constructing an account of how and why the carrying game developed.

Much of the confusion over Webb Ellis' role can perhaps be attributed to the wording of the plaque on the Close at Rugby School. Erected in 1900, the plaque was meant to express their understandable pride in the game which had developed there, but instead created a myth. The committee's findings about the gradual acceptance of the carrying game had been overlooked and the 'Big Bang' story was born.

THIS STONE
COMMEMORATES THE EXPLOIT OF
WILLIAM WEBB ELLIS
WHO WITH A FINE DISREGARD FOR THE RULES OF FOOTBALL
AS PLAYED IN HIS TIME
FIRST TOOK THE BALL IN HIS ARMS AND RAN WITH IT
THUS ORIGINATING THE DISTINCTIVE FEATURE OF
THE RUGBY GAME
A.D. 1823

It did not take long for the myth to become firmly embedded, as described by Harry Stevenson (one of the most intuitively gifted sportsmen ever to play for the Academicals in the late 1880s and early 1890s) in a letter to *The Scotsman* newspaper in November 1937, in which he wrote:

> Many years ago when I had occasion to hunt for the origins of rugby, I discovered that the High School [of Edinburgh] played a carrying game round about 1810. This fact I mentioned to some of my old English football friends and others when we gathered at Rugby in 1923 as representatives of the carrying game to help celebrate the centenary – so called. When told that they had given the name 'rugby' to the game but they certainly did not invent it as it had been played in Scotland for unknown years before 1823, and by the High School about 1810, some of them were very annoyed.

We might not know the intricate details of how the game was played at other schools in 1823, or what exactly the rules were in the various festival day games which had taken place in towns and villages the length and breadth of the country for many years previously, but we are pretty certain that players had run with the ball before. The fact that it took approximately 23 more years before three pupils at Rugby School wrote down the rules as they understood them for the first time, and 48 more years before a uniform set of rules was recognised nationwide, surely undermines the suggestion that Webb Ellis changed the nature of the game in one single afternoon.

As Sandy Thorburn points out:

What Rugby School did was produce the first set of printed rules and they must be given credit for that. But the game that they played had been part of the fabric of the British Isles and Western Europe for centuries. It certainly was not invented at Rugby School by William Webb Ellis or anybody else.

It seems that ball games were played at the Edinburgh Academy from its earliest days. We know that even during the planning stages, it was anticipated that pupils would play ball games in the school's spacious playground during recesses. During the summer of 1824, when the new school building was in its final stages of completion, the directors spoke about the possibility of building a wall to serve as bounds for the playing of ball-games against, but it was decided that the cost (£600 or £800) was prohibitive, and settled instead for a railing to be erected to close off the steep bank at the north end of the playground (Magnusson).

The influence of a master named Thomas Harvey (who joined the school in 1847 and was often commended for joining pupils in their games) appears to have had a major impact in terms of encouraging ball games to become more formalised. And the opening of Raeburn Place as a playing field for the Academy in 1854 reinforces the impression that the penchant for organised sport at the school was gaining momentum. However, the arrival in Edinburgh of the brothers Alexander and Francis Crombie in 1853 was surely the key moment in this process.

The brothers had been pupils at Durham Grammar School (as it was then known), where the rules according to Rugby School had already been adopted. Alexander, or 'Joe' as he was generally called, came north in December 1853 to study law at Edinburgh University; with Francis, who was two years younger, following six months later and attending the Edinburgh Academy from 1854 to 1856.

Francis became the Academy's first Captain of Football in 1855–56, while Alexander fell into the habit of joining former pupils of the school in informal matches with current pupils at Raeburn Place. It is believed that it was around about this time that the Rugby School rules were introduced – although there is some dispute about when exactly this happened.

R.J. Phillips, in *The Story of Scottish Rugby*, says it was in 1851, but gives no authority for his assertion. Meanwhile, Hely-Hutchinson Almond thought that it was 1855 and he was well placed to know the facts of this case, having been an assistant master at Loretto in 1857–58 and at Merchiston in 1858–62, before playing a crucial role in the early development of the game in Scotland during his long tenure as headmaster of Loretto from 1862 to 1902.

When the Edinburgh Academical Football Club was set up in January 1858, the elder Crombie brother was elected the club's first captain, an office he would hold for eight seasons in total. He then served as president of the club between 1880 and 1882.

He was also a keen cricketer. Good enough to be described in *The Scotsman* as 'the best fast bowler in Edinburgh', and later served as secretary of the Academicals Cricket Club.

He remained an enthusiastic supporter of the Academicals throughout the remainder of his life. After his death in London on 13 June 1914, *The Chronicle* carried a touching obituary.

> . . . his interest in the games of the school continued for long afterwards. At the end of the session he used frequently to have the principal members of the eleven to stay with him at Thornton Castle for a fortnight's cricket, and there must be many who look back with pleasure to his generous hospitality.

Francis Crombie went straight from the Academy to Trinity College, Cambridge, to study Mathematics, after which he entered the church and served in various ministries throughout England, as well as in Ghazipur in Calcutta and in Bengal, meaning that his involvement with sport at Raeburn Place did not extend beyond his school days.

*. . . the moving spirit was the late Robert Balfour, C.A., who was the 'guide,
philosopher and friend' of Academy boys of that day, to whose exertions are
chiefly due the Raeburn Place ground . . .*

James Wallace, EAFC captain 1868–69,
Writing in the *Academy Chronicle* of May 1908

WHEN FIFTEEN RUGBY ENTHUSIASTS connected to the Edinburgh Academy met one
January morning in 1858, they could not possibly have envisaged the lasting
significance of their decision to form the Academical Football Club. The opening
page of the brand new Minute Book for the club records that:

The First General Meeting of the Academical Football Club was held in Mr
Balfour's Office, 21 St Andrew Square, on the   day of   January 1858.
                              [The actual date was not inserted.]
Mr Alexander Dunlop was called to the Chair.
The following were then agreed as the general Laws of the Club.
  (1) That the club be composed exclusively of those who are or have
       been connected with the Academy.
  (2) That a General Meeting be held annually in the end of October for
       the purpose of electing a Captain, a Treasurer, and a Committee,
       who shall have power to fix the length of the Season.
  (3) That the committee do consist of five Members (of whom one at
       least shall be a present pupil of the Academy) and that the Captain
       and Treasurer be chosen from them.
  (4) That the subscription shall be such sum as the Committee may
       consider necessary for the expenses of the Season.
  (5) That at all Meetings of Committee there shall form a Quorum, one
       of whom must be the Captain or the Treasurer, and the Captain or in
       his absence the Treasurer shall when necessary have the casting
       vote.

(6) That on a Field-Day any Member may introduce a friend with the permission of the Captain or Treasurer, or in their absence, one of the Committee.

(7) That the Captains of sides shall always if possible be selected from the Committee.

(8) That any member leaving a Game before it is concluded without the permission of the Captain of his side shall be liable to a fine of 6d.

(9) The Committee shall have power to arrange matches with other Clubs and to select players for such matches.

(10) Any member who does not appear on the ground after having agreed to play a Match and who fails to give due Notice of his inability to do so, shall be fined 1s.

The following Office-Bearers were then elected:–

Honorary President: Robert Balfour, Esqre.

Captain: Alexander Crombie, Junr.

Secretary & Treas.: William Blackwood.

Committee: Alexander Crombie, Junr., William Blackwood, Alexander Dunlop, John Mackenzie and Robert Lyall.

That same day, the new committee met, once again in Robert Balfour's office, with Alexander Crombie as Chairman.

According to the Minute Book the following decisions were made –

(i) That the season for Football be continued to the end of February.

(ii) That the following be the rate of Subscription for the Season, viz., For Old Scholars 3s, For Present Scholars, Upper School [left blank], Lower School [left blank], and Directed the Treasurer when receiving payment of their Subscriptions to give credit to such members as had already subscribed for the sums subscribed by them respectively.

(iii) The Committee further agreed that the Game be played by the Rules used at Rugby and directed the Treasurer to have same printed along with the Rules of the Club.

There then follows the Treasurer's account of Charge and Discharge in 1857–58.

Charge (summarised)

			£	s	d
Payments:	'from Lyall' (Dec. 21)	£	–	8	–
	'from Crombie' (Dec. 22)		–	17	–
	3 @ 1s. [possibly fines]		–	3	–
Subscriptions:	17 @ 3s, 24 @ 2s.		4	19	–
'Amount collected for Tent' (Jan. 23)			–	13	–
		£	7	–	–

Discharge
1857

Dec. 21	Account Book	£	–	–	6
	Footballs		1	–	6
	Repairing do., Covers and Bellows		1	–	–
	Postages		–	–	6
	Printing Club Rules Etc		1	6	6

1858

Jan. 23	Beer for Military Match		–	7	6
	Tent		–	15	–
	Flags and Flag Posts		1	5	–
March 18	Balance, paid Mr Balfour		1	4	6
		£	7	–	–

It is worth making a number of observations at this stage.

Firstly, we can see from these minutes and accounts that this group had met at the beginning of 1858 to formalise something which was already in existence, which explains why 1857 is recognised as the year of the club's formation. The first recorded game against the university began on Boxing Day of 1857 and there were probaly games before that.

Secondly, it is explicitly stated in bye-law 1 that while the new club required members to be 'connected' with the Edinburgh Academy, there was absolutely no necessity for members to be former pupils. Indeed, Alexander Crombie, the club's first captain and a driving force in those early years, had not gone to the school. He qualified as a member though his younger brother, Francis, who was at the school.

Similarly, the Reverend Samuel Goldney had not attended the Academy, but he had been at this inaugural meeting, and he appears again in the Minute Book as a member of the committee and as Clerk of the Course at the Academy Games in April 1858. Of the 14 others at the meeting, 13 can be identified as Academicals, and one – Johnstone (no initial given) – may have been.

The wording of this bye-law is the same as that used by the Academical Cricket Club at that time, and differs from the Academical Club itself, which was strictly confined to 'gentlemen who have studied in any class of the Edinburgh Academy'.

Thirdly, it is clear that at this early stage this was also a club for boys still at the Academy – and not just for 'Old Boys'. This is also evident from the payment of 8s from Lyall (who was Captain of Football at the Academy in 1857–58 and 1858–59) in the club accounts. He was presumably handing over the subscriptions of a number of pupils at the school who wished to join the club.

Finally, the club at this early stage was called the Academical Football Club. There was no 'Edinburgh' and no 'Rugby'. These words were unnecessary because no other Academical clubs existed at the time, and it wasn't until the 1860s that association football and rugby officially became two different sports.

For the record, the full list of Academicals present at this inaugural meeting of the club is as follows: Robert Balfour, J. Montgomerie Bell, R. Craigie Bell, William Blackwood, Alex. Dunlop, D. Dunlop, W.S. Fraser, D.R. Lyall, J.H.A. Macdonald, J. Mackenzie, Duncan McNeill, Tom Patterson and J. Tod. All except Balfour were in their teens or early twenties.

As well as hosting the meeting at which the Academical Football Club was founded and providing some invaluable guidance to the young men behind this venture, Robert Balfour had been instrumental, some five years earlier, in the acquisition of Raeburn Place – the field which soon became known as 'the cradle of Scottish rugby', having provided a base for the country's oldest club for all of its 150 years and the venue of the world's first rugby international between Scotland and England on 27 March 1871.

Balfour was a pupil at the Academy from 1827 to 1834. He served as secretary of the Academical Club from 1845 until his death at the age of 50 in 1869, and was a director of the Academy from 1861 to 1869. After the acquisition of Raeburn

Place in 1853 he served as treasurer of both the Field Committee and of the Academical Cricket Club. He was also, of course, the first president of the Academical Football Club.

In the Minute Book of the Football Club, on 22 October 1869, the members recorded 'their deep and heartfelt sense of the severe loss they have sustained in the sudden and lamented death of Mr Robert Balfour, who, since the foundation of the Club in January 1858, has filled the office of honorary president. To the success of the club, as well as of all matters connected with the Academy, Mr Balfour contributed very largely; and the members feel that the blank thus caused will be with difficulty supplied, and they have lost one upon whose friendly advice and co-operation they could with the utmost confidence rely.'

An ambitious and energetic administrator with an infectious enthusiasm for all things relating to the Edinburgh Academy, and the young men that the school produced, he was involved in countless enterprises which have benefited the school and the various Academical clubs immeasurably over the years, but his most important and long-lasting legacy was surely the acquisition of Raeburn Place in 1853.

As R. Craigie Bell, who was another enthusiastic Academical, serving as president of the Football Club between 1897 and 1902, wrote in *The Accountants Magazine* in February 1901, some 32 years after Balfour's death:

Of all the Academy matters with which the name of Robert Balfour is still and always will be identified, that of the cricket-field takes leading place. When cricket began to be a popular game in this country, it became exceedingly desirable to get a cricket-ground for the school in a locality suitable for purpose. The burden and responsibility for the necessary arrangements fell mainly on Mr Balfour. To find a suitable bit of ground at a convenient distance from the school, to bargain for it, have it enclosed, levelled, and properly turfed, were steps quite foreign to his usual avocations, but he persevered and eventually triumphed.

Bell continued:

He took an enthusiastic interest in all sport of the Academy boys, partly . . . because they were congenial to his own active and physical frame, but mainly, we are persuaded for the wholesome influence which he thereby acquired over many promising boys and young men: for Robert Balfour was an earnest Christian, with a deep and simple faith, seldom losing sight of his responsibilities and his opportunities of doing good. He was regarded by many as the radiant, cheery, energetic promoter of cricket, football, golf and other outdoor sports . . .

The other key player in the acquisition of Raeburn Place in 1852 was the Reverend John Hannah, the Rector of the Academy at that time. According to the Academical Club Minute Book the idea of a separate playing field for boys at the Academy to play cricket was first mooted at a meeting which took place at Balfour's St Andrew Square offices on 18 April 1853.

Mr Balfour (secy) reported that he had summoned this meeting in consequence of a letter which he had received from the Rector of the Academy who was anxious to secure a field for the use of pupils for cricket and should wish to know whether the club would be disposed to aid in accomplishing this object. After some conversation the committee were of the opinion that the object was a desirable one and that they should aid the Rector and a subcommittee was appointed.

John Hannah, Edinburgh Academy Rector 1847–54

While Hannah probably had a certain amount of empathy with the concept of muscular Christianity as promoted by the likes of Hely-Hutchison Almond, from what we know about his seven-year spell as Rector at the Academy, as it struggled to overcome a crippling debt which had threatened the school with closure, it is not hard to jump to the conclusion that his enthusiasm for this venture had more to do with encouraging well-to-do families to send their children to the school than any particular love of sport.

According to Canon Gregory, a childhood friend, Hannah had been a shy, bookish child 'with no love for the ordinary game and active pursuits in which most boys delight', and had probably never played a game of football or cricket in his life – but he had a shrewd nose for success and the foresight to recognise the value which would soon become attached to having such a facility at the school's disposal.

The first cricket match between Eton and Harrow was in 1822 while the first Oxford versus Cambridge match was in 1827, and from then on the popularity of the sport grew exponentially. The Grange Cricket Club, which initially played at Lovers Loan in the Grange area of Edinburgh, then Grove Street in Fountainbridge, then at Fettes College, before eventually ending up next door to Raeburn Place from 1872 onwards, had started organising annual visits to Edinburgh by the All-England XI in 1849, and in 1851 more than 7,000 spectators turned up to watch the All-England XI play against a 22 of the Clydesdale Club at Kinning Park in Glasgow. Spectators generally seemed to be from the wealthier end of society, with one newspaper report referring to a 'splendid display of private carriages', prompting Magnus Magnusson to speculate in *The Clacken and the Slate* that 'Hannah must have realised that these were all potential parents of boys for the Academy'.

After moving to Glenalmond in 1854, Hannah achieved something similar when he provided that school with a cricket ground which remains one of the most attractive in all of Scotland.

Whatever their motivation, both Hannah and Balfour, and the three other men on the sub-committee which looked into the acquisition of a cricket field – Messrs Mackenzie, Kirk and Marshall – wasted no time in setting about their task.

At the next Academical Club meeting, only ten days later, on 28 April 1853, the secretary reported that:

> The Committee elected at the last Meeting had waited upon the Rector in regard to the Cricket field, that along with the Committee of Masters and Pupils various fields had been examined, that the most suitable appeared to be a field on the Estate of Inverleith immediately behind Raeburn Place which extended to ten Imperial Acres, the Rent being £53 17s. 4d., and that from enquiries made at the present Tenant and at the Agent of the proprietor it appeared not improbable that arrangements might be made for getting immediate entry, and for a lease for several years. The Committee continued with the addition of Mr. William Moncreiff to make enquiries . . .

And in his annual report to the directors of the school, dated 27 June 1853, Rector Hannah advised:

> The Committee of the Academical Club have also joined most kindly in another Scheme, which I hope to see carried out next Session, that of providing a cricket-ground for the exclusive use of the Academy, in which boys may enjoy their exercise without the chance of interruption.

The field which is now the Grange Cricket Ground was considered, but apparently its 'uneven nature' deemed it unsuitable; however, the adjoining field clearly met with approval, and at the annual general meeting of the Academical Club, on 25 July 1853, the members were informed that there was every likelihood 'that an exceedingly eligible Cricket Field in the neighbourhood of the Academy will be ready by next Spring'.

It went on:

> In order to prevent any possibility of the Club being involved in connection with this scheme, four members, vizt., the Rev. Dr. Hannah, Mr. Kenneth Mackenzie, Mr. Thomas Cleghorn and Mr. Robert Balfour have agreed to take upon themselves the whole pecuniary responsibility. The ultimate management will probably be conducted by a joint Committee of the Club and of the Pupils, and the Field will be open only to such Members of the Club and to pupils at the Academy as may be disposed to subscribe a small sum annually. Among many other advantages which may be anticipated from this arrangement, the Committee regard as not the least important, the facilities which will thereby be given to former pupils for meeting with present pupils.

By August 1853, negotiations for a six-year lease at a rent of £53 17s 4d had been completed, and over the winter work continued at a steady pace so as to make Raeburn Place fit for purpose for its opening in May 1854. According to the field's Annual Accounts, ploughmen were employed, grass seed was purchased, as were larch flakes for fences, and money was paid to a 'Mr Peter Anderson for cutting turf at Fisherrow for the cricket field'. In total £87 10s 5d was spent getting the field ready, and that was more than offset by donations and annual subscriptions for that year of £95 8s 6d.

Aerial view of Raeburn Place, September 1949

When the annual general meeting of the Academical Club took place on 24 July 1854, it was recorded that the objectives outlined at the previous meeting in 1853 had been met.

After an examination of the different fields in the neighbourhood of the Academy, one of them, situated between Comely Bank and Stockbridge and within a few minutes' walk from the School, seemed so suitable, that although considerably larger than was required, a lease for it was taken for six years. About six acres were set apart for a Cricket Field, and the remainder was sub-let. Being sensible of having the cricket field in the most excellent order possible, it was carefully levelled, cleaned, fenced and resown with grass, a portion in the centre being laid down with turf for bowling. Although these operations were conducted at some disadvantage owing to the advanced season of the year at which they were commenced . . . the field was ready for play this Summer, having been opened upon 17 May. The scheme received the cordial sanction and approval of the Directors and the management of the field has been conducted by a Committee, consisting of two of the Directors, the Rector, and two of the masters, several members of the club, and seven pupils.

It had all been achieved in just over a year, which is remarkable for such an ambitious project – as was highlighted in the book *One Hundred Years of Raeburn Place: A Short History of Edinburgh Academy's Playing Fields*, which was produced in 1954 by the Edinburgh Academical Club to commemorate the ground's centenary:

A small boarding-school, as, for instance, Merchiston then was, used an adjacent field for playing cricket and other games, but in the early 1850s the provision of a cricket ground for a day school of the size of the Academy (350 boys) was something unheard of in Scotland. Fourteen years later the Royal Commission of Education of 1868 stated that 'within comparatively recent times, some of the more important Burgh schools, following the lead of the Edinburgh Academy, have provided fields as play grounds for their pupils, at a convenient distance from the school'. It went on to say that 'the play grounds of all the day schools put together would not form a place of recreation of the same size of the "playing fields" of Eton or "the Close" at

Rugby . . . With the single exception of Irvine Academy, which has three acres in extent, there are not, to the best of our recollection, two acres of grass set aside for the use of any of the schools, except the Cricket field of Edinburgh Academy.'

The provision of this Field was therefore a momentous enterprise, requiring farsightedness and courage, enthusiasm and organising ability. These qualities were provided by two men, the Rev. John Hannah . . . and Robert Balfour.

The 'want of any space for play ground' had been one of the key criticisms levelled against the High School and the various small private schools which had sprung up in the late eighteenth and early nineteenth centuries, when Henry Cockburn and Leonard Horner first raised the idea of setting up a new school in Edinburgh's elegant New Town. And the first explanatory statement of the Academy scheme emphasised that the site 'in the field to the north of the New Town' contained 'ample space for play ground'. The growth of organised sport had rendered the yards at Heriot Row inadequate, but now the Academy had a facility which would soon become one of the most famous sporting grounds in the world.

Raeburn Place was an instant success, and more than lived up to the expectations of the two men who provided the impetus behind its acquisition and development into a sports field. The Rev. Hannah would have been gratified to learn that a year after he left the school, the Academical Club Report for 1855 stated that the field had 'attracted a considerable amount of public attention . . . and in the plan of the Academy as published and issued by the Directors, it is now recognised as one of the distinctive features of the School'.

Meanwhile, Robert Balfour would have been delighted to learn that during the first year alone nearly 200 Academy pupils paid the field subscription of 6 shillings for senior boys and 4 shillings for the juniors.

A committed Christian, Balfour must surely have been in celestial bliss as he watched the Academicals celebrate their 150th birthday against the Barbarians on 9 April 2008, from his specially reserved spot atop the long gone but not forgotten Mound at Raeburn Place. The club which he had such an important role in setting up is still going strong, and it is still playing its home games on the field which he found, helped purchase and originally renovated.

. . . the cradle of Scottish rugby . . .

Anon

THE WIDE OPEN SPACES OF Raeburn Place might have been the envy of all other Scottish day schools and fledgling sports clubs back in the 1850s, but by 21st-century standards the facilities were very basic. When one of the club's founding members, J.H.A. Macdonald, addressed the EAFC Jubilee Dinner in 1908 (by which time he had assumed the judicial title of Lord Kingsburgh, having been appointed to the bench as Lord Justice Clerk in 1888), he spoke about the primitive facilities at Raeburn Place 50 years earlier.

> A small loft over an outhouse in the garden of a villa in the corner of the field, approached by a wooden ladder . . . no basins, no lockers . . . The only thing we could do after we had played our match (we came out quite as dirty as you do now) was to go up into that loft and smoke until it was sufficiently dark and we could go through the streets without being mobbed.

The ground derived its name from the street running westwards from Stockbridge towards Comely Bank, the former mansion estate of Sir William Fettes – whose bequest led to the foundation of Fettes College in 1870. The street itself got its name from the St Bernard's estate of Sir Henry Raeburn R.A., and began to be developed for housing in about 1814. By the mid-1830s three handsome villas had been built on the northern side of the street, on what was then the absolute edge of the city, and would 20 years later be the south-eastern corner of the playing fields. Two of these buildings were later demolished to make way for tenements, with the remaining one coming to be known as Somerset Cottage, and more recently as the Raeburn House Hotel. It seems likely that it was in the outhouse of this villa (which was demolished in 1930 to make way for squash courts), that Lord Kingsburgh and his team-mates hid until it was possible to escape home undetected under the cover of darkness.

The ground became very busy very quickly. The first cricket match at Raeburn Place for which a score has been recorded was reported on in *The Evening Courant* on 17 April 1855, when the 1st XI of Academy pupils defeated 11 of the school's masters. The following week, the Academy defeated the High School in the first recorded match against 'foreign' opposition at Raeburn Place, although it is likely that the High School had played there in 1854.

By the summer of 1856, Dr J.S. Hodson, who had replaced the Rev. Hannah as Rector of the Academy, felt compelled to write in his annual report about 'the freedom from illness which we have enjoyed, as evidenced by the unusually small number of absentees, during a season of much sickness around us'.

He continued:

> I cannot but believe that we owe much of this good health to the successful establishment of the Academy Cricket Ground, and to the general support it has received from the present and former Pupils, as well as from the Parents and Masters. The frequent presence of many of the latter on the ground has a salutary effect. To Mr. Harvey [afterwards Rector of the Academy, 1869–88] more especially we are greatly indebted, as, besides his indefatigable and most successful care of his two Classes (the First and Fifth) within the walls of the Academy, he has regularly superintended and shared their Games in the Cricket Field, himself affording a proof that the most refined Scholarship is not incompatible with the love of manly sports: and truth of which we have another example this year amongst ourselves, since the Dux of our whole School (R.B. Ranken) is our best Cricketer and the Captain of our Eleven.

Clearly, Raeburn Place and the games which took place there had already become a major part of life for those connected with the Academy and the Academical Club.

There is no mention in the Minute Book of football being played at Raeburn Place until the winter of 1857–58, when the ground was 'for the first time opened for football', but circumstantial evidence suggests that informal games were played there from 1855.

Over the years, Raeburn Place has been used for a diverse range of activities. The ground started hosting the Academy's Annual Games in May 1858. In 1877 a lacrosse match between Loretto and an Academical team was arranged to be played at Raeburn Place, at a time when both those schools as well as Fettes and Merchiston were experimenting with the sport, however we cannot be sure that the game ever actually took place. In 1878 the Edinburgh University soccer team was granted use of the ground for a match against Cambridge University, though not without some discussion at committee level as to the rectitude of encouraging the Association game. And in 1884 the contest for the Scottish lawn tennis title was held outdoors for the first time, on the wicket at Raeburn Place (the game had been introduced to Scotland by former Academy pupil Sir James Patten Mac-dougall in 1874). More recently it has hosted among other things summer softball leagues, local primary school sports-days, mixed hockey leagues, Edinburgh Festival Fringe shows and women's international rugby matches.

Back in the summer of 1859, before the original lease ran out, a new 15-year deal was agreed at an increased rent of £73 17s. By then the Rev. Hannah had moved on to Glenalmond, so he dropped out of the tenancy agreement. Mackenzie, Cleghorn and Balfour continued as before, and they were joined by James Mylne, W.S. (an Academy director and president of the Cricket Club) and Alexander Crombie (who was, of course, the first captain of the Academical Football Club).

The contracted land was described in the lease as:

9.232 Imperial acres and consisting of the portion of the field or park being the West Haugh or the Westmost portion of the Haugh lands on the entailed estate of Inverleith lying to the east and south of the Burn or Ditch which runs through the said field, bounded on the East partly by a Cottage erected for the Farm of Inverleith Mains and partly by a private Road leading to the said Farm, on the south by a Wall separating the said Lands and the Turnpike Road, on the West and North by the said Burn and Ditch.

The 'said Burn and Ditch' still runs along the northern boundary, but was covered over in about 1891, although its exit point into the Water of Leith is still visible from the top end of Reid Terrace as you look back towards Arboretum Avenue.

The renewal of the lease and the increase in activity at the ground warranted the erection in 1859 of a small pavilion and the bringing into use as playing fields of three acres which had been previously sub-let. The Academical Club Report, issued in July 1859, reveals that the committee felt that the time was right for 'certain important improvements' to be made. 'In particular,' the report continued, 'it is indispensable to erect a Pavilion as there is at present no accommodation for the players and no shelter from wet either for players or spectators.'

In the winter of 1858–59 'old scholars and others interested in the school' responded generously to an invitation to subscribe towards the cost of a pavilion, and it was ready for use by the beginning of the cricket season in 1859. Described as 'an elegant and commodious structure' and costing about £150, it was built on to the north gable of the small cottage where the original club members had hidden until dusk a few years earlier, and consisted of a central 'dining hall' with a room on either side.

At a meeting of the Cricket Club committee on 7 February 1866, the Secretary reported that 'the gale of the preceding morning had blown out the back wall of the pavilion'. He 'was authorised to execute the necessary repairs at once', and presumably did so to everyone's satisfaction as there is no further mention of it in the Minute Book.

In 1857, John Sands, from Sussex, became the first groundsman and cricket professional to be employed at Raeburn Place (for the summer months only). He came back in 1858 and 1859, and was followed by five others who stayed for varying lengths of time, until the appointment of Tom Sellars in 1876. As with his predecessors, he was originally engaged for the summer months only, but was later appointed groundsman for the whole year round. He was essentially a cricket appointment, but his influence was far wider reaching than that, as *One Hundred Years at Raeburn Place* points out:

> A native of Nottinghamshire, Sellars came to Raeburn Place after three years at Fettes. It is fortunate for the Academy that Fettes decided, on the grounds of economy, to do without a professional for 1876. In the *Fettes Register* it is stated that 'no school could desire a better coach, bowler or groundsman than Tom Sellars'. To him it is largely due that Academy cricket kept up a reasonable standard during the 'lean years'. Sellars was also a groundsman to the Grange and its neighbours, the Dyvours Lawn Tennis Club and the Coates Curling Club, and a first-class umpire. In all he gave forty-four years of conscientious service in Scotland, twenty-four of which were to the Academy. In the 1870s and 1880s it was customary to include

the professional in the School XI when a club side was met – 'the Academy (with Sellars)', as it was styled. He was a good forcing bat and a slow medium bowler of good length and peculiar action (described by a fellow professional as a 'God Save the Queen' action), and he could turn the ball a bit both ways. For all his service to the Academy and its playing-field, Tom Sellars deserves special mention in any history of Raeburn Place.

In 1882, Raeburn Place, along with the lands occupied by the Grange Cricket Club, the Coates Curling Club and the Dyvours Lawn Tennis Club (approximately 18 acres in all), was purchased from the Inverleith Estate at a cost of £9,500. The Academical and Grange Trust was constituted 'to secure to the said Club's and Company permanent possession of the grounds they occupied'. The eight original trustees were William Moncreiff and Alexander Crombie (Grange Cricket Club), Dr Thomas Harvey and R. Craigie Bell, W.S. (Academical Cricket Club), Harry Cheyne, W.S., George Cunningham (Coates Curling Club), James Lutyens Mansfield, Advocate and James Patten, Advocate (Edinburgh Lawn Tennis Company, parent company of the Dyvours tennis club). While the football club was not yet officially involved in taking responsibility for Raeburn Place, this list of names included a number of individuals who were closely associated with the club.

The appeal for funds for this purchase produced over £6,000 and the balance of the purchase price was raised through the issue of a bond over the ground. To cover the interest payable on the bond, as well as rates, taxes and other costs, the grounds continued to be let by the trustees to the four clubs. The bond was later held partly by the Academy Endowment Fund and partly by the Academy itself, before being paid off in 1945. The share allocated against Raeburn Place was £1,715, and was personally repaid by R.G. Simpson, who was the chairman of the Academical Club committee at the time, and later served as president of the club.

Two years after the initial purchase from the Inverleith Estate, the Cricket Club committee set about upgrading Raeburn Place. A 'Grand Bazaar' held in the school Music Hall on 1 and 2 February 1884 produced £1,430, and the lion's share of that (£1,150) was spent on erecting a new pavilion, which is described in detail in *One Hundred Years at Raeburn Place 1854–1954*.

This building partly occupied the same site as its predecessor, but was a much more elaborate affair. It comprised two dressing-rooms and a luncheon hall on the first floor, and below that there was two more dressing-rooms and a kitchen 'communicating with the upper flat by means of a stair and a lift, and also a large store room for roller, cutting machine, goal posts, footballs, flags, &c., &c'. In front, protected by a roof, there were six rows of terraced wooden seats, 'forming a stand capable of accommodating upwards of 250 onlookers'. This stand was, of course, too far away from the main pitch to be of any use for watching football matches. The Minute Book mentions 'Range and Boiler for Kitchen', but hot water for washing purposes does not seem to have been provided until the 1890s. The hot-water boiler then installed continued in use until 1927. In the same year electric light replaced gas.

A permanent scoring-box was also erected and an underground water pipe to the cricket square was installed.

A number of factors, such as the introduction of compulsory games at the Academy, the rising roll at the school and the increased demands on the ground by the Academical clubs, led to the purchase by the school of New Field in the late 1890s. Over the years, through the generosity of the school, that ground has been made available to the Academical Football Club and Cricket Clubs on the many occasions in which demand for pitches had outstripped supply.

Responsibility for the general administration of Raeburn Place initially rested on the shoulders of the Academical Cricket Club, but then in 1900 the Academical Club was reconstituted with the Cricket Club and the Football Club both being brought under its umbrella. At this point, the care of Raeburn Place was entrusted to a field committee – comprising of two representatives from the Football Club, two representatives from Cricket Club and a field secretary. That basic structure with some tinkering lasted until the mid-1970s when the Edinburgh Academical Sports Centre was set up to provide a more efficient way of running the ground, and act as a buffer protecting Academical interests after the football club went 'open' in 1973. Then, in August 2008, the arrangement with Festival Inns, which facilitated the total redevelopment of the clubhouse, necessitated another restructuring of the tenancy agreement, with a newly created company called Raeburn Place Sports Limited taking on responsibility for running the ground.

It was fortunate that the field committee made the excellent choice of S.C. 'Sidney' Freeman as the first ever field secretary. He continued in that role with untiring zeal until his death in 1936. His dog, a Scottish terrier called Accie, was a familiar character around Raeburn Place at this time, collecting cricket balls during practice and featuring in several football team photographs. Freeman left behind a fascinating scrapbook which has been of great use in the compilation of this work. He was secretary of the Football Club 1899 to 1902, and was the first honorary secretary and treasurer of the Scottish Cricket Union after its formation in 1908, staying in that role for about a dozen years.

The most distinctive feature of Raeburn Place during the early years was the grassy knoll known as The Mound, which dominated the playing fields until its removal in 1946.

For a long time it was assumed that The Mound was an ancient bow-butt, and in support of this theory it was often pointed out that there had been a similar hillock in the Grange field just over 200 yards away – which is one of the distances fired by the Royal Company of Archers. However, when it was eventually decided to remove this famous Raeburn Place landmark, the Inspector of Ancient Monuments and the Society of Antiquaries of Scotland were both informed and two archaeologists were appointed to carry out a preliminary investigation. They reported back that the Mound was 'of no archaeological importance'. This conclusion was supported by later investigations during the levelling of the pile by a bulldozer, when pottery and china fragments from the nineteenth century were unearthed amidst other made-up materials which had been dumped on top of a natural low embankment of boulder clay to form an artificial and more conical hillock.

Had The Mound been on the boundary of the field it would probably still have been in existence today, but unfortunately it impinged dramatically on the seconds' pitch, which became known as 'the Mound pitch' or sometimes as 'the small goals'. The west touchline of the pitch ran over the shoulder of The Mound, meaning that a wing three-quarter throwing the ball in from touch might be anywhere from eight to ten feet higher than the last man at the line-out.

When Loretto played the Academy on 5 November 1887, *The Lorettonian* magazine reported:

Owing to the fact that Edinburgh and Glasgow Academicals were also playing at Raeburn Place, we had to be content with the 'Small Goals', which ground, including as it does a great portion of 'The Mound', gave the game quite an Alpine character.

At one point, the Academy were pressing hard, and, according to *The Lorettonian*:

> . . . playing with great vigour and dash, took the ball well into our part of the field and up the higher slopes of 'The Mound', but our superior weight drove them back down the steep again . . .

The Mound's companion across the way was levelled as soon as the Grange took possession of their field in 1871, and throughout the 1880s and 1890s the issue of removing the distinctive landmark from Raeburn was regularly debated at committee level, with a sub-committee even recommending at one point that 'the Mound be removed forthwith'. But it survived for another 50 years – largely because of the affection with which it had come to be regarded. The Mound might have been a nuisance when second teams were trying to play serious games of rugby on a pitch more suited to cross-country skiing, but it was an intrinsic part of Raeburn Place life – and it had its uses too, as *The Chronicle* explained:

> As a vantage point at football matches, especially in the days when Internationals were played at Raeburn Place, as a delightful slope to recline on in the sunshine during the cricket season, and as a feature which gave the Field a character of its own, the Mound will be long remembered with affection.

CHAPTER SIX

Indeed, it is wonderful that the game survived at all.
R.J. Phillips *The Story of Scottish Rugby*, 1925

WHILST THE CLUB'S FIRST Minute Book contains records of proceedings at all annual general meetings and many of the committee meetings which took place during the early years, it does not, unfortunately, record anything about the matches played at this time

With no other clubs in Scotland to play against, we can assume that matches against the Academy, and alongside Academy boys against Merchistonians (who, like the Academicals, were a boys' and old-boys' organisation at this time), provided the main form of on-field activity for the first decade of the club, with bye-law 6 in the original rules of the club indicating that 'Field Days' would be special occasions when visitors could be introduced.

It is a shame that the well-documented proceedings of the club's Jubilee Dinner – held in the main hall of the Academy on 20 March 1908 – cannot provide a better insight into what happened on the pitch during the club's formative years. At the dinner, John Chiene, who had been an Academy schoolboy when the club was set up, said that he had hoped Craigie Bell, one of the two founding members present at the dinner (Lord Kingsburgh was the other), 'would have told us something about the first match that was played, because my mind is an entire blank on the matter. I have a dim idea that Jimmie Mansfield brought down a number of Scotsmen who had been up at Rugby and they showed us how to play the game'. Apart from the rather disorientating geography of this statement, Chiene's words are interesting because they indicate that despite the influence of the Crombie brothers, the rules of Rugby had not yet been fully embraced. Unfortunately there is no record of Craigie Bell saying anything about this first match.

There were a couple of matches against opposition outside the Accie–Merchiston duopoly, including the first two matches about which we have any real details. The first of these games was against a side from Edinburgh University

36

which had actually begun before the club's inauguration, but because it took place over four Saturdays, from 26 December 1857 to 16 January 1858, there is a good chance that the game had not yet finished when that meeting at Robert Balfour's office took place. There was no university club at the time, so this team would have been a group of students looking for some entertainment in the city during their Christmas holidays.

A report of the match appeared in the *Edinburgh Evening Courant* on 19 January 1858:

THE UNIVERSITY V. THE ACADEMICAL CLUB

This match which was commenced in December last was brought to a close last Saturday. The match was for the best seven goals, the number of players on each side being 25. On the first Saturday the University obtained one goal; on the two next succeeding Saturday neither party obtained a goal. Last Saturday (16 Jan.) which was the fourth day of the match, the numbers on each side were increased to 30. The play began at a quarter to two o'clock, the University having one goal in their favour, and also being much superior to their opponents in point of weight; but such was the activity and skill displayed by the Academicals that before half past three they had kicked all of the four goals required, without the University obtaining any, or even having a 'try at goal'. The Academical Club, therefore, were declared the victors, beating the University by three goals. Much of the success of the Academicals was due to three or four of their number who had learned to 'drop-kick' and played the game in England.

It is possible that this was the same game that John Chiene alluded to at the Jubilee Dinner. The Head Boy at Loretto in 1856 was a future Edinburgh Advocate called James Mansfield, who then had a brief spell at Rugby School before going to study Law at Cambridge University. It is entirely conceivable that he would have had friends at Edinburgh University at the time so could have organised a match whilst on his Christmas break in the city.

Alternatively, Mansfield might have organised a game with his friends from Rugby School against the Academicals at some point before the University match. Unfortunately we can only speculate on this:

The period almost up to 1870 is enshrouded in mist, records are meagre, and altogether the impression conveyed is that players must often have struggled against circumstances that were not encouraging. Indeed it is wonderful that the game survived at all.

A week after the university match the Academicals played a military team. The accounts in the EAFC Minute Book tell us that a tent, flags and flag-posts as well as 7s 6d worth of beer had been purchased for the occasion, but we know very little about the event apart from that.

We only know of three games being played the following season (1858–59) – two of which involved the school side but not the Academicals. The first of these matches was between the Academy and Merchiston Castle on 11 December 1858, and this remains the longest-standing continuously played rugby fixture in the world.

Merchiston had already played in the first ever inter-school match against the High School on 13 February 1858, although it is worth noting that efforts had been made to organise a fixture between Merchiston and Edinburgh Academy a few months earlier. A letter from a Merchiston pupil, dated 9 November 1857, to an old friend who had left the school the previous year, tells us: 'We are playing at Football now and expect to come to close quarter with the renowned Edinburgh Academy'. Twelve days later he wrote: 'We intended to have a match at Football to-day with the Edinburgh Academy, but as half of us are unable to play on account of a general cold, which is prevailing amongst us, it has been postponed until next Saturday when I hope we will come off victorious' (*The Merchiston Castle School, 1855–68* David Murray). Evidently it proved impossible to rearrange this fixture for that date, so it would be another year until the two schools locked horns for the first time, on 11 December 1858.

A detailed report of this match appeared in the *Merchiston Magazine* of January 1859, and was reproduced almost in full in *One Hundred Years at Raeburn Place*.

The Academy scored two tries, but as neither was converted and only goals counted, the result was a draw. The first try produced the sort of argument which helps demonstrate how vague the rules of the game still were.

Lyall [the Academy captain] made a rush, and to our astonishment runs into 'touch' right behind our goal. Here an expostulation was made on the plea that the rules prohibited running into 'touch', but finding that it only related to side touch, we were obliged to yield and allow the 'try at goal'.

At Merchiston the convention was for matches to be played over the area of the whole field, from the wall on one side to the paling on the other, so there was no 'side touch'. Lyall's try was also appealed against on the grounds that no player could cross the line whilst holding the ball. The rule at Merchiston up until this point had been that the player must let go of the ball and kick it over the line before he touches down. As there was no referee or umpire these legal problems had to be resolved by the captains.

The game lasted two and a half hours without (it seems) a break. Seventeen names of Academy players are given, they are: A. Cheyne, H. Cheyne, Chiene, Findlay, Forman, Gordon, Gore-Booth, Jackson, Lloyd, D. Lyall (captain), W. Lyall, Maclure, Melville, Moncreiff, Moore, Simpson, Smith.

A month later, on January 8 1859, Merchiston and the Academy joined forces to take on the Academicals at Raeburn Place. The combined team was made up of eight Merchiston boys (Brown, Burlton, Ewing, McCallum, McFie, McLean, McNeel and Tennent), two Merchiston masters (Almond and Rouse) and ten Academy boys (Beaton, Cheyne, Chiene, Jackson, Lloyd, Lyall (captain), Melville, Paterson, Simpson and Smith).

This match provides us with the earliest recorded Academical team, which consisted of: A.B. Bell, John Bell, Joseph Bell, R.C. Bell, W. Bell, Cage, Crombie (captain), D. Dunlop, J. Dunlop, Goldney, H. Hamilton, J. Hamilton, Hill, McDonald, Moncreiff, Moody, Murdoch, Sellar, Thompson, Tod, Hills.

The schools team won the match, thanks to the first recorded goal at Raeburn Place, scored by McNeel of Merchiston. There had been two tries scored in the Academy versus Merchiston match but no goals, and although there were five goals scored throughout the course of the university match there is no record of who the scorers were.

Towards the end of the season, a return match between the Academy and Merchiston again resulted in a draw. On this occasion Merchiston included two masters in their side, while the Academy were reinforced by two Academicals.

We have no record of the Academicals playing any matches during the 1859–60 season, but the *Merchiston Chronicle* tells us that the Academy and

Merchiston played each other twice, with the spoils shared. There are also reports of junior matches between equivalent classes in the two schools taking place.

For the following season the committee made two amendments to the rules used by the club. It was decided 'that there should be no "knocking-on"' and 'that a ball going into "touch"' should be thrown out from the spot where it went in'. The 1860–61 season also witnessed the start of matches against the Merchistonian club, on 17 November. The Merchistonian XX was made up of six former pupils, two masters and 12 current pupils; while the Academicals, who won by a goal to nil, had 16 old boys and four current pupils in their side. For the return match it was agreed to limit the number of former pupils on each side to seven. The Academicals dominated this game, and scored several tries – but no goals were kicked, so the match ended in a draw.

Publication of the *Merchiston Chronicle* was discontinued after February 1861 and for the next two seasons we have very little information about the games played. However, the EAFC Minute Book provides an uninterrupted record of the office-bearers at the club and the state of the club funds during these early years. Any credit balance at the end of the year was paid over to the Cricket Club, who took responsibility for looking after Raeburn Place. Any deficits were also absorbed by the Cricket Club, although the amounts involved were always very small.

CHAPTER SEVEN

Very few of you have ever seen a real scrum. Have you ever seen a haycock that was put up when the hay was wet, and the smoke or steam was rising from it fourteen or fifteen feet in the air? That was just what a scrum was in those days – absolutely still and steaming.

Lord Kingsburgh
at the Edinburgh Academical Football Club Jubilee Dinner, 1908

AT THE TIME OF THE CLUB's 100th anniversary it was thought that no original copies of the laws of the game, as agreed at that inaugural meeting, had survived. But in August 1969 a 16-page pamphlet was discovered in a deed box among the Academy archives, which was entitled: *Academical Football Club: General Laws and Rules of the Game*, January 1858, Edinburgh, printed by W. Blackwood & Sons:

1. KICK OFF must be from MIDDLE and a place kick.
2. When the ball is touched down behind goal, if touched by the side behind whose goal it is, they have a KICK OUT; but if by the opposite side, they may have a TRY AT GOAL.
3. KICK OUT must not be from more than 25 yards out of goal.
4. FAIR CATCH is a catch direct from the foot, or a knock on from the HAND of the opposite side only.
5. A CATCH from a throw on is not a fair catch.
6. CHARGING is fair, in the case of a place kick, as soon as the ball has touched the ground; in case of a kick from a catch, as soon as the player offers to kick, but he may always draw back unless he has actually touched the ball with his foot.
7. OFF SIDE. A player is off his side when he is behind all the players on the opposite side, or in front of the kicker of his own side.
8. A player being off his side is to consider himself as out of the game and is not to touch the ball in any case whatever (either in or out of

touch) or in any way to interrupt the play, and is of course incapable of holding the ball.

9. It is not lawful to take the ball off the ground, except in touch, for any purpose whatsoever.

10. It is not lawful to take the ball when rolling as distinguished from bounding.

11. RUNNING IN is allowed to any player on his side, provided he does not take the ball off the ground, or through touch.

12. RUNNING IN: If, in the case of a run in, the ball be held in a maul, it shall be lawful for a player on either side to take it from the runner in.

13. No player out of a maul may be held, or pulled over, unless he is himself holding the ball.

14. Though it is lawful to hold any player in a maul, this holding does not include attempts to throttle and strangle, which are totally opposed to all the principles of the game.

15. No one wearing projecting nails or iron plates on the soles or heels of his boots or shoes shall be allowed to play.

16. TRY AT GOAL: A ball touched between the goal posts may be brought up to either of them, but not between; but if not touched between the posts the posts must be brought up in a straight line from where it is touched.

17. The ball, when punted, must be within, and when caught, without the line of goal.

18. The ball must be place kicked or dropped, but if it touches two players' hands the try will be lost.

19. It shall be a goal if the ball goes over the bar (whether it touch or no) [*sic*] without having touched the dress or person of any player; but no player may stand on the goal bar to interrupt it going over.

20. No goal may be kicked from touch or by a punt at any time.

21. TOUCH: A ball in touch is dead; consequently the first player on his side must in any case touch it down, bring it to the edge of touch and throw it straight out, but may take it himself if he can.

22. No player may stop the ball with anything but his own person.

23. Heads of sides, or two deputies appointed by them, are the sole arbiters of all disputes.

A foreword to this set of rules states: 'The following are taken from the Book of Rules used at Rugby' – however, there appear to be a number of minor differences between the two documents. For example, in the Rugby School rules, it is stated that 'it is not fair to hack and hold at the same time', while the issue of hacking is not addressed at all in the Academical rules. Also, in the Rugby School Rules a fair catch is 'a catch direct from the foot'; whereas in the Academical Rules a fair catch can also be from 'a knock-on from the HAND of the opposite side only'.

As for how these rules translated onto the pitch, we can be grateful to the *Merchiston Magazine,* which published in 1859 a uniquely detailed description of the sport as it was played in Edinburgh at that time. The account is retold in the *EAFC Centenary History.* It begins with a description of the posts:

> . . . two very portentous looking erections . . . facing each other at a distance of about 150 yards. Each of these consists of two poles about 13 feet high, and 14 feet apart, with a horizontal bar across, at a distance of almost 10 feet from the ground.
>
> At the beginning of matches the ball, consisting of a tightly-blown India rubber bladder, with a leather covering of an oval shape, is placed half-way between the goals. The players are divided into two bodies, each attacking their opponents' goal, and protecting their own, the ultimate object of each side is being to kick the ball over one of the cross bars spoken of above.
>
> This, it is evident, is a feat of no easy accomplishment, as the space to be defended is very narrow, and indeed, the weaker side, though 'penned' close to their goal the whole time, can often manage to stave off actual defeat during a match of several hours' duration.
>
> The ball being kicked off by one side or the other in the direction of the opposite goal, the two sides, which have been drawn up in battle array, like miniature armies, rush together, each leaving a reserve behind, and then comes the tug of war. Each player must keep with his own side as much as he can, for when in front of the ball, he is debarred by the rules of the game from taking any part in it whatever, until he has become 'on-side' again. The beauty of the rule is, that it makes a side keep together, and work hard, and prevents games being won by some good-for-nothing 'loafer', waiting with his hands in his pockets in the enemy's quarters until the ball happens to

come his way. And now the ball, carrying the tide of battle with it, surges from side to side, and . . . [an uninitiated spectator] . . . has no doubt that the game has begun, but cannot make it out at all why we don't pay some people to undergo such violent exertions, instead of undergoing them ourselves. He has, however, a lurking suspicion that we are losing our tempers, and that our sport is becoming earnest, a suspicion which soon becomes a certainty, for a 'stalwart youth', who has been keeping rather out of the thick of the fight, catches up the ball, and runs off with it bodily, evidently resolved to put an end to the quarrel by removing its cause. But, alas! His good intentions are nipped in the bud, by that lithe, active little fellow, who springs on him like a mad wild cat, and pulls him right down on top of himself, with his struggling arms, legs, and body twined round him in such desperate contortions that the petrified spectator asks in ill-disguised alarm which might be the warrior's body, which is leg, which is arm. But the fury of both sides will not permit the issue to be decided by single combat. All the bravest and the best rush like bulldogs on the prostrate combatants, and immediately the ground is covered by a struggling, rolling heap, two or three deep, and evidently bent on mutual extermination . . . tugging, pulling and tearing at each other with all their might and main . . .

[Eventually there emerges] . . . our wiry friend . . . with the ball under his arm. Brushing past the outsiders before the 'maul' is fairly disentangled, he knocks over some small boys in the middle of the field, dodges past one goal-keeper, and slips like an eel from the embraces of the other, and pitches down the ball right behind the adversary's goal-posts.

But the game is not won yet, and now is the time for a sure foot and a steady nerve. All the side whose goal is threatened have to retire behind it while the ball is carried out some distance to the front, and the surest kicker on the attacking side prepares to 'try at goal'. One of his own side holds the ball an inch or two from the ground and puts it down as the kicker runs at it. Woe betide him if his nerve fails, for as soon as the ball touches the ground, the besieged, as we may call them, sally forth with an Indian yell. But if the goal-kicker is fit for his post of honour, the ball sails away over his adversaries' heads and goal-bar, and the goal is won.

Chapters might be written on different kinds of 'tries at goal', on drop-kicking, punting, placing a field, keeping a reserve, and other delicate points of a game, on which the winning and losing of a match often turns. We have merely endeavoured to sketch some of the leading features of our great and noble winter game, for which, in its now developed perfection, we are indebted to Rugby School.

Forty years after the club's birth, one of its founding members, Lord Kingsburgh (previously J.H.A. Macdonald), wrote about the sport as it was in the mid nineteenth century, and he was quoted at length in the *EAFC Centenary History* book:

> We then played twenty a side, and a scrum was a scrum indeed – fifteen pushing against fifteen in a tight maul, which often was immovable for several minutes. The steam rose from the pack like the smoke from a charcoal-burner's pile. It was much more straining and fatiguing than the more open game of to-day. During the years of my football work I was never able to cross one leg over another on a Sunday if I had been playing a match on the previous Saturday, and as for shins, the breaking up of a maul when it came meant vigorous kicking ahead, on the chance that ball and toe might meet.

It should be noted that the purpose of a scrum at this time was to drive the ball forward, and not to heel. Even as late as the 1890s a scrum was still defined in the laws as being when the ball had been put down 'and all who have closed round on their respective sides endeavour to push their opponents back, and by kicking the ball to drive it in the direction of the opposite goal line'. Back then, players in a scrum would stand, more or less, upright.

CHAPTER EIGHT

What you rugby types have managed to do to such a simple object as the ball
appals me. Thank goodness you weren't around when the wheel was invented.

John Rafferty,
former association football correspondent of *The Scotsman*

WHEN FORSYTH'S *RUGBY RECORD* used to publish a list of 'Scottish Club Champions',
the Academicals were given that honour for the first six years recorded, from 1865–
66 to 1870–71. In a review of season 1870–71, during which the Academicals lost to
St Andrews University and West of Scotland, *The Scotsman* newspaper stated that
'these two matches were the first, we believe, the Academicals have lost for seven
years'. All very impressive, but we must remember that not many games were
played at that time – probably fewer than half a dozen a season.

The fact that the game was still in its infancy is well demonstrated by the
story of the Academicals going to St Andrews in February 1871, and arriving there
five men short of a full team. Given that the Academicals were at that time the
leading club in the country, this can be taken as symptomatic of the difficulties
clubs had in building player numbers and organising meaningful matches during
these early years of the sport.

West of Scotland are believed to be the Academicals' oldest club opponents.
This fixture was started thanks to the initiative of W.H. Dunlop, who had been
honorary secretary of both the Academical Cricket Club and the Academical
Football Club in 1864–65, before moving to Glasgow and becoming involved with
West. According to Dunlop's diary, the Academicals travelled to Glasgow for that
first game between the two clubs by train, and the match took place at Partick on
16 November 1867, with the home team having 'rather the better of it'. Later,
Dunlop tells us that the return fixture at Raeburn Place on 14 December was a
'fine game'. The game was followed by a meal at Dejays New Luncheon, Dinner
and Supper Rooms on Princes Street, which was 'great fun', before the visitors set
off for home, arriving back in Glasgow at 1 a.m.

The match at Raeburn is one of the first to be reported in *The Scotsman* –

The weather was very unfavourable and from the soft state of the ground running and kicking (both place and drop) were very difficult. Notwithstanding the inclemency of the day, several ladies were present. The match, which was well contested, resulted in favour of the Edinburgh Academicals, by three tries. The former match, played at Glasgow on the 16th ult., was drawn.

EAFC played St Andrews University twice that season. The first of these encounters was at home and the Academicals won by a goal and a try. But in the return fixture they were beaten by the same margin and the day ended in acrimony, with the Academical captain withdrawing his men during the third quarter on account of 'the irregularities of the opposition' [*EAFC Centenary*, p.24].

It wasn't until the early 1870s that the spread of the game allowed the club to expand its fixture list. The decade began with Accies adopting their now widely recognised blue and white uniform, which replaced the plain blue jersey which had been worn since 1864.

James Wallace, who captained the Academicals from 1868–69, provided a detailed insight into some of the more notable EAFC players of that era and the nature of the game at this time in an article he wrote in *The Chronicle* in May 1908.

We played twenty a side, and 'hacking' and 'tripping' were part of the game, while it was unlawful to pick up a ball unless bounding. Perhaps the less said about hacking the better, although I don't think that the effects, though painful at the time, were very serious. 'Tripping', however, was a fine art and in my day George Chiene and Andrew Gemmell were past masters of it, while the Hon. James Moncreiff was a good third. The skill in 'tripping' consisted of catching the heel of the runner with the toe of your boot and bringing him to the ground. As a rule he fell quite gently to mother earth, but sometimes the toe of the boot caught him on the shin instead of the heel, when, in addition to the shock of sudden collapse, the abraded shin caused considerable pain, not felt so much at the time as after the game was over; and many of us were in the habit of walking to church on a Sunday with a limp. Serious accidents, however, were few, and in my opinion more disasters happen now in charging and standing up to a heavy opponent in the endeavour to stop him.

A maul with twenty a side, all playing forward with the exception of one full back and two halves, was a serious affair, and as they occasionally lasted for ten or twelve minutes, till the ball was 'put down' the condition of exhaustion was considerable, especially if you happened to be on the ground in the middle of the seething mass of humanity. The steam would be rising in a cloud from the bodies of the players, and at the close you would see individuals being dragged out by their legs or arms, in a condition in which their best friends could with difficulty recognise them.

Harry Cheyne was a very difficult man to pass; and as for charging him, you might as well charge a stone wall; while the hug he gave you when he did get hold of you, squeezed all the breath out of your body, and left you limp and powerless in his mighty embrace. The hardest man I ever tried to tackle was Frank Moncreiff. He was fast and strong, and had a way of wriggling and throwing you off with his arm, which made it most difficult to secure hold of him.

Back play was not so much in evidence as now, and 'passing' was unknown, but we had many good backs and drop kickers. One of the best was Robert Sanderson, who was equally good with his left or right foot. It was a treat to see him pick up the ball on the outside of a scrimmage and run round, letting fly at goal with his left foot . . . One of the fastest men I ever saw on the football field was the Hon. and Rev. Robert Moncreiff who occasionally played with us and was a perfect clipper . . . Another magnificent runner was W. Kinross Gair, whose graceful style and splendid stride were the admiration of all who saw him run at the Academy and University. Other famous players of those days were Arthur Cheyne, Sherriff Lees, 'Gurdy' Dunlop, also one of the best cricketers the Academy ever produced, Tom Torrie the 'Woolwich Infant' and . . . Duncan Robertson.

The growing popularity of the game made it increasingly apparent that some sort of consensus as to the rules of play would have to be established. In the beginning the schools and clubs which had pioneered the development of formalised ball games throughout Britain played to whatever rules had been agreed to before the match – there was no single recognised code, and even those who used the Rugby School rules were quite prepared to amend them if they saw fit without reference to any other organisation. However, a growing desire for a uniform code to be established led to a meeting of representatives of 11 London schools and clubs in 1863, some of whom favoured the Rugby game and others the dribbling version which had developed at a number of schools, including Charterhouse and Shrewsbury.

The conference first agreed to form an association, to be called the Football Association, before a heated argument erupted over what the precise nature of the laws should be for this game to which all members were going to subscribe. At first it appeared as if the 'handlers' would win, but eventually the 'dribblers' prevailed. The adopted code included two decisive rules:

1. No player shall run with the ball.
2. Neither tripping nor hacking should be allowed, and no player shall use his hands to hold or push an opponent.

Blackheath and several other clubs were against these stipulations, so they withdrew – and the split between 'Rugby' and 'Association Football' was complete.

In Scotland, the move towards uniformity was rather less divisive. In 1865, the EAFC committee had discussed the idea of holding a meeting with representatives from Merchiston and Loretto to rationalise the rules, but nothing had come of this. Then, in November 1867, the club approved some alterations to the rules then in use for their own purposes.

A copy of this set of amended rules has not survived but we can visualise the intention of an addition to Rule 6, which read: 'In the case of a maul, however, a player having entered on side cannot get off side unless he leaves or be taken out of the maul.' More startling is the sentence inserted in Rule 18, which read: 'No player except the first on his side may be hacked.' At the time, the rules dictated that a result could be decided by goals only, so it was an obvious improvement to add: 'In the event of no goal being obtained by either side, the match will be decided by the number of tries obtained by either side, and one try will be held to decide the match.' This innovation, however, does not seem to have met with general approval and 'goals only' continued to be the sole method of scoring until 1875, which led to a ridiculous situation in 1873 when the Academy scored seven tries to Loretto's nil and the result was still officially a draw.

A month after these new law changes had been adopted a letter arrived from Hely-Hutchison Almond, the Headmaster of Loretto, proposing a meeting at which a uniform set of rules could be drawn up. The EAFC committee authorised Harry Cheyne, the club captain, along with G.T. Chiene, Jun., the honorary secretary, 'to meet with delegates from Loretto, Merchiston and, if possible, the West of Scotland, to have the rules adjusted so as to prevent confusion and disputes in future matches'. A series of conferences took place in Edinburgh and there was also a summit in Glasgow (after the Academicals' first ever game against West of Scotland), which eventually led to a new set of rules being submitted to the EAFC general committee for approval on 7 December 1867. At this meeting there was considerable support for a counter-proposal – to continue as before, playing the Rugby rules with adjustments being made as and when the club saw fit – but in the end a narrow majority (12 versus 10) voted in favour of the new rules.

In February 1868, Chiene sent a proof of these rules to Almond so that they could be printed. In the covering letter, Chiene wrote: 'After we have got the proof finally adjusted, clear proofs should, I think, be sent to St Andrews, Merchiston and the West of Scotland. I hope the two former will adopt them though I have considerable doubts about Merchiston doing so'. He added a postscript: 'I think we may put on the title page "The Laws of Football as played by the Principal Clubs in Scotland"'.

So, as Sandy Thorburn points out:

Three years before the formation in London of the Rugby Union the Scottish Clubs had produced and printed their set of Laws, which became known as the Green Book.

In the same passage Thorburn also states:

It is disappointing to find that so far no copy has turned up, for almost certainly it would be these Laws that were used in the first International match in March 1871.

CHAPTER NINE

Flodden is at last revenged!
James 'Skinny' Carmichael, a master at the Academy, 22nd March 1871

NOT ONLY DID RAEBURN PLACE host the first international rugby match, the club also played a key role in the protracted negotiations leading up to this historic occasion.

In March 1870, the Football Association, inspired by the success of two 'district' matches between London and Sheffield, decided to arrange a match at the Oval cricket ground which it advertised as 'England v Scotland'. This was rather misleading, as the 11 'Scottish' players all came from the London area, and many had extremely tenuous links with the country they were representing. It was rumoured that one qualified because of his admiration for whisky and another because he went north every year to shoot grouse.

This did not detract from the success of the match, so C.W. Alcock, the secretary of the FA, arranged for another game under the same banner to be played in November 1870, and on this occasion he wrote to several Scottish newspapers inviting clubs to nominate players for a Scottish XI. However, this only produced one player, who had already moved to London for business reasons, which was not surprising given that only four clubs – Queen's Park (1867), Thistle (1868), Hamilton (1869) and Airdrie (1870) – were playing under the FA rules at that time.

After the match, a letter in *The Scotsman* newspaper suggested that Scotland's rugby clubs should send ten of their players down to join the same number in London to challenge the FA. The challenge was quickly accepted by Alcock, with the proviso that the team sizes be limited to 11. 'With greater numbers it is our opinion that the game becomes less scientific and more a trial of charging and brute force'. This provoked a letter from H.M. (identified as Almond of Loretto by R.J. Phillips in his *History of Scottish Rugby*) who retorted: 'Mr Alcock is a very leading supporter of what is called the "association game" which is to Rugby football or whatever its detractors may please to call it as moonlight unto sunlight and water unto wine.'

But the seed had been sown, and on 8 December 1870, there appeared in *Bell's Life in London* and *The Scotsman* the following letter signed by the captains of five senior Scottish clubs:

Sir,

There is a pretty general feeling among Scotch football players that the football power of the old country was not properly represented in the late so-called International Football Match. Not that we think the play of the gentlemen who represented Scotland otherwise than any good – for that it was so is amply proved by the stout resistance they offered to their opponents and by the fact that they were beaten by only one goal – but that we consider the Association rules, in accordance with which the last game was played, not such as to bring together the best team Scotland could turn out. Almost all the leading clubs play by the Rugby code, and we have no opportunity of practising the Association game even if willing to do so. We therefore feel that a match played in accordance with any rules other than those in general use in Scotland, as was the case in the last match, is not one that would meet with support generally from her players. For our satisfaction, therefore, and with a view of really testing what Scotland can do against an English team we, as representing the football interests of Scotland, hereby challenge any team selected from the whole of England, to play us a match, twenty-a-side, Rugby rules either in Edinburgh or Glasgow on any day during the present season that might be found suitable to the English players. Let this count as the return to the match played in London on 19 November, or, if preferred, let it be a separate match. If it be entered into we can promise England a hearty welcome and a first-rate match. Any communications addressed to any one of us will be attended to.

We are, etc.,

    A.H. Robertson, West of Scotland FC
    F. Moncrieff, Edinburgh Academical FC
    B. Hall Blyth, Merchistonian FC
    J.W. Arthur, Glasgow Academical FC
    J.H. Oatts, St Salvator FC, St Andrews

Not surprisingly Alcock ignored the letter, but an acceptance of the challenge on behalf of the rugby-playing clubs in the London area was received from B.H. Burns, secretary of Blackheath (and incidentally a former pupil of the Edinburgh Academy), and so the match was scheduled to be played at Raeburn Place on Monday 27 March 1871.

A committee of six – comprising H-H. Almond of Loretto, J.W. Arthur of Glasgow Academicals, B.H. Blyth of Merchistonians, A. Buchanan of RHSFP and two Edinburgh Academicals in the shape of Dr J. Chiene and F.J. Moncreiff – was formed to make the necessary arrangements; and two trial matches were played – the first in Glasgow on 11 March and the other in Edinburgh on 20 March.

Negotiations were initiated with the Academical Cricket Club committee for the use of Raeburn Place, and eventually a majority voted in favour of allowing the ground to be used for this historic occasion. Apparently there were some serious reservations within the committee about allowing the ground to be used for this purpose, but those concerns surely disappeared when the club's treasurer reported after the match that 'the large sum of £13 was obtained from the Football Fund, being balance of gate money on the day of the First International Match after deducting expenses'.

The original challenge had suggested playing in either Glasgow or Edinburgh, but Raeburn Place was the obvious choice. Hamilton Crescent in Partick was the only appropriate venue in the west and at this time it was some distance outside the city, which would create all sorts of logistical problems for both players and supporters. Meanwhile, Raeburn Place, which was the most easily accessible venue for such a game in Edinburgh, was only a ten-minute cab ride from the New Town area, where the players would almost certainly lodge and change, and spectators would be able to use the local service to Stockbridge. Edinburgh was also easier for the London contingent of the English team to reach, via the east coast rail route. The fact that all but one of the committee members for the Scottish team were based in Edinburgh, and 13 of the 20 Scottish players were also resident in the city, must also have been a factor when the decision was made.

In London, a similar committee had been formed with B.H. Burns as secretary, but no trial matches were played.

Two days before the match, the *Glasgow Herald* had reported that the Rugby School rules would be used, with two minor alterations, both of which were customary in London. Firstly, the ball, on going into touch, was to be thrown into the ground again from the spot where it crossed the line, and not where it first pitched in touch; secondly, for a try at goal, the ball was to be brought out in a straight line from where it was touched down, thus eliminating the original Rugby School rule whereby the position of the kick at goal was established by punting the ball back into the field of play from the spot where it had been touched down.

It was also noted that in London the convention was that the ball could be picked up regardless of whether it was rolling or bounding. The Scottish clubs only allowed the latter, and this was the rule which applied in this match.

The match was to be umpired by that giant of Scottish rugby during the early years, H-H. Almond, and by an Englishman, A. Ward.

The Scottish team, who wore blue jerseys and cricket flannels, contained six Edinburgh Academical players – T.R. Marshall, J.F. Finlay, R.W. Irvine, W.J.C. Lyall, J.A.W. Mein and F.J. Moncrieff, who captained the side – as well as G. Ritchie, who played for Merchistonians but had been at the Academy between

The 1871 Scotland XX

Back: R.Munro, J.S. Thomson, J.W. Arthur, T. Chalmers

Middle: A. Buchanan, A.G. Colville, J. Forsyth, J.A.W. Mein (Edinburgh Academicals), R.W. Irvine (Edinburgh Academicals), W.D. Brown, A. Drew, W. Cross, J.F. Finlay (Edinburgh Academicals), F.J. Moncreiff (*Captain*, Edinburgh Academicals), G. Ritchie (Merchistonians)

Front: B. Ross, W.J.C. Lyall (Edinburgh Academicals), T.R. Marshall (Edinburgh Academicals), J.H.L. Macfarlane (Edinburgh University), A.H. Robertson (Edinburgh Academy)

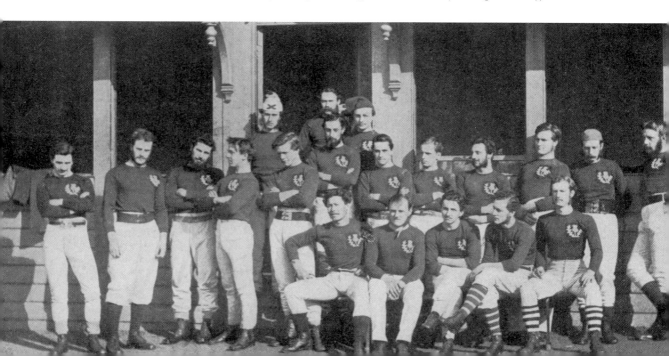

1858 and 1861, and A.H. Robertson, who played for West of Scotland but had been a pupil at the Academy from 1863 to 1865. There might well have been two more Academicals in the team, but W.K. Gair, a brilliant runner, lost a probable place through being injured in the second trial, and L.M. Balfour (afterwards Balfour-Melville), the Academy captain, was ruled out after being bitten by a dog.

Meanwhile, the English, who were in all-white except for the red rose on their shirts, had an Academical in their team too. B.H. Burns, who had taken such a prominent role in the lead-up to this match, ended up playing for his adopted country when there was a late call-off. Their team was made up of 12 London based players, and four each from Liverpool and Manchester. Apparently no fewer than ten of the team were Old Rugbeians.

The weather conditions on the day were delightful, apart from a gentle breeze. A crowd of around 4,000 paid an admission fee of one shilling to J.H.A. Macdonald (Lord Kingsburgh), who sat behind a deal table with an earthenware bowl to hold the takings, as they entered the ground from the south-west corner of the field.

The pitch was in more or less the same position as it has been throughout the long history of Raeburn Place. Measuring 55 yards across and 120 yards in length, it was a good deal smaller than the English were used to, and this almost certainly worked in the home team's favour because the visiting backs had hoped that they would be able to use their superior pace to outflank their opponents. Since neither North Park Terrace nor Inverleith Pond existed at that time, the rising ground over the burn to the west and north of the pitch was used by the spectators, whilst the east touchline and the famous Mound were reserved for Academicals and their guests.

According to R.W. Irvine's contemporary account, the Scottish team had prepared as well as they could for the match, but still went into the game without a clue as to what was awaiting them.

The men were requested to get into training and did it. It was twenty-a-side, and the Scotch forwards were heavy and fast. We were ignorant what team England would bring, of what sort of players they had, and of how they would play; and though assured by Colville, a London Merchistonian – and a rare good forward, too – that we would find their size strength and weight not very materially different from our own, many of us entered that match with a sort of vague fear that some entirely new kind of play would be shown by our opponents, and that they would out-manoeuvre us entirely. The day of the match soon unsettled that uncertainty. The English twenty were big and heavy – probably bigger and heavier than ours, but not overpoweringly so.

Before we had played ten minutes we were on good terms with each other. Each side had made a discovery – we that our opponents were flesh and blood like ourselves, and could be mauled back and tackled and knocked about just like other men; they that in this far north land rugby players existed who could maul, tackle and play-up with the rest of them.

After a deadlocked first half, Scotland won the match by a goal and a try to a single try by England, although both Scottish scores were disputed.

With the first score, the umpires had awarded a scrummage five yards out and the Scots mauled the ball over the line and A. Buchanan of Royal High School FP grabbed the try. The English complained that the surge had been made before the ball had been properly put down, but the umpires sided with the Scots. Buchanan might have touched the ball down, but as a try in those days only provided that team with the right to have a 'try' at goal, the honour of scoring the first points in international rugby went to W. Cross of Glasgow Academicals, who kicked the conversion from close to the touchline. It was that kick which prompted James Carmichael to throw his tall hat into the air and exclaim the immortal words: 'Flodden is at last revenged.'

The second Scottish try came after the ball had gone into touch near the English try line. A long throw-in went over the heads of the forwards to J.W. Arthur, of Glasgow Academicals, but the ball rebounded forwards off him into the hands of Cross, who touched down for the try. The English players immediately protested that the ball had been knocked-on, but the Scottish interpretation of the laws of the game at this time was that this was only an offence if it was intentional, so both umpires agreed that the try should stand. Cross missed the conversion but his previous goal was enough to eclipse England's solitary try by R.H. Birkett, which F. Stokes had failed to convert.

Umpire Almond left his own account of the match, demonstrating some incontrovertible wisdom when justifying his controversial decision to allow that first Scottish score to stand:

The Calcutta Cup match at Raeburn Place, 1886, by W.H. Overend and L.P. Smythe

I do not know to this day whether the decision which gave Scotland the try from which the winning goal was kicked was correct in fact . . . I must say, however, that when an umpire is in doubt, I think he is justified in deciding against the side which makes the most noise. They are probably in the wrong.

The other major controversy the umpires had to deal with related to the vexed issue of hacking. That practice had not yet been officially outlawed, but by 1871 it was on the way out, with club after club deciding that there was no room in the game for such brutality. According to Irvine, the decision to ban the practice in this first international match proved troublesome, especially as nerves frayed and tempers flared.

There was one critical time during the match. Feeling was pretty highly strung. It was among the first no-hacking matches for many of the players on both sides. Now, hacking becomes an instinctive action to one trained to it; you hack at a man running past out of reach as surely as you blink when a man puts his finger in your eye. There were a good many hacks-over going on, and, as blood got up it began to be muttered, 'Hang it! Why not have hacking allowed? It can't be prevented – far better have it.' The question hung in the balance. The teams seemed nothing loth. The captains (Moncrieff and Stokes) both looked as if they ought to say 'no' but would rather say 'yes', and were irresolute, when Almond, who was umpire, vowed he would throw up his job if it were agreed on, so it was forbidden and the hackers were ordered to be more cautious.

Irvine added that:

Although many matches have been played since between the two countries, there has not been one better fought or more exciting than this, the first one. The Scotsmen were exultant and the winning ball was hung for many a day in the shop of Johnnie Bowton, at the Stock Bridge, adorned with ribbons like the tail of a Clydesdale stallion at a horse show. With this match and victory the life of rugby football as a national institution fairly commenced.

Scottish rugby football may be said to have sprung up from boyhood to robust manhood with the first international match in 1871.

CHAPTER TEN

A meeting will be held on Monday the third of March, in the Glasgow Academy, Elmbank Street, at 1/2-past four o'clock (immediately after the conclusion of the international match), to consider as to the propriety of forming a Football Union in Scotland, upon a similar basis to the Rugby Union in England. All members of clubs playing the Rugby Union Rules are invited to attend.

Public notice placed in Scottish newspapers
on the morning of Scotland versus England
match at Hamilton Crescent in Glasgow, 3 March 1873.

IT DID NOT TAKE LONG for the concept of representative rugby to catch on, with the first Edinburgh versus Glasgow inter-city match being played on 23 November 1872 at Burnbank, the home ground of Glasgow Academicals. On that occasion the Edinburgh team, containing six Academicals – T.R. Marshall, J.A.W. Mein, F.J. Moncrieff, R.W. Irvine, E.M. Bannerman and J. Finlay – defeated Glasgow by a drop-goal (scored by Marshall) to nil.

This was the beginning of a period of rapid growth in the popularity of the game. In March 1873, *The Scotsman* noted:

> The number of spectators which two or three years ago would not have exceeded two or three score, can now be reckoned by hundreds, and has necessitated the charging for admission to some of our leading football club grounds, and in one case – the Edinburgh Academicals – the ground had to be fenced round in addition.

This boom in interest was not restricted to those wishing to watch matches. Playing numbers were also increasing. During the 1873–74 season an Academical second team made occasional appearances, and during the following season it became a regular side.

Elsewhere in Scotland, the game was growing in popularity, and the 1870s was the decade in which the Scottish Borders first emerged as a stronghold of the sport. Langholm led the way by founding a club in 1871, followed by

Hawick in 1873, Gala in 1875, Kelso in 1876, Melrose in 1877 and Jed-Forest in 1885.

The game was also growing in England, and the need for some sort of uniformity in the rules led to a meeting of delegates from 21 clubs, almost all from London, at the Pall Mall Restaurant, on 26 January 1871. At that gathering the Rugby Football Union was officially constituted and a three-man committee appointed to draw up a definitive set of laws – which included the prohibition of hacking. Legend has it that there would have been 22 delegates present but the Wasps representative went to the wrong establishment and decided to stay there.

In October of 1871, the Academicals adopted the RFU's laws, and the following year the club joined that organisation. Five other Scottish clubs – West of Scotland, Glasgow Academicals, Edinburgh University, Royal High School FP and Edinburgh Wanderers – also threw their lot in with the RFU around about this time. This meant that they had to accept English opposition to the practice of hacking – but this wasn't a complete shock to the system.

For several years the issue of hacking had been a hot topic in Scotland. Indeed, it had become such a contentious issue that the players and committee men of the day were probably quite relieved to abrogate responsibility to the RFU.

In November 1869, *The Scotsman* had noted: 'The semi-barbarous habit of "hacking" we are glad to see getting out of fashion in this part of the country. Though it was indulged in last Saturday by Craigmount [at that time a boy's school on the south side of Edinburgh] and Merchiston in their match, the game at Raeburn Place, on Saturday [between the Academy and Merchiston] was conspicuous for its absence.' Strangely, the report of that match in the same newspaper paints a rather different picture, with hacking apparently being 'indulged in somewhat freely' during the final ten minutes. A week later, the Acadamy and Craigmount were due to meet at Raeburn Place, where there was 'a large turnout of ladies and gentlemen'. In the preliminary discussion, the captains had agreed that there should be no hacking, but the Academy team refused to play under these conditions and, as Craigmount were under strict orders not to play with hacking, the match was abandoned, with the two sides not meeting again until six years later. At the Academicals' AGM in October 1870, 'it was agreed that the Club play with hacking but that in school matches it be left to discretion'.

This alliance between Scottish clubs and the RFU was destined to be a stop-gap measure. The growing popularity of the game north of the border, allied with a desire for Scotland to replicate in its own right the aims and successes of the RFU, meant that the establishment of an independent Scottish governing body was inevitable.

When it happened, Edinburgh Academicals were, once again, in the thick of the action. As James Wallace (who captained the club during the 1868–69 season) later recorded in *The Chronicle* (May 1908):

> The EAFC were largely instrumental in founding the Scottish Rugby Union [the name was changed in 1924]. The first steps were taken at a dinner in the University Club, and there were present, if memory serves me rightly, Albert Harvey of Glasgow, B. Hall Blyth of Merchistonians, John Chiene, Harry Cheyne, Craigie Bell, and myself of the EAFC.

Even the first two names on this list had strong connections with the club. Harvey was a Glasgow Academical but had been a pupil at Edinburgh Academy for a couple of years between 1854 and 1856; while Hall Blyth had five brothers at the school. Most of those present at the dinner went on to hold high office in the Union. John Chiene was the first president, Harvey the second, and Hall Blyth the third, while Wallace was the first secretary.

The outcome of this discussion was a notice inviting representatives of all Scotland's rugby clubs to a meeting on 3 March at Glasgow Academy. At the meeting Dr Chiene was called to the chair, and it was agreed that a union of clubs in Scotland should be formed, with the aim of providing funds for a cup, bringing into closer connection the clubs then playing, and forming a committee for the selection of future Scotland international teams.

A provisional committee, consisting of the captain and one other member of each of the eight founder member clubs, was nominated to draw up the bye-laws of this new organisation. These bye-laws would be ratified at a general meeting to be held before the start of the next (1873–74) season.

The eight founder member clubs in this new association were: Edinburgh Academicals, Edinburgh University, Glasgow Academicals, Glasgow University, Merchistonians, Royal High School FP, St Andrews University and West of Scotland.

The first AGM of the Scottish Football Union was held in Keith & Co.'s Rooms, 65a George Street, Edinburgh on 9 October 1873. Harry Cheyne was in the chair and the meeting first approved and then passed the bye-laws of the new Union. It is interesting that the idea of running a cup competition was discarded, and it would be another 100 years before any Union-run club competition materialised, with the introduction of National Leagues in 1973.

Once the bye-laws had been dealt with, Wanderers FC and Warriston FC were admitted as member clubs. So, while the eight clubs in the original committee could be described as founder members, those two clubs could accurately be labelled as original members of the Union.

Warriston did not survive long. It had been formed by some Academicals who were not satisfied with the way their club was being run, but the persuasive efforts of R.W. Irvine – who had played in the first international match and was secretary, treasurer and captain of EAFC at the time – managed to smooth things over.

Another Academical, H. Radcliffe, played a leading role in starting Wanderers, and that club quickly emerged as one of Scotland's most prominent clubs. Occasionally, Academicals played for Wanderers in important matches when their own club did not have a game.

Unlike the RFU, the SFU decided not to extend membership to school sides, which was a brash move considering the central role certain schools had played in the game's development up to this point. Not surprisingly, Almond of Loretto strongly criticised the decision. Writing in Marshall's *Football* 20 years later, he deplored the way the game had been allowed to develop to suit the adult player rather than the schoolboy.

> The great end of this game . . . [is] . . . to produce a race of robust men, with active habits, brisk circulations, manly sympathies, and exuberant spirits. I don't think I am overstating my charge when I say that they [the SFU] regard it far too much as a means of attracting spectators. That is in itself an evil. When a man is past playing football, which is ten years sooner in the modern game than by the old one, he ought as a rule to be taking hard exercise in some form himself whenever he gets the chance and not spending his Saturday afternoons as a stationary and shivering spectator.

It was agreed that this new Scottish Union should work with its English counterpart, but it quickly became clear that this well-intentioned aim would not be as easy to achieve in practice as had been hoped.

CHAPTER ELEVEN

In one match the Geits (the youngest boys in the School) found try scoring very
easy but goal kicking very difficult. Out of 22 tries scored during the game, only
one was converted – and the Geits lost by 21 tries to 1 goal!
from *The Edinburgh Academical Football Club Centenary History*, published 1958

IN DECEMBER 1875, THE SFU committee decided that from the start of the following
season the new scoring system which had recently been drawn up by the RFU
should be adopted. This meant: 'A match shall be decided by a majority of goals,
but if the number of goals be equal, or no goal be kicked, by a majority of tries; if
no goal be kicked or try obtained, the match shall be drawn'.

This did not happen soon enough to prevent the Academy team of 1873–74
from returning a set of results for that season which did not do justice to the
dazzling talent in that side.

The team was captained by J.H.S. Graham, and included N.J. Finlay, W.E.
Maclagan and P.W. Smeaton, all of whom went on to play for Scotland, as well as
J.J. Moubray, who played for Oxford in the University Match three times between
1876 and 1878. The side was described by R.J. Phillips as 'the first great school
combination in the game', yet it only managed two draws versus Merchiston, and a
win and a draw versus Fettes. The lack of a decent goal-kicker had proven to be an
insurmountable hurdle. In one of the matches against Merchiston, the score was
two tries to nil in the Academy's favour, but as neither of those scores was
converted the match ended in a draw. The drawn match against Fettes was even
more one-sided, with the Academy scoring seven unanswered tries but failing to
kick any goals.

The nucleus of the 1873–74 Academy team stayed together for the 1874–75
season, during which N.J. Finlay became the first of four Academy boys to be
'capped' whilst still at school (the others were Charles Reid for Scotland against
England in 1881, Frank Wright for England in the same match and W.M.C.
McEwan for Scotland against Wales in 1894). Then, during the 1875–76 season,

63

1873–74 Academy XX

Back: S.L. Sharp, C.E. Wood

Second Row: W.E. Maclagan, A.M. Kennedy, J.A. Gardner, G.T. Lyell, M.H. Gardiner, P.W. Smeaton,
H.L.M. Dunlop, E.W. Anderson, G.S.R. Smith

Third Row: N.J. Finlay, J.G. Macnair, F. Fraser, J.H.S. Graham (*Captain*), L.J. Aitken, J.J. Moubray

Front: A. Brebner, J. Younger, J.G. Durie

W.E. Maclagan captained the Academy to a third consecutive undefeated season. This period of excellence at the Academy provided the backbone of the success enjoyed by the Academical sides of the mid to late 1870s.

During the 1870s, the number of inter-club matches being played in Scotland increased at a steady rate. Edinburgh Academicals first played Glasgow Academicals in January 1872, and this quickly became the crucial club game in Scotland's rugby calendar.

The first match between the two clubs ended in a scoreless draw, largely thanks to the fair-minded spirit of the Glasgow side, who crossed the line for what initially appeared to be a good try until two players from their team spoke up. They 'had misgivings as to the handling of the ball in a scrummage, immediately preceding the touchdown, informed their side of the same, and the ball was at once resigned to Edinburgh's care' *(The Glasgow Academy, 1846–1946)*. Despite the lack of scoring, this was apparently a 'really fine' game, which is not surprising given the number of leading Scottish players taking part – with eight current or future internationalists playing on each side.

The Edinburgh Academicals side that day, as listed in *The Scotsman* newspaper (without positions), was: T.R. Marshall (captain), L.M. Balfour, J.F. Finlay, R.W. Irvine, J.A.W. Mein, D.R. Irvine, J.A. Ross, W. Blackwood, D. Robertson, R.G. Dunlop, T.A. Bell, A.B. Finlay, T.W. Lang, R.E. Wood and C.K. Scott Moncrieff.

Of this team, Leslie Melville Balfour (who became Leslie Melville Balfour-Melville when his father succeeded to the estate of Mount Melville near St Andrews in Fife) is particularly worthy of mention.

His family were the Balfours of Pilrig, and he led almost as exciting a life as his fictional relative David in Robert Louis Stevenson's novel *Kidnapped*. However, while Stevenson's character was preoccupied with surviving the sinister attentions of his evil uncle and various other villains during the aftermath of the Jacobite Rising in eighteenth-century Scotland, the real-life Balfour was more concerned with outwitting fast bowlers and chipping in birdie shots from off the green – for he was probably the greatest Scottish athlete of all time.

Balfour played rugby for Scotland against England at Kennington Oval in 1872, at the age of seventeen years and ten months, and that would have been his second cap had he not been bitten by a dog before the inaugural international match of 1871. If he had been fit to play in that game he would still be Scotland's youngest ever international player. As it was, Scotland lost in 1872, and in those days when the annual match against England was the beginning and end of the international season, Balfour was never selected again.

Instead, he had to content himself with other sporting successes in a range of diverse fields. He won the British Amateur Golf Championship at St Andrews on the 19th hole in 1895, beating the reigning Open champion John Ball, who had been the first man to hold both the Open and Amateur titles at the same time. Each of the last three ties on the way to becoming champion went to play-offs: on each occasion he put his approach shot into the Swilcan Burn and had to lift out and count a penalty stroke. He was runner-up in the Amateur Championship in 1889, and reached the semi-final a further six times between 1888 and 1897. He won 31 medals in Royal and Ancient competitions and is the only player to have won the King William IV medal on four occasions.

Balfour also won the Scottish Lawn Tennis Championship in 1879 and was a beaten finalist in 1878 and 1880; a Scottish champion at billiards and the long jump; and an internationalist at skating, curling and athletics.

However, the greatest moment of Balfour's sporting career was on 29 July 1882, when he was captain, wicket-keeper and opening batsman in the Scottish XI which defeated Australia by seven wickets in a one-day match at the Grange. Balfour scored the winning runs with a six dispatched to the Academical ground next door, and then insisted that his team bat on so that the spectators at the ground could get full value for their money. Scotland needed 123 runs to win the match but ended up with 167, of which 73 were scored by Balfour, before he was captured leg before wicket by the Australian captain, W.L. Murdoch.

One month later, more or less the same Australian team gained their first victory over England by seven runs, in the match which gave birth to the Ashes legend, when one distraught Englishman, Reginald Brooks, posted a mock obituary in *The Sporting Dispatch* lamenting the death of English cricket and signing off with the immortal words: 'NB – The body will be cremated and the ashes taken to Australia.'

Known as 'the W.G. Grace of Scotland', Balfour was a near automatic choice for the national cricket team between 1874 and 1893, and he was recalled to the side to play against Ireland in 1909 and in 1910, by which time he was well into his 50s. He was 14 years old when he played his first game for the Academy XI, and 56 years later, in 1924, he turned out for the Old Academy Captains XI, at the age of 70.

Balfour also contributed hugely to Scottish sport as an administrator. He served as president of the Scottish Rugby Union for the 1893–94 season; was captain of the Honourable Company of Edinburgh Golfers in 1902–03 and captain of the Royal & Ancient Golf Club of St Andrews in 1906–07; was president of the Academical Cricket Club in 1908; and was elected first president of the newly re-organised Scottish Cricket Union in 1909, thereby gaining the rare distinction of playing for his country whilst serving as president.

Remarkably, Balfour managed to combine all these sporting achievements with a highly successful career as a lawyer, he was a Writer to the Signet, and in later life became a Justice of the Peace. His son, James, was also a very good cricketer, playing twice for Scotland in 1913, but was killed in action in the First World War the following year.

This remarkable man died on 20 July 1937. He was 83 years old. In 2002, he was one of the initial 50 inductees into the Scottish Sports Hall of Fame.

The Glasgow Academicals game was one of only five matches played by the Academicals in the 1871–72 season, but that number increased to ten the following year and included the first match against an English club when a Liverpool team fielding four Academicals – including the captain, G. Dunlop – played out a no-scoring draw at Raeburn Place. The visiting side also contained J.R. Hay-Gordon, a future Scotland cap who had gone from the Academy to Harrow, but had retained enough affection for his old school to make intermittent trips back to Edinburgh to assist the club in important matches.

With R.W. 'Bulldog' Irvine as captain, the Academical side of 1873–74 went the whole season unbeaten. That campaign witnessed the revival of matches against Royal High School FP after a three-year lapse. To celebrate the occasion, the game was played under the 'old rules' and a dinner was held at the Castle afterwards. *The Scotsman* reported: 'The game played was the old Rugby, that is picking up only on the bound (with the exception of goal keepers); and consequently the game, though perhaps more open, had not the same relish with some people as that presently in force.'

Perhaps the most noteworthy aspect of this match was that five Finlay brothers played in the Academical team. There were seven brothers in total – six of whom played for the Academicals at various times, and three of whom represented Scotland.

The only Finlay brother who was not a footballer was the eldest, R.B. (Robert Bannatyne), who would become Viscount Finlay of Nairn and serve as Lord Chancellor from 1916 to 1919. At the Academy Centenary Dinner in 1924, this early 20th century giant of British political and legal life recalled an incident which demonstrated how rugby had already developed that priceless ability to capture the imagination.

A young man was told about me by a connection of mine. He listened with languid interest but when he was told that I was a brother of Ninian Finlay, the Scottish half-back in the International matches, his whole attitude changed and the toleration he had been previously disposed to extend was replaced by profound respect for the brother of so great a man.

Of all the Finlay brothers, Ninian [N.J.] was undoubtedly the rugby star. An expert drop-kicker at a time when drop-kicking was used not only as a scoring mechanism but also for touch-finding, he also handled beautifully, possessed a splendid physique and had a startling turn of pace which he used to great effect in both defence and attack.

Scotland v England, 5th March 1877

Back: H.M. Napier (West of Scotland), C. Villars (Edinburgh Wanderers), J.R.H. Gordon (Edinburgh Academicals), J.H.S. Graham (Edinburgh Academicals).

Middle: H.H. Johnston (Edinburgh University), J.R. Reid (Edinburgh Wanderers), R.W. Irvine (*Captain*, Edinburgh Academicals), A.G. Petrie (RHSFP), T.J. Torrie (Edinburgh Academicals), J.S. Carrick (Glasgow Academicals).

Front: D.H. Watson (Glasgow Academicals), M. Cross (Glasgow Academicals), J. Junor (Glasgow Academicals), R.C. MacKenzie (Glasgow Academicals), E.I. Pocock (Edinburgh Wanderers).

He was an early bloomer and was selected for Scotland to play against England whilst still at the Academy on the back of a remarkable performance a few months earlier for Edinburgh in that season's inter-city match against Glasgow. Despite the treacherously wet conditions the match proved to be a classic, with

Finlay at the centre of much of the excitement. With only a few moments left to play and the scores level, G. Heron, one of Glasgow's international forwards, broke with the ball from around the halfway line.

According to R.J. Phillips in *The Story of Scottish Rugby*:

Nothing, it appeared, could possibly prevent a score. The crowd were already cheering the success, when Ninian Finlay flashed into sight and went in pursuit. The shouting increased in volume and the excitement in intensity as the race between the pair proceeded. Yard by yard the Academy boy gained, and almost as Heron was stepping over the line his pursuer was on him, and had him down outside. One of the old chroniclers described the incident as 'the most thrilling bit of play ever to be seen on a football field . . .'

Phillips also recounts an episode in the 1879 international between Scotland and England.

Scotland's equalising score was characteristic of Ninian Finlay. It often took two or three men to bring him down. J.H.S. Graham, at the end of a Scottish forward rush, picked up the ball and passed it to Gordon Petrie. The Royal High School man in turn handed it to Ninian Finlay, who made a direct course for the line. The way was blocked, but, with a couple of Englishmen hanging onto him, Finlay got in his drop and sent the ball over the bar. Cheering and enthusiasm did not subside, one report says, for fully five minutes.

The greatest half-back of his time, and one of the greatest players who have appeared in the game, Ninian Finlay was the accepted standard of comparison for International half-backs [the modern three-quarters] for many years after his retiral.

Ninian Finlay might have been the first superstar of Scottish rugby, but he was by no means the only brilliant player to represent the Academicals at this time.

James (J.F.) Finlay, the fourth of the seven brothers, had played in the first international match in 1871 and was an ever-present in the Scotland side until he retired in 1875 after the match against England in which two of his younger brothers, Ninian and Arthur, made their debuts. R.J. Phillips described him as 'one of the heaviest, most powerful, and athletic of the Scottish forwards. Inside the 25 there was no stopping him if he got fairly set for the line'. According to an account of that first international match in the Rev. F. Marshall's book *Football: The Rugby Union Game*, he was involved in a spectacular collision with an equally fearsome Englishman.

> Finlay had got well away with the ball and was sprinting for the English line at hundred yards speed when Osborne, folding his arms across his chest, ran full tilt at him, after the fashion of a bull charging a gate. Both were very big, heavy men, and the crash of the collision was tremendous, each reeling some yards and finally falling on his back. For a few seconds, players and spectators alike held their breath, fearing terrible results, but the two giants promptly resumed their places, apparently none the worse for wear.

R.W. Irvine continued to captain the Academicals for three seasons on the trot, during which time the club lost only one match, against Glasgow Academicals in the 1875–76 campaign. A doctor to trade, he was a splendid forward and an inspiring leader. He has been widely credited with doing a great deal to ensure that the EAFC remained a major force in the sport when the rapid spread of the game might have found the oldest club in Scotland falling off the pace. He was one month short of his eighteenth birthday when he played in the first international match in 1871, and appeared in every match against the old enemy in ten successive years until 1880, which is a record only equalled by Sandy Carmichael between 1965 and 1977. He was Scotland captain during the last five of these games.

Irvine's successor as captain at the club was J.H.S. 'Gissie' Graham, who was described in glowing terms by Phillips:

> One of the greatest forwards the game has seen. A fair-haired, enthusiastic schoolboy, he possessed from his early days the gift of leadership, and as the captain of the champion school team, captain of a great Academical champion team, and captain of the International team, he gained all the honours the game could give. Of very powerful physique, it was his skill as a dribbler that carried him into the first International match in 1876. He played the game heartily and vigorously, and was always as willing to make

concessions to an opponent as he was ready to acknowledge the merits and encourage the efforts of his own players. No forward of his day played the game with more intelligence, skill and effect than Graham. He was one of the most advanced players of his time, and one of the great products of Scottish football.

Graham captained the Academicals for four seasons, from 1876–77 to 1879–80, during which time they were champions three times. The best of those seasons was 1877–78, when the Academicals won all 11 matches they played, scoring 14 goals and 14 tries, and with no score whatsoever being conceded.

1878–79 1st XV

Back: G.W.L. McLeod, C.E. Wood, J.P. Bannerman, N.J. Finlay, L.J. Aitken, E. Ross Smith, T.W. Tod, P. Russel

Middle: W.E. Maclagan, R.W. Irvine, J.H.S. Graham (*Captain*), D.R. Irvine, P.W. Smeaton

Front: G.Q. Paterson, J. Younger

An article in the *Evening Dispatch* in 1914 attributed the success enjoyed by the Academicals at this time to 'the combination and thorough understanding which permeated the team'.

Academicals agree that to J.H.S. Graham more than any other player this was due. More than that, it was not due to precept so much as to example. From the first days when Jim Graham played for the Academy down to his last international match he was always the same, steady, determined, hard-worker – never a showy player. By his sheer hard work in the scrimmage he inspired others to do likewise, and so founded what we may term the first 'School' of Scottish Rugby.

The game as it was played in those days was very different from what it is to-day [1914], but no team that the writer can recall could quite equal the Academicals of the latter '70s for sure, hard, resolute tackling.

Once the ball got in the scrum it was kept there – wedged probably tight between one of the leading forwards' feet – and the opposing side were surely and steadily shoved towards their goal line. Such a thing as 'heeling out' would have been promptly condemned as 'bad form', and when the ball did get loose in a forward rush, the great object of Graham and his fellows was never to let it more than a foot in front of them, and in a loose scrimmage they were so well together that practically no side could withstand them . . .

The essential difference between Scottish Rugby and the game played in each of the other three countries has been forward, and it is not too much to claim that the Academicals, with J.H.S. Graham at their head, were the real originators of the Scottish style of game.

While the Academical forwards received much of the credit for the success the team enjoyed at this time, the value of some exceptionally gifted backs should not be overlooked. As well as Ninian Finlay, there was, for example, G.Q. 'Quinty' Paterson, who was prevented by a lack of weight from being a success at international level – he was only capped once, against England in 1876 – but whose skill as a quarter-back in club matches was long remembered. Weighing just under nine stone, he remains the lightest player ever to have represented Scotland.

After Paterson retired from the game, J. Younger and P.W. Smeaton – who was capped three times for Scotland in the early 1880s – were the usual quarter-backs. And behind this pair, playing either as a three-quarter or as a full-back, was W.E. (Bill) Maclagan.

According to the *EAFC Centenary History*:

It was in defence that Maclagan excelled. He was splendid in facing a forward rush, and his kicking was long and accurate. His tackling was not only extremely reliable but was made even more effective by a remarkable judgement that enabled him to deal with a player faster than himself. In attack he was an expert at drop-goals and difficult to stop in a short dash to the line, although he was not exceptionally fast. 'Great as a player of the Rugby game,' the *Chronicle* has recorded, 'he was almost greater as a captain. Tall, erect, alert, resourceful, he inspired confidence, and his keenness commended itself to the team.'

He was in the Scotland team for 13 seasons, between 1878 and 1890, and he captained the side during the last six of those years. After leaving the Academy in 1876 he played regularly for the Academicals until moving to London in 1881, whereupon he was instrumental in turning London Scottish into one of the leading clubs in the capital. He remained a loyal and committed Academical and often travelled back to Edinburgh to help his old team out in important matches. He was president of the club for three seasons from 1905–06 to 1907–08, and at the club's Jubilee Dinner in 1908 it was fitting that he was in the chair.

In 1891, at the age of 33, his standing in the game was recognised when, at the request of the RFU, he was made captain of the first British team to visit South Africa.

This was the tour which formalised the concept of international rugby competition, with the tourists playing three Test matches. However, the South Africans were only just beginning to get to grips with the game and were unable to cope with the dribbling skills of the British forwards and the passing skills of the backs. Once Maclagan's team had got used to the hard grounds and the thin atmosphere on the high veldt, they proved far too strong for their hosts. They won all 19 of the matches played, scoring 224 points and conceding only one – a try in the first match of the tour. It was more of a missionary exercise than anything else, and in that regard it can be considered an unqualified success. At the farewell dance before the tourist departed for home at the end of the tour, Maclagan predicted a great future for the game in South Africa – he could not have been more prescient.

One lasting legacy of this trip was the handsome silver cup which had been donated by Sir Donald Currie of the Union Caste Shipping Line, to be presented to the team which did best against the Brits. That honour went to Griqualand West, who only lost by three points to nil. The trophy was held by that club until the next season and was then contested for by all the clubs of South Africa. The Currie Cup remains the holy grail of the South African Provincial Championship.

CHAPTER TWELVE

When the match is going against you and you've striven hard to win,
When the forwards rush the scrimmage and the halves keep romping in,
When the score's three goals to one,
With ten minutes more to run,
And victory seems hopeless, and you're very tired and lame,
Remember, schoolboy pluck,
Will often turn the luck:
Play up! Play up! Play up! Play up and win the game!

From the *Academy Chronicle*,
quoted in Sidney Freeman's scrapbook.

IN 1881, THE EDINBURGH ACADEMY achieved the unique distinction of being the only school to have ever had two current pupils playing in the same international match. When Scotland played England, at Raeburn Place on 19 March of that year, there was one Academy schoolboy on each side. Charles 'Hippo' Reid, the Academy captain, had already played against Ireland and retained his place in the national team for the visit of England; while F.T. Wright was called upon to fill a last-minute vacancy in the visiting team.

The match, which had already been postponed twice, was played on a Tuesday afternoon in front of 12,000 spectators, with a temporary stand being constructed to help accommodate the bumper crowd. It was a fast and open game in good conditions. Scotland, playing with the wind at their backs, got the better of the first half, and R. Ainslie of Edinburgh Institution FP crossed for a try, but T.A. Begbie failed with his conversion attempt. His effort from close to the touchline hit the post just above the crossbar and rebounded back into play. Under the rules of the time, the game was still alive and Reid was the first to react, collecting the ball six yards from the line and fighting his way over, only to be denied the score when he was dispossessed in a maul with three Englishmen. On the stroke of half-time, J.A. Campbell of Glasgow Academicals touched down in the north-east corner of the field, but the score was disputed and eventually yielded because he had knocked the corner flag down.

England, playing with ten forwards, started to dominate after the break, and midway through the second half Lennard Stokes, captaining the visitors, kicked an astonishing 80-yard drop-goal (apparently his effort was from the touchline and 16 yards inside his own half). Then H.C. Rowley gave England the lead with an unconverted try. On the stroke of full-time, Ninian Finlay broke away and after a long run dropped at goal. He missed, but J.B. Brown was following up, and was able to gather the ball and touch down despite being tackled as he crossed the line. Begbie's conversion rescued a draw for Scotland.

It had been a thrilling afternoon, but there was barely a moment to draw breath for the two Academy pupils, who were straight back to school the following day. H.J. Stevenson, who would carve out his own place in Scottish rugby history a few years later, recorded the scene at 'Prayers' in the main hall that Wednesday morning:

> Tommy Harvey was the Rector. 'Hippo' and Frank came in with their class just as Tommy did to say prayers. There were no prayers that day! We cheered and cheered and cheered – and Tommy gave it up!

Sadly, this was one of only a few highs for rugby at the school during the 1880s. Good players that Reid and Wright were, that 1880–81 team were hopelessly out-weighed and lost all matches against Fettes, Loretto and Merchiston. In fact, throughout this decade the Academy won only one match against these schools, and that was largely due to Loretto being under-strength when the two teams met during the 1882–83 season. Apparently the Academy struggled so much during this decade that there was a danger that fixtures against the other leading school teams might be discontinued. Time and again, teams from the school were forced to batten down the hatches and defend grimly for long periods just to keep the score respectable, and they were not always successful in achieving even this rather modest aim.

The decline was partly caused by a fall in the number of boys at the school, and the situation was exacerbated by the fact that Academy pupils tended to leave school earlier than boarding-school pupils, which obviously reduced the number of senior boys available to the 1st XV. Charles Reid, for instance, was 17 when he left school and the average age of his XV had been 16 at the start of season, compared to nearly 17 at Fettes and Loretto.

The strength of these boarding schools was demonstrated in 1881 when the Academicals played Loretto on one of the afternoons which had been freed up by the repeated postponements of the Scotland–England match. It was a strong Academicals side, containing several players who represented Scotland that season – J.H.S. Graham, Ninian Finlay, P.W. Smeaton, plus the two Academy boys, Reid and Wright – but they were well beaten on the day. The club side may have been guilty of taking their opponents too lightly at first, but that should not detract from the school team's achievement in setting up a two-score lead in the first half before defending splendidly for the remainder of the match to hold on for a well-deserved victory, by one goal and two tries to two tries. That season, Loretto beat Fettes but lost twice to Merchiston.

The standard of day-school football was well below that of the boarding schools, and throughout the 'depression' the Academy could still defeat most of the day schools they met, until George Watson's College graduated from playing the 2nd XV in 1885, and went five years without losing a match to the Academy.

The Academy's problems on the rugby field had inevitable ramifications for the Academicals. The stars of the 1870s had either retired or were reaching the twilight years of their playing careers, and while the school was producing some very good players, there was not enough young blood coming through to fill the gaps left by the likes of 'Bull-Dog' Irvine. The problem was exacerbated by the number of players produced at the Academy during this period who moved away from Edinburgh after leaving school and could only intermittently play for the club. For example, C.H. Sample, E.L. Strong and Frank Wright all played for England, but they were never regular Academical players.

In 1880–81, when the Edinburgh Institution FP were heading for their first championship success, Bill Maclagan came up from London to play against them, and he did so again the following year. Academicals lost both those games, but the value of these sorts of reinforcements was shown in November 1882, when Maclagan (London Scottish) scored the Academicals' only try in a draw with Glasgow Academicals, and a week later A.P. Reid (West of Scotland) performed a similar feat to help Academicals to a one try to nil victory over Edinburgh Institution FP

The 1880–81 season was disrupted by seven weeks of frost, but was enlivened by a dispute over the Scottish captaincy – with the Academicals, as usual, at the centre of the controversy.

With 'Bulldog' Irvine having retired, the captaincy of the Scotland team was passed to J.H.S. Graham, his brilliant but relatively inexperienced club-mate. However, a number of players in the national side felt that A.G. Petrie of Royal High School, who was the most senior member of the team, having first played for Scotland in 1873, should have been given the job.

According to Phillips 'the Royal High School section blazed up in their wrath and were supported "on principle" by the [Edinburgh] Institution and [Edinburgh] University. The boys met in their crowds in "Daish's", the "Albert" and the other howffs, and let loose their indignation'.

As Phillips explains how the argument escalated, it is hard not to see comparisons with some of the more recent bouts of bickering which have blighted the game in this country during the last decade or so.

> It did not require a great deal to ignite a fire. They were inflammable material, and cared less for Petrie's wrongs than they did for a good row. Representatives from clubs as far remote as Thurso and Earlston were said to have attended the indignation meetings, but it need not be assumed that the country was agitated from end to end. It was easy to procure a mandate for a local supporter who was indignant enough to deserve it.

By now club rivalries were fairly well established, and there was none fiercer than that between the Academicals and Royal High School – which had its roots in the controversy surrounding the foundation of the Academy in 1824. Referring to some of their earlier matches, a sports article in 1889 noted: 'It was never quite clear what the football was brought onto the field for, as after the first kick most of the players forgot it was there and they are said to have marched off the field one time and left the ball behind them' (from Thorburn, p. 45). The strained relationship between the two clubs was surely an important factor in this nasty little spat. But Royal High were not alone in their opposition to Graham's appointment. The Academicals had been the dominant club in Scottish rugby for 20 years, and this had perhaps given rise to resentment amongst rival clubs.

When John Chiene and R.W. Irvine wrote a letter to *The Scotsman* suggesting that the players should choose the captain themselves, it was met with a stern reply from R.S.F. Henderson, the Edinburgh University captain. He pointed out that this assumed 'that the team chosen would be a satisfactory one. That it certainly would not be if we are to take the team chosen against Ireland as an example; and every rugby player knows to which club the captaincy in that event would fall'.

A handful of players from Royal High, Edinburgh Institution and Edinburgh University withdrew from the team which lost to Ireland on 19 February, and at a hastily convened special general meeting of the Scottish Football Union a motion was presented which called for the resignation of the Union committee. This was eventually withdrawn, but only after the committee had been forced into making a number of concessions, which included allowing the selected players to appoint their own captain in future.

The upshot of all this was that Graham retained the captaincy while Petrie never played for Scotland again. However, the Royal High man was elected president of the Union at the next AGM, when there were wholesale changes throughout the committee.

As an interesting footnote to this story it is worth quoting Jacques McCarthy, an Irish reporter with a colourful turn of phrase, who chronicled that Ireland versus Scotland match in 1881, which ended with the Irish scoring a late drop-goal to grab their first victory in an international match.

They commenced fiercely but after Spunner and big Jock Graham had gotten black eyes, and a certain hot Scotsman had come second best out of an independent boxing match with Browning, milder methods were adopted. No tangible score was gained in the first half, but in the second McMullen making a mismatch at a long kick (. . . from Maclagan) placed the whole of the Scottish team onside, and Graham, who was leaning against the Irish goal post, rubbing his shin after a recent hack, leisurely limped over and touched the ball down . . . some slight was forthcoming when Begbie missed the kick which was as easy as possible . . . Only five minutes remained . . . Taylor got possession after a drop out and ran and worried his way amidst frantic exhortations up to the Scottish 25 where he passed to Johnston who returned him the leather on the very verge of the Scottish line. Here it was heeled out to Johnston who amidst vociferous profanity missed his pick-up and Campbell shot the ball into touch ten yards down. Hughes, however, rapidly realised the situation and threw it out to Taylor before the Scotsmen could line up, and Taylor transferred to Johnston, who quicker than you could think or write tossed to Bagot who dropped the ball over the goal.

The political manoeuvring which is endemic in modern rugby might already have begun, but the game itself was clearly still a very different sport back in 1881.

For the Academicals, 1881–82 was a disastrous season during which they suffered a succession of defeats. And the following campaign was not much better, although it did include an Academical victory by a try to nil over Watsonians in the first fixture between the two clubs. The match was played on 6 January 1882, and the Academicals were bolstered by the availability of J.G. Tait (back from Cambridge University) and L.F. Robertson (who was playing regularly for

1883–84 1st XV

Back: R.C. Matthew, P.W. Smeaton, M.C. McEwan, P.M. Matthew, F. Saunders, G.H. Carphin

Middle: O.S.M. Fraser, G.R. Macdonald, C. Reid (*Captain*), A.P. Moir, H.H. Littlejohn, R.O. Adamson

Front: T.W. Irvine, D.M.M. Orr

Richmond and Cooper's Hill College in London). The captain this season was J.A. Gardner, who was honorary secretary of the SFU from 1883 until his death at the early age of 30 in 1887.

The following year, Charles Reid took over the captaincy – and during the next five seasons he was to oversee a revival in the fortunes of the club after a couple of tough seasons.

Scotland team that beat Ireland in Edinburgh on 7 March 1885

Standing: J. Gordon Mitchell (West of Scotland), Dr J. Dod (Watsonians), T.W. Irvine (Edinburgh Academicals),
H.L. Evans (Edinburgh University).

Middle: P.H. Don Wauchops (Fettesian Lorettonians), G. Maitland (Edinburgh Institution FP),
J.P. Veitch (Royal High School FP), T. Ainslie (Edinburgh Institution FP).

Sitting: W.A. Peterkin (Edinburgh University), J.B. Brown (Glasgow Academicals), W.E. MacLagan (*Captain*,
Edinburgh Academicals), A.R. Don Wauchope (Fettesian Lorettonians), J. Jamieson (West of Scotland),
J.G. Tait (Edinburgh Academicals).

Front: C. Reid (Edinburgh Academicals).

Reid was a big man. Standing 6ft 3in and weighing between 15 and 16 stone, he dwarfed virtually all of his contemporaries. But he carried very little excess weight, and the nickname 'Hippo' did not come from any physical resemblance to the animal – rather more mundanely it came from his schooldays when he could not give the word for 'horse' in a Greek lesson.

Rugby was in Hippo's genes. His brother, James, had already played four times for Scotland by the time Reid made his international debut against Ireland in 1881, and the two would play twice together that season – but it was the younger sibling who was destined to become a genuine Scottish great.

Remarkably, Hippo was exactly the same age as Ninian Finlay when he made his international debut (both were 17 years and 36 days old). Finlay, however, had lived through one less leap year than Reid, so he is generally regarded as being the youngest ever Scottish cap.

1887–88 1st XV

Back: R.O. Adamson, J. McEwan, W.C. Dudgeon, T.W. Irvine, T.B. White, A.T. Clay, C.G. Glawford

Middle: R.D. Jameson, M.C. McEwan, H.H. Littlejohn, C. Reid (*Captain*)

Front: J. Methuen, J. Duncan, R.H. Johnston, H.J. Stevenson

Reid went on to represent his country 21 times in total between 1881 and 1888, during which time he scored four tries. He finished on the losing side only four times in international matches. He captained Scotland to its first outright championship win in 1887.

He was fast for his size, which inevitably made him difficult to stop. His powerful running was never more evident than during the Scotland versus Ireland match of 1888, when, according to one contemporary newspaper, Reid made a long run 'with the bulk of the Irish forwards hanging onto him'. He also had a particularly long place kick, and a reputation of sending the heavy balls of that era beyond the dead ball line straight from kick-off.

Shortly after Reid's death in 1909, A.T. Clay, who had been a team-mate at both club and international level, wrote in the *Academy Chronicle* about the great man.

He may not have had the irresistible dash of forwards of the type of the Ainslies [the brothers who played for Edinburgh Institution FP] in Scotland and some of the Blackheath and Yorkshire men in England; he may not have had the panther-like spring in defence of T.W. Irvine, which brought a three-quarter apparently hopelessly out of reach to a dead stop; he was not, partly from his height and bulk, the deadly scorer ten yards from the line that McEwan was; but no one could gain more ground with the ball at his feet than Reid, and it was a not uncommon sight, even in International matches, to see him dribble through nearly all the opposing backs . . . with the ball under his arm he was speedy on the field, and one of the most difficult men to stop. He usually had a hand in most of the scoring of his side, but his most striking and rare characteristic was his quickness to see an opening, and the lightning-like rapidity with which he seized the opportunity. In this, to my mind the highest quality in a football player even in a forward, I never saw his equal. Much has been said of the strenuous nature of the Academical team's play. Some teams are apt to forget, particularly when playing a losing game, that football is not a drawing room game; and it could never be said of Reid that he made undue use of his strength. I have frequently seen him, when holding a man smaller than himself, lift his opponent off his feet and lay him gently on his back with a look almost of apology. He played hard, but he always played with his characteristic good nature. If, however, he was roused by unfair play in an opponent he did not hesitate to his disapprobation by the way he handled him. I once saw him when so roused lay hold of a man who had the ball, and was quite his own weight, lift him off his feet and throw him into touch with such force, that the post with which the opponent came into contact was snapped through

Scotland v Ireland, Belfast, 19 February 1887

Back Row: D. Lang (Paisley), H-H. Johnston (Edinburgh University).

Middle Row: J.R.H. Gordon (Edinburgh Academicals), J. Junor (Glasgow Academicals), J.R. Reid (Edinburgh Wanderers), J.H.S. Graham (Edinburgh Academicals), C. Villars (Edinburgh Wanderers).

Sitting: D.H. Watson (Glasgow Academicals), M. Cross (Glasgow Academicals), R.W. Irwine (*Captain*, Edinburgh Academicals), R.C. MacKenzie (Glasgow Academicals).

On Ground: S.H. Smith (Glasgow Academicals), E.I. Pocock (Edinburgh Wanderers), H.M. Napier (West of Scotland).

the middle. Perhaps the best test is that Reid was universally popular amongst the players of opposing teams. Particularly was this the case with the Border teams, and it is safe to say that no player before or since has been better known or more universally beloved.

R.J. Phillips believed that Reid's Academical side contained the 'greatest pack that has played in Scottish club football' and he insisted that he was not alone in holding that view.

A mistaken idea seems to prevail as to the weight and physique of C. Reid's forwards. He himself was a giant amongst men. About 6 feet 3 inches and between 15 and 16 stone – nearer 15 perhaps – he carried no superfluous weight, and was as active as a well-trained 10 stone man. M.C. McEwan would be about 14 stone, and A.T. Clay and T.W. Irvine about 12 stone each. T.B. White . . . would be fully half a stone lighter, and the others, except J. Methuen, who would be nearer 13 than 12 stone, were all a little over 12 stone or thereabouts. Their power lay in their combination, quick breaking up, and tackling.

Reid had little use for players who could not tackle and bring the man down. He had them drilled to perfection, and held a complete command over his team. On a big occasion no back division could settle down against these forwards.

Four of them – 'the quartette' – Reid, McEwan, Irvine, and Clay – were first choice International forwards for several years, and T.B. White latterly increased the number to five. Reid still stands as Scotland's greatest forward production. No player has yet appeared who could do on the field the things that Reid did.

M.C. (Matthew) McEwan was the eldest of four brothers who all played for the Academicals [the youngest of his brothers, W.M.C. (Willie), also played for Scotland and is spoken about later in this text]. Known as 'Saxon' on account of his fair hair and fine physique, he was a resourceful and intelligent player, and later in his career he was an excellent captain of both club and country. Under his leadership, Scotland were convincing winners of the Triple Crown in 1891.

M.C. McEwan

McEwan was vice-president of the SFU for the 1894–95 season and was due to take over as president, but in March 1895 he moved to America to take over as financial manager of a thread manufacturing company, leaving Bill Maclagan to serve a second term as head of the organisation.

Before leaving for America, McEwan was guest of honour at a dinner hosted by a number of Academicals and other friends in the Waterloo Hotel, for which a menu was produced which was embellished with a photo of the famous Scottish XV he captained to the Triple Crown in 1891. Before departing he was also presented with a gold watch by Craigie Bell, another Academical enthusiast, who served as president of the Football Club from 1897 to 1902. Four years after arriving in America, McEwan died in Chicago after an attack of pneumonia.

McEwan had been a key figure during the preliminary negotiations which led to the amalgamation in 1900 of the various sports clubs connected with the Academy under the central authority of the Edinburgh Academical Club. He did not live to see his vision realised, but his dedicated service to the club and the school was recognised when the clock above the old pavilion at Raeburn Place was named in his honour.

T.W. 'Wattie' Irvine was not as tall or heavy as McEwan but had a 'panther-like spring' which he used to devastating effect as one of the great tacklers of his generation. 'When he burst through the maul in pursuit of a ball just ahead of him, no quarter-back and few half-backs had a chance of getting under way,' noted the *EAFC Centenary History*. 'He had great speed and the courage to spring at an opponent apparently out of reach and seldom failed to bring him down. For five years he was a member of the Scots XV.'

Alec Clay was a different type of forward. Short but with a powerful, bulldog-like build, he did much of the unseen hard work in the maul, and his dribbling and tackling were as devastating as any of the others'.

Tom White was described by Phillips as the 'prettiest dribbler and most scientific player in the team.' He might have been one of the lightest players in the pack, but he punched well above his weight when on the charge.

Just as had been the case with 'Gissie' Graham's great team of the previous decade, this impressive Academical pack was complemented by some outstanding backs.

H.J. (Harry) Stevenson was good enough to be described in *The Scotsman* newspaper as 'the greatest football player in the world', and he would certainly have earned more than 15 caps for Scotland if he had been prepared to play the 'wide passing' game-plan laid out by the Union's committee – but he disapproved of this tactic and as a result he was moved from centre to full-back, and on one occasion dropped from the national team altogether. In rugby, as in the rest of life, he was a free thinker – prepared to override established conventions in order to find a new and improved method of gaining an advantage on the pitch.

According to Phillips:

When it was the practice for a back to fall on the ball in front of a forward rush, Stevenson nipped the ball from their toes, kept on his feet, and replied by kicking or breaking through. No one had ever seen saving done in that fashion.

In attack his strong running, sudden twists, and dummy passes enabled him to draw the opposition – and then out went a pass to a speedy wing with a fine chance to score.

In his book, *Play*, N.L. Stevenson (no relation) wrote:

It was a treat to see him nip in and gather the ball, side-step the onrushing forwards, 'dummy' a couple of opposing backs, and, with a perfectly timed pass, send his wing in for a score.

Stevenson had been a quarter in a desperately weak Academy side and after leaving school he had initially played for the Academicals second XV. However, it was not long before he was promoted to the first team, in 1887, and when R.H. (Herbert) Johnston and J. (James) Duncan joined him in the side later that year he became the fulcrum in one of the great half-back lines (more closely resembling a three-quarter line by today's norms) of early Scottish club rugby.

On 15 March 1889, the *Evening Dispatch* reported:

Mr Stevenson's career as a player has been brief, but eventful. It is barely three years since he first became associated with first-class football, and up to the time of his entering the senior fifteen of the Academicals quarter-back play was supposed to be his *forte* . . . One often hears it said that to be successful as a half-back weight and speed are absolutely indispensable. The Academical 'crack' is a striking proof of the ancient adage that every rule has its exception. He is wiry, but not weighty; dodgy, but not speedy. Mr Stevenson, however, is the happy possessor of qualities much beyond these. Marvellous judgment, coolness, and decision, and above all, unselfishness. He is one of those exceptional players who invariably do the right thing at the right moment. His passing is wonderfully well timed, his partner always receiving the ball at the very moment he can make the most of it. R.H. Johnston, for instance, who is the great try-getter of the Academicals, owes most of his points to his comrade. As a saver he stands unrivalled; he is no mean drop; he can punt well; and as a dodger, no better has been seen since the palmy days of the great Don Wauchope.

Initially, Stevenson's half-back partners were George Carphin and Harvey Littlejohn. Carphin was a powerful runner whose career was cut short by injury. Littlejohn made up for a lack of inches by being a courageous tackler of opponents of any size. He moved to quarter-back after Johnston and Duncan arrived on the scene.

Johnston had learned most of his rugby at an English public school where he had also been a good enough cricketer for W.G. Grace to describe him as the best schoolboy wicket-keeper he had ever seen. Johnston's great strength on the rugby field was his pace, although he seems to have been too fast for his own good at times. 'Stevenson had to nurse him,' says Phillips. 'If he sent him off too soon, he was sure to fall before he got to the line. His brain was too active to get the response from his body, and the goal-line did not come to him soon enough.'

According to Phillips, it says much about Duncan's natural ability that he was able to hold his place in such a distinguished Academicals side given his lack of interest in the sport.

J. Duncan's heart was not in football. As a schoolboy he kept tally of the salmon he had landed on the Tay, and though he was a good cricketer and a marvellous fielder at point, and might have been a first class wing half, give him a rod and a line and you might have had all the glories of the football or cricket field for those who desired them.

This half-back line containing Stevenson, Johnston and Duncan made an immediate impact. In their first season together – the 1887–88 campaign – the Academicals won the championship, remaining unbeaten throughout and conceding only two tries.

The following year Stevenson made his international debut against Wales, and his arrival in the national side took the club's representation up to seven, which was a record that lasted until the game went 'open' in 1995. Stevenson made a promising debut for Scotland in a match which was lost in controversial circumstances, as Phillips explains:

Wales won the 1888 match at Newport by a try scored by T.J. Pryce Jenkins (London Welsh) from a run remarkable in that a goodly part of its course was in touch. Some of the Scottish defenders [including Stevenson] allowed him to go, and although his tracks were quite discernible, he got his try.

Scotland were not so fortunate. Five times the ball was touched down for a try over the Welsh line, and on each occasion it was disallowed. They were still fighting adversity and hoping that a sixth appeal on numeric grounds, if on no other, could be withstood when time was called. That was the first Welsh triumph over Scotland.

Against Ireland, in his second match, Stevenson played a crucial role in the game's only score – collecting possession from A.R. Don Wauchope and cutting out a devastating path through the Irish defence before releasing his left wing, D.J. McFarlan, with a clear run at the line.

Stevenson quickly established himself as one of Scotland's most important players, rarely turning in a poor performance and frequently emerging as the team's star turn. He kicked a tremendous drop-goal into the wind to defeat Ireland in Belfast in 1889 and against Wales the following year he played a key role in Bill Maclagan's try.

Scotland v Wales 1888

Back: M.M. Duncan, C.P. Fraser, T.W. Irvine, W.E. Maclagan, A. Duke, A.T. Clay

Middle: L.E. Stevenson, D. Morton, C. Reid (*Captain*), M.C. McEwan, C.W. Berry, H.F. Chambers

Front: H.J. Stevenson, T.B. White, C.E. Orr

In 1891, Stevenson was moved from centre to full-back, so that Gregor McGregor, of Cambridge University, who was also a Test match wicket-keeper, could play the wide passing game which the selectors were keen to see adopted by Scotland. It proved to be an inspired decision. McGregor's brilliant hands were ideally suited to the style of rugby the Scottish selectors wanted to play and Stevenson's aggressive defence, brilliant kicking and audacious counter-attacking brought a new dimension to the team's back play. Scotland, captained by Stevenson's club colleague M.C. McEwan, enjoyed a magnificent season, winning the Triple Crown for the first time and running in 14 tries.

SCOTLAND v ENGLAND AT RAEBURN PARK EDINBURGH MARCH 5TH 1892.   J. PATRICK.

The following season, Scotland defeated Wales and Ireland but lost 5-0 to England in a Triple Crown decider at Raeburn Place. Stung by the lack of bite exhibited by their pack the previous year, England had brought eight Yorkshiremen into the side for the 1892 campaign, and this certainly seemed to bring the sort of hard edge which the selectors had been looking for. Not only did they remain undefeated throughout their three matches, but they did so without conceding a single point. The Scotland–England match was a particularly hard-fought encounter, as noted by one English report: 'Activity and skill were at a discount and very rough play was indulged in by both sides, the brandy bottle having frequently to be requisitioned for the knocked out ones.'

The match remained a forward battle throughout, but Stevenson still managed to make his presence felt. His willingness to attack from full-back was once again evident, and in defence a series of 'breathtaking' tackles managed to limit the English to only one score.

Inexplicably, the Scottish selectors then decided to drop Stevenson at the start of the 1893 Championship. In his absence, Scotland slumped to a 9-0 defeat at home to Wales in a match which was to have major repercussions on the way the game was played in Scotland in the future.

Wales had been playing with four three-quarters in the side for a number of years, but this was the first time Scotland had been on the losing side when playing against that formation. With nine forwards playing against eight, the Scots had clearly expected their pack to dominate the match and in the process prevent the Welsh backs from making the most of their extra man behind the scrum – but things did not go according to plan for the home team. The Scots had failed to anticipate that a controversial alteration in the game's laws in 1892, which permitted the 'heeling out' of the ball in a scrum, played into Welsh hands because it meant they could avoid becoming embroiled in a long and arduous shoving contest. Furthermore, a lack of practice due to frost was said to have affected the home team's fitness, and with Stevenson, G.T. Campbell (London Scottish), W. Neilson (Cambridge University), J.D. Boswall and J.E. Orr (both West of Scotland) all missing for a variety of reasons, the Welsh scored three unanswered tries and a drop-goal to record only their second victory over Scotland. All the points were scored during the second half, with Wales producing such a sparkling exhibition of continuous running and passing rugby that the possibility of introducing a similar formation in Scotland all of a sudden became a burning issue.

There was, however, considerable resistance to this change, not least from the great Charles 'Hippo' Reid, who wrote to the *Athletic News*:

> Give me a forward team like we had on Manchester in 1882 and I don't care how many three-quarter backs you have, we could go through them. We dribbled very close, and one backed up the other so well they could not get away, and they had fliers like Bolton against us. Dribbling and tackling are the characteristics of the Scottish forwards, and on them we depend to win.

Reid was not alone in his assessment. Several other notable players and former players agreed with him, including R.G Macmillan, who had captained the Scotland side that day, and A.R. Don Wauchope, who had taken over the captaincy from Reid in 1888. However, they could not stem progress, and by the start of the next season Scotland were experimenting with the new formation.

Two weeks after the Wales debacle, Scotland scraped a 0-0 draw away to Ireland before Stevenson returned for the final match of the season against England. Inevitably, he was one of his team's best performers on a day in which the Scots overcame the wet conditions overhead and a loose, slippery playing surface at Headingley to record an 8-0 victory.

Sadly, this was to be his last appearance for Scotland on the rugby field. He retired from the game at the end of the 1893 season to concentrate on his business concerns. He was only 26 and still at the peak of his powers, so his departure from the game naturally caused widespread consternation, not only in Academical circles, but throughout Scottish rugby.

At least he was not completely lost to the world of sport. He continued to play cricket in his own inimitable way, for several more years. He was good enough to play for Scotland at that sport, and once scored 151 for Edinburgh versus the South. On another memorable occasion he smashed the legendary W.G. Grace clean out of Raeburn Place.

If anything, his aggressive batting was surpassed by his success as a bowler. In 1886 he took five wickets in successive balls for the Academicals against Craigmount; and, amazingly, he performed exactly the same feat against Gala in 1894. This is all the more remarkable given the eccentric style he employed. Apparently he used to throw innocuous looking underarm lobs towards the batsman, rush up the wicket after them, and take astonishing off-the-bat catches – leading one bemused victim to comment that it was the first time he had encountered a silly mid-on, a silly mid-off and a silly bowler all at the same time.

'Hippo' Reid's first season as captain (the 1883–84 campaign), had been fairly unremarkable, and the start of the second year didn't look too promising either, with the Academicals losing three out of their first four games. But the team then went the rest of the season with only one further defeat, to a last-minute try at Bradford, who were regarded by many as being the premier club in England at that time.

Two games in particular stand out. When the Academicals defeated West of Scotland on 20 December it was described in one newspaper as 'one of the great surprises which has been seen in Scottish rugby football for some years.' A week later the first match between the Academicals and a London Scottish team captained by Bill Maclagan, ended in a draw at Raeburn Place. The match marked the opening of the club's new pavilion, which was the largest in Scotland, and a dinner was laid on in the Waterloo Hotel – with Alexander Crombie, one of the pioneers of the game in Scotland 30 years previously, in the chair.

The 1885–86 season started with a bang. Early in the campaign Bradford travelled to Edinburgh to take on the Academicals in a match which wasn't for the faint-hearted. The *EAFC Centenary History* gives a detailed account of this game and its aftermath:

> This match was undoubtedly a memorable occasion, an historic encounter, a tremendous battle – but it was also just too vigorous. Who was responsible for starting the 'rough stuff' is not clear – one report says the Academicals were responsible for doing so but adds that they were incensed by the unfair

tactics of their opponents (which makes the obscurity more obscure). But once it was started each side gave as good as they received. On one occasion 'during a specially stiff and prolonged maul the ball was suddenly hooked out and sent far down field, upon which the maulers quickly broke up, leaving, however, to the amusement of the spectators, the centre forward on each side hammering his opponent's shins, oblivious of the fact that they were alone and in full view of the field'.

Half a dozen of the Bradford team had played or were to play for England and their skilful backs were always dangerous. Fortunately, 'Wattie' Irvine, famed for his tackling, was in fine form for the home team. He halted both Robertshaw and Bonsor when each was racing down the touchline, apparently clear of all opposition; and on another occasion, when all seemed lost, he cut across and brought down the Yorkshire 'flyer', Ritchie, with a tremendous tackle. Mid-way through the second half, following a throw near the Bradford line, Moir gained possession and made a dash for the line, when he was tackled by the Bradford full-back, but Orr was up to take his pass and touch down for the only score of the game.

The Academicals team which won this historic match by a try to nil was: F. Saunders; G.H. Carphin, H.H. Littlejohn, R.H. Johnston; D.M.M. Orr, H.G. Kinnear; C. Reid, T.W. Irvine, M.C. McEwan, A.T. Clay, A.P. Moir, R.O. Adamson, P.M. Matthew, V.A Noel-Paton, P.W. Hislop.

W.J. Stuart, who was present as a schoolboy at this match, remembers it vividly – 'a very rough game', he calls it. It was 'a memorable occasion' in that, for probably the first and only time, 'bookies' appeared on the Field at Raeburn Place, standing on stools and shouting the odds – with Bradford as favourites.

On the following day Bradford returned to Raeburn Place to play Edinburgh University. 'Unlike the contest of the previous day, which has created no little talk in rugby circles, the match was of the most pleasing description.' *The Scotsman* also noted Reid, the Academical captain, who was assisting the University (he was a medical student), as 'fairly excelling himself'. He, apparently, was none the worse from the previous day's experiences! On both sides, however, there had been some casualties and relations between Bradford and the Academicals were somewhat strained. Reid made a point of going to the station to see the Yorkshiremen

leave for home and his courteous bearing did much to improve matters –
though nearly forty years elapsed before the Academicals and Bradford
played each other again.

The match caused quite a stir in the newspapers of the time, especially in
Yorkshire, where they took the defeat of their local heroes very much to heart.
The *Bradford Post* accused the Academicals of 'brutal and cowardly treatment' and
claimed that Bradford had been 'first crippled and then apologised to'. The
Academicals were accused of 'caddish blackguardism' and were described as
'barbaric' and 'muscularly violent scholars'. The paper even attempted compar-
isons with the Battles of Rorke's Drift in Africa, and the Battle of Tel-el-Kebir in
Egypt, to help illustrate its version of events.

Meanwhile, the *Yorkshireman* described the Academicals as 'devils in human
shape' and said that the game was 'the most brutal exhibition ever seen . . .
characterised by some of the foulest play ever perpetrated by a club having any
claim to stand in the first rank'. Apparently a telegram was received by friends of
one of the Bradford forwards on Monday night, which said: 'I am alright; not one of
the team injured', before running through a list of hurt players:

Bonsor	Finger broken in two places.
Wright	Foot badly crushed and severe shock – result of kicks and terrible rushes.
Ritchie	Ankle severely sprained – believed to be broken.
Robertshaw	Badly knocked about. Had to go to bed on Monday immediately after the game and was totally unfit to play on Tuesday, although he turned out.
Hickson	Used very roughly.

The correspondent for the *Scottish Athletic Journal* gave the Academicals a
more sympathetic hearing:

A great event has rolled into history . . . Some papers have taken to
blackguarding the Academicals. We are told that they, and they alone,
did the dirty work. Now that is a most unfair charge to make. The one side
I blame just as much as the other. The main count in the libel against the

Academy is that of 'knocking'; but was the knocking indulged in not due to the exasperation at some of Bradford's unfair tactics? . . . Things cropped up that provoked the Academy, who, incensed at these things, let out with a vigour which touched and occasionally bordered on the brutal; and, on the other hand, things cropped up that provoked Bradford, who, incensed at these things, let out with a vigour which touched and occasionally bordered on the brutal. In the face of that, then, is the one side not as much to blame as the other for the polished brutality which characterised this game?

The hangover from the Bradford match had serious implications on that year's championship challenge. The following week the Academicals were without three key players – G. Carphin, H. Littlejohn and A.P. Moir – when they took on Wanderers, and lost by a goal to nil. The only other match the Academicals lost during the 1885–86 season was to Royal High School FP at Grange Loan in a match which was brought to a premature end. Royal High had taken the lead early in the second half through a Wilson try, prompting some frantic catch-up play from the Academicals. Eventually, Churnside made it over the line, but Royal High insisted that the ball was dead and the Academicals left the field in disgust. Accies defeated West of Scotland by a goal to nil at the end of the season, but that was the only defeat suffered by the Glaswegians that season and they finished the season as champions.

The 1886–87 season was the first in which Harry Stevenson played for the 1st XV, and with T. White now also established in the side the famous Academical quintet of international forwards was now complete. However, defeats to Glasgow Academicals (by one try to one goal) and Royal High School (this time by two tries to one goal and one try), meant that they once again missed out on finishing top of the unofficial championship.

After a slow start to the decade, the Academicals were back at the top of the Scottish game; and this resurgence reached its zenith during the 1887–88 season, when the club won all 14 matches played. Surely it is no coincidence that this was the first season in which Stevenson, Johnston and Duncan teamed up as the Academicals' half-back line.

The record for the 1887–88 season was:

Played: 14; Won: 14; Goals: 25; Tries: 25; Tries Conceded: 2.

The results for that season were:

Opponents	For	Against
St George	1 goal 1 try	nil
Hawick	1 try	nil
Merchiston	2 goals 4 tries	nil
Collegiate	7 goals 6 tries	nil
Glasgow Academicals	6 goals 4 tries	nil
Edinburgh University	1 try	nil
RHS FP	2 goals	nil
Institution FP	2 goals 1 try	nil
Hawick	3 goals	1 try
West of Scotland	5 tries	nil
Fettesian-Lorettonians	1 goal	1 try
Watsonians	1 goal 1 try	nil
RHS FP	1 goal	nil
Manchester	1 try	nil

The usual team for this extraordinary season was: C.G. Glassford, J. Duncan, H.J. Stevenson, R.H. Johnston, H.H. Littlejohn, R.D. Jameson, C. Reid, M.C. McEwan, T.W. Irvine, A.T. Clay, T.B. White, R.O. Adamson, W.C. Dudgeon, J. McEwan, J. Methuen.

Reid retired from the game at the end of this season, and 'Saxon' McEwan took over as club captain for the 1888–89 campaign. The club did not manage to repeat the success of the 1887–88 campaign, but with only two losses they were still clearly a force to be reckoned with. The two games the Academicals lost that season were to Wanderers (2-8) and to West of Scotland (2-4).

That season, Scottish clubs played under a new scoring system which gave teams four points for a goal, three points for a drop-goal or a goal from a mark and two points for a try, a penalty being worth nothing. Two years later, with the formation of the International Board, the scoring system was brought into line with that used in England, which was two points for a try, five points for a goal from a try, three points for a penalty goal, and four points for any other goal.

There were three defeats in the 1889–90 season, to Watsonians (4-8), Cambridge University (8-10) and Fettesian-Lorettonians (0-8). The *EAFC History* tells us that the Cambridge game had a particularly exciting climax.

The University were leading by 10 points to 6 when in the last minute the Academicals 'came down the field in one of their famous rushes' and Dudgeon crossed for a try in the north-west corner (8-10). A goal was required to make the scores equal and McEwan's effort from the touch-line all but succeeded. An eye-witness reports: 'It was a beautiful long high kick. It fell on the cross-bar and bounced very high off it; hit the far away post near the top; bounced back; hung in the air; fell again on the bar; bounced again quite high off it, and fell, just grazing the cross-bar, but on the wrong side – no goal!'

1889–90 1st XV

Back: D.G. Newton, H.F. Cadell, F.B. Marjoribanks, H.L. Usher, A.H. Boyd, W.R. Ferguson, W.C. Dudgeon

Middle: E. Glendinning, A.A. Scot-Skirving, M.C. McEwan (*Captain*), H.J. Stevenson, J. Duncan, A.W. Mosman

Front: J.D. Boswall, A.W. Livingston, McIvor Campbell

At the end of the campaign a brilliant try by Stevenson not only gave Hawick their first defeat, but was also the first time the Borderers' line had been breached all season.

With the likes of Royal High, Edinburgh Wanderers and Edinburgh University all enjoying golden periods, and clubs such as Watsonians and Hawick also emerging as genuine forces in the game, this was a boom period for Scottish rugby.

The Academicals might not have managed to emulate their remarkable achievement of 1887–88, but they were still a major force in Scottish rugby. Their record during the six years from the start of 1885–85 season to the end of the 1889–90 season makes impressive reading: the club played 92 matches, of which they won 69, drew 11 and lost 12.

CHAPTER THIRTEEN

One of the curiosities of cricket is that an umpire is powerless to give a batsman 'out' unless there is an 'appeal' from the fielding side. Which, as mathematicians might say, is absurd. For many years Rugby Football suffered from the same kind of absurdity but it grew out of it, with immense benefit to all concerned.

from *EAFC Centenary History*, published 1958

THE *EAFC CENTENARY HISTORY* provides a comprehensive summary of the changing role of referees and umpires in rugby matches during the 1880s:

It was not until 1896 that appeals were rendered unnecessary in Rugby Football, but in the 1880s good progress was made in this direction. The introduction of a referee, and in 1885, the provision of a whistle were the first steps – for the idea of a whistle Association Football must be given credit. For many years the referee had to operate in conjunction with two umpires, each with a stick. In contrast to the touch judges, by whom they were replaced in 1890, the umpires moved about the field of play. If a player appealed and the umpire upheld the appeal, he raised his stick. On this, if the referee allowed the appeal he blew his whistle and the game stopped. If the referee did not agree with the umpire, he took no action and the game proceeded. If *both* the umpires raised their sticks, however, the referee *had* to allow the appeal and blow the whistle. Later, the referee was authorised to allow an appeal without waiting for any action by an umpire, and eventually he was given powers to act without any appeals.

Prior to the introduction of a referee [in the 1870s], the two captains or two umpires were arbiters and disputes were frequent. Sometimes it was agreed to leave the point at issue undecided, possibly to be referred to some authority after the game, and the match went on producing results like: 'January 1880: Academicals 1 goal (disputed), RHS FP nil'; and 'November 1880: Loretto 2 goals (1 disputed), Academy nil'.

Sometimes agreement to defer a decision could not be reached, and then one or other of the teams walked off the field and the match was recorded as 'Unfinished'. This occurred in a match between the Academicals and Edinburgh University in December 1881. The University claimed a try which the Academicals disputed on the ground that the ball had been 'fisted', which was forbidden. The umpires disagreed. There was no referee. The University captain proposed to take the kick at goal and refer the matter to the S.F.U. The Academicals refused and walked off the field and the match was abandoned with the score: Academicals 1 drop goal; University 1 try ('disputed and not allowed to be placed').

In November 1885 a match between the Academicals and RHS FP was 'played under the new rules as to umpires and referee . . . and gave satisfaction. The umpires were each provided with small flags and the referee with a whistle . . .' The new system may have given satisfaction, but that did not prevent the match from having an abrupt conclusion during the second half. One of the Academicals crossed the High School line 'after what seemed to be a dead ball outside. The point was disputed by the School whose umpire promptly gave dead ball: the Academical umpire gave a reverse decision, while the referee was unable to see. Considerable discussion ensued and neither captain would yield the point. The referee ordered the ball to be hacked off, but this was not agreed to by the Academical captain and the teams then left the field.'

These arguments were also found in International matches, and that in the Scotland–England match of 1884 is usually referred to simply as 'The Dispute'.

In the first half of this match, J. Jamieson, the West of Scotland forward, had scored a try for the Scots, but C.W. Berry failed to convert. After the break, R.S. Kindersley touched down for England, but Scotland protested that the try should not be allowed, and the argument which followed was to have a profound effect on the future of the game. G. Rowland Hill, secretary of the RFU, said:

In the course of play the ball was knocked back by a Scotsman [C.W. Berry], one of the English team secured it and a try was obtained. The Scots claimed that 'knocking back' was illegal; the English held that it was not an illegal act and even though it had been, the act was done by a Scotsman and as no Englishman claimed for it, the Scotsmen could not claim for or profit by their own infringement.

Meanwhile, A.R. Don-Wauchope, the great Scottish quarter-back from the Fettesian-Lorretonian club, had a very different point of view:

> In those days there were two umpires who carried sticks, not flags, and a referee without a whistle. The ball was thrown out of touch, an appeal was made, the umpire on the touchline [J.H.S. Graham of EAFC] held up his stick, all the players with the exception of four Englishmen and two Scotsmen, stopped playing and England scored a try. The only question of fact decided by the referee was that a Scotsman knocked the ball back. This, according to the Scottish view of the reading of the rule, was illegal and the whole question turned on the interpretation. The point that no Englishman had appealed was never raised at the time and to judge by the fact that eleven of the English team ceased play, it would appear that their idea was that the game should stop.

The issue basically boiled down to a lack of uniformity in the interpretation of the rules, through Scottish resentment over the try is easier to empathise with if we recognise that the advantage law was not introduced until 1896.

After half an hour of fierce debate the two sides remained at loggerheads, so the Scots allowed England to kick for goal under protest, with the point to be referred to the Rugby Union Committee. W.N. Bolton was successful with his conversion, and the final score for the match was recorded as an England victory by a goal from a disputed try against a try. But this was only the beginning of the quarrel.

The disputed try had brought into sharp focus a simmering resentment over the RFU's determination to be the sole arbiter of the laws of the game. The SFU annual general meeting in 1884 determined that the English should not be allowed to ride roughshod over the rights of Scotland, and it would soon become apparent that Ireland and Wales were similarly minded.

> That the recent match in March between Scotland and England may be held null or a draw, or be satisfactorily settled by reference; that the independence of the Scottish union be fully recognised and arrangements

be made for the settlement of future disputes by reference; and that when these points are settled the Secretary shall issue or accept a challenge for the ensuing season.

The SFU entered into correspondence with the RFU, and whilst the former remained adamant that the try was invalid they did offer to have the question adjudicated by a neutral body. In response, the RFU insisted that the referee, having made a decision on a question of fact, must have his authority on the field upheld. It was stalemate, and as a result no match between the two countries was arranged for the 1885 season.

It looked as if a solution to this impasse might be reached when the four Home Unions met in Dublin in February 1886 and Scotland agreed to concede the 1884 match so long as England agreed to join an International Board, comprising of an equal number of representatives from each Union, which would decide on such points of law that might arise during international matches. But when the board met for the first time in Manchester a few weeks later the RFU were not present, and they later refused to accept the constitutional terms previously agreed for the new body. With more clubs than the other three Unions, they felt they were entitled to a greater representation on the board.

It was clear that the RFU was not prepared to yield its position as lawmaker for the game. They did offer the other three Unions representation and the right to vote at any committee meeting dealing with possible alterations in the rules, but this was not acceptable to the Irish, Scottish and Welsh. Instead the English found themselves on the receiving end of an ultimatum in December 1887, which insisted that the International Board rules must be used in all international games, and warned that England would be unable to find anyone to play against unless they signed up. The RFU stuck to their guns, and as a result England played no international matches in 1888 and 1889.

For both sides of the argument, it was a classic case of: *can't live with them, can't live without them.* Eventually, in December 1889, the RFU took the decisive step of offering to submit the dispute to a board of two, one member nominated by the International Board and the other by themselves.

This arbitration process led to the creation of a new constitution for the International Board which somehow managed to reconcile the interests of all parties. The three Celtic Unions got the Code of Laws they were after, which were to be maintained and administered by the new board and which would be sovereign in all international matches. Meanwhile, the RFU were satisfied at having six members on the board as opposed to the two from each of the other three Unions. The RFU might have blinked first, but a 50 per cent representation on the new International Board more than offset this minor loss of face.

From beginning to end, the EAFC, or more accurately some of its leading members, played a central role in this saga. The umpire in the 1884 match who 'held up his stick' was J.H.S. Graham (that great Academicals and Scotland forward, who captained his club for four glorious seasons between 1876 and 1880 and his country twice, against Ireland and England in 1881); the secretary of the SFU and one of the leading negotiators in the dispute was J.A. Gardner (EAFC captain in 1882–83); and when the case was finally submitted to arbitration, the man entrusted by the Celtic Unions to find a sensible solution was Lord Kingsburgh (that great Accies stalwart, who, as J.H.A. Macdonald, had been a founding member of the club and had collected the gate money at Raeburn Place before the first international match in 1871).

Macdonald had recently taken the title Lord Kingsburgh, after being appointed Lord Justice Clerk of Scotland in 1888. A measure of the debt of gratitude felt towards him for his part in bringing to an end this ugly spat can be deduced from the handsome silver bowl with which he was presented and which he later bequeathed to the school. It bears the emblems of the four Home Unions and the inscription:

> Presented to the Right Hon. John Hay Athole Macdonald, Lord Justice Clerk of Scotland, by the Football Unions of England, Scotland, Ireland and Wales, in grateful acknowledgement of his Services as Arbiter with Major Francis Mandarin, R.E., C.M.G., in the settlement of the international difference between the International Football Board and the Rugby Football Union, April 1890.

Lord Kingsburgh

CHAPTER FOURTEEN

– Oh Accies, let it out – this is most exhausting!
– Nonsense, Fatty, we're enjoying ourselves. Push away, man, push away!
An exchange between A.G. Cairns (Oxford, Watsonians and Scotland)
and L.H.I. Bell (Edinburgh Academicals captain)
after a particularly long maul, circa. 1902.
Overheard by W.J. 'Pussy' Stuart.

AFTER THE DIFFICULTIES of the previous decade, the 1890s witnessed a period of regeneration for rugby at the Academy. For the first time since the 1870s a day school was successfully challenging the boarding schools, with R.J. Mackenzie, who had been appointed rector in 1888, the driving force behind this remarkable turnaround. When he took over at the school he inherited an institution on the wane, with inadequate facilities, antiquated methods and, not unnaturally, a steadily decreasing roll. On the football field, the XV was suffering regular crushing defeats from Fettes, Loretto and Merchiston – with one loss by nine goals and five tries appearing to be the record. By the time Mackenzie retired due to ill health in 1901, the Academy had taken on a new lease of life both academically and in a sporting context.

In football, the Academy was successfully competing against all the leading boarding schools. Mackenzie was an Old Lorettonian and he certainly seems to have inherited Almond's enthusiasm for physical exercise – and particularly rugby. In his first report as Rector of the Academy he stressed the value of school games, which he said developed:

. . . physique, endurance, presence of mind – qualities of the highest value in practical life . . . Football to which objection is most frequently taken on the ground of danger, is no longer with us, as in the early days of the game, a barbarous pastime. Whatever the risks may be for men who play the game in a brutal spirit, they are immensely over-estimated for boys. On the other hand, the risks of not playing should be considered. If I were asked what was the most dangerous occupation for a boy's leisure, I should at once name 'loafing'. As an outlet for manly energies, and an education in manly virtues and public spirit, I commend the School games to the cordial support of the Parents.

Two years later Mackenzie went a step further and made games compulsory for all pupils at the school. He also appointed a number of young masters to the staff, mostly from England, and this played a big part in improving the organisation of games at the school. One of this number, L.G. Thomas (who taught at the school from 1893 to 1930), appears to have been the first Academy master to have played for the Academical XV. He played centre during the 1893–84 season.

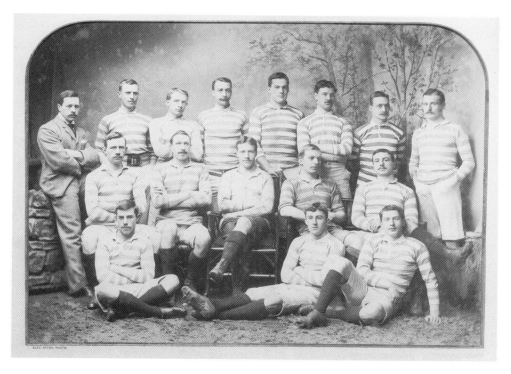

1890–91 1st XV

Back: C. Chirnside, D. Macnair, E. Glendinning, H.L. Usher, A.H. Boyd, F.B. Marjoribanks, D.G. Newton, A.W. Mosman

Middle: H.F. Cadell, W.R. Ferguson, H.J. Stevenson, M.C. McEwen, A.A. Scot-Skirving

Front: R.D. Jameson, J.D. Boswall, A. Livingstone

The Academy 1st XV of 1892–93, captained by George Moncreiff, was the team which finally ended the disastrous sequence of results against the boarding schools, with their goal-to-nil victory over Merchiston being the school's first win against those opponents in 12 years. The following week Loretto were defeated for the first time in eight years, again by a goal to nil. Four of that team – J.M. Reid, J.I. Gillespie, J.H. Dods and W.M.C. McEwan – went on to play for Scotland. Meanwhile, E.R. Balfour became the first Academical to captain the Oxford XV and also rowed twice in the Boat Race, F.C. (later Sir Frederick) Thomson played several times in the Oxford XV and L.B. Bradbury played for Sandhurst and in a Scottish trial. Another notable member of that team was Donald Hall, whose prowess as a goal-kicker was recalled at the school for many years through a tankard awarded annually in his name for 'Football Kicking'. [The prize is still awarded, but sadly it is no longer known as the Donald Hall Tankard.] J.H. Dods' team of 1893–94 perhaps did not reach the same heights as the previous year, but did succeed in beating Fettes for the first time since 1875.

It took a few years before the improvements in rugby at the school filtered through at club level. Harry Stevenson took over the captaincy of the club in 1891–92 and continued in that role for three seasons. All three campaigns were distinctly average, with the team struggling to come to terms with life after Hippo *et al.* By the start of the 1892–93 season, Stevenson was the sole survivor from that great Academical side of 1887–98.

Harry Stevenson

There were occasional high points, most notably on 19 March 1892, when an undefeated Watsonians side hosted the Academicals knowing that a draw would give them the championship. A sparkling display by Stevenson, playing out of position at 'quarter' (half-back in today's parlance), in-spired the visitors to a surprise victory, with an H.N. Boyd try the only score of the match. That result meant Watsonians had to share the title with West of Scotland.

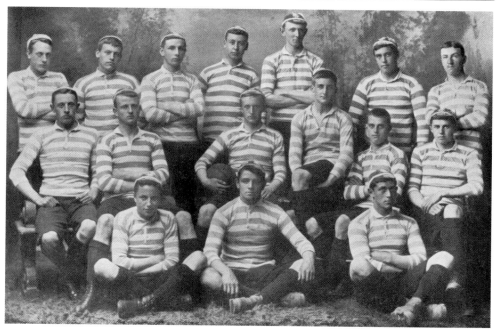

1894–95, Academy 1st XV

Back: E.R. Moncreiff, J.E. Hotson, G. Cook, A.D.G. Glassford, W. Dove, FP Dods, A.W. Robertson

Middle: J.G.H. McIntosh, L.B. Bradbury, H.W. Moncreiff (*Captain*), J. Ballantine, J.I. Gillespie, T.A. Nelson

Front: J.D. Harvey, A.S. Pringle, L.H.I. Bell

After Stevenson decided to give up rugby at the end of the 1892–93 season, he was replaced as captain by Boyd – who would later serve for several years on the SFU Committee. He was a popular and hard-working individual, who helped lay the foundations for the successful years that followed – but for the time being the club continued to struggle.

According to the *EAFC Centenary History*:

With reduced numbers the Club found difficulty in fielding two XVs, and as Academicals at the time (and at other times too perhaps?) were not very good at replying to postcards, Ben Bell, the Captain and Secretary of the 'A' XV, was accustomed to invite more than fifteen players each Saturday, being confident that some would not turn up. Once, however, they all did. On that occasion, when half-time had been reached, the solitary spectator said to the Academical Captain: 'Ben, you should protest to the referee – the other side are playing sixteen men', whereupon Ben laid a finger along the side of his nose and said 'Wheesh-sh-sh! We've got seventeen.'

From the club's earliest days it had fielded players who had been to other schools as well as the Academy. However, not since the days of Alex Crombie, the club's first captain, had the team been led by a player who had received any of his schooling elsewhere. That all changed during the 1895–96 season when C.P. Finlay – who had also attended Loretto – took on the role. He was a good forward who had played in two inter-city matches and had looked likely to go further when he died suddenly in the spring of 1897 at the age of 26. His two seasons leading the club were years of striking progress. In 1895–96, victories once more exceeded defeats and the club drew twice with Watsonians and once with Clydesdale, who shared the championship in a triple tie with Jed-Forest. The following season was another success, with Accies winning 15 matches and losing only four – during which time they conceded only one try, to Hawick. This Academical XV was also the first team to beat both Oxford and Cambridge in the same season. It was the beginning of another golden era for Academical rugby.

W.M.C (Willie) McEwan took over the captaincy for the 1897–98 season and although the 'double' over Oxford and Cambridge was not repeated, the team had a better record overall, with their only defeat being against Oxford (5-3). In 22 matches played, only 11 points were conceded (one goal by Oxford and a try each by Wanderers and Jed-Forest). With an unbeaten record in Scotland for the first time in ten years, the Accies were champions.

They clinched the championship with a 12-3 victory over Jed-Forest in the last match of the season. Before that match a poem was sent to McEwan entitled: 'To the "Accies" – for Saturday first'. Penned by a 'Stockbridge follower of the Academicals', it seems to have been reproduced on card for the purpose of wider distribution. The former field secretary, Sydney Freeman, preserved two copies of the poem in his fascinating scrapbook.

> Now Mr. McEwan, mind what you're doin',
> For the champion game – you must *win it* –
> Keep your heads level, and play like the d—l,
> And 'Jeddart' will never be *in it*.

That 'Jeddart' can go, you very well know,
Yet "Sonians' (oh) *they* tried the same,
But, the good old 'Accies,' withstood all the hackies,
And proved *two* could play a like game.

Well, the season is o'er, and your bones may be sore,
But fame and good fortune are thine,
Long, long may the true, good white and blue
Exist, in Auld Reekie to shine.

When next year comes round, I'll be on the ground
With a hearty hip, hip, hurrah.
Now, to Forwards and Backs, and Try-getting Cracks,
I wish you a pleasant ta, ta.

'Accie' follower
Stockbridge, March 1898

While injuries meant that the team did change a few times during the course of the season, the line-up was usually: J.M. Reid; W.H. Morrison, P. Turnbull, A.W. Robertson-Durham and A.M. Bucher; J.I. Gillespie and J.N. Morrison; W. McEwan, L. Crawford, G. Moncreiff, H. Moncreiff, W. Dove, L.H.I. Bell, T.P. Dods and D.G. Hall. Three of the forwards – McEwan, Dods and Bell – played for Scotland; while the whole back division with the exception of J.N. Morrison were similarly honoured.

Willie McEwan was first capped against Wales in 1894, when he was still a pupil at the Academy. Robert Mackenzie, the Rector at the Academy at that time, only allowed him to play on the understanding that he would not be selected for the next game against Ireland, and would not attend the public dinner after the match. He was, however, back in the side when England came calling for the last international game of that season. That match also featured W.G. Neilson of Merchiston Castle (who joined his brother Willie in the team, having been drafted into the side in place of another brother, George, who was injured). McEwan and Neilson were the last schoolboys ever to represent Scotland.

McEwan went on to play 16 times in total for Scotland in an international career which spanned seven seasons up to 1900, and he undoubtedly would have won more caps had he and L.H.J. Bell not volunteered during the Boer War. He captained the Academicals for three of the most successful years in the club's history, from 1897–98 to 1899–1900, during which time the club played a total of 60 games, winning 50, drawing six and losing only four. Having taken up permanent residence in Johannesburg after the Boer War, he was capped twice for South Africa in 1903 against Mark Morrison's British Isles touring team.

He was the youngest of four McEwan brothers, all of whom were good footballers. The eldest, Matthew ('Saxon'), was probably the most accomplished, but Willie was not far behind. His main attribute was his exceptional strength. He was seen once at the carnival in Waverley Market using dumb-bells weighing 112lbs for all the usual exercises – including putting them up full stretch above his head. It is claimed that he then tried out his weight-lifting powers on a machine which registered up to 54 stone. He lifted until the dial (which he couldn't see) recorded 54, gave an extra heave – and ripped the handle out of the machine.

Perhaps McEwan's finest performance on the rugby field was the 1896 inter-city match, when the Edinburgh pack was reduced by injuries to seven, then six, and during the last ten minutes to five players. Despite this Edinburgh manage to restrict Glasgow to a 3-0 victory, thanks largely to McEwan's inspirational leadership and never-say-die determination.

The success enjoyed by the Academicals during the tail-end of the nineteenth century points to a high level of dedication and determination; however, a couple of stories recounted in the *EAFC Centenary History* illustrate that it was not all hard work and no play for McEwan and his team-mates:

Once Alick Robertson, the speedy centre, had been repeatedly criticising the forwards (as three-quarters often do), with cries of 'Play-up, forwards – you're slacking!' 'We'll show you,' said the captain, Willie McEwan, 'how hard forwards have to play' and next Saturday Alick found himself detailed to play as a forward. At half-time, an exhausted man sat on the ground, feely admitting that he had never realised that the maul was 'such a hell'.

Another time, when the team was taking the field, an argument arose as to what would happen if no one kicked. The general opinion was that the team that did this would be beaten. 'I don't believe it,' said McEwan, and gave the order, 'No one is to kick to-day.' And that afternoon the Academicals entirely refrained from punting or drop-kicking the ball, which sometimes passed from hand to hand a dozen times, and the match was won easily.

With practically the same team as the previous year, the 1898–99 season brought a particularly impressive set of results. The club's only defeat was versus Oxford, their only draw was against Cambridge, and all 17 Scottish matches were won. Their record for that season was:

Opponents	For	Against
Glasgow Academicals	11	0
Panmure	31	0
Partickhill	19	0
Watsonians	16	3
Edinburgh University	3	0
Royal High School	10	3
West of Scotland	3	0
Wanderers	11	0
Cambridge University	0	0
St George	50	0
Clydesdale	8	0
Kelvinside Academicals	3	0
Oxford University	0	3
Edinburgh Wanderers	8	0
Royal High School	9	0
Stewart's College (FP)	19	3
West of Scotland	6	0
Glasgow University	9	0
Watsonians	15	0

The usual team for this season was:

*J.M. Reid; *W.H. Morrison, *Phipps Turnbull, *A.W. Roberston (later Robertson Durham), *A.M. Bucher, *J.I. Gillespie, *J.N. Morrison (with F.C. Ferguson deputising from January onwards); *W.M.C. McEwan (captain), L. Cauford, G. Moncreiff, H.W. Moncreiff, W. Dove, *L.H.I. Bell, W.J. Stuart, *FP Dods. (R.H. Carlisle played several matches as a three-quarter, as did D.G. Hall in the forwards.)

(*denotes an international at that time or later)

As well as the capped players listed above, W.J. 'Pussy' Stuart was a reserve for Scotland, and W. Dove was a Scotland trialist. Dr A.B. Flett, of Edinburgh University and Scotland, was a contemporary of both players. He described the former:

Always in the pink of condition, Stuart was the mainstay of the pack and was skilled in the art of forward play. Even in his hospital resident days, when he was on duty 18 hours out of 24, he donned his jersey and shorts to run round the meadows at midnight to keep himself in training. As an apostle of physical exercise, he remains a shining example.

Meanwhile, when discussing the extraordinary height of Dove, it might just be possible that the good doctor was guilty of telling more than one sort of tall tale:

One felt he could reach the crossbar if he extended his long arms and I can remember penalty kicks which seemed safe being deflected by Dove's extraordinary reach. In the line-out he was at his best, but all over he was an asset to his side and a personality on the field.

Of all the backs who represented the club with distinction during this era, the most notable were Phipps Turnbull and J.I. (Johnnie) Gillespie. Dr Flett was certainly in no doubt about the rugby prowess of these players.

According to him, Turnbull was:

. . . a star of the first magnitude . . . an incomparable centre three-quarter, certainly one of the most polished who have ever played the game. Tall and not very robust, he was a fearless tackler and his handling of the ball was unsurpassed, but it was as a runner that he excelled. With a very long stride, he seemed to glide through the opposing defence at high speed, apparently without effort.

The *EAFC Centenary History* tells us:

To Phipps Turnbull goes the distinction of scoring a 'field goal' for the Academicals – the only one scored for the club of which we have any record. Up till 1905 it was possible to score a goal by kicking the ball over the bar from the field of play during the course of the game. This earned four points (the same as a drop goal) but was seldom seen. Against Hawick, however, in February 1900, one of these did occur – by accident! The Academicals were playing with a very strong wind and Phipps fly-kicked the ball past the full-back, intending to follow up, but the latter, in the excitement of the moment, tackled him. Phipps was one of the best-tempered players there has ever been but on this occasion he rose in a violent temper and claimed a try. The referee, however, had already blown his whistle, for the wind had carried the ball high over the cross-bar and a 'field goal' had been scored.

1900–01 1st XV

Back: A.S. Pringle, F.P. Dods, W.H. Morrison, W.J. Stuart, P. Turnbull, J.N. Bell, J.M. Bell, A.G. Ramage

Middle: H.S. Reid, D.G. Hall, 'Accie', J.M. Reid, J.I. Gillespie (*Captain*), A.W. Robertson Durham, H.W. Moncreiff, R.M. Neill

Front: O. St J. Gebbie

Turnbull formed one of the great Scottish three-quarter lines alongside the Edinburgh University triumvirate of W.H. Welsh, A.B. Timms and A.N. Fell, which marched to the Triple Crown in 1901. But he was blighted by ill-health, and despite playing in all three Scottish matches in 1902 his powers were clearly on the wane. He did not play for Scotland again, and only occasionally for the Academicals during the next two seasons. He died in 1907 at the tragically young age of 29.

Meanwhile, Dr Flett regarded Johnnie Gillespie as:

. . . one of the best and most efficient and most original half-backs Scotland ever had. He was always in command of the game however tense the situation might be. He handled the ball beautifully and his defence was clever and effective, while his unorthodox methods kept opponents in a state of bewilderment. In the Welsh match of 1901 Scotland was pressing Wales in their 25 and the forwards heeled quickly. Gillespie, instead of passing out to his three as expected, kept the ball on the ground and like a flash dribbled right through his opponents and scored between the posts. His footwork was exceptional and he could dribble like a soccer professional. He scored the first try in each of the three matches in that champion year.

He had a strong sense of humour and during the match would give a running commentary on the game in a low but audible voice, and his wit and good-humoured sarcasm gave delight to friend and foe alike, not to mention the referee!

When Scotland won the Triple Crown in 1901, it was Gillespie who opened the scoring in each match. His half-back partner in the last of these games – an 18-3 victory over England at Blackheath – was his club-mate R.M. Neill. The other Academical to make the national side that season was the forward FP Dods, who picked up his one and only cap against Ireland.

The following year, Gillespie was capped against Ireland and Wales, but was replaced by E.D. Simson of Edinburgh University for the England game. He then took up refereeing, but he resurrected his playing career in time to tour South Africa with Mark Morrison's British side in 1903 – playing in all three Test matches – and was then an important player in Scotland's successes over Ireland at Lansdowne Road and England at Inverleith in 1904, before retiring for 'positively the last time'. Another Academical half-back of this era, R.M. Neill, also made the trip to South Africa in 1903, but was not selected for the Test team.

The Accies team was also bolstered by occasional appearances from J.E. Crabbie and T.A. Nelson during this period, both of whom were internationalists and Oxford captains.

Another Academical of this vintage who deserves a mention is Oswald St John Gebbie, who attended the school between 1895 and 1897, and then played for the Academicals until 1901, before moving to Argentina with Ashworth & Co Merchants (later working for the New Zealand and River Plate Land Mortgage Company). He played for the 1st XV of the Buenos Aires Football Club (now the Buenos Aires Cricket & Rugby Club) from 1902 to 1910 and was captain from 1904 onwards.

In 1910 a 'Combined British' team managed by Major R.V. Stanley, the Oxford University and England selector, visited Argentina. That side, made up predominantly of Englishmen with a smattering of Scots, played three games against guest sides Olimpicos (Olympians), the River Plate Rugby Union and Argentina Natives. Playing at centre, St John Gebbie captained the home team in each of these matches, scoring a try in a 13-19 loss in the first of those matches and kicking two goals in a 10-41 loss in the third match.

The match against the River Plate Rugby Football Union (the precursor of the *Unión Argentina de Rugby*), was played on 12 June and resulted in a 3-28 win for the tourists. That match has come to be regarded as Argentina's first Test match (although it is not recognised as such in the IRB World Rugby Yearbook), so perhaps Oswald St John Gebbie's name should be added to the long list of Academical internationalists.

He was also president of the River Plate Rugby Football Union from 1936 to 1939. His brother, Tom, was president of the same organisation from 1915 to 1919 and president of the Buenos Aires Football Club for nine years. *The Edinburgh Academy Register* records that his hospitality was enjoyed by many visiting Academicals over the years.

Back on home soil, the 1899–1900 season brought two defeats against Scottish opponents for the Academicals, versus Edinburgh University (with whom they shared the championship) and Wanderers; and both games against Watsonians were drawn. Johnnie Gillespie took over the captaincy for the 1900–01 season, and once again the Academicals were unbeaten in Scotland, with 15 wins and one draw versus Edinburgh University. Their only two defeats that year were to last-minute scores by both Oxford and Cambridge universities.

The club had won the championship in each of the last four seasons – three times outright and sharing the honour once with Edinburgh University.

The 1901–02 season, which was heavily disrupted by frost, saw a decline in the club's fortunes, with four defeats coming against Edinburgh University (12-0), Oxford (12-5), Edinburgh University again (5-0) and Jed-Forest (8-6). By the high standards set during the previous five years, this was a disappointing campaign, but far from an abject failure. Going into their second last match against Edinburgh University, the Academicals were still in with a shout of winning the championship, and a large crowd turned up at Inverleith to watch a thrilling contest.

The club's record during this period is impressive:

Scottish Matches	P.	W.	L.	D.	Points	
1896–97	17	13	4	0	170	7
1897–98	19	16	0	3	203	6
1898–99	17	17	0	0	231	9
1899–1900	18	14	2	2	289	13
1900–01	16	15	0	1	188	20
1901–02	14	10	3	1	140	35
	101	**85**	**9**	**7**	**1,221**	**100**

All Matches	P.	W.	L.	D.	Points	
1896–97	19	15	4	0	187	17
1897–98	22	18	1	3	214	11
1898–99	19	17	1	1	231	12
1899–1900	19	15	2	2	292	13
1900–01	18	15	2	1	200	37
1901–02	15	10	4	1	145	47
	112	**90**	**14**	**8**	**1,269**	**137**

These statistics are particularly formidable given the standard of competition in Scottish club rugby at that time, with the Edinburgh University team which pipped Academicals at the post in the race for the championship in 1901–02 the strongest of the lot – at least on paper. That side had 11 players who were current Internationalists or would go on to be capped the following season; and such was the strength in depth at the university that their 'A' team had E.W. Baker in the centre, who was a reserve for England, and J.S. Macdonald on the wing, who was a reserve for Scotland and would go on to be capped five times between 1903 and 1905.

Watsonians were also strong and encounters between these two teams tended to be particularly robust affairs – although the true rugby spirit would usually prevail. *The EAFC Centenary History* recounts a tale of an Academical and a Watsonian nipping behind the pavilion after the game to settle a dispute which had started on the field. They ended up the best of friends and went off together to celebrate the occasion with strong ale at a penny a pint.

Another story, which is probably apocryphal, relates to a match between the two clubs at Raeburn Place which became so heated that one leading newspaper of the day reported that another such game would kill rugby football in Scotland. During the course of this battle the ball was kicked out of the field, and while it was being retrieved an impartial but very interested spectator sitting on the wall shouted: 'Get on wi' the game! You dinna need a ba'!'

CHAPTER FIFTEEN

The game has changed very much in appearance, but, as a matter of fact, it is very difficult to point to any great difference that has taken place. There are really very few, although they have had considerable effect. First of all, coming down from twenty to fifteen made an enormous difference. After that there was the growth of less foot and more hand, which was very gradual and probably reached its height of excellence in Harry Vassall's Oxford years [1879–82], and has since probably been a little overdone. Then there was the change introduced by Wales, called by most people the four three-quarters. I think that is probably the proper name for it; but it took several years for it to find favour; and in my humble opinion might never have found favour, might absolutely have died in inanition, but for the introduction and permission of heeling out. I advisedly say permission, because I am not quite satisfied in my own mind that it really is legalised, to this day. There is one remark I would like to make. Year after year, and several times during the year, people come to me and say, 'Don't you think this game is not so good as it used to be?' and I am tempted to say, 'Certainly not'; but in my inmost soul I think and believe the game has improved.

Bill Maclagan,
speaking at the Academical Football Club Jubilee Dinner in 1908

DURING THE PERIOD BETWEEN 1902 and 1914 the Academicals maintained their place among the leading Scottish clubs, and they were 'Champions' in 1905–06. However, these sides were never able to reach the same dizzy heights as the teams of Hippo Reid and Willie McEwan had managed during the last two decades of the previous century. Perhaps the chief reason for this was that an increase in boarders at the Academy meant that fewer boys stayed in Edinburgh after leaving the school; and this problem was amplified by the fact that more boys who might previously have gone to Edinburgh University were going on to Oxford or Cambridge after leaving school, or joining the Regular Army. Some of these players made occasional appearances for the Academicals during vacations or while on leave, but few were regularly available.

This was counter-balanced to a degree by the growth of the Academy prep school, which meant that there was an increasing number of boys who had spent their early school years as day pupils at the Academy before going off to boarding schools elsewhere. Many of these former pupils returned to live in Edinburgh after leaving school and viewed the Academicals as the natural club to join. For example, J.M.B. Scott, G.H.H. Maxwell (Sedburgh) and J.D.B. Campbell (Fettes) all gave good service to the club during this period.

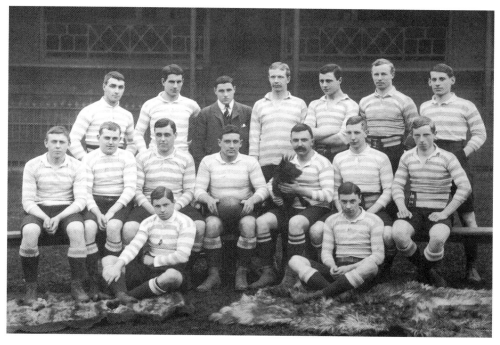

1902–03 1st XV

Back: J.N. Bell, P.C. Young, G. Crabbie, Dr W. J. Stuart, J.A.R. Cargill, J.C. Murray, A. Wyllie

Middle: H.S. Reid, J.L. Gillespie, FP Dods, L.H.I Bell (*Captain*), 'Accie', Dr D.G. Hall, R.M. Neill, D. Cotterill

Front: J.E. Crabbie, D.M. Wood

The 1902–03 season seems to have been a particularly frustrating campaign, with injuries and the retiral of several senior players taking its toll on the team. There were a few very good results that season, such as an 18-0 victory over Cambridge University, a 27-3 triumph against West of Scotland and a hard-fought

4-3 win over a Canadian touring team in miserable conditions on Christmas Day at Inverleith. However, these lone beacons of hope were not enough to divert attention fully away from an overall record for the season of five losses and two draws from 17 Scottish matches played. The final match of the campaign was an 11-0 defeat to Watsonians at Myreside, prompting a scathing review of the season to be published in *The Chronicle* in April 1903:

> This is our second defeat in the season by Watsonians, which has not happened since 1894, and our fifth defeat in Scotch football for the season, which is a terrible fall from former heights.

The correspondent was in no doubt as to where the problems lay:

> The system at the school which has prevailed in the past few years of allowing the backs to monopolise practice games, though it has produced a lot of good three-quarters and halves, has totally stopped the supply of hard-working forwards which is absolutely essential to the style of game necessitated by the muddy grounds which are so prevalent in Scotland; and this applies as much to the School as to the Academicals. If we are to regain the position we once held we must rear forwards, who can push, dribble, and tackle low, not mere heeling-out machines who do not even get the ball to heel. The school three-quarter play has reached a state of very high efficiency, and there is no reason why the forwards should not do the same; if that can be brought about there is no fear for the future of the Academicals.

This analysis was perhaps a tad melodramatic. The 1902–03 season had hardly been a classic, but the club lost to only three Scottish clubs – Watsonians (twice), Edinburgh University (twice) and Glasgow Academicals – and during the next five years these three clubs and Jed-Forest were the only Scottish sides to beat the Academicals.

The 1st XV's record during this period might not have been exceptional, but neither was it disastrous:

Scottish Matches	P.	W.	L.	D.	Points	
1902–03	17	10	5	2	217	85
1903–04	19	13	4	2	182	38
1904–05	18	10	5	3	173	49
1905–06	20	14	1	5	214	42
1906–07	14	11	2	1	163	41
	88	**58**	**17**	**13**	**949**	**255**

All Matches	P.	W.	L.	D.	Points	
1902–03	20	12	6	2	227	101
1903–04	21	14	4	3	200	41
1904–05	21	13	5	3	196	54
1905–06	22	15	2	5	252	67
1906–07	17	11	5	1	171	73
	101	**65**	**22**	**14**	**1,046**	**336**

With Lewis Bell serving a second term as captain during the 1903–04 season, the Academicals came within a whisker of finishing top of the championship, for each of their four defeats was by a very narrow margin. *The Chronicle* described the record for that season as 'very poor' but added that many 'still believe the full Academical side was the best in Scotland'. That season the club defeated Cambridge University and drew with Oxford. From this team Bell and the brothers Jack and 'Gee' Crabbie were capped, while Russell Cargill would later become president of the Middlesex County Rugby Union and help to introduce Sevens to London. The Middlesex Sevens trophy is named after him.

The 1904–05 season brought a similar set of results, with the Academicals being edged out by narrow score-lines in a handful of key matches. The Academicals drew once and lost once to champions-elect Glasgow Academicals, the double was achieved over Cambridge and Oxford Universities, and a strong London Scottish side was held to a draw.

Bobby Neill was captain during the 1905–06 season, when the Academicals were champions for the first time since 1900–01 and for the last time until 1929–30. The season started with a 9-0 victory over Heriot's in the first match ever played between these two clubs, while the 14-8 defeat of Watsonians in a thrilling match a

1905–06 1st XV

Back: A.D. Anderson, J.M. McKeand, J.H.B. Smith, P.M. Murray, J.D.B. Campbell, J.M.B. Scott, M.B. Anderson, C. Anderson

Middle: J.C.M. Bell, J.A.R. Cargill, G.E. Crabbie, R.M. Neill (*Captain*), H.S. Reid, J.C. Murray, D. Cotterill

Front: G.G. Blackwood

few weeks later seems to have been a defining moment in the season. A second victory over Watsonians in the last game of the season secured the title. There was only one defeat to Scottish opposition that season, against Glasgow Academicals towards the end of the campaign; and five draws, against Edinburgh University, Royal High School FP, West of Scotland, Edinburgh Institution FP and Edinburgh University again.

The 1906–07 season was a reasonably successful one. Frost reduced the number of fixtures played to 17, of which 11 were won and one was drawn. The Cambridge, Oxford and London Scottish matches were all lost, but none of these were heavy defeats, and the only club in Scotland to overcome the Academicals were Watsonians, who did so twice. (The exploits of the club this season were overshadowed by the achievements of A.B. Mein's Academy XV, which went the whole season without tasting defeat – winning nine matches, drawing one, scoring 202 points and conceding only 33.)

1906–07 Academy 1st XV

Back: R.C.C. Campbell, K. McLean, J. Prosser, R.C. Blackwood, J.G. Monteath, A. Gilmour

Middle: W. Ross Stewart, P.A. McKeand, T.M. Anderson, A.B. Mein (*Captain*), H. Martin, J.T.R. Mitchell,

C. Mackintosh

Front: W. Milne, J.R. Milligan

It may appear as if the suggestion made in *The Chronicle* back in 1903 that the Academicals would suffer because of a lack of hardy forwards being produced at the Academy was slightly premature. However, similar sentiments were being voiced by such knowledgeable rugby experts as Johnnie Gillespie, the Academical and Scotland international half-back, in a letter published in *The Chronicle* in December 1907:

It seems to me that there is something radically wrong with the system of teaching the young boys at the Academy how to play forward. I am very strongly of the opinion that the proper way to teach the junior practices is to play the old forward game of nine forwards and to instil into their heads that the first duty of a forward is to shove for all he is worth . . . I think everyone will agree with me that in the last fifteen years we have turned out very few first-class forwards in comparison with the number of backs who have got representative honours. This would seem to me to show that there is not enough trouble taken in the teaching of forward play, which after all, in Rugby Football is the chief controlling power of the game. I would suggest that all practices up to the first practice go back to the old game of nine forwards, and that neither side should be allowed to have the ball out of the scrum until they are well within their opponents' 25. Once they learn how to wheel a scrum, the backs on both sides will find that they get plenty of running about.

Steps were taken to improve forward play at the school. S.H. Osborne – an old Fettesian, who had played in the pack for England against Scotland in 1905, whilst a student at Oxford University – had joined the Academy staff, prompting Rector Reginald Carter to state in his annual report of 1907–08:

> Young boys who are learning the game should not be allowed to heel out in ordinary practices, otherwise they will not learn how to shove hard, to get possession of the ball, and to dribble strongly. The instructions given by Mr Osborne in these matters will, I hope, be fruitful in the future.

Within a couple of years the school was once again producing forwards of the desired quality. In 1909–10, David Bain captained a young but plucky Academy team which won seven out of the ten school matches they played – losing once to Glenalmond and twice to Fettes. *The Chronicle* described Bain succinctly as 'one of the best forwards we have had for many years. Combines pace with weight and cleverness. Particularly dashing near the line'. He was chosen as a reserve for the Scotland team which played England that year, gained a cap and an Oxford Blue the next season, and went on to play in 11 international matches in total and in four varsity games.

Bain wasn't the only exceptional forward to emerge from the school at this time. F.W. Thomson and J.G. Monteath also became Oxford Blues, and in 1912 there were five Academical forwards – Bain, Thomson, Monteath, E.S. Fiddes and J.D.O. Coats – in the Oxford side which gave the touring South Africans a run for their money.

Eleven of Bain's XV returned to the school the following season, and that year the team led by H.F.W.W. Buchan swept all before them – winning all 11 school matches played and seven out of seven matches played against club opposition; scoring 409 points and conceding only 54.

While this renewed emphasis on forward play certainly doesn't seem to have done the Academy XV any harm, the benefit at club level was not immediately apparent. Between 1907 and 1914 the Academicals were infuriatingly inconsistent, as the *EAFC Centenary History* explains:

> They would rise to great heights on occasion against powerful opposition – and then fade away quietly in matches they were expected to win. Some of the defeats they suffered were so heavy that the 'old brigade' must have shaken their heads very sadly over the failing of these 'young chaps'. Then would come some great achievement – and the sun shone again.

Jubilee Dinner menu featuring portraits of past captains

Two of those heavy defeats came during the 1907–08 season, when the gloss was rather taken off the club's jubilee celebrations by a 35-8 defeat to Cambridge University and a 43-3 loss to London Scottish. These results stood in stark contrast to the impressive performances of the team against Watsonians (11-6 and 5-5), Glasgow Academicals (0-0 and 5-0) and Hawick (16-0).

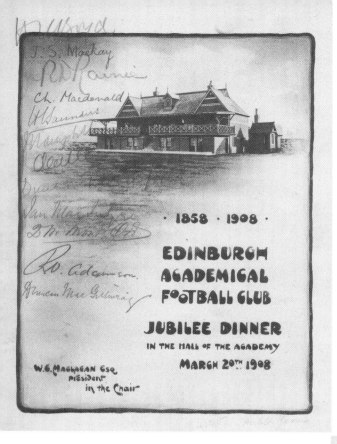

Front cover of the Jubilee Dinner
menu, signed by players, 1908

Back cover of the Jubilee Dinner
menu, listing Academicals to have
played international rugby

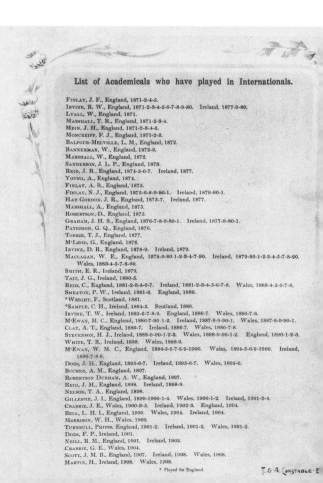

List of Academicals who have played in Internationals.

FINLAY, J. F., England, 1871-2-4-5.
IRVINE, R. W., England, 1871-2-3-4-5-6-7-8-9-80. Ireland, 1877-9-80.
LYALL, W., England, 1871.
MARSHALL, T. R., England, 1871-2-3-4.
MEIN, J. H., England, 1871-2-3-4-5.
MONCREIFF, F. J., England, 1871-2-3.
BALFOUR-MELVILLE, L. M., England, 1872.
BANNERMAN, W., England, 1872-3.
MARSHALL, W., England, 1872.
SANDERSON, J. L. P., England, 1873.
REID, J. R., England, 1874-5-6-7. Ireland, 1877.
YOUNG, A., England, 1874.
FINLAY, A. B., England, 1875.
FINLAY, N. J., England, 1875-6-8-9-80-1. Ireland, 1879-80-1.
HAY GORDON, J. R., England, 1875-7. Ireland, 1877.
MARSHALL, A., England, 1875.
ROBERTSON, D., England, 1875.
GRAHAM, J. H. S., England, 1876-7-8-9-80-1. Ireland, 1877-9-80-1.
PATERSON, G. Q., England, 1876.
TORRIE, T. J., England, 1877.
M'LEOD, G., England, 1878.
IRVINE, D. R., England, 1878-9. Ireland, 1879.
MACLAGAN, W. E., England, 1878-9-80-1-2-3-4-7-90. Ireland, 1879-80-1-2-3-4-5-7-8-90.
    Wales, 1883-4-5-7-8-90.
SMITH, E. R., Ireland, 1879.
TAIT, J. G., Ireland, 1880-5.
REID, C., England, 1881-2-3-4-6-7. Ireland, 1881-2-3-4-5-6-7-8. Wales, 1883-4-5-6-7-8.
SMEATON, P. W., Ireland, 1881-3. England, 1883.
*WRIGHT, F., Scotland, 1881.
*SAMPLE, C. H., Ireland, 1884-5. Scotland, 1886.
IRVINE, T. W., Ireland, 1885-6-7-8-9. England, 1886-7. Wales, 1886-7-8.
M'EWAN, M. C., England, 1886-7-90-1-2. Ireland, 1887-8-9-90-1. Wales, 1887-8-9-90-1.
CLAY, A. T., England, 1886-7. Ireland, 1886-7. Wales, 1886-7-8.
STEVENSON, H. J., Ireland, 1888-9-90-1-2-3. Wales, 1888-9-90-1-2. England, 1890-1-2-3.
WHITE, T. B., Ireland, 1888. Wales, 1888-9.
M'EWAN, W. M. C., England, 1894-5-6-7-8-9-1900. Wales, 1894-5-6-9-1900. Ireland,
    1896-7-8-9.
DODS, J. H., England, 1895-6-7. Ireland, 1895-6-7. Wales, 1895-6.
BUCHER, A. M., England, 1897.
ROBERTSON DURHAM, A. W., England, 1897.
REID, J. M., England, 1898. Ireland, 1898-9.
NELSON, T. A., England, 1898.
GILLESPIE, J. I., England, 1899-1900-1-4. Wales, 1900-1-2. Ireland, 1901-2-4.
CRABBIE, J. E., Wales, 1900-3-5. Ireland, 1902-3. England, 1904.
BELL, L. H. I., England, 1900. Wales, 1904. Ireland, 1904.
MORRISON, W. H., Wales, 1900.
TURNBULL, PHIPPS, England, 1901-2. Ireland, 1901-2. Wales, 1901-2.
DODS, F. P., Ireland, 1901.
NEILL, R. M., England, 1901. Ireland, 1902.
CRABBIE, G. E., Wales, 1904.
SCOTT, J. M. B., England, 1907. Ireland, 1908. Wales, 1908.
MARTIN, H., Ireland, 1908. Wales, 1908.

* Played for England.

T. & A. CONSTABLE. E

The victory over Glasgow Academicals must have been particularly satisfying given that they had beaten London Scottish that season. Hamish (J.S.) Allan had been a 3rd XV player at school but through enthusiasm and hard work he eventually become vice-captain of the Academical 1st XV, and also represented Edinburgh versus Glasgow. This was one of his first appearances for the Academical 1st XV and he scored the only try of the match. He also scored a vital try against Watsonians in the last game of the season which allowed J.C. 'Sausage' Murray to kick the goal which tied the match.

'Sausage' Murray was undoubtedly one of the great characters in the club's long and colourful history. Time and again he stepped forward to kick crucial goals for the club, and according to *EAFC Centenary History* never once wavered:

Tall, good-looking, immaculately dressed and usually wearing white kid gloves, he added an air of distinction to any game in which he took part. Some slight physical weakness had kept him off football in his last year or two at School, but he outgrew this and became a fine player who went near an international 'cap'. Possibly his adventurous outlook was held against him. He was always eager to turn defence into attack and frequently caused his colleagues palpitations with the risks he took.

His punts were of tremendous length, straight up the touch-line and curling in at the end of their flight to gain every possible foot, and his place- and drop-kicking could be magnificent. Two of his best efforts occurred in rapid succession at Myreside in 1907, each penalty goal from half way, the first a drop, the second a place. The second was from a point within a yard of the touch-line, and when 'Sausage' said, with his usual confident air, 'Oh, I'll have a try', it was easy to see that many of the onlookers thought that this was just 'pure side'. The touch judges evidently thought the same because neither went behind the goal posts. Had it not been for the sportsmanship of J.L. Forbes, the Watsonian and Scottish centre, who caught the ball as it fell behind the bar and who indicated that it had indeed gone over, the referee would not have known that it was a goal. And so taken aback were the spectators that there was hardly any applause for an astonishing feat.

Another character from this era was George Blackwood, who was essentially a full-back, but used to fill in elsewhere in the backline if required. According to the *EAFC Centenary History*:

1907–08 1st XV

Back: G.G. Blackwood, T.M. Anderson, J.S. Allan, J. Prosset, T.R. Binnie, F.C. Muirhead, W. Bruce, M.B. Anderson

Middle: C. Anderson, A.D. Anderson, J.C. Murray, J.C.M. Bell (*Captain*), J.M. McKeand, J.M.B. Scott

Front: A.S. Aikman, W. Ross-Stewart

By the time he retired he had occupied every position in the Academical 1st XV except one – scrum half. Some years after he had retired, he was strolling along Princes Street on a Saturday, having just had a lunch complete with vintage port, when he was suddenly seized by 'Bunjy' Watson [the club captain in 1912–13] who said that he had been searching for Blackwood, as the Academicals were short-handed. George protested that he had not even run for two or three years and that he had just had an excellent lunch – but what position required to be filled? When 'Bunjy' said 'Scrum half', there were no further protests. George duly turned out as scrum half, and, though he 'never felt nearer death than after the first five minutes', he got his second wind, scored a try, and lasted the game before going into retirement again with his record of appearances for the Academicals now 100 per cent complete.

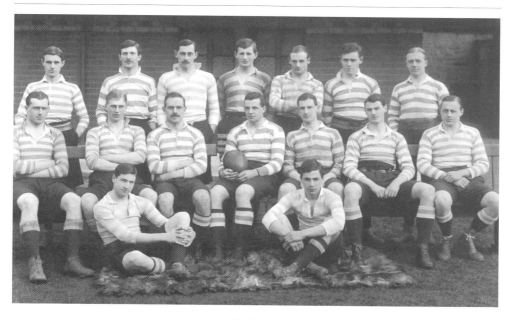

1909–10 1st XV

Back: G.W. Wallace, A.G. Moir, P.M. Campbell, K. McLean, J.H.D. Watson, A.M. Stewart, A.B. Mein

Middle: T.R. Binnie, W. Bruce, J.C.M. Bell, J.M.B. Scott (*Captain*), Dr J.M. McKeand, J. Prosser, J.S. Allan

Front: W.J. McKeand, R.B. Anderson

The Academicals lost their first five matches of the 1908–09 season, and over the course of that campaign defeats exceeded victories. The record was slightly better the following year; and despite losing Jim McKeand, the newly elected captain who was forced to retire from the game through illness before the season had started, this slow but steady progress continued into the 1910–01 season. McKeand, who played centre, was a fearless tackler and powerful runner, who had the most bewildering double swerve which often confused his team-mates as much as it did the opposition. He was the second Academical to play for the Barbarians, after Tommy Nelson in 1898–99, and was a reserve for Scotland on at least one occasion.

The 1911–02 season brought the Academicals 11 wins and seven losses in their matches against Scottish opposition, which was enough to see them described in *The Chronicle* as a side 'of more capabilities and lasting powers than had been seen at Raeburn in recent years'. Their final record for that season would have been a lot more impressive if they hadn't lost three of their last four matches. Jock Scott

1910–11 Academy 1st XV

Back: R.D. Milligan, W.M. Wallace, R. Clark, N.G. Salvesen, W.K. White, R.G.S. Durward, J.C.G.C. Muirhead

Middle: G.E.F. Campbell, E.S. Fiddes, W.M. Crabbie, H.F.W.W. Buchan (*Captain*), J. Fleck, C.D. Ritchie, R. Carlyle

Front: W.F.T. Haultain, H. Alexander, A.T. Sloan

was outstanding amongst the forwards who 'as a whole came nearer to what we should like to consider as the Academical standard'. Faint praise indeed, especially when followed up with an expression of regret at 'a tendency to overstep the limits of healthy robustness into an unnecessary roughness and pugnacity which is to be deprecated, if for no other reason, for the waste of energy entailed, which might be turned to account in the game'.

Meanwhile, the three-quarter line was both the most dangerous and disappointing section of the team. Individually, each was very good in attack, but somehow as a line they seldom functioned smoothly. In defence they did extremely well, admirably supported by George Wallace at full-back until he was injured.

The Chronicle concluded:

On the whole, the team may be congratulated on a promising season and justified their title in the Championship as a spoiling side, whether it was their own position on the list or that of others they were spoiling.

1911–12 1st XV

Back: G.D. Ferguson, W.M. Crabbie, R.B. Anderson, G.H.P. Maxwell, H.F.W. Buchan, R.D. Milligan, J. Fleck

Middle: G.W. Wallace, P.M. Campbell, J.S. Allen, J.M.B. Scott (*Captain*), J.H.D. Watson,
A.M. Stewart, C. Mackintosh

Front: H.J. Davidson, A.T. Sloan

The 1st XV that season was: G.W. Wallace (R.B. Anderson); H.F.W. Buchan, C. Mackintosh, J.S. Allan, J.H.D. Watson; A.T. Sloan, H.J. Davidson, J.M.B. Scott, P.M. Campbell, G.H.H. Maxwell, A.M. Stewart, W.M. Crabbie, R.D. Milligan, C.D. Ferguson, J. Fleck.

The captain for the 1912–13 season was J.H.D. (Digby) Watson, who played on either the wing or at centre. Watson had come to the Academy from King's School, Canterbury, bringing with him an odd name for a pencil eraser. When, shortly after his arrival, he sought to borrow a 'bunjy' the word became associated with him and from then on he was known as Bunjy Watson.

He played brilliantly in the inter-city match in 1911, and after being named as a reserve for the match against England later that year he came within five minutes of becoming a Scottish internationalist. R.F. Simson, one of his closest Academy friends, only arrived at the ground just before kick-off, at which point Bunjy was stripped and ready to take his place.

His heart, however, was really set on playing for England, so after he had finished his degree at Edinburgh University he moved back south, joining Blackheath, and before long he had forced his way into the England team, playing against Wales, Scotland and France during the 1913–14 season. The Scottish selectors had allowed a rare talent to slip through their fingers, as was made painfully clear during that season's Calcutta Cup clash at Inverleith, when Bunjy played a key role in all three of C.N. Lowe's tries in a thrilling 16-15 victory for the visitors.

Bunjy had a quick eye for an opening and the speed and skill to make use of it. A long and distinguished international career seemed to be his destiny, until the war came and he volunteered for the Royal Navy. He went down with HMS *Hawke* in October 1914.

Probably Bunjy's finest performance as an Accies player was against Watsonians in October 1912, when he scored all but three of his team's 18 points. The first try came from a scrum on the Watsonians line, the ball came out and Bunjy, feinting beautifully, cut through a gap and scored between the posts. For the Academicals' second try he broke from his own 25, and when confronted by the opposition full-back he was able to offload to Jock Scott, who showed plenty of pace to race home from the half-way line despite the close attentions of J. Pearson, the Scottish three-quarter. Shortly before the end, Bunjy broke through to get his second and his team's third try of the match. As well as kicking all three conversions, he also dropped a beautiful goal and kicked a fine penalty. In defence he kicked long and accurately for touch and tackled superbly. That 18-3 victory was the first Academicals win over Watsonians in five years.

Another game of particular note that season took place on 21 December, when the Academicals visited Manchester. Play was extremely fast, with both sides better in attack than they were in defence. By half-time the Academicals had scored two goals and a try against three tries for Manchester, but that was nothing compared to what followed during the second half. The lead changed hands six times with Accies eventually running out 31-25 winners, thanks to two tries in the last five minutes. The visitors had scored five goals and two tries against two goals, three tries and two penalty goals. Surely it was no coincidence that his high-scoring, free-wheeling encounter occurred the night after Bunjy Watson promoted the hypothesis that crème-de-menthe was the ideal refreshment for the evening before a match, with that theory being rigorously and vigorously tested during the journey to Manchester.

The 1912–13 season was also Jock Scott's last with the team. He had been an invaluable player for the Academicals and for Scotland since the 1906–07 season, during which time he had picked up 21 caps. According to *The Chronicle*, he had an uncanny knack of being 'often found in places where he was required but not expected'. That try against Watsonians in October 1912 was typical of Scott, for he had good hands and an exceptional turn of pace for a forward. In later life he wrote a rugby manual on the game entitled *Rugby Football & How to Play It*, which was published in 1922.

Despite the departure of two such important stalwarts of the side as Watson and Scott, the 1913–14 season got off to an encouraging start with a convincing 19-6 victory over Gala, but then injuries and call-offs for other unspecified reasons began to take a toll. Against Cambridge University at Raeburn Place, six regulars were missing, and despite scoring in the first minute the Academicals were completely outclassed, eventually losing by 56 points to three. Some improvement was shown when Watsonians arrived at Raeburn at the end of the season looking to avoid defeat in order to regain the championship. The visitors were made to fight every inch of the way before eventually running out winners by a goal to nil.

That match not only brought down the curtain on the season, but it was also the last game played by the Academicals before the outbreak of the First World War. On 18 June 1914, the annual general meeting of the club was held in the pavilion at Raeburn Place, at which G.H.H. Maxwell was elected captain and A.T. Sloan vice-captain. The other appointments were: G.W. Wallace, honorary secretary; E.J. Thomson, captain and secretary of the 'A' XV; I.A. Johnson-Gilbert, captain and secretary of the 'B' XV.

On 11 September, a special general meeting was held 'to ascertain what attitude the Club should adopt to the playing of football during the War'. It was unanimously agreed that:

Owing to the War between Great Britain and Germany and Austria, when the feeling was that the playing of football was out of place and when the majority of the Club's members were absent serving their country, all fixtures for Season 1914–15 should be cancelled.

It was not until five years later, on 4 October 1919, that an Academical XV took to the field again.

CHAPTER SIXTEEN

Men who had learned to 'play the game' on football grounds might be trusted to do no less in the greater game of war . . . he [the rugby player] answered the call of his country as he would to the whistle – without question.

L.R. Tosswill in
Football: The Rugby Union Game, 1925

LIST OF ACADEMICALS WHO WERE KILLED IN ACTION, DIED OF WOUNDS, OR DIED ON SERVICE DURING THE FIRST WORLD WAR

Adams, Ord
Addis, Ronald Forrester
Aitken, John Malcolm
Allan, James Stanely
Almond, George Hely-Hutchison
Alston, John Douglas
Alves, John William Jerome
Anderson, Archibald Mitchell
Anderson, Edward Darnley
Anderson, Francis
Anderson, Robert Ballantyne
Anderson, Thomas Binnie
Angus, Archibald
Angus, Stewart
Arnott, Robert Louis Irving
Bain, David McLaren
Bain, William Graham
Balfour, Isaac Bayley
Balfour-Melville, James Elliot
Banks, Henry Crawford
Beattie, Charles

Bell, Adam Dickson
Birrell, William George
Black, John
Black, William Macmillan
Blair, Patrick Edward Adam
Bogle, Andrew Blyth McCulloch
Boswall, James Donaldson
Boyd, Nigel John Lawson
Boyd, William Noel Lawson
Brickman, Frederick William
Brickman, Hugh Morton Gavin
Brickman, Noel
Briggs, George Clark
Brodie, Walter Lorrain
Brown, James Macpherson Gordon
Brown, John Caldwell Cochran Cook
Brown, Robert Lowis Campbell
Bruce, Alexander Charles Arbuthnot
Bruce, John Russell
Buchan, Leslie Alexander
Burn-Murdoch, William Callander

Cadell, Richard Lewis
Cadenhead, George
Cairns, George Morton
Cameron, Colin Neil
Cameron, Ian Gilmour
Campbell, George Edward Forman
Campbell, Robert Charles Cowburn
Cargill, Duncan Campbell
Carlyle, Robert
Carmichael, Edward William Scott
Cheyne, Harry
Christie, Lindsay Bruce Stark
Christison, Frederick John
Clark, Richard
Clement, Hubert Arnold
Conduitt, Robert Bruce
Cook, Walter Lorrain
Cotterill, Denis
Cowan, George Deas
Craig, Frederick Claude
Cullen, William Geoffrey Langley
Cundall, James Tudor
Cunningham, Stewart Gordon
Cunynghame, Ronald Ogilvy Blair
Cuthbert, Reginald Vaux
Dalmahoy, John Francis Cecil
Dangerfield, William Cecil Hay
Davidson, Francis Charteris
Davidson, Thomas
Davis, Robert
Dawson, John Douglas
Dewar, Alexander
Dickson, Archibald William
Dixon, Norman Ferguson
Dobbie, Alexander Middleton

Douglas, Archibald Halliday
Douglas, John George
Duncan, Ronald Wingrave
Durwald, Robald Gibson Stewart
Dyer, William Oscar
Egerton, James Boswall
Ellington Leslie, Leslie Francis
Falconer, William Keay
Ferguson, Arthur Douglas
Ferguson, George Douglas
Ferguson, James
Ferguson, Stanley McEwan
Fergusson, James Scott Elliot Gillon
Ferryman, William Edward
Flockhart, John
Foot, David Victor
Fordyce, James Dingwall
Fraser, James Lovat Hosack
Fraser, Patrick Neill
Fraser, William St John
Galletly, Ian
Gardiner, Ilay Ferrier Forrest
Geddes, Alisdair Cosmo Burton
Georgeson, Dan Horace
Gibson, Mungo Campbell
Gibson, Robert Horsburgh
Gillies, Halliday Gordon
Gilmour, Allan
Gordon, Reginald Glegg
Gordon, William Hyde Eagleson
Gowans, Alexander Douglas Stuart
Graham, Henry Balfour
Graham, John Hamilton Thom
Graham, Richard
Grant, Ivor Forsyth

Gray, Edward Leadbetter
Gregory, James Langdale
Grierson, James Gilbert Hamilton
Haddon, Walter
Haldane, Robert Patrick
Hall, Henry
Hamilton, Kenneth
Harrison, William
Henderson-Begg, Robert
Hepburne-Scott, Alexander Noel
Herdman, Thomas Anderson
Herford, Francis Mackay
Hewat, James Govan Argyll
Hewitt, William George
Hole, William Arthur
Horn, Robert
Horne, Thomas Wardlaw
Horsburgh, Robert Patrick
Howard, Stewart Chouet
Hunter, Norman Frederick
Hunter, Robert Gibson
Hunter, Douglas Campbell
Inglis, James Arthur Chetwynd
Innes, John Stuart Brodie
Jalland, Boswell Victor
Johnston, Robert Graham
Johnston, William Savile
Jones, Charles Kenelm Digby
Kennedy, Gilbert Stuart
Kennedy, Thomas Christian
Kindersley, Douglas Cumming Paget
King, Alexander Duncan Campbell
Lamb, Everard Joseph
Latta, Alexander James Joff
Latta, Charles Keith

Latta, Robert William Campbell
Lawrence, Frank Deane
Lawson, Arthur Creswell
Lawson, John Lawson
Lennox-Conyngham, Hubert Maxwell
Lennox-Conyngham,
   John Staples Molesworth
Liddle, William
Liebenthal, Louis George
Liston-Foulis, Archibald Primrose
Lorimer, James Bannerman
Lundie, Robert Charles
Macdonald, Evan Ronald Horatio
   Keith
Macdonald, John Doran
Macdonald, John Row Mackenzie
MacDougall, Stewart
MacEwen, David Campbell
Macfarlane, Alastair Hunter
McFarlane, Donald MacIntyre
McIntosh, Henry Beveridge
Mackay, Ian
Mackay, Ian Forbes
Mackenzie, Kenneth
McKerrell, Martin Mungo Mure
Mackintosh, James Lawton
McLaren, James
McLaren, Quentin
McLaren, William Somerville
McLeod, John Kelty
McLintock, Arnold
Macnicol, Horatius Bonar
Macrae, Alexander William Urquhart
Macwatt, Norman Ian
McWilliam, James Julian Gordon

Matthew, Francis Henry
Maule, Robert
Maxwell, John Rennie
Menzies, Arthur John Alexander
Middleton, Alexander Samuel
Middleton, George Hilton
Middleton, James Russell
Mill, Robert Cowpar King
Mill, William Henry Jun.
Miller, Archibald William Buchanan
Miller, Charles Wallace Strettell
Miller, Henry William Watson
Miller, Thomas Alexander Grant
Milligan, Alastair
Milligan, James Henry
Milligan, John Richard
Milne, William
Mitchell, James Thomson Rankin
Moir, Archibald Gifford
Moncrieff, William Scott
Morrison, William Fleming Oliphant
Mosman, Hugh
Muir, George Watson
Muir, John Wallace
Murray, John Congrieve
Mylne, James Graham
Nairne, William Graham
Nelson, Thomas Arthur
Nicol, David
Norie, Evelyn William Medows
Notman, William Graham
Paterson, William Paterson
Pattison, Peterswald
Peddie, Allister William Ponsonby
Pender, George

Pender, Hamish Grainger Geils
Pollard-Urquhart, William Edward
Porter, William Guthrie
Pott, James Gideon
Pringle, Arthur Stanley
Pringle, James
Pringle, Robert William Hay
Prosser, John, Jun.
Reid, William Morison
Ritchie, Thomas Arthur
Robertson, Sydney
Robertson Duram, William Hugh
Russell, James Forteath
Russell, Patrick Alfred
Salvesen, Christian Raymond
Salvesen, Eric Thomas Somervell
Sanderson, Frederick Borthwick
Sanderson, Harold Scott
Schafer, Thomas Sydney Hermann
Scott, Thomas, Jun.
Seater, George Harold
Shennan, John Eric
Sime, William Francis Watson
Simson, Ronald Francis
Skirving, Thomas Mylne
Sloan, Thomas Ian Thomson
Small, Norman Howard
Smeaton, John Burgh
Smith, Harry Graham
Smith, Ian Frazer
Standring, Frederick John
Steele, James Hume
Steuart, Norman Kennedy
Stevenson, Robert Dennistoun
Stewart, Charles Edward

Stewart, Frederick Arnold
Stewart, John James Erskine Brown
Stewart, John Walcot
Stewart, Ronald Dundas Falconar
Steyn, Stephen Sebastian Lombard
Taylor, Stanley Gordon
Thatcher, Francis Geoffrey
Thomson, Arthur John Gordon
Thomson, Alan Graham
Thomson, Eric James
Thomson, Francis Wishart
Thomson, John Harvey
Thomson, Kenneth Douglas
Thomson, Patrick Grant
Thyne, Kenward John
Tod, William Lennox
Trotter, Warren Francis
Turnbull, David Stevens
Turnbull, William Elliot
Twynam, Cyril Francis Frederick
Veresmith, Daniel Christopher
Waddie, Thomas Wallace

Walker, William
Wallace, William Middleton
Watson, James Henry Digby
Watson, William George Douglas
Weir, George Gordon
White, Alexander
White, John Gardner
White, Robert Edward
White, William Kenneth
Whyte, William
Wilkie, George Spence Maclean
Wilson, Robert Sym
Wilson, Rodney
Wood, George Douglas Harry
Wood, John George
Wood, Oswald Ireland
Wood, Russell Eliott
Wyllie, Alexander
Wyse, Roderick Wynfield
Yorston, James Gifford
Young, Norman Mitchell
Young, William Barrie

CHAPTER SEVENTEEN

In the hope that, by next season, there will be a sufficient number of Academicals in Edinburgh and district to enable the Football Club to resume play, we are of opinion that, if possible, a small Committee should be formed now, in order to have everything ready when the time comes.

Will old members of the Football Club and any ex-members of the School XV who are stationed near Edinburgh, and who can attend a meeting with a view to appointing this Committee of re-construction, kindly communicate with Major J.M.B. Scott at Radcot, Colinton, Midlothian?

Further arrangements will be announced by means of the Chronicle *in due course.*

John M.B. Scott
G.W. Wallace

advert in the *The Chronicle*, December 1918

ON 26 JUNE 1919 THE CLUB'S first post-War general meeting took place in Dowell's Rooms on George Street, at which J.E. Crabbie was elected club president and A.T. Sloan was voted in as captain. It was initially decided to arrange fixtures for only one team because nobody was quite sure how many players would be available. However, it quickly became apparent that people were desperate to return to some sort of normality after the long hard years of war, and the success of an inter-Services tournament the previous winter – between teams from the 'Mother Country', the RAF, Australia, Canada, New Zealand and South Africa – had clearly reinvigorated interest in the sport. So, by the time the fixture card was printed a 2nd XV schedule had been drawn up as well. Furthermore, during the season a 3rd XV also played intermittently.

At this meeting it was decided to arrange fixtures for only one team because nobody was quite sure how many players would be available. However, it quickly became apparent that people were desperate to return to some sort of normality after the long hard years of war, and the success of an inter-Services tournament the previous winter – between teams from the 'Mother Country', the RAF, Australia, Canada, New Zealand and South Africa – had clearly reinvigorated interest in the sport. So, by the time the fixture card was printed a 2nd XV schedule had been drawn up as well. Furthermore, during the season a 3rd XV also played intermittently.

The Academicals' first post-war match was supposed to be against Gala at Raeburn Place on 4 October 1919, but a railway strike intervened and the Borderers could not travel, so Heriot's (who were still being referred to as Heriotonians in *The Chronicle*) stepped in at short notice. The Academicals had played a practice match the previous weekend but this does not seem to have been sufficient preparation for the challenge of taking on a Heriot's side which had already beaten Hawick and were clearly the fitter of the two teams. Heriot's won a fast game by 19 points to 14, and they went through that season undefeated to become champions for the first time in the club's history.

The Academical team for that first post-war match was: I. Kerr; G.A. Usher, J.C. MacKay, D.S. Weir, G.B. Crole; A.T. Sloan, E.G. Dalziel; J.W.F. Neill, J.D.O. Coats, E.S. Fiddes, R.I. Marshall, T. Gibson, V.F. Noel-Paton, J.N. Shaw, A.K. Mackintosh.

Throughout the 1919–20 season the Academicals showed plenty of potential but lacked consistency, and ended up losing nine out of the 22 matches they played.

The 1920–21 season got off to a promising start with a rather fortuitous draw away to Gala followed by seven consecutive victories – including a Jack McCrow-inspired triumph over Watsonians, who only lost twice that year and finished the season as champions. But injuries became a major stumbling block, with the 1st XV never able to field the same back division in consecutive matches, and the undefeated run came to an end on 15 November when the Academicals contributed fully to an exciting encounter at Oxford University but eventually went down by 14 points to seven. Five days later a crowd estimated to be in the region of 5,000 congregated at Raeburn Place to watch Stewart's FP bring the Academicals' undefeated record against Scottish opposition to an end. It was a tense encounter until two late tries from the visitors gave them a 14-6 victory. The Academicals ended the season with a record of 12 wins and two draws out of 19 championship matches played. They also played five matches against English opposition, winning two and losing three.

1919–20 1st XV

Back: T. Gibson, W.R. Dawson, J.A. Wright, J.L. Stewart, J. Lindsay, J.C. MacKay, H.M. Somerville

Middle: R.I. Marshall, J.N. Shaw, J.W.F. Neill, A.T. Sloan (*Captain*), L.H.T. Sloan, J.D.O. Coats, V.F. Noel-Paton

Front: J.D. Cairns, E.G. Dalziel, J.W.S. McCrow

Four players from this 1919–20 team won caps. According to the *EAFC Centenary History*:

Allen Sloan, who was capped for Scotland both before and after the War, played in three different positions in Internationals – stand-off, centre and wing. Of medium height, he was fast and elusive and was remembered for several exceptionally brilliant tries, notably one against Wales at Inverleith in 1920 in which he ran diagonally across the field from near the centre to the corner – 'an electrifying try, one of the finest ever seen in an international'. His two sons, W.H. and D.A. both played for the Academy and the Academicals and D.A. also played for Scotland, to provide the first instance of father and son who were both Academicals and Internationals. When Donald gained his first cap, the SRU marked the occasion by inviting Allen to attend the International Dinner following the match.

J.W.S. McCrow

W.E. Maclagan, c1920. His international career spanned the years 1878–91. He led a British Isles touring side to South Africa in 1891. *Getty Images.*

Hamish Shaw became president of the SRU in 1949–50. Only six Academicals have held that office [there have now been eight] and Shaw was the first to be so honoured since W.E. Maclagan in 1896. To the Academical Football Club he presented the four touch-flags used by the Scottish touch-judges during his year of office, and these now make a splendid display in the Pavilion at Raeburn Place.

Jack McCrow was badly wounded during the War and it says much for his courage that he had such a distinguished career as a footballer. On one occasion after his playing days were over, he was persuaded to play in an 'Old Crocks' Seven. Always a neat and clever player, Jack was still able to produce a side step and with this he found his way right through the defence. There was no one near him and a clear passage to the line, 30 yards away. But this prospect was too much for his weary legs, so he stopped dead on the '25' line – and dropped a goal.

Jock Stewart, the remaining member of the Club quartet capped against Ireland, though remarkably agile, was an exceptionally large and heavy forward in a weighty pack. The size of some of the Academical forwards at this time caused one interesting comment at Langholm. The club there had, in those 'pre-bus' days, great difficulty getting fixtures with Scottish clubs outwith the Border League, and in October 1920, at the request of the SRU, the Academicals paid a visit to Langholm. The Academical team changed in a hotel and as they were emerging, one tall forward after another, a wee Langholm laddie was heard to exclaim: 'Cripes! They've sent the Scots Guards!'

Another internationalist from this era with a strong Academical connection was G.H.H.P. Maxwell, who had been capped out of the club five times in 1913 and 1914, and had been elected 1st XV captain in 1914 before all club activity was suspended for the war. He was listed as an RAF player when playing against Wales and England in 1920, and then, after being demobbed, picked up six more caps as a London Scottish player – against France, Wales, Ireland and England in 1921, and against France and England a year later.

That 1920–21 season was as good as it got for the Academicals until the arrival of G.P.S. McPherson in 1926–27 heralded the start of a steady climb towards the 'Championship' success of 1929–30. There were some great moments, such as a four points (one drop-goal) to nil victory over Heriot's which was one of only two defeats suffered by the Gold-enacre side during the 1921–22 season; a 23-3 win over Cambridge during the 1922–23 season; and a splendid display in a 10-6 victory at Bradford a year later in the first match between the clubs since the great battle of 1885. But inconsistency was an ongoing problem and these encouraging results tended to be followed up with infuriatingly poor performances and frustrating defeats.

Injuries and other factors such as university exams took their toll, but this sort of consistent inconsistency over such

G.P.S. McPherson

an extended period of time suggests that the problem was more deep-rooted than that, and it is surely no coincidence that the troubles experienced by the Academicals during these immediate post-war years mirrored a problem at the Academy. Similarly, the growing success of the 1st XV through the latter half of the 1920s and into the 1930s coincided with an improvement in standards at the school.

Schools rugby had carried on throughout the war, but inevitably at a much reduced level – with the activities of the Officer Training Corps taking precedence. Also, boys leaving school earlier to join the war effort meant that the average age of teams dropped; and younger masters, whose coaching and inspiration meant so much, disappeared into the Forces. All schools were affected, but the Academy seemed to suffer more than most.

The link between club and school is well demonstrated by the 1915–16 Academy side, which was the only time between 1914 and 1930 that the school managed to win more matches than it lost, with Alan Foster leading the team to four wins and a draw in seven matches played. That side provided a number of players who would be key figures in the Academicals' relatively successful 1920–21 season – including Jack McCrow (a future internationalist), Ian Marshall (a future Scotland reserve) and John Wright (who, for eight consecutive years between 1920 and 1928, played in every Academical 1st XV match except one and every sevens tournament the club entered).

Similarly, when the Academicals began to build towards their championship success during the latter half of the 1920s, the foundations laid down at school level were once again evident.

During the 1923–24 season the Academy under-15 team defeated both Fettes and Loretto, and in the first of these two matches it was noted that B.R. (Ben) Tod 'as usual, did the work of three men in defence, played a good attacking game, and gave his side an excellent lead'. The following year Tod was made captain of the Academy 1st XV and under his leadership the team turned a corner, with an exciting 17-16 victory over Watsons on 12 December 1925. During the previous five seasons the Academy had managed only four victories over Glenalmond, a draw against Merchiston and suffered 34 defeats.

Tod retained the captaincy for the 1926–27 season, and after five consecutive wins over club sides the school claimed a 30-9 victory over Loretto. There were also victories over Watson's and Merchiston that season. Although the Academy's teams struggled for consistency throughout the remainder of the decade, at least they were no longer being hopelessly outclassed by the other leading schools, and they were producing a steady stream of players who would go on to play an important part in the resurgence of the Academicals as a leading force in Scottish club rugby.

CHAPTER EIGHTEEN

Macpherson was well known for his tactical sense and study of his opponents'
weaknesses. His generalship and inspiration were invaluable both in the
international and in the club sphere.

As a player he could find a way through an almost invisible gap by a variety
of methods – a sudden burst of speed, a swerve, a baffling 'jink' of a kind of stop-
start without actually stopping – and he excelled in making openings for his
wings.

Jack Dunn in *The Scotsman*, 3 March 1981

A CENTRE THREE-QUARTER who combined tactical good sense with creative genius
to devastating effect, George Philip Stewart Macpherson was by common consent
the outstanding player of a golden era for Scottish rugby – and arguably the
greatest player the country has ever produced.

He was born in Newtonmore, Inverness-shire, on 14 December 1903, but
spent the first few years of his life in India, where his father, Sir Stewart, was a
career civil servant. He returned to Edinburgh at the age of six and attended the
Edinburgh Academy for seven years before earning a scholarship to Fettes
College in 1916. At this point his natural sporting prowess was already evident,
and he excelled at cricket, the long jump and hurdling, as well as rugby. His
academic ability was almost as impressive and in 1921 he went from Fettes to
Oriel College, Oxford, where he gained a double first in Classics.

It was during his time at Oxford that the full extent of Macpherson's rugby
ability became apparent. He played in three Varsity matches between 1922 and
1924, captaining Oxford to victory in 1923; and made his international debut in a
3-3 draw over in France on 2nd January 1922. In 1925 he was captain of the side
when the Oxford University three-quarter line – consisting of Ian Smith,
Macpherson, George Aitken and Johnny Wallace – inspired Scotland to its first
ever Grand Slam success.

Ian Smith might have been the headline grabber in that team, with eight
tries in four matches that season and 24 tries in 32 matches throughout his

career, but it was Macpherson's quick thinking and innovative attacking ploys which created the opportunities for the flying winger to rack up this remarkable scoring tally. Of his 24 tries for Scotland, 21 were scored in the 17 matches he played outside Macpherson. When Scotland thumped France 25-4 at the start of the 1925 campaign, Macpherson did not cross the whitewash himself, but he had a hand in all seven of Scotland's tries that day – including the four scored by Smith.

He played two games for the Academicals whilst on vacation from Oxford during the 1924–25 season, and *The Chronicle* noted that 'from the start he made his presence felt'. After finishing his degree, Macpherson spent a year in the USA as a Davison scholar at Yale, before returning to Edinburgh to qualify as a chartered accountant. He began to play regularly for the club during the 1926–27 season and his arrival at Raeburn Place coincided with an influx of good players directly from the Academy and also from other schools. With John Moffat providing vigorous leadership in the pack, and Macpherson the inspiration behind the scrum, the Academicals began to build the team which would win the championship three years later.

Perhaps the clearest indication that this Academicals side was beginning to make some serious progress as a team – and not just because of its star player – came during the 1928–29 season, when a Cambridge University side containing 13 of the team which had beaten Oxford some weeks earlier were defeated 7-5 at Raeburn Place. Macpherson was unavailable for this match, so S.L. Robertson, who was at that time a forward for the 2nd XV, deputised, and his close marking of C.B. Aarvold, the Cambridge and England centre, was crucial to the Academicals' success that day.

Macpherson captained the side for three consecutive seasons between 1928–29 and 1930–31. In the second of those seasons (1929–30) the Academicals won their first championship since 1906–07. The campaign started with five consecutive victories, including a first triumph over Glasgow Academicals for nine years. There was a disappointing defeat at Cambridge, where everything that could possibly go wrong did go wrong in a heavy defeat, but the undefeated run against Scottish opposition continued for another eight matches – with seven wins and one draw – before a 14-5 defeat at Hawick blew the championship wide open. Apparently there was little between the two sides on the day and certainly not the difference that the final score seemed to suggest. A number of accounts state that the Academicals were unlucky, but, as *The Chronicle* rather sagaciously pointed out: 'We have had our full share of luck this season and by its aid we have scraped through at least three games – Selkirk, Glasgow High School and Gala – when we were decidedly not at our best – so that there were no grounds for complaint when things went the other way for a change.'

Hawick had already lost to Heriot's that season, so their victory in this match brought them level with the Academicals at the top of the championship table, and set up a tense finale to the campaign. In the end, the Academicals were able to hold their nerve to collect seven wins from their seven remaining matches, while Hawick lost once more.

There were, however, two near disasters before the championship was finally secured. The first of these was against Heriot's at Goldenacre, when the Academicals found themselves 23-3 behind at half-time, but a stunning performance by Macpherson, who ran half the length of the field on at least five occasions, turned the match on its head and secured an improbable 25-23 victory.

The Academicals team that day was: J.L. Tod; F. Ranken, H.H. Turcan, G.P.S. Macpherson, G.M. Dacker; B.R. Tod, G.M. Crabbie; F.M. Roughead, J. Moffat, J.C.K. Miller, J.A. Wright, G.G.P. Dodds, R.J. Henderson, L.H. Hill, F.A. Wright.

A month later, at Melrose, the Academicals again came from behind to save the day, in a match which was just as exciting but not of the same high standard as the game at Goldenacre. The Academicals were without Macpherson, who was playing at Twickenham, and they found themselves 18-3 down with 20 minutes to go. Defeat seemed inevitable when, according to *The Chronicle*:

> Hill gained possession in our 25 and ran strongly past half-way, handing off several would-be tacklers, and pulling his scrum cap straight on the way. When finally held up, he passed to Turcan, who flashed through, with Dacker at his side for the latter to score between the posts. Todd converted.

That made it 18-8 to Melrose, but the Academicals had finally found their feet and they scored three further tries, two of which were converted, to put themselves 21-18 ahead at the final whistle.

The Academicals' results for this championship winning season were:

Watsonians	15-9	Glasgow HS FP	3-3
Edinburgh University	34-3	Kelvinside Academicals	10-3
RHS FP	9-3	Gala	8-6
Glasgow Academicals	3-0	Hawick	5-14
Bradford	14-9	Jed-Forest	11-0
Cambridge University	3-34	Hillhead HS FP	18-0
West of Scotland	42-5	Heriot's FP	25-23
Stewart's FP	34-5	Edinburgh University	18-11
Institution FP	49-3	Watsonians	16-3
RHS FP	11-0	Melrose	21-18
Selkirk	8-6	Wanderers	15-5
London Scottish	19-9		

Scottish Matches: Played: 20; Won: 18; Lost: 1; Drawn: 1; Points For: 355; Points Against: 120.

All Matches: Played: 23; Won: 20; Lost: 2; Drawn: 1; Points For: 391; Points Against: 172.

F.A. Wright was the only other member of this Academical team, apart from Macpherson, to play international rugby, but a few others came pretty close. R.J. Henderson lost a probable cap through an injury in the Final Trial, while Turcan and F.M. Matheson (who played occasionally during the season) became Scottish reserves. Eight others – Dacker, Hill, Moffat, A.M. Prain, Ranken, B.R. Tod, J.L. Tod and J.A. Wright – played in the inter-city at one time or another.

Without Macpherson, however, the side would never have achieved what it did. Not only did he provide the inspiration through his performances on the pitch, but his ability to analyse the strengths and weaknesses of the opposing team and formulate a game-plan suited to the challenge ahead was invaluable. Just as he was the creative genius behind Ian Smith's remarkable try-scoring record in international rugby, at club level he also excelled at creating openings for his wingers (particularly for George Dacker) with his razor-sharp breaks and well-timed passes.

Macpherson was also a superb Sevens player and his time with the Academicals coincided with a period of unprecedented success for the club on the Border circuit. In 1927 they reached the semi-finals at Melrose, Hawick and

Jedburgh; and a year later they won at Melrose, which was the club's first success in any of the Border competitions. The team that day was: G.M. Dacker, G.P.S. Macpherson, N.M.S. Macpherson, K.A.W. Slater, J. Moffat, J.A. Wright and N.J. Graham-Yooll.

1929 Champion VII – Winners at Murrayfield, Hawick and Langholm

Back: A.M. Prain, F.A. Wright, G.M. Dacker, G.M. Crabbie

Middle: J. Moffat, G.P.S. Macpherson, B.R. Tod

Front: K.A.W. Slater

The following year the Academicals won three tournaments at Murrayfield, Hawick and Langholm. And then, in a near perfect ending to their championship-winning season, they won the Melrose Cup again in 1930, with the team on this occasion being: G.M. Dacker, G.P.S. Macpherson, B.R. Tod, G.M. Crabbie, J. Moffat, F.A. Wright and R.J. Henderson.

Two innovations of the 1920s deserve a mention – the installation of flood-lighting at Raeburn Place in 1928 to make it easier for players training in the evening, and the introduction of a weekend tour to Bradford on the Saturday and Oxford or Cambridge on the Monday became a regular feature of the fixture list.

1929–30 1st XV – Winners of the Scottish Rugby Club Championship. Played 23, Won 20, Lost 2, Drew 1.

Back: G.G.P. Dodds, F. Ranken, H.H. Turcan, R.J. Henderson, A.M. Prain, F.A. Wright, L.H. Hill, G.M. Dacker, S.L. Robertson

Middle: J.A. Wright, B.R. Tod, F.M. Roughead, G.P.S. Macpherson, J. Moffat, J.C.K. Miller, G.M. Crabbie

Front: J.L. Tod, J.S. Macfie

The championship-winning season of 1929–30 heralded the beginning of a joyous decade for the Academicals. Although the 1st XV did not manage to finish top of the unofficial league table again during this period, they were runners-up in 1931–32 and they remained one of the strongest teams in Scotland throughout. It was, however, in terms of playing numbers and sociability that the club exceeded what had previously been achieved. By 1932–33 the club was fielding six teams on a regular basis, and club spirit was encouraged by weekend 'tours' at New Year or in the spring and other innovations – such as the institution of a Football Club Dance at the Plaza in Morningside, catering for players in the junior teams as well as for the 1st XV.

At this time, the 2nd XV were generally called the 'A' team and the 3rd XV were the 'B' team. When the number of teams increased to four in 1923–24, the 3rd XV became the 'A2' team with the 4th XV inheriting 'B' team status. Then, when a fifth team was set up seven years later, in season 1930–31, it was called the 'B2' team. When a sixth team came into being for the 1932–33 season, the nomenclature was thankfully changed altogether, to 1st, 2nd, 3rd, 4th, 5th and 6th XV – which was clearly a more logical system, even if it might have sounded a lot less impressive for a social player to say that he was a member of the 5th XV rather than the 'B2s'.

The fact that the 1st XV did not win more championships during this period can be partly attributed to the loss of players such as R.J. Henderson through injury, and partly to the fact that several of the best players produced by the Academy at this time did not go on to play regularly for the club. For instance, not one of seven successive Academy captains became regulars at Raeburn Place after leaving school, amongst whom were future internationalists W.A.H. Druitt (Oxford University and London Scottish), H.M. Murray (Glasgow University), D.J. Macrae (St Andrews University) and R.B. Bruce Lockhart (Cambridge University).

Most of the players who took part in the 1929–30 season were available for the next campaign, with the exception of John Moffat and J.A. Wright, who had both retired. However, injuries and players missing matches for other assorted reasons meant that results were mixed. The best performance of the campaign was at Oxford, when the Academicals won 15-0, prompting *The Chronicle* to report that 'the whole side played magnificent football, with Macpherson the outstanding three-quarter'.

The quality of this team had clearly not gone unnoticed. Sandy Thorburn's summary of the SRU Annual Diary, which was published in *The Scottish Rugby Union Official History* in 1985, records that during this season: 'an eyebrow-raising complaint was received from Edinburgh Academicals FC stating that two of its members had been approached by Border clubs seeking their services. This despite the fact that the players in question had no connection whatsoever with the clubs concerned'.

154

At the start of the 1931–32 season a combined Edinburgh and Glasgow Academicals side took on a Fettesian-Lorettonian XV as part of the latter club's jubilee celebrations. J.L. Tod, G.M. Dacker, R.R. Tod, R.J. Henderson, A.M. Prain and F.A. Wright all played for the joint Academicals team in a 21-16 victory over a Fettesian-Lorettonian side containing G.P.S. Macpherson.

This match coincided with the opening of the Academical season and a weakened side lost at Carlisle to a Cumberland County XV. On the following Saturday the Academicals were back to full strength but had clearly not yet found their stride and lost 18-16 to Watsonians in a well-contested match at Raeburn Place. There followed a splendid run of ten consecutive victories, interrupted by two defeats in three games to Oxford University and London Scottish, but as both these results were against English opposition the Academicals' push for their second championship in three years was still very much on track. However, a draw against Gala, a defeat to a Stewart's FP side which had been defeated 29-9 earlier in the campaign and another defeat to Melrose on the last day of the season, meant that the Academicals had to settle with being runners-up to Gala.

There were several big victories that year, including a 35-6 defeat of Bradford, a 52-0 demolition of Edinburgh Institution FP and a 54-0 victory over Jed-Forest, when club captain Ben Tod was successful with nine of his ten conversion attempts and also kicked a penalty. But the best performance of the season was almost certainly against Glasgow High School FP, who were also in with a chance of winning the championship when the two sides met. According to *The Chronicle*, it was 'an excellent and hard-fought game, played in the very best spirit throughout and thoroughly enjoyed by both sides'. All three tries were scored in the first half, with the High School taking the lead and the Academicals equalising shortly afterwards after a determined run by Dacker. Then, just before half-time, a burst by Turcan led to some inter-passing among the forwards before Prain touched down over the line. The second half witnessed a great fight, with attack, counter-attack and narrow escapes at both ends – but neither side could break the deadlock and the match finished with the Academicals 6-3 ahead. Apart from being a great contest, this match was notable because both sets of players were numbered and a match programme was produced – something which, according to *The Chronicle*, had not happened in a match between two Scottish clubs before. At the Academical Football Club AGM in June 1931 it was unanimously agreed that 'the committee should arrange for the numbering of players at all games where such a course is practicable'. A year later the SRU, which had been holding out against the numbering of players in international matches, finally decided to fall in line with the other countries in this respect.

Ben Tod and R.J. Henderson were re-elected captain and vice-captain for the 1932–33 season, but both players missed large chunks of the campaign. Early in November, Tod went abroad on business, and then Henderson was injured in the Final Trial and did not play again that season (and hardly at all thereafter). In their absence, F.A. Wright led the side. This lack of stability in leadership might partially explain the Academicals' inconsistency. Highlights included a 40-6 victory over Watsonians at Raeburn Place and a second consecutive success at the Murrayfield Sevens, but these achievements were offset by disappointing defeats against Hillhead High School FP, Heriot's and Melrose.

1932–33 1st XV

Back: G.E. Pott, F. Ranken, L.H. Hill, J.J.S. Binnie, J.G.R. Guthrie, G.M. White

Middle: D.B. Black, J.M. Henderson, F.A. Wright, R.J. Henderson, G.P.S. Macpherson, H.H. Turcan, K.W. Marshall

Front: J.L. Tod, C. Alexander

The 2nd and 3rd XVs had good seasons, losing three out of 20 and four out of 16 games played respectively, and at the end of the campaign came the first appearance of the Geits touring side, who had a weekend trip to Carlisle and Langholm. The *EAFC Centenary History* tells us: 'George Waterston's enthusiasm and organising genius made the Geits a success from the start. From 1933 to 1939 their forays, from Inverness in the north to Stranraer in the south-west, and mid-week evening matches nearer home, contributed greatly to the spirit and effectiveness of the Academical Football Club. The Geits had their own tie, a variation of the standard Academical colours.'

Barbarians Easter Tour, 1933. Mac Henderson is second in on the far right of the second row from the back.

Also during the spring of 1933, J.G. Fraser led a side known as the 'Raeburn Casuals' to success at the Highland Rugby Club's Sevens. That began a long association with the Inverness club, and for seven consecutive years between 1933 and 1939 this tournament was won by Academical teams. In 1934, two sevens from the club competed, with the 'Casuals' of the previous season now being regarded as an official Academical side. They made a valiant effort to retain the Lauder Cup, but in the best tie of the tournament they were defeated by the Geits, who went on to win the trophy.

Season 1933–34 was G.P.S. Macpherson's last as an Academical player. He did not feature in the side until Christmas Day, but against London Scottish he soon showed that the old magic was still there. Within a few minutes of kick-off he had cut straight through the opposition and sent H.J.S. Matthew over between the posts. Matthew added a second try and before half-time Macpherson was once again involved in the lead-up to a third Academical try, scored by Turcan. London Scottish rallied well in the second half, scoring two goals, a drop-goal and a try, but the Academicals managed to keep their noses in front with a G.E. Pott try, for an 18-17 victory. Macpherson's last appearance in Accies colours was in the second of two victories over Watsonians that season, when he played at stand-off in place of B.R. Tod, who was injured. According to the *EAFC Centenary History*, he 'was in good form and his anticipation was invaluable in stemming the Watsonians' attacks'.

The best performance of the 1934–35 season was against Cambridge University at Raeburn Place. Despite fielding ten 'Blues' in this match, including six in the pack, the students were, according to *The Chronicle*, 'well beaten in all departments of the game'. In one of his rare appearances since being injured two years earlier, R.J. Henderson provided the forwards with an inspiring lead. Meanwhile, D.B. Black was a constant threat at scrum-half and K.W. Marshall was superb in defence. H.M. Murray and H.J.S. Matthew scored two tries each and 'handyman' G.M. White, who was deputising for B.R. Tod, kicked a goal to make the final score 17-0.

This year also saw the Geits go from strength to strength, winning the Inverness and Langholm Junior Sevens tournaments, and also visiting Dumfries and Stranraer – with both of these trips meriting a special mention in the *EAFC Centenary History*.

1934–35 Academy 1st XV

Back: W.F.R. Walker, N.J. Mackay, R.B. Galloway, F.A. Macrae, D.H. Orrock, J.S.G. Munro, I.C. Henderson

Middle: A.D.R. Macphail, W.W. Ballantyne, W.H. Stevenson, R.B. Bruce Lockhart (*Captain*),
R.I. Alexander, W.R. Norman, A.G.M. Watt

Front: G.M. Hector, C.A. Young

The Stranraer match was a triumph of organisation. It had been intended to go to Inverness but word came that the 'Sevens' there had been postponed because of frost. Those who had been going on the trip foregathered in some convenient hostelry, when it was decided to go somewhere else and that Stranraer would probably be free from frost. George Waterston went away to telephone and ten minutes later a match had been arranged with the Wigtownshire Club and cars were starting to leave for Stranraer.

[Meanwhile] Dumfries was the occasion of a notable drop goal. Arthur Walker, who had been a hard-working forward in Academical XVs for about a dozen years, had intimated that this was to be his last appearance. He had also mentioned, in passing, that one of his regrets was that throughout his career as a player he had never dropped a goal. The match turned out to be very one-sided and the Geits soon piled up a commanding lead. At one point Arthur broke away and went over between the posts with no one within yards of him. He was about to touch down when there were shouts of 'Drop a goal!' So he ran back into the field of play, turned round, and with great deliberation and from a range of about ten yards, achieved his ambition.

The 1935–36 season was badly interrupted by adverse weather conditions. A third of the matches arranged for the five regular Academical XVs had to be cancelled, including eight out of the 25 matches scheduled for the 1st XV. And when matches were not called off due to frost, the pitches tended to be wet and heavy. Despite this the 1st XV results were reasonably good, and included a 13-8 victory at Raeburn Place over an Oxford University side containing Alexander Sergeevich 'Obo' Obolensky (the exiled Russian prince who scored two tries on his International debut for England versus New Zealand later that year), and a Ben Tod-inspired triumph at the Hawick Sevens. The 2nd XV ended the season with a commendable record of 15 wins and a draw from 18 matches played, with 302 points scored and only 72 conceded. The Geits once again won at Inverness and Langholm, and visited Annan at New Year.

1935–36 1st XV

Back: I.L. Young, R.I Alexander. A.G.M. Watt, C.W.A. Falconer, M.D. Kennedy, H.J.S. Matthew, E.M. Matthew

Middle: R.E. Harvey, K.W. Marshall, F.A. Wright, B.R. Tod (*Captain*), I.A. Crabbie, I.M. Macrae, G.M. White

Front: K.J. Dunlop, A. Lyell

At the AGM in June 1936, a presentation was made to R.K. Cuthbertson, who retired after 15 years as honorary secretary of the club. 'Capable Cuthbertson' was elected to the SRU committee that same summer, and for the next 20 years he gave sterling service to that organisation as well as the International Board. He was elected vice-president of the SRU for the 1958–59 season and was president the following year.

Cuthbertson was succeeded as honorary secretary of the club by another great enthusiast in the shape of Francis Wright, and at the same meeting George Waterston was appointed honorary junior secretary. The War limited this pair's period in office to three years, but the *EAFC Centenary History* says: 'these two achieved a very great deal during that short space of time'. After 1945, Wright returned to club duty as a member of the committee and continued to be a valuable servant at Raeburn Place until his untimely death in 1959 at the age of 49.

Perhaps the most impressive thing about Edinburgh Academicals during the immediate pre-war years was their strength in depth. Their record for the 1936–37 season read:

Team	Captain	P.	W.	L.	D.	Points F.	A.
1st XV	B.R. Tod	26	18	8	0	333	222
2nd XV	G. Waterston	21	17	3	1	341	97
3rd XV	H. Dacker	18	15	2	1	336	27
Junior XV	—	1	1	0	0	27	3
4th XV	B.A. Stenhouse	19	14	4	1	504	111
5th XV	D.F. Jardine	19	15	4	0	345	89
6th XV	—	11	7	4	0	187	89
		115	87	25	3	2,073	638

Whilst the 1st XV were statistically the least successful side in the club, they still recorded some notable victories, including a double over Oxford and Cambridge universities (21-9 and 21-12 respectively). Meanwhile, the 4th XV's points total of 504 remained a club record until Jeremy Richardson's 1st XV clocked 699 points in 34 games during the 1988–89 season (according to the records available). But even this was overshadowed by the achievements of the 3rd XV, which started the season with 11 wins and one draw, scoring 234 points and conceding none. On 9 January they lost to a strong Dunbar 1st XV and only two other sides succeeded in scoring points against them that season.

The Geits sent three Sevens to Inverness and that captained by R.A. Sim brought back the Cup. In addition, the Langholm Junior Trophy was won for the third year in succession, with J.H.B. Munro captain of the winning side.

1936–37 4th XV

Back: H.H. Brown, G. Dempster, H.J. Macpherson, C.F. Hogg, W.M. Munro, B.C. Harding-Edgar,
G.D. Hunter, A.E.S. Wood

Front: B.C.E. Richardson, T.B. Moodie, D.F. Anderson, B.A. Stenhouse (*Captain*), D.S. Mackenzie,
C. Ritchie, G.D. Bonner

The 1937–38 season was Ben Tod's last as a player, and his final appearance for the club in a 15-a-side match was against the Wanderers at Murrayfield in March. This fixture had been restored the previous season, having lapsed after 1931 because of difficulties in finding a date which suited both sides. Tod finished his 11th season at the club playing scrum-half in the Spring Sevens, with Accies reaching the final at Melrose before losing to Heriot's.

The Geits once again triumphed in Inverness, and, 600 miles south, history was made when an Academical side made the club's first appearance in London – which is surprising given that this was the club's 80th season and during the previous eight decades strong links had been built up with several English clubs, including London Scottish.

The match was between a scratch Academical side made up of mainly 1st and 2nd XV players, organised by H.G. Fraser, and a collection of London club and county players calling themselves 'The Noggins'. The game was played at Teddington on the morning of Wilson Shaw's Triple Crown match. Most of the Academical side had travelled south the previous day, apart from four unnamed heroes who motored through the night in an Austin Seven and arrived just in time for some light refreshment in lieu of breakfast before taking the field. Not surprisingly, the visitors took some time to settle and they trailed 3-0 after 15 minutes of play, but they soon found their feet and eventually ran out 35-3 victors, with the magic moment of the match being a monstrous 40-yard drop-goal from full-back J.A. Stevenson. This match was a precursor of the first official Academical match in London against Wasps eight months later.

The Academical team for this match was: J.A. Stevenson; R.E. Harvey, H.G. Fraser (capt.), R. Tod, W.E. Scott; J. Jardine, R.A. Sim; G.M. Menzies, D.W.L. Menzies, I.A. Menzies, I.S. Ritchie, A.G.M. Watt, W.H. Stevenson, R.I. Alexander, H. Dacker.

The last season before the war was full of ups and downs. Captained by A.G.M Watt, with A.I.S. Macpherson as his vice-captain, the Academical side during the 1938–39 campaign contained a number of excellent forwards. I.N. Graham, I.C. Henderson and G.H. Gallie all played for Scotland that season (albeit in a team which lost all three of its matches), while Watt was capped after the war and M.D. Kennedy played in a Services International against England in Leicester in 1943. However, the team also contained several youngsters who were clearly still finding their feet in senior rugby, and this contributed to a less than impressive start to the campaign, with a first defeat in 16 years to Melville College FP being one of nine losses suffered in 15 matches before Christmas.

As the season wore on, the potential of this side began to shine through and, after four blank weekends between mid December and mid January due to frost,

I.C. Henderson

the Academicals won seven and drew one of their ten remaining fixtures – in the process chalking up impressive victories over Hawick, Hillhead High School FP (their first defeat that year) and Watsonians.

At Sudbury, the Academicals played superbly to defeat Wasps 22-13, with *The Chronicle* reporting that 'it was a fine, fast and open game, with every player going as hard as he could, and there was no lack of excitement as only one point separated the sides until twenty minutes from the end'. The team on this occasion was: B.C.E. Richardson; H.A.C. Mackenzie, J.A. Stevenson, G.A.F.R. Gibson, E.M. Matthew; R. Tod, C.A. Young; M.D. Kennedy, I.N. Graham, I.C. Henderson, A.G.M. Watt, B.A.H. Newton, C.W.A. Falconer, T.B. Moodie, G.H. Gallie.

Throughout the 1930s, the number of rugby clubs and rugby-playing schools steadily increased, but the improvised nature of the unofficial championship meant that the standard of play in Scottish club rugby was often difficult to measure. Because the championship was not run by the SRU but by the newspapers of the day, and relied on clubs to organise their own matches, there was always the danger of a team with an easy fixture list finishing higher up the table than their performances merited. This was demonstrated during the 1938–39 season, when Allan Glen's FP were included in the table for the first time. They finished the season as champions having won ten and drawn the other two of the 12 matches they played, but there was considerable unease at the time about the validity of their claim to be the top club in Scotland. They had played about half as many counting games as their main rivals and, although they recorded wins over Melrose and Selkirk, the names of most of the other leading clubs in Scotland at that time were missing from their list of scalps. The rigidity of club fixture lists at this time, allied perhaps to a little bit of snobbery, meant that the Bishopbriggs side found it difficult to organise fixtures against many of the more established sides. For example, that year they recorded a 9-0 victory over an Academicals 2nd XV, but were not allowed a crack at the 1st XV.

Not that this anomaly really impacted on the Academicals' season on this occasion. They finished 13th in the unofficial table with nine wins, ten losses and a draw from 20 matches.

The shadow of Hitler's increasingly aggressive behaviour on the continent might have loomed large during the summer of 1939, but at that stage the scale of the conflict which lay ahead was not yet fully apparent to the vast majority of the British population, and the Academicals clearly felt that the 1939–40 season would go ahead as normal. Watt and Macpherson were re-elected as captain and vice-captain and fixtures for all six XVs were arranged. The annual match with Cambridge had lapsed because the university's Scottish tour had been discontinued, so for the Monday following the Bradford game a match against Otley, another Yorkshire club, had been arranged. However, the Academicals were unable to keep that appointment, because on 3 September 1939 Britain and France declared war on Germany and the club almost instantly suspended its fixture list.

CHAPTER NINETEEN

Older men declare war but it is the youth that must fight and die.

Herbert Hoover, 27 June 1944

LIST OF ACADEMICALS WHO WERE KILLED IN ACTION, DIED OF WOUNDS, OR DIED ON SERVICE DURING THE SECOND WORLD WAR

Adams, Robert Frederick Wilfred
Addis, Eric Elrington
Adshead, Patrick James Neil
Ainslie, Francis George
Ainslie, Tom Dale
Aitken, William Archibald
Alexander, Kenneth
Allsebook, Antony John
Anderson, Lawrence Charles
Austin, Alexander Berry
Bell, Alan John Newall
Bell, John Lawrence
Blair, James Michael
Blair, William
Blair-Imrie, Hew Angus Christopher
Brackenbridge, Robert Robertson
Brash, James Gowans
Brown, Robert
Browne, Henry Gallaugher
Bruce, Alexander Charles Arbuthnot
Bruce, William
Burney, Stephen Henry D'Arblay
Cameron, Donald

Cameron, James Douglas
Campbell, Ian
Carmichael, Eoghan Lyon
Chambers, Joseph Macrea
Cousens, Richard Allinson
Cowan, Alan Archibald
Crombie, John Milward
Cunningham, John Laurence Gilchrist
Cuthbertson, Norman Henderson
Dalziel, John Graham
Davidson, John Henry
Down, John Roderick
Dryburgh, Neil Ged
Dryerre, Harry Winton
Dundas, James Strathearn
Dundas, Robert Charles
Eason, John Patrick
Egerton, Wion de Malpas
Elgin, Ralph
Elliot, Edward Ian Cameron
Fahmy, Eric Milne Chalmers
Ferguson, John Guthrie
Fletcher, Ian Douglas Wolfe

Forbes, John Gordon
Forbes, John William Sivewright
Forrest, James
Gallie, George Holmes
Gallie, Robert Eric
Gibson, John Charles Fraser
Gill, Alastair Hadley
Gillan, John Hamilton
Gillan, John Woodburn
Glasfurd, Charles Eric
Grant, Leslie Alexander Stuart
Grigor, James MacLeod
Hair, George William Fyfe
Hair, John Gilbert Martin MacGavin
Hamilton, Claud Eric
Hart, Arthur Michael
Harvey, Robert Edwards
Hebeler, Christopher Rendel
Henderson, Kenneth Gerald
Herdman, James Kenneth
Hogg, Charles Stuart Flockhart
Hogg, Hamish Reid-Henry
Irvine, Douglas King Lindsay
James, Arthur Hood
Jardine, Alexander Russell
Jeffrey, Alastair John Oswald
Kilgour, Hugh McPherson
Laird, John
Lane, Hugh William Edward
Lang, John Anderson
Langwill, Peter Graham Wilson
Lees, Ian Allister
Lees, Walter Carr
Levack, John Sutherland Lidgey
Liddle, Denis Bemister

Logan, Kenneth William Innes
Lorimer, Duncan
Lusk, Andrew Ronald
MacArthur, Duncan Alastair
MacArthur, John Bisset,
Macdonald, Donald Kennedy
McKendrick, John Gray
Mackenzie, Ian Drummond
Mackenzie, Kenneth William
Mackie, Alexander Stuart
McLennan, George Alastair
McLennan, Kenneth Leslie
McLeod, William Arnott
Martin, Norman Magnus MacLeod
Mathieson, Robert
Mathieson, Robert Harley
Middleton, Donald Stewart
Millar, Noel Legat Wilkie
Mitchell, Craig Bentley
Moodie, Duncan McNaught
Moodie, Thomas Blane
Moore, Lewis Peter
Morris, Alfred Dayrell
Muir, Thomas Temple
Newton, Basil Arthur Herdman
Noble, Roderick
Officer, John Moore
Oliphant, Colin Duff
Orr, John Allan
Orrock, Denis Heriot
Paterson, George Carfrae
Paton, Charles George
Pattullo, Colin Arthur
Paul, George Graham
Paulin, David Alastair

Phillips, Ronald George
Pirie, William Munro
Pitcairn, Andrew Alexander
Primrose, Robert Cairns
Richardson, Thomas Herbert Ottewill
Roach, Frank Alexander
Robb, Hamish William
Robertson, Donald
Robertson, Harold Graham
Robson, David Alan Hope
Rose, Brian Westland
Rose, Walter Ross Taylor
Ross, Hamish
Roynon-Jones, Edward
Roynon-Jones, James
Ryan, Allen William
Sandeman, Gordon Chisholm
Scott, John Edgar
Scott, John Younger
Scott-Moncrieff, Colin Herbert
Shearer, Charles Alexander
Shepherd, William Kyd Ogilvy
Simson, David James Robert
Simson, Hugh James
Sinclair, Ian Hector
Smith, Harry Noel
Smith, Robert Douglas
Steele, Norman Graham
Steven, William Mitchell
Stevson, William Reynolds
Stewart, Ronald

Stracey, Ian
Stuart, Joseph Gordon
Symon, John Parker
Thom, Derrick Maurice St Clair
Thomson, Evelyn Claude Ogilvie
Thomson, Ian Scott
Thorburn, Douglas Glendinning
Turcan, James Prentice
Turcan, Ronald Somerville
Tweedy, Timothy Christopher
Urquhart, Stanley Clarke
Walker, Douglas Grant
Walker, John
Walker, James Cadenhead
Walker, John Gordon
Walker, William Fitzgerald Redmayne
Warren, John Gunn
Waterston, Malcolm
Wedderburn, Ernest Alexander
    Maclagan
Weir, Robert Gordon
Wilson, Kenneth Evelyn Adey
Wilson, Norman Gladswood
Wilson, Norval Murray
Wilson, Thomas Leslie Lyall
Winchester, Charles Campbell
Wood, George Bertram Mure
Wright, Alexander Campbell Smith
Wright, John Dale
Young, Charles Alastair
Young, Robert Gordon

CHAPTER TWENTY

Who is there who has been at Murrayfield and seen Douglas Elliot swinging a
man by one hand and tossing him into touch like a bag of potatoes and has not
realised even to-day we have mighty men?

Dr A.B. Flett (Scotland Internationalist 1901–02),
quoted in *EAFC Centenary History*, 1958

IN CONTRAST TO THE First World War, there was not a complete cessation of club rugby between 1939 and 1945. A very happy partnership was arranged with Edinburgh Wanderers and for eight years the Academical-Wanderers – 'Accie-Wanderers' – provided an immense amount of pleasure and exercise to those club members and rugby fans still in Edinburgh. Raeburn Place was the home ground of this temporarily amalgamated club until it was ploughed up in 1942, then home games were played at New Field and after the war at Murrayfield until the partnership was amicably dissolved in 1947.

The combined club was set up within weeks of the outbreak of war, playing and winning (33-23) their first match against Edinburgh Borderers on 30 September. That season they also played Melville College FP (39-6 win), Watsonians (9-0 loss), Edinburgh University (0-0 draw), a team called Outcasts (16-10 loss), RHS FP (25-6 win), Outcasts again (15-8 loss), Depot Royal Scots (38-8 win), Stewart's College FP (5-14 loss), Edinburgh Dental Hospital (8-9 loss), Watsonians (3-6 loss), RHS FP (13-10 win), Heriot's FP (0-11 loss) and RHS FP (30-17 loss).

A scratch 'Wednesday' team played a handful of matches in October and November 1939, against the likes of Royal (Dick) Vet, Edinburgh University and City Police, while a 3rd XV played fairly regularly up to the middle of December, but did not appear again after the middle of that month.

The association went from strength to strength during the 1940–41 season, with three teams taking to the field on a regular basis throughout the winter. The 1st XV were unbeaten in their first ten games up until mid December, before losing 6-0 to Heriot's FP, but then slumped to five straight defeats, against Heriot's

FP, Glasgow Academicals, City Police, Watsonians and Boroughmuir FP The team then rallied slightly with wins over St Andrews University and Rover Scouts, followed by a draw against Edinburgh University, before Heriot's once again got the better of them at Raeburn Place in the last game of the season.

Thanks to the hard work and perseverance of a small band of dedicated members from both clubs, the Accie-Wanderers fielded teams throughout the course of the war, and in the process provided a much needed release from the grind of everyday life during these difficult years. The club also helped raise funds for the Red Cross through collections at games.

The EAFC committee held its first post-war meeting on 12 March 1946 and made arrangements for a general meeting of the club on 24 April, when it was agreed to continue the partnership with the Wanderers for another season but to elect separate office bearers at both clubs with a view towards them going their separate ways at the end of the 1946–47 season. For the Academicals, W.T.F. Haultain was elected president, I.C. Henderson was elected captain, B.A. Stenhouse was appointed honorary secretary and A.H. Elder was appointed honorary treasurer. R.K. Cuthbertson, F.A. Wright, W.I.D. Elliot and R. Tod made up the committee.

During the 1946–47 season the Accie-Wanderers' 1st XV matches were a carefully arranged mixture of those usually played by the two constituent clubs, so as to reserve spaces in the fixture cards of both clubs ahead of them going their separate ways at the start of the following season. This included a match against London Scottish on Christmas Day, which the Accie-Wanderers won 17-3, in front of a crowd in excess of 3,000 at Murrayfield.

The team that day was: R.R. Macnaughton; C. Ritchie, D.A. Roberts, W.H Sloan, T.Elliot; A.A.S. Scott and D.A. Crabbie; C.W.A. Falconer, A.D. Govan, M.D. Kennedy, R. Cadzow, R.R. McEwan, W. Elliot, J. Kirk, W.I.D. Elliot.

The combined club also managed to field 2nd, 3rd and 4th XVs this year, with the 2nd XV going the season undefeated under the captaincy of R. Tod.

The biggest problem facing EAFC when it was eventually rehabilitated for the start of the 1947–48 season was finding somewhere to play home games, as Raeburn Place was still out of action after being ploughed up in 1942 as part of the war effort. The Academy provided facilities at New Field for training and for some junior fixtures, but increasing numbers at the school and difficulties in collecting an entrance fee made it unsuitable for 1st XV matches. Inquiries were made about various other venues in the city and the club were very fortunate that the SRU and several other Edinburgh clubs granted the use of Murrayfield, Craiglockhart, Goldenacre, Inverleith, Myreside and Jock's Lodge until Raeburn Place was once again ready to host rugby matches. This led to the rather novel situation of the Academicals playing at home and collecting the gate money for a match against Watsonians at Myreside.

Edinburgh Academicals v Edinburgh Wanderers. Murrayfield, 4 October 1947.

Back: R.R. MacNaughton, J.A.R. Macphail, J.S. van Niekerk, P.R. Masters, B.A. Timbs, H.G. Hay, D.A. Sime, A.F. Gardiner, R.B. McEwan

Second Back: J.E.I. Grey, I.S. Dougal, R.C. Murray, J.C. White, A.R. Woods, C. McLay, A.B. Murray, D.A. Sloan, J. Newall, C. Ritchie, J.O. Grieve

Second Bottom: J.S. Macfie (*Hon. Secy.,* Academicals), I.D. Mair, B.A. Stenhouse (*Hon. Secy.,* Academicals 1946–47), W.F.T. Haultain (*President* Academicals), G.H.S. Rome (*Captain* Wanderers), I.C. Henderson (*Captain* Academical-Wanderers and Academicals), A.A.S. Scott (*Vice-Captain* Academical-Wanderers), F.S. Mackenzie (*President* Wanderers), E.G. Mackean (*Hon Secy.,* Academical-Wanderers and Wanderers), D.A. Roberts (*Vice-Captain* Academicals), D.M. Ferguson (*Hon. Treas.* Academical-Wanderers and Wanderers)

Front: H.L. Pearse, W. Elliot, M.G. Armour, W.I.D. Elliot, R.A. Cadzow, D. Crabbie, J.A. Eddison, T. Elliot

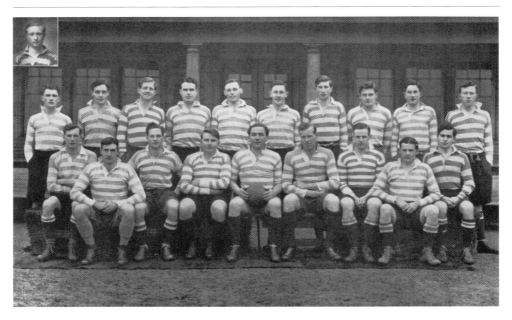

1947–48 1st XV

Top: J.C. Wregg, J.M. Martin, R. Keltie, R.K. Hamilton, A.F. Gardiner, W.C.D. Hare, W.H. Sloan, M. Walker, D.A. Sloan, C. Anderson

Front: C. McLay, T. Elliot, H.G. Hay, J.A.R. Macphail, I.C. Henderson (*Captain*), W.I.D. Elliot, C. Ritchie, J.C. White, D. Crabbie

Inset: D.A. Roberts (*Vice-Captain*)

It was appropriate that the Academicals' first match of the 1947–48 season was against Wanderers (a 14-13 victory), which was followed by a dinner at which the 'Accie-Wanderers' Club was dissolved amid mutual expressions of appreciation and good will. While the fixtures were very similar to those in 1938–39, there were a few new opponents, including Aberdeen Grammar School FP, Greenock and a composite Kelvinside-West XV. The vigorous play and enthusiastic leadership both on and off the field of captain Ian Henderson was essential in helping the club get back on its feet during this difficult year. The 1st XV played 28 matches in total, of which 13 were won, 13 were lost and two were drawn. Notable scalps included Heriot's FP (8-6,) Stewarts FP (9-6), and Aberdeen Grammar (8-7 despite being two men short for more than half the game). The weekend tour to London was revived with matches against Wasps (12-3 win) and

Oxford University (23-3 defeat), but the highlight of the weekend seems to have been when Ian Henderson treated the passengers on a London Tube train to a blast of bagpipe music.

A near constant stream of injuries throughout the season meant that consistency in team selection was hard to achieve. Among those who did feature at one point or another were: W.C.D. Hare, I.S. Dougal; T. Elliot, C. Ritchie, D.A. Sloan, D.A. Roberts (the vice-captain who missed most of the season through injury), W.H. Sloan, J.C. Wregg, M. Walker; H. G. Hay, D. Crabbie; I.C. Henderson, J.A.R. Macphail, J.C. White, C. McLay, A.F. Gardiner, W.T. Lyell, R. Keltie, W. Elliot, J.M. Martin, C. Anderson, W.I.D. Elliot.

The club was able to field four teams during this first season back, and the following year a 5th XV made occasional appearances. It was just as well that there was this sort of depth in playing resources because during the 1948–49 season the 1st XV were once again badly affected by injuries. The record for that season was distinctly average, with seven wins, four draws and 14 defeats from 25 matches played.

An invitation to play Blackheath in London on Boxing Day was accepted and the team travelled south overnight following the London Scottish match on Christmas Day, only for the game to be cancelled due to frost. Another feature of the season was the reappearance in the side of K.W. (Kenneth) Marshall, after several years of globetrotting, and he was still an excellent full-back at the age of 37. During his travels he had played for British Columbia against the Australian touring team of 1948, and also in 'upcountry' matches in New Zealand.

Club captain this season was hooker J.A.R. Macphail, who would later play twice for Scotland, versus England in 1949 and South Africa in

J.A.R. Macphail

1951. In his professional life Macphail was chief executive and then chairman of the Edrington Group, one of Scotland's leading premium spirit suppliers. When he died in the summer of 2004 his family and the trustees of his estate established a scholarship in his memory, which pays for one talented young Scottish rugby player to experience a summer playing rugby abroad. The first recipient of the scholarship, in 2005, was John Barclay, who spent that summer playing rugby in Wellington in New Zealand, and went on to make his international debut against New Zealand in the 2007 Rugby World Cup.

The 1947–48 season ended on a high with an Academicals Seven consisting of M. Walker, D.A. Sloan, H.G. Hay (captain), J.C. Wregg, W.I.D. Elliot, R. Keltie and C. McLay winning the Melrose Sevens. Both the Academical tries in the final against Stewart's FP were scored by Elliot, at the end of long-range dashes.

1st VII, Winners at Melrose, 1949

Back: M. Walker, J.C. Wregg, C. McLay, R. Keltie

Front: D.A. Sloan, H.G. Hay, W.I.D. Elliot

Born in Stow in the Scottish Borders, Elliot attended Edinburgh Academy from October 1935 to December 1939. He left the school at the age of 16, having only played four games for the 1st XV, all of which were on the wing. It was playing for the Accie-Wanderers during the war whilst farming at Stow that his full potential as a rugby player began to emerge.

He made his Scotland debut in the non-cap 1946 international against the touring New Zealand Army side, which had swept through Britain playing an exciting brand of open rugby. That match could hardly have gone any better for Elliot or the Scottish team. Scotland was the only country to beat the Kiwis and afterwards *The Scotsman* reported:

> There was not a better forward on the field than Elliot, whose physique more than any of his colleagues', approximated more closely to that of the Kiwis. Time and again he was at the head of frantic Scottish forays. Besides, he linked up cleverly with his backs to prove that the tourists had not a monopoly of forwards who could run like three-quarters.

Very much a player for the big occasion, he had a lot of pace, boundless natural stamina and the rugged strength of a Border farmer. He also had good hands, once moving to scrum-half in an injury-strewn district match and proceeding to deploy an unexpectedly dexterous service. Similarly, when Scotland played England at Twickenham in 1947, he picked up a knee injury in the opening minutes which meant that he could not carry on in the pack, so he moved to full-back where he acquitted himself well in difficult circumstances.

He was the outstanding Scottish rugby player of the immediate post-war years, and was asked to tour New Zealand and Australia with Karl Mullen's British and Irish Lions squad in the summer of 1950. But in those days the squad travelled by ship, played some 30 matches and were away from home for about six months – which was too long for Elliot to leave his farm. So he volunteered to fly out at his own expense at a later date, only to have that offer declined by the home unions committee. After drawing their first Test in New Zealand, the Lions were beaten 8-0, 6-3 and 11-8 in the three remaining matches in the series. Contemporary thinking was that Elliot's pace, power and big-match temperament might just have been enough to turn these narrow losses into wins.

W.I.D. Elliot

Ian Henderson piping the
Scottish team out ahead of
playing Ireland at Lansdowne
Road on 28 February 1948

Probably his finest performance in a Scotland jersey was at Murrayfield on 3 February 1951, against a Welsh side which contained 11 players who had been on that Lions tour the previous summer and which had already trounced England 23-5 on the opening weekend of the championship. In front of a then record crowd of approximately 80,000, an inexperienced Scottish side, of which Peter Kininmonth was the only Lion, harried and harassed Wales mercilessly on their way to an astonishing 19-0 victory – with Elliot causing mayhem.

The Scottish back-row at this time normally played left and right but, against Wales that afternoon, Elliot played essentially as a specialist open-side flanker because, as he had remarked, chillingly: 'I know which way Glyn Davies sidesteps'. The stylish Welsh stand-off endured a torrid afternoon, and Elliot wrought such havoc in the enemy midfield that the captain, John Gwilliam, felt compelled to move the young Lewis Jones from centre to stand-off. Davies never played for Wales again. Fellow Academicals D.A. Sloan (centre) and H.M. Inglis (second-row) also played that day.

That victory was Scotland's last until they defeated the same opposition again four years later. During this appalling run of 17 consecutive losses, which included the 'Murrayfield Massacre', when South Africa helped themselves to 44 unanswered points on 24 November 1951, Elliot continually managed to rise above the mediocrity which so often surrounded him.

Shortly after Douglas' death in March 2005, Allan Massie wrote in *The Scotsman* newspaper of watching the great man in action for Scotland more than five decades earlier:

> The years after the war were as difficult for Scottish rugby as the present days are, though they didn't start badly. Scotland won the unofficial 'Victory' internationals played in the spring of 1946, and also defeated the strong New Zealand Services team. Douglas thought that the best Scottish XV he ever played in.
>
> Form and selection were haphazard in the post-war years, but Douglas was capped 29 times between 1947 and 1954, and, uniquely for a player of that time, was never dropped. He missed a number of matches, including the whole of the 1953 series because of injury, but there were many days

when he alone seemed to stand between Scotland and disaster, and he was one of the few who survived the 44-0 defeat by South Africa with his honour untarnished.

A big man, 6ft 3in and more than 14st, he was for years the only possible rugby hero for a Scottish schoolboy. He roved the field like the most predatory and destructive of his Border reiving ancestors. Few more secure and powerful tacklers have worn the blue jersey. He was also a fine ball-player, good with it in his hands and a master of the lost art of dribbling.

One of Elliot's last great days in a Scotland shirt was against New Zealand in February 1954. For the first time there was some criticism of his selection. He had missed almost all of the previous season through injury, and had been out again for six weeks over Christmas, so there were major doubts about his match-fitness. But on the day he was outstanding, captaining Scotland and leading by example as his side pushed the mighty All Blacks all the way before going down to a single penalty goal.

Elliot captained the Academicals during the 1951–52 season and was club president for three seasons between 1975–76 and 1977–78.

At the start of the 1949–50 season, rugby posts went up again at Raeburn Place, and on 24 September the pitch was played on for the first time in a decade, when the Academicals defeated a Select XV led by A.G.M. Watt, the club's last pre-war captain.

The restoration of Raeburn Place and reconstruction of the pavilion and squash courts after years of neglect during the war was paid for by the Academical War Memorial Fund. A plaque was erected at Raeburn Place.

The improvements mentioned on the plaque relate principally to the flattening of The Mound, which was paid for by A.M. Carmichael and his five sons J.R., D.D., A.M., G.C. and I.R., as their contribution to War Memorial Fund.

The fact that Raeburn Place was ready to reopen on time was thanks largely to the hard work of several club supporters, and particularly F.A. Wright, the Field Secretary, who, according to *The Chronicle*, 'did not spare himself to ensure the Field was ready for use for September'.

The War Memorial plaque at Raeburn Place

Francis Wright had been nicknamed 'Fatty' whilst at school, and that moniker stuck with him into adulthood – but it was never really justified because he was, in fact, tall and rather lean of build. He had been a mainstay of the Academical pack for ten years from the mid 1920s through to the mid 1930s, captaining the side during 1933–34 season and taking the role of vice-captain in three other seasons. In 1932 he was capped against England.

After hanging up his boots he moved into rugby administration, excelling at both club and international level. Wright served as secretary and treasurer of the SRU from 1947 and, although ill-health forced him to give up those positions in 1954, he was later appointed as the governing body's auditor.

He was a member of the EAFC committee from 1946 until his death in 1959, at the tragically young age of 49, and he played a leading role in organising the club's centenary celebrations during the 1957–58 season. However, it was as field convener between 1947 and 1954 that he rendered his greatest service to the club – taking responsibility for restoring the ground. And his strenuous efforts – along with those of J.C. White – were instrumental in the construction of the new 'stand' at Raeburn Place in 1949, which ran along part of the west side of the pitch, in more or less the same position as the present stand is located. Building restrictions limited its size, but it was a great asset until the Butler Stand of the same dimensions, the first covered enclosure Raeburn Place had ever had, replaced it in 1981.

Wright was to be the committee's nomination for president for the 1959–60 season, and after his death his years of dedicated service to the club were recognised with the construction in 1961 of the Wright Memorial Gates in the south-western corner of the ground. These gates are to be incorporated within the new set-up at Raeburn Place when the redeveloped pavilion is completed in September 2009.

The first match in front of the new stand took place on 12 December 1949, against Cambridge University – on their first visit to Edinburgh since 1938. The university side contained 14 'Blues' (including 13 who had played against Oxford the previous week), and the Academical forwards, who were without regular hooker J.A.R. Macphail, struggled for possession against their much heavier opponents. But the whole team defended heroically, and the backs were quick to seize any chances which came their way. D.A. Sloan was particularly sharp and he scored two tries and a conversion in a magnificent 11-3 victory. The other Academical points came from a Hay conversion.

The 1949–50 season had started well, and by the time the 1st XV played Cambridge they had already won nine and drawn two out of 11 matches played, but the loss of key players such as Elliot, Sloan, Macphail and Hay to national trials and international matches was one of the contributing factors when results started to tail off during the second half of the season. There were a couple of good results, such as an 11-0 victory away to Jed-Forest at the start of February and a 6-0 win over Oxford University at Raeburn Place in March, but these were offset by disappointments such as a 14-5 home defeat to Musselburgh in mid January and a 15-0 hammering at home to Melrose in the penultimate game of the season. The junior teams also struggled for consistency and several games were called off because of the state of the ground. However, the number of players at the club was encouraging. 'It has not been possible to give everyone a game every Saturday. There have been just too many players for four XVs and not quite enough for five', noted *The Chronicle*.

Accies v Oxford University, March 1950

Over the next two seasons results were, on the whole, disappointing. However, during this period several youngsters who would go on to become key players for the club – such as the brothers David, John and Robin Marshall, Tommy McClung, Keith Paterson-Brown, John Adam and Sandy Simson – began to establish themselves.

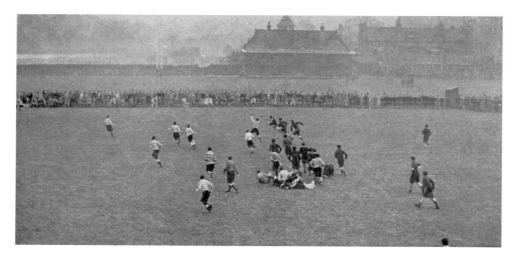

Academy v Merchiston, Raeburn Place 1949

Notable victories during these years included a 14-5 win at Wasps on 11 November 1950, followed by a 16-0 success over Guy's Hospital two days later in the first ever match between these two famous old clubs. On Christmas Day 1950 a last-minute frost prevented the Academicals from playing rugby against London-Scottish at Raeburn Place, so a soccer match took place instead, which the Academicals won 5-3. A day later, an 'Accie-Wanderers' XV lost 9-3 to Blackheath at the Rectory Field in London. Also that season, H.G. (Graham) Fraser, who had been playing regularly for the 4th XV at the age of 40, was called upon to play full-back for the 1st XV against St Andrews University, and produced an excellent performance – tackling splendidly and kicking two penalties. He continued to play occasionally for the 1st XV, and in 1956–57, at the age of 47, appeared in the same junior XV as his two sons. Also during the 1956–57 season an even older veteran in the shape of J.G.C. Buchan played occasionally for the 4th XV in his 50th year.

At the other end of the spectrum, the future health of the club seemed assured with three successes in four years in the 'Under 20' Sevens at Goldenacre. The Academicals won that tournament in 1952, 1954 and 1955, whilst captained by J.A. Adam, J.A. Simson and M.J. Sands respectively.

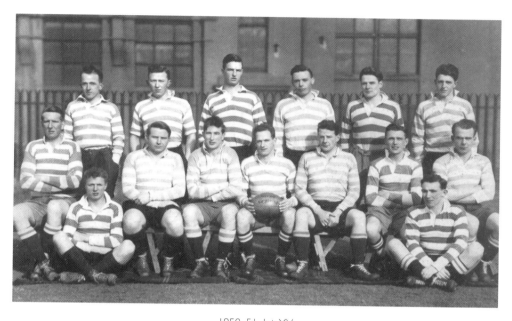

1950–51 1st XV

Back: C.J.R. Mair, C. Anderson, D.J. Marshall, A.F. Gardiner, M. Walker, R.I. Marshall

Middle: G.H. Matthewson, J.A.R. MacPhail, W.H. Sloan, H.G. Hay, W. Wregg, T.D.G. White

The man I give most credit to for the success we enjoyed is Colin Mair. He was a disciplinarian, and before he became captain we Accies didn't understand what the word 'discipline' meant — or at least we didn't want to understand what it meant.

We suddenly had to start going on the pitch with a clean strip . . . spotless . . . white shorts . . . and we were smart. We also started training properly — not like they do today, but more seriously than we ever had before.

And when you begin winning every Saturday you soon get the message . . . that all the work is worthwhile.

Keith Paterson-Brown

WITH C.J.R. MAIR TAKING over the captaincy from W.I.D. Elliot, the 1952–53 season saw the Academicals beginning to come of age as a team, and commence their march towards becoming Scottish champions three years later.

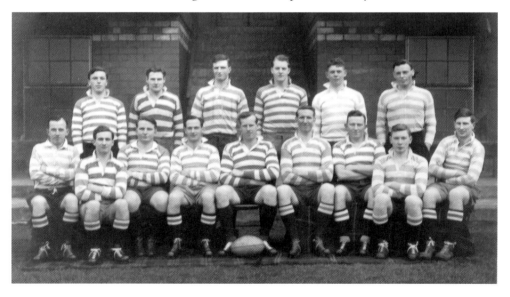

1951–52 1st XV

Back: A.I. McCrostie, M. Walker, D.J. Marshall, R.W. Meikle, T. McClung, A.F. Gardiner

Middle: C.J.R. Mair, J.A.R. Macphail, H.G. Hay, W.I.D. Elliot (*Captain*), G.H. Mathewson, C. Anderson, W.H. Sloan

Front: D.F. Foster, J.A. Adam

The sense that this was a new beginning for the Academicals was asserted by a change in the club uniform. A set of numbered jerseys was acquired and against Watsonians, in the fourth match of the season, the 1st XV played in white (as opposed to blue) shorts. This inevitably prompted some head shaking amongst some of the more conservative members of the club – who failed to recognise that white shorts had been worn up to the 1890s – but generally the change met with approval.

The Chronicle commented:

The improved appearance of the team was most marked and there can be few who will disapprove of the return to our former custom. The game itself was one of the best of the season. Right from kick-off, while we were still admiring our white shorts, Watsonians scored a very fine try – incidentally this was the first time our line had been crossed this season. We fought back vigorously and ten minutes later Mair levelled the score with a penalty from the touchline. In the second half Watsonians, repeatedly securing possession, pressed continuously, apart from some gallant and very neatly successful forays by our forwards. Truly magnificent defence kept them out and the match ended without further scoring. The manner in which our backs downed their man time after time was an object lesson, and the game itself a refutation of the theory that club rugby is in a bad way.

The Academicals' defensive solidity was once again evident when they became the first Scottish team to fly to London for their game against Wasps later in the season, and held on to an 8-3 lead despite enduring a tremendous onslaught from Wasps during the last 20 minutes of the match. 'This was Rugger at its best and once again we owed our success to the fighting spirit of the whole team', noted *The Chronicle.*

That flight from Turnhouse to London prompted one London-based newspaper to publish the headline: 'Scots Make an Air Raid on the Wasps'. To commemorate the occasion, the BEA presented the tourists with a miniature rugby ball inscribed with the motto 'the Flying Accies'.

While the overall record for this season was unremarkable – played 27, won 14, lost 9, drawn 4, points for 207, points against 134 – the fact that no tries were conceded in 17 of the 27 matches played, and only 18 tries were conceded all season, testifies to the sort of progress the team was making. W.I.D. Elliot missed

H.M. Inglis

most of the season through injury, but the hard work of H.M Inglis, J.A.R. Macphail and C. Anderson ensured that he wasn't too great a loss to the pack.

At the end of the season *The Chronicle* reported:

> With some qualms it was decided to run a Junior XV this season with the twin aims of keeping together a young side of promising players and keeping these players out of the hurly-burly of senior Rugger until they were physically strong enough to cope with it. Though this has meant a weaker 2nd XV than usual, and the results of the Junior XV have been mixed, the experiment has been an undoubted success. The side has played good Rugger and shown excellent spirit.

Despite a slow start to the season, the 1st XV's overall record for 1953–54 was similar to that of the previous campaign – played 29, won 15, lost 11, drawn 3, points for 199, points against 173. With the 2nd and 3rd XVs showing considerable improvement, and the under-20s lifting the Goldenacre Cup, the club was clearly in good all-round health – even if the experiment of fielding a Junior XV had to be abandoned due to a lack of numbers.

1953–54 1st XV

Back: J.M. Martin, G.W. Simpson, W.H. Sloan, M.T.R. Marwick, I.R. Beale, R.W. Meikle, R.I. Marshall, J.A. Adam

Middle: K.W. Paterson Brown, J.T. Williamson, H.G. Hay, C.J.R. Mair (*Captain*), W.I.D. Elliot,

H. Wregg, A.F. Gardiner

Front: D.D. Walker, M.J. Sands

According to *The Chronicle*, that season's match at Wasps was an epic encounter.

We pressed from the start and after five minutes a cross-kick by Sloan resulted in a loose scrum near the post. A quick heel, a pass from Adam to

Wregg, and Williamson went over for a 'copy-book' try (3-0). A few minutes later we suffered what seemed a disastrous blow when Wilson was carried off on a stretcher. But from this point the whole side fought with a determination which refused to admit defeat. After half an hour Mair kicked a penalty goal from 40 yards out (6-0) and just before half-time the same player was successful with another long range penalty.

Against the breeze and the slope in the second half we had to do some grim defence. Wasps concentrated on getting the ball to Woodward, the English International, who again and again seemed to be 'well away', but always someone stopped him – very often Hamish Wregg, who must have been giving away about five stone. Quite early in this half Wasps scored an unconverted try (9-3), which spurred them on, but our whole team worked like Trojans and refused to let them pass. The forwards, out-weighted even when they were at full strength, often carried play into the enemy's territory, while the backs not only defended grimly but looked dangerous with the few chances they had in attack.

With 14 minutes to go Stalder scored a brilliant try for Wasps which Sykes converted (9-8). In the hectic finish which followed, we not only kept them at bay but came very near scoring ourselves. The final whistle found us exhausted but triumphant winners of a memorable game. We should like to mention the excellent refereeing of Group Captain G.A. Walker and the tremendously encouraging support from the London 'Accies'.

Once again we were most hospitably entertained by the Wasps, and, following a week-end just as restful as ever, we defeated St Thomas's Hospital (19-0) on the Monday to conclude a most successful and enjoyable tour.

Other notable results that year included a 3-0 victory over Oxford University, despite losing John Adam with a knee injury in the first minute, and a 14-6 victory over Wanderers on the last day of the season, which prevented them from finishing top of the championship.

At the end of the season, an Academical Seven – consisting of G. McClung, J.T. Williamson, W.H. Sloan (captain), J.C. Wregg, A.F. Gardiner, M.T.R. Marwick and J.M. Martin – won at Inverness for the first time since the war. It was just as well that the victory over Aberdeen Grammar School FP in the final was a

Raeburn Place, 1954

decisive one (18-3), as the referee was D.J. Macrae, an Academical who had relocated to Dingwall, and whose impartiality was not entirely convincing. Apparently during the final, before a set scrum, one of the Academicals asked: 'Whose ball?' to which Macrae replied: 'Ours'.

H.G Hay replaced Mair as captain for the 1954–55 season, and despite another slow start the 1st XV ended up with a record of 22 games played, 13 won, six lost and three drawn, having scored 198 points whilst conceding 123, which made it their club's best season since the early 1930s. Lack of match practice was perhaps an understandable excuse when the first game of the season was lost 20-6 to a Bradford side which had already played three matches, but to lose 14-13 to Wanderers after leading 13-3 at half-time and then draw 10-10 with Watsonians after leading 10-0 at the break could not be so easily explained away. The press at the time suggested that there must be something wrong with the Academicals' training and preparation, while *The Chronicle* argued that a lack of a good leader in the forwards was the key problem.

Raeburn Place Pavilion, 1954

This is surprising because although the team was young, the pack still contained a number of strong characters, including Douglas Elliot, who had been Scotland captain up until the end of the previous season, and vice-captain Mike Marwick, who would lead the championship-winning team the following year.

Whatever the cause of these early season jitters, the team soon turned things around; and with I.R. Beale showing up well in the pack they embarked on an impressive winning streak – beating Aberdeen Grammar (13-3), West of Scotland (18-3), Glasgow Academicals (6-0) and Newcastle Northern (8-6) to put their season back on track.

One notable feature of the side was the presence of three brothers in the pack. David, John and Robin Marshall were all important players for the club during the mid to late 1950s. They were the sons of R.I. Marshall, who had captained the Academicals during the 1921–22 season. R.I. Junior was the club's vice-captain in 1955–56 before taking over the captaincy in 1956–57, and he was succeeded by his brother, J.H., in 1957–58. There is no other instance of father and son having captained the Academicals, far less father and two sons. A.F. Gardiner was also an important player in the pack during a season in which the forwards bagged 40 per cent of the total tries scored.

Of the backs, P.F.S. Kittermaster, who played for the first half of the season, showed up well as an attacking stand-off. The others, if not strong in attack, defended well. J.T. Williamson, the most consistent performer, played one or two exceptionally good games; and at full-back, H.G. Hay, the captain, did a power of work in defence and was always ready to open the game up when the opportunity arose.

CHAPTER TWENTY-TWO

A serious neck injury stopped David Fairbairn from playing just when he was developing into a very fine full-back. Many tremendous winning contributions came from the powerful Tommy McClung, great defence and also strength in attack from Sandy Simson, the silky running of Gilbert McClung and Campbell Walker, the reliability of Martin Sands on the left wing, the sheer enthusiasm of Dougie Jardine, and the effervescence and confidence of Bruce Adam at full-back, the latter not always shared by those in front of him! All contributed to a very talented back line.

David Marshall was a quite outstanding second-row forward and probably still the best never to get Capped. Physical contact with David, as opponents and, hilariously, some of his own found, was a bruising affair. His brothers, John, a very fine hooker, and Robin, a fine wing forward, played in the same Accies pack. Surely something that will not often be repeated. Mike Marwick was a footballing powerful No. 8 and captain of the Championship winning side. There were solid front rows with Charlie Sleigh, Roy Meikle, Sandy Gardiner, the late greatly missed Dr George Simpson and latterly Brian Neill. We had hard grafting performances from Jake Millar and his brother Ian, tragically killed so young in a road accident, and the speed of Keith Paterson-Brown, the Neil Back of his era, and the footballing all-round skills of John Adam. They all combined to give us a fine set of forwards.

My apologies to those who played during this time and are not mentioned.

Stan Coughtrie,
quoted in the programme for the club's 140th Celebration match

W.I.D. ELLIOT RETIRED FROM rugby at the end of the 1954–55 season and his loss after nine seasons of dedicated service to the club since the end of the war was undoubtedly a blow; however, this was offset by the arrival of superb reinforcements at half-back for the start of the 1955–56 season in the shape of Tommy McClung (who had spent his formative school years at the Academy before being sent to Sedbergh School in Cumbria when he was 11, and was now back in

Edinburgh full-time having played intermittently for the club since 1951 whilst studying at Cambridge) and Stan Coughtrie (home from National Service and living in Glasgow, but persuaded by club secretary J.A. 'Jim' Stevenson to travel by tram, train and bus to play at Raeburn Place). The team was also bolstered by the decision of the previous season's captain, H.G. Hay, to play one more year after toying with the idea of retiring.

H.G. Hay (right), 9th December 1945

M.T.R. Marwick had taken over the captaincy of the club, and after a 22-3 victory over a Select XV, raised by former captain C.J.T. Mair and made up of retired and semi-retired players, the season proper got off to an inauspicious start with a 17-10 loss to Bradford and a 6-6 draw with Wanderers. But once the early season cobwebs had been blown away, the Academicals embarked on a run of ten wins against Scottish opponents – interrupted only by a narrow 5-3 loss away to Wasps on 12 November. Then, after defeats to Cambridge University and Glasgow Academicals on consecutive weekends during December, the Academicals recovered their winning form and remained undefeated throughout the remainder of the season, with only one draw against Oxford University in the penultimate match of the season.

1955–56 1st XV – Winners of the Unofficial Championship

Back: C.F. Sleigh, J.M. Barber, R.W. Meikle, J.H. Marshall, J. Forrest, S. Coughtrie, J.D.L. Fairbairn

Middle: T. McClung, K.W. Paterson Brown, R.I. Marshall (*Vice-Captain*), M.T.R. Marwick (*Captain*), H.G. Hay, D.J. Marshall, M.J. Sands

Front: H.M.A. Rowan, J.A. Simson

The best performance of the season was probably the 6-0 victory over Hawick – champions the previous season and eventual runners-up this time round – in front of a big Raeburn Place crowd on 28 January 1956.

The Chronicle reported:

The Hawick pack was more than held, and our halves and three-quarters appeared superior to theirs. McClung and Coughtrie combined brilliantly and seemed untroubled by the Hawick wing forwards. It was with very great regret that we received information from Gordon Hay that he would play no more 1st XV rugger after this match. It was a fitting tribute to him that he was asked to captain the side on that day, and it was even more fitting when he was carried shoulder high from the field at the final whistle.

Raeburn Place Pavilion, 1956

The season record was: played 27, won 21, lost 4, drawn 2, points for 336, points against 94. In Scottish matches, the record was: played 20, won 18, lost 1, drawn 1; points for 278, points against 51. The team scored 75 tries and conceded only 13. In the ten matches played after the New Year, only three scores were conceded – a goal by Watsonians and two penalty goals by Oxford.

The results that year were:

Opponents	For	Against
Bradford	10	17
Wanderers	6	6
Selkirk	29	6
Watsonians	6	5
Aberdeen GS FP	9	3
West of Scotland	15	0
Glasgow Academicals	11	0
Newcastle Northern	14	0
Wasps	3	5
St Thomas's Hospital	11	6
Stewart's FP	11	6
Melville FP	12	3
RHS FP	17	3
Cambridge University	8	9
Glasgow Academicals	0	8
London Scottish	6	0
Glasgow HS FP	13	6
Greenock Wanderers	40	0
Musselburgh	32	0
Hawick	6	0
Hillhead HS FP	20	0
Heriot's	12	0
Edinburgh University	8	0
Watsonians	11	5
Melrose	17	0
Oxford University	6	6
Wanderers	3	0

At this time, some newspapers were changing their system for calculating the unofficial 'Scottish club championship', from least games lost against other championship sides to the percentage of games won. It was a source of great satisfaction within the club, and a demonstration of how successful this side had been, when the Academicals were held to be champions irrespective of the methodology employed.

Much had depended on the last match of the season against Wanderers at Murrayfield on Wednesday, 21 March. The Academicals, who needed to avoid defeat to ensure that they would be champions, were playing their third hard game in five days – having recently defeated Melrose on the morning of the Scotland versus England international, and drawn with Oxford on the Monday after that match. They were weakened by the absence through injury of vice-captain R.I. Marshall, tearaway flanker K.W. Paterson-Brown and reliable prop R.W. Meikle, while T. McClung had not entirely recovered from a leg injury he had picked up playing in the Calcutta Cup match four days earlier. It was a nerve-racking afternoon for players and spectators alike. A try by M.J. Sands, created by T. McClung, in the tenth minute was the only score, and for the next hour the Academicals had to defend doggedly, and rely on Wanderers failing with a number of penalty attempts, before breaking out during the last ten minutes and pressing hard for a second try, with both Inglis and Coughtrie being held up over the line.

T. McClung

The team for this championship season was usually selected from: J.D.L. Fairbairn (after H.G. Hay retired in January); J. Forrest, H.M.A. Rowan, J.A. Simson, M.J. Sands; T. McClung, S. Coughtrie; C.F. Sleigh, J.H. Marshall, R.W. Meikle, D.J. Marshall, H.M. Inglis, J.M. Barber, R.I. Marshall junior, M.T.R. Marwick, K.W. Paterson-Brown.

A comprehensive review of the season appeared in *The Chronicle* (July 1956):

Stan Coughtrie

The team was successful because of the excellent spirit which prevailed amongst the players and because of their keenness and insistence on regular and thorough training in all weathers throughout the

season. Not a little praise and thanks must be to Sergeant-Major Atkinson, who put the team through fifteen minutes' hard physical training every Tuesday and Thursday evening in the open.

The captaincy of M.T.R. Marwick was sound and thoughtful and the leading of the forwards by R.I. Marshall, Jr., was vigorous and inspiring.

One of the keys to success was the acquisition of a scrum-half in S. Coughtrie. His long, accurate service enabled our backs to take the ball on the move and penetrate the opposing defence. Both H.G. Hay and latterly, J.D.L. Fairbairn performed well at full-back. Forrest and Sands were strong running wings although the former lacked pace, Simson was brilliant at times in the centre. McClung at stand-off was often unavailable owing to Inter-District Matches, Trials, Internationals and injury but was outstanding when we had his services. He has magnificent hands, is a very powerful kick and while he does not use much of a swerve or a hand-off has a natural ability to beat his man by change of pace and by what might be described as 'power running'.

J.H. Marshall's hooking was another key to success and he was well supported in the front row by Sleigh and Meikle. In the second row D.J. Marshall was often prominent but was frequently called away to Trials. Inglis, before he went South, and Barber played several good games. The final key to success was Paterson-Brown, who is probably the fastest wing forward over twenty yards in this country: he broke up countless opposition attacks by reaching the stand-off at the same time as the ball and he virtually destroyed the chances of Hawick and London Scottish of scoring against us. He also used his speed most effectively in attack and scored a number of match-winning tries. The covering of Marwick and R.I. Marshall was of tremendous value and it was due to their efforts in this direction that our opponents throughout the season were only able to score 13 tries against us, whereas we crossed their line on 75 occasions.

On 4 May 1956, a special Football Club Dinner was held in the Royal British Hotel to celebrate the 1st XV's success. The guests for the evening were all those who had played during the past season and also all available members of the 1929–30 team, the last Accies side to be recognised as Scottish champions. B.G.W. Atkinson, the club president, was in the chair and a gathering of 72 enjoyed a very

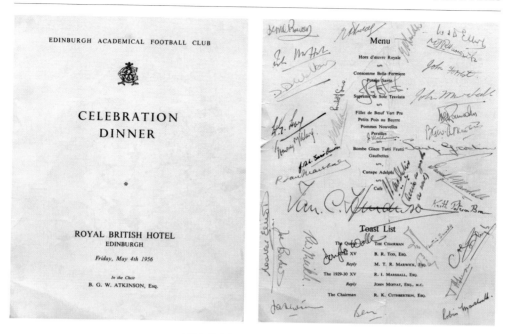

1956 Celebration Dinner Menu

successful evening, with speeches from the chairman, B.R. Tod, M.T.R. Marwick, John Moffat, R.I. Marshall and R.K. Cuthbertson.

With youth on their side, virtually all the players from the championship winning campaign were still available for the 1956–57 season, and with the addition of J.C. Walker and G. McClung arriving from Oxford and Cambridge respectively, there was an air of confidence around the club as the campaign got under way on Tuesday, 18 September with a 14-10 victory over a fairly strong side raised by former club captain H.G. Hay. Not for the first time a lack of match practice was evident when the season proper started the following weekend with a comprehensive 29-15 defeat to Bradford. However, a series of solid victories over Wanderers, Watsonians, Aberdeen GS FP, West of Scotland, Kelso and Newcastle Northern got the season back on track. For the West of Scotland game, Tommy and Gilbert McClung swapped position to good effect, with the former making some fine breaks in the centre and the latter handling the ball beautifully at stand-off.

A slightly unfortunate 5-3 defeat to Wasps in London was followed by a run of six straight victories, including a 6-3 win over Glasgow Academicals, who had

199

1956–57 Academy 1st XV

Top: H.J. McDougall, A.F. Wilkie, A.B. Paton, D.R.D. Hutton, G.H. Crombie, W.R. Dunbar, K.R.L. Turner

Middle: D.M. Mowat, P.J. Burnet, J.G.G. Hunter, I.M. Millar (*Captain*), J.E.N. Harris, D.M. Henderson, K.L.G. Sinclair

Front: A. Macfarlane, A.M. Mowat

been the only Scottish side to defeat the Academicals the previous season. There followed a 0-0 draw against Boroughmuir after a titanic forward struggle, a 12-9 victory over London Scottish on Christmas Day and an 11-0 victory over Glasgow HS FP on 29 December. The side had remained unbeaten in Scotland up to 12 January, but four defeats during the second half of the season to Gala (12-8 at Netherdale), Musselburgh (8-6 at Raeburn), Jed-Forest (3-0 at Raeburn) and Melrose (11-9 at the Greenyards) put an end to the club's aspirations of being outright 'Champions' for a second successive year. The Musselburgh game was a particular low, with *The Chronicle* (March 1957) lamenting:

> Our play reached the lowest level for a very long time. Our forwards seemed to be tired and stale. They were held in the line-out and scrum and looked beaten from the early stages. The worst feature, however, was the exhibition of passing by the three-quarters which was almost too bad to be true. Three times we had the Musselburgh line at our mercy and on each occasion the final pass went astray or was knocked on.

Raeburn Place Pavilion, 1956

There was, however, a highly gratifying 3-3 draw with Hawick in front of a huge crowd at Mansfield Park on 26 January, when Accies scored an excellent try in the first half, with Simson and D.D. Walker working a dummy-scissors which opened the way for T. McClung to send Sands over in the corner. A 17-6 victory over Watsonians on 9 March, with T. McClung the outstanding player on the park, was another high.

This season was not quite as successful as the previous year in terms of Scottish matches:

1955–56	P: 20	W: 18 L: 1	D: 1	Points: 278-51
1956–57	P: 23	W: 17 L: 4	D: 2	Points: 264-86

But the overall record was almost as good:

1955–56	P: 27	W: 21 L: 4	D: 2	Points: 336-94
1956–57	P: 28	W: 20 L: 6	D: 2	Points: 344-134

The Academicals finished the season as joint champions with Jed-Forest, going by the number of games lost criterion.

The 1st XV this year was usually selected from the following: J.D.L. Fairbairn; J.C. Walker, J.A. Simson, G. McClung, M.J. Sands; T. McClung, D.D. Walker, S. Coughtrie; C.F. Sleigh, J.H. Marshall, R.W. Meikle, D.J. Marshall, R.S. Wilson, A.F. Gardiner, R.I. Marshall Junior, J.C.N. Darling, M.T.R. Marwick, K.W. Paterson-Brown.

CHAPTER TWENTY-THREE

This great inheritance which has been handed on to the young members of this Club has not only been safeguarded but has achieved additional lustre in the past fifty years. To be able to claim that you have been a hundred years in existence is in itself something of an achievement, but during those one hundred years that you have achieved such a grand record of results in your football is something of which every Edinburgh Accie should be really proud. Throughout their long history the Accies have produced many first-class and excellent footballers, and to the great names of the first fifty years, Irvine, Finlay, Graham, Maclagan, Reid, McEwan, Stevenson and Scott have to be added the great names of the second fifty years – Sloan, Macpherson, Marshall, Macrae, Henderson, Elliot and your president, Ben Tod.

Changes are bound to have taken place and one is tempted to ask how the Academical of today compares with his counterpart of 1857. In the early days of the Academicals they had blue jerseys with a white badge, white knickerbockers, and a blue nightcap. Today the blue jersey has been replaced by a blue and white jersey, which we all know so well; and the blue shorts which were worn in my day have now given place to white. I wonder if it is too much to suggest that as a gesture to this centenary season the committee should make an issue of nightcaps to the 1st XV? But what is more important is that having discarded knickerbockers and dundreary whiskers, the Academical of yesterday emerges clearly distinguishable as the Academical of today, a likeable chap, a great sportsman, and a citizen well above the average.

Mr W. Maxwell Simmers of Glasgow Academicals
– proposing the toast to the club at the
Edinburgh Academical Football Club Centenary Dinner
26 October 1957

HOPES THAT BRITAIN'S OLDEST rugby club would be able to celebrate their centenary season in the best possible fashion were raised when the 1957–58 campaign got off to a flying start. With more or less the same team as the previous season, apart from J.A. Simson, who was out until November with a wrist injury, the team took advantage of the hard ground to play some excellent running rugby on the way to four decisive victories over Bradford (17-6 at home), Selkirk (26-6 away), Wanderers (25-0 at home) and Watsonians (30-0 away) in their first four matches. There was a setback on 19 October, when the team travelled north to play Aberdeen Grammar School FP without six players were who were representing Edinburgh against the South that day and three more were smitten by the flu epidemic which was doing the rounds that autumn. That match was lost 6-3, but by the following Saturday all of these missing players, with the

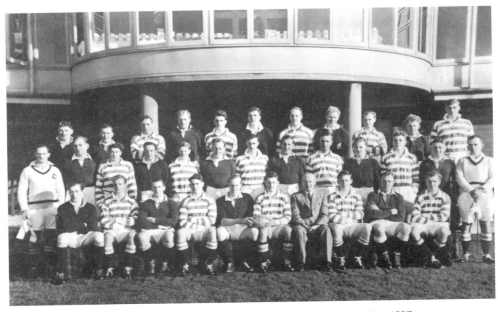

Centenary Match – Academicals v International XV. 26 October 1957

Back: J.H.F. King (Selkirk), I.H.M. Thomson (Heriot's FP), A.F. Gardiner, J.E. Woodward (Wasps), R.I. Marshall, A.J.F. O'Reilly (Old Belvedere), R.W. Meikle, J.T. Greenwood (Perthshire Academy), W.A. Simpson, R. Burnett (Newport), J.K. Millar

Middle: H.G. Hay (*Touch Judge*), H.M. Inglis (London Scottish), M.J. Sands, D.A. Sloan (London Scottish), D.D. Walker, J.C. Dawson (Glasgow Academicals), S. Coughtrie, J. Johnston (Melrose), D.J. Marshall, K.R. Macdonald (Stewart's College FP), G. McClung, A.F. Dickie (*Referee*), C.J.R. Muir (*Touch Judge*)

Front: R.C.C. Thomas (Swansea), J.D.L. Fairburn, R. Willis (Cardiff), T. McClung, W.I.D. Elliot (*Captain, Edinburgh Academicals*), J.H. Marshall (*Captain*), B.R. Tod (*President EAFC*), M.T.R. Marwick, T. Elliot (Gala), K.W. Paterson-Brown exception of J.C. Walker (who was still ill) were available again for the first of three special matches played at Raeburn Place that season to mark the club's centenary.

The game was against an International XV captained by the great W.I.D. Elliot. It was an open and fast encounter which the Academicals ended up winning 24-10. The guest side was hit by a number of late call-offs due to illness, injury and a continental transport strike, which stranded the great French flanker Jean Prat at Toulouse Airport. Accies had offered to pay for a specially chartered flight to get him to the game on time, but were prevented from doing so by a lack of airport staff in France.

The Internationalists also lost a few players to injury during the course of the game. But despite all this they contributed fully to an entertaining contest played in front of a bumper crowd of around 5,000, on a gloriously sunny afternoon in Stockbridge.

The teams that day were:

Academicals: J.D.L. Fairbairn; W.A. Simpson, T. McClung, G. McClung, M.J. Sands; D.D. Walker, S. Coughtrie; R.W. Meikle, J.H. Marshall (captain), A.F. Gardiner, D.J. Marshall, J.K. Millar, R.I. Marshall Junior, M.T.R. Marwick, K.W. Paterson-Brown.

International XV: I.H.M. Thomson (Heriot's FP and Scotland); J.E. Woodward (Wasps and England), A.J.F. O'Reilly (Old Belvedere and Ireland), D.A. Sloan (London Scottish and Scotland), K.R. Macdonald (Stewart's FP and Scotland); R. Burnett (Newport and Wales), R. Willis (Cardiff and Wales); T. Elliot (Gala and Scotland), J.H.F. King (Selkirk and Scotland), J.C. Dawson (Glasgow Academicals and Scotland), J. Johnston (Melrose and Scotland), H.M. Inglis (London Scottish and Scotland), J.T. Greenwood (Perthshire Academicals and Scotland), R.C.C. Thomas (Swansea and Wales), W.I.D. Elliot (captain) (Edinburgh Academicals and Scotland).

Referee: A.I. Dickie (Gala).
Touch judges: C.J.R. Mair and H.G. Hay (Edinburgh Academicals)

ACADEMICAL XV

DAVID LAWSON FAIRBAIRN

JAMES CAMPBELL WALKER

THOMAS McCLUNG

GILBERT McCLUNG

MARTIN JOHN SANDS

DAVID DOUGLAS WALKER

STANLEY COUGHTRIE

ROY WALKER MEIKLE

JOHN HANNAH MARSHALL (Captain)

ALEXANDER FRAZER GARDINER

DAVID JOHN MARSHALL

JAMES KINGHORN MILLAR

ROBERT IAN MARSHALL

MICHAEL THOMAS ROBSON MARWICK

KEITH WISHART PATERSON-BROWN

M. J. SANDS   G. McCLUNG   T. McCLUNG

J. H. MARSHALL   A. F. GARDINER   D. J. MARSHALL

EDINBURGH ACADEMICAL FOOTBALL CLUB

CENTENARY MATCH

PLAYED AT

RAEBURN PLACE, EDINBURGH

on

SATURDAY, 26th OCTOBER 1957

KICK-OFF 2.45 P.M.

OFFICIAL 1/- PROGRAMME

ACADEMICAL XV

1. J. D. L. FAIRBAIRN
2. J. C. WALKER
3. T. McCLUNG
4. G. McCLUNG
5. M. J. SANDS
6. D. D. WALKER
7. S. COUGHTRIE
8. R. W. MEIKLE
9. J. H. MARSHALL (CAPTAIN)
10. A. F. GARDINER
11. D. J. MARSHALL
12. J. K. MILLAR
13. R. I. MARSHALL
14. M. T. R. MARWICK
15. K. W. PATERSON-BROWN

Touch Judge: C. J. R. HAIR

INTERNATIONAL XV

1. J. G. M. W. MURPHY — Army
2. J. E. WOODWARD — Wasps
3. A. J. F. O'REILLY — Old Belvedere
4. D. A. SLOAN — London Scottish
5. T. G. WEATHERSTONE — Stewart's College F.P.
6. R. BURNETT — Newport
7. W. R. WILLIS — Cardiff
8. T. ELLIOT — Gala
9. J. C. DAWSON — Glasgow Academicals
10. J. JOHNSTON — Melrose
11. H. M. INGLIS — London Scottish
12. J. T. GREENWOOD — Perthshire Academicals
13. R. C. C. THOMAS — Swansea
14. W. I. D. ELLIOT (CAPTAIN) — Edinburgh Academicals
15. J. PRAT — Lourdes

Touch Judge: H. G. HAY

Before the commencement of the game music will be played by the Pipes and Drums of The EDINBURGH ACADEMY C.C.F.

KICK-OFF 2.45 p.m.

Referee: A. I. DICKIE (Gala)

INTERNATIONAL XV
As selected

J. G. M. W. MURPHY (Army)

J. E. WOODWARD (Wasps)

A. J. F. O'REILLY (Old Belvedere)

D. A. SLOAN (Edinburgh Academicals and London Scottish)

C. L. DAVIES (Cardiff)

A. J. F. O'REILLY   D. A. SLOAN

J. E. WOODWARD

J. G. M. W. MURPHY

R. BURNETT (Newport)

W. R. WILLIS (Cardiff)

T. ELLIOT (Gala)

J. C. DAWSON (Glasgow Academicals)

J. JOHNSTON (Melrose)

H. M. INGLIS (Edinburgh Academicals, London Scottish, and Army)

W. R. WILLIS

T. ELLIOT

H. M. INGLIS   J. JOHNSTON   J. C. DAWSON

J. T. GREENWOOD (Perthshire Academicals)

R. C. C. THOMAS (Swansea)

W. I. D. ELLIOT (Edinburgh Academicals) (Captain)

J. PRAT (Lourdes)

J. T. GREENWOOD

R. C. C. THOMAS

W. I. D. ELLIOT

J. PRAT

Centenary Match programme.

The Chronicle carried a lengthy report of this historic match:

Before the start of the game, the pipe band of the Academy C.C.F. made an excellent impression on the spectators, who included the Lord Provost of Edinburgh (present in his private capacity as an Academical), the President of the Scottish Rugby Union, and many of his committee, as well as a host of well-known Rugger personalities.

Our opponents (who included three Academicals – Sloan, Inglis and Elliot) were a most impressive team. Of the regular Academical XV, J.C. Walker was unable to play owing to influenza.

Right from the kick-off it was obvious that both sides intended to make the most of the dry ball and the firm turf, and after an initial spell of pressure from the Internationals, a fumble by the full-back from a kick ahead by Paterson-Brown put the Academicals on the attack. Sands just failed to gather a pass from Coughtrie on the blind side, which might have led to a score, but immediately after, from a short penalty kick, G. McClung broke through and Marwick was up to score at the corner. The long kick was not converted, but almost from the restart G. McClung again made a beautiful opening with a long diagonal run, but after beating the full-back he was tackled by Woodward. The visitors worked their way down to the Academical 25, helped by several darting runs from Burnett, and from one of these, started by a long pass from a line-out by Elliot, the ball

Accies Centenary Match v International XV, 1958

travelled to O'Reilly, who roused great enthusiasm by racing over for a try, which was converted by Thomson. Unfortunately, O'Reilly appeared to damage a thigh muscle and moved to the wing. The visitors were having the best of the set scrums, but the Academicals more than held their own in the loose, and they were rewarded when Paterson-Brown picked up a ball on the 25 line and went at high speed to score a typical opportunist try. T. McClung could not convert, but soon after he intercepted a pass and ran with great determination – Thomas being on his heels for nearly 40 yards – to score far out, and this time he made no mistake with the kick. Inglis suffered a back injury and had to go off, and Macdonald, also, was hurt and moved to the wing. Half-time came just after a fine dribbling rush headed by Elliot, with Academicals leading by 11 points to 5.

The visitors' seven forwards resumed with refreshed energy, Dawson especially playing a remarkable game for a veteran, and Thomas had two galloping runs which were finally stopped by good tackling. A period of ineffective play suddenly ended when Sloan intercepted, and a well-timed pass left the limping O'Reilly with a simple try. Thomson converted with an excellent kick to make his side only one point behind. The Internationals then put on great pressure, and Woodward, a very difficult man to stop, and the nimble Burnett, who was receiving a perfect service from Willis, caused the Academicals many anxious moments. However, when Macdonald tore a ligament and had to leave the field, the visitors had virtually shot their bolt.

Centenary Match,
1958

After a 50-yard rush by the Academicals forwards, G. McClung put over a well placed cross-kick and Sands romped over for a try, which T. McClung converted. Burnett made a fine dash shortly afterwards, beating several men before being tackled by Paterson-Brown. The pace was now telling on the veterans, especially as they were two men short, and in the last ten minutes, Walker scored a good try after a 'dummy' drop at goal and T. McClung converted. In the closing minutes G. McClung again made a glorious thrust through the centre and scored the final try, which was not converted, the Academicals thus winning by 3 goals 3 tries – 24 points – to 2 goals – 10 points.

The Internationals are to be congratulated most heartily on their showing in this fast and open game, and on the way in which their remaining 12 players (their other missing player being the injured O'Reilly) refused to give in. Nevertheless the Academicals deserve great praise for overcoming such a talented opposition, and, on this performance, John Marshall's team must rank as one of the best all-round teams in the history of the Club. A worthy game for a historic occasion, helped in no small measure by the refereeing of A.I. Dickie.

That evening 275 Academicals and 193 guests attended the club's Centenary Dinner at the Assembly Rooms and Music Hall on George Street in Edinburgh. Among the speakers was: The Right Honourable I. A. Johnson, Lord Provost of Edinburgh and captain of the Academical 'B' XV in 1914; SRU president R.J. Hogg; EAFC president B.R. Tod; E. Watts Moses, a past president of the RFU; G.P.S. Macpherson; W.I.D. Elliot, and club captain J.H. Marshall.

The actual foundation of the club was commemorated by a meeting of the general committee on 29 January 1929. This was held at 21 St Andrew Square, in the office of a firm in which a future club president R. Tod was the senior partner. It was in Robert Balfour's office at this same address that 100 years previously Alexander Dunlop had presided over 'The First General Annual Meeting of the Academical Football Club'.

After three more victories, over Kelso (22-3), Wasps (19-3) and St Thomas's Hospital (11-5), the Academicals played their second centenary celebration match on 16 November against Blackheath, one of England's oldest clubs. Unfortunately, six first-choice players had been laid low with the flu, including captain J.H. Marshall,

Centenary dinner programme – front, back and inside covers, Saturday 26 October 1957

EDINBURGH ACADEMICAL FOOTBALL CLUB

his brother D.J., vice-captain T. McClung and S. Coughtrie. In their absence R.I. Marshall led the side. Keith Paterson-Brown deputised at scrum-half, where he had played in his youth before moving to flanker, and was a constant source of irritation to Blackheath through his willingness to break from the base.

Despite taking an early lead when J.C. Walker capitalised on D.D. Walker's diagonal kick, the Academicals were trailing 8-3 at the break. The second half also got off to a promising start with a series of determined assaults on the Blackheath line, but after 20 minutes of soaking up the pressure the visitors broke away and their Scottish centre, A.C.J. Sharp, broke through to score the game's decisive try, after some fine dribbling by their hefty pack – described in *The Scotsman* as 'giants' with an average weight of just 14 stone. The match ended with Blackheath 13-3 victors.

The Academicals team for this match was: J.A. Simson; J.C. Walker, H.M.A. Rowan, G. McClung, M.J. Sands; D.D. Walker, K.W. Paterson-Brown; R.W. Meikle, R.I. Marshall Junior (acting captain), A.F. Gardiner, R.S. Wilson, J.K. Millar, W.D.C. More, M.T.R. Marwick, B.K. Mann.

On paper the team appeared to be back to full strength when Stewart's College FP arrived at Raeburn Place the following Saturday, but some of the forwards were clearly still feeling the effects of their illness. The Academicals scored two excellent tries early on through J.C. Walker (made by T. McClung) and Paterson-Brown, but with hardly any possession they could not hold on to their 8-3 half-time lead and ended up losing 11-12 – although they could have won the match right at the end if T. McClung had been successful with his conversion attempt of M.J.B Sands' late try. This was the first time in three years that the club had lost to another Edinburgh side; and to add injury to insult J.D.L. Fairbairn got hurt and did not play again that season, while T. McClung damaged his leg and only managed one more appearance. The loss of McClung was a particularly grievous blow. By now he was a Scotland regular, and he had been in particularly devastating form for the Academicals in the nine matches he had played so far that season, with 11 tries and 27 successful kicks at goal.

As well as this pair, the Academicals were without G. McClung, D.J. Marshall, M.T.R. Marwick and K. Paterson-Brown, who were playing for Edinburgh against Glasgow, when they faced Melville College FP the following week – but they still managed an 8-3 away win. They then dispatched RHS FP (17-0 at home), before welcoming to Raeburn Place an excellent Cambridge University XV.

According to *The Chronicle* the students were 'most impressive in all departments' and provided a 'magnificent display of open football', winning the match convincingly 17-3.

With injuries to S. Coughtrie, G. McClung and H.M. Inglis further disrupting the side, the stretch between mid-December and mid-February was difficult, and although the Cambridge match was the only loss during these winter months, there were four low-scoring draws against London Scottish, Gala, Musselburgh and Heriot's FP

However, as the weather improved so did the Academicals' form. Five victories in a row over St Andrews University (5-3 away), Edinburgh University (9-8 away), Watsonians (11-3 at home), Melrose (11-0 at home) and Boroughmuir FP (16-0) at home revived the prospect of winning the unofficial championship again, but for that to happen a victory over Wanderers in the last match of the season against Scottish opposition was imperative.

Having defeated the same opponents 25-0 at Murrayfield at the start of the season, confidence was high, and for the first half hour it seemed as if this self-belief was well placed. With the breeze at their backs the Academicals raced into an 8-0 lead within 15 minutes, and would have gone even further ahead if a vital pass had not been dropped. Wanderers, however, were by now a much more accomplished side than they had been at the start of the season, and stand-off T.A. Hall scored twice for Wanderers in quick succession to reduce the gap to 8-6 at the break. The lead changed hands three times during the second half, and with the score 11-14 in Wanderers' favour as the game entered the final minute the Academicals were awarded a penalty in a very kickable position. J.H. Marshall opted to go for the win rather than settling for a draw, and took a short penalty to launch one last frantic attack, which was eventually stopped by some desperate Wanderers defence just short of the try line – and the whistle was blown for no-side.

After the high expectations of the autumn, the season had ended in anti-climax – and this was reflected in the small crowd which turned up at Raeburn Place for the final match of the campaign against Oxford University on the Monday after the Wanderers defeat. It was a shame, because despite the miserable weather, both teams did well to produce an entertaining and well-balanced match – which was eventually decided by an Oxford penalty goal kicked from the half-way line.

The season was not a complete disaster. Injuries had made things difficult for the Academicals, and their form had often been disappointing, but they still managed to finish alongside Stewart's FP and Melrose at the top of the championship in terms of games lost – and fourth under the newly styled percentage points system, behind those same two teams and also Wanderers.

All Matches   P: 28   W: 18   L: 6   D: 4   Points: 339-134.
Scottish Matches: P: 19   W: 13   L: 3   D: 3   Points: 248-65.

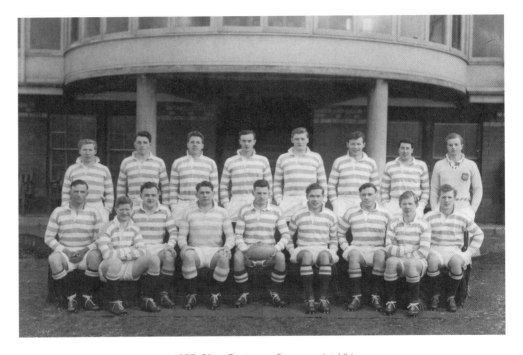

1957–58 – Centenary Season – 1st XV

Back: J.B. Neil, R.I. Marshall, G. McClung, S. Coughtrie, J.K. Millar, M.T.R. Marwick, M.J. Sands, J.D.L. Fairburn

Middle: D.J. Marshall, J.A. Simson, T. McClung (*Vice-Captain*), J.H. Marshall (*Captain*), J.C. Walker,
A.F. Gardiner, K.W. Paterson-Brown,

Front: D.D. Walker, T.L.B. Adam

Eight members of the team played for Edinburgh this season – T. McClung, S. Coughtrie, G. McClung, D.J. Marshall, J.H. Marshall, M.T.R. Marwick, J.K. Millar and K.W. Paterson-Brown – while one of the side's most reliable performers was A.F. Gardiner, now the team veteran, having appeared for the Academical 1st XV in every season since the resumption in 1947.

At the end of this historic season the club was invited to take part in the Middlesex Sevens at Twickenham as one of two guest sides, but a team consisting of J.C. Walker, G. McClung, D.D. Walker, K.W. Paterson-Brown, M.T.R. Marwick, J.H. Marshall and F.H.D. Wright lost 8-10 to the Woodpeckers, a combined Oxford and Cambridge universities touring rugby side, in their first tie, after leading 8-0 at half-time.

The 2nd XV had an exceptionally good season and finished with their best record since the war (P: 20, W: 15, L: 4, D: 1, Points: 249-173). This was a particularly creditable achievement given that they lost three of their first five matches, and were frequently called upon to release players to the 1st XV when injuries began to take their toll. The highlight of the season for the 2nd XV was their tour to Dublin, organised by H.M.A. Rowan, on the weekend of the Scotland versus Ireland international match. Mater Hospital had played the 2nd XV at Raeburn Place on the corresponding weekend the previous year, and this return fixture was the first time an Academicals team had played in Dublin. It was an exciting match which ended with the honours shared 16-16.

The third and final centenary match did not directly involve the Academicals. On Monday, 23 December, Raeburn Place hosted a match between 'A Scottish Schools XV' and 'An English Schools XV'. This match was arranged to emphasise the Academical Football Club's connection with school football, especially in its early years when it was a combined school-and-old-boys' club. The Scottish XV, led by Academy captain (and future Scotland Internationalist) P.J. Burnet, was drawn from fewer schools than their opponents, and this clearly aided team cohesion. The Scots won the match 16-0.

The two teams that day were:

Scottish Schools XV: P.J. Burnet (*Captain*, Edinburgh Academy); P.E. Murray (Glenalmond), I.M. Macmichael (Glenalmond), J.A.P. Shackleton (Fettes), I.A. Wetherspoon (Keil); J. Blake (RHS), G.E. Farlowe (RHS); N.D.R. Harris (Loretto), J.G.R. Percival (Loretto), M. Jack (Paisley Grammar School), W.A.M. Crow (Merchiston), I.G.C. McLaren (Merchiston), J.P. Fisher (RHS), J.C. Brash (Fettes), G.M. Reid (Glenalmond).

English Schools XV: A.J. Howard Baker (Clifton); J.C.W. Madge (St Paul's), R.M. Trembath (Dulwich), J. Taylor (*Captain*, Cheltenham), S.H. Lloyd (Cheltenham); W.G. MacDonald (Oundle), R.E. Spirit (Durham); R.J. Hargreaves (Giggleswick), B.A. Isbill (King's Canterbury), R.H.C. Wagstaff (The Leys), N.C. Wakefield (St Bees), J.P.L. Glover (Harrow), H.D.C. Williams (Rossall), R.H.C Page (Tonbridge), J.F. Svejdar (Stowe).

Scotland side that played England at Murrayfield, 16 March 1957

Back: Mr R. Mitchell (*Referee*), R.K.G. MacEwen (London Scottish), K.R. Macdonald (Stewart's College FP), G.K. Smith (Kelso), J.W.Y. Kemp (Glasgow High School F.P), J.L.F. Allan (Cambridge University), T. McClung (Edinburgh Academicals), K.J.F. Scotland (R. Signals and Heriots FP), Mr C.W. Drummond (*Touch Judge*).

Middle: E.J.S. Michie (London Scottish), T. Elliot (Gala), A. Robson (Hawick), J.T. Greenwood (Perthshire Acads, *Captain*), A.R. Smith (Cambridge University), H.F. McLeod (Hawick).

Front: G.H. Waddell (London Scottish), A.F. Dorward (Gala).

CHAPTER TWENTY-FOUR

In rugby you are only as strong as your weakest link and there was no real weak link in that side. We used to win the ball in the tight, we used to win the ball in the loose and we used to be very constructive when the backs got the ball. Guys like Pat Burnett were bloody good and they could make the breaks, so for a back-row forward, who was racing around all over the place, it was great – they got us in the positions where we could just pick up the ball and be away. It was brilliant . . . just fantastic.

The lack of facilities was definitely made up for by a real respect in the team. There's no doubt about that. They were great guys, they were really nice people, they were good rugby players, and there was a real comradeship. They were a tight-knit group – we'd do a lot of socialising together. They were very forward looking, very embracing of other clubs and other people. That was a real ethic for the club.

Rodger Arneil

THE 1958–59 SEASON FOLLOWED a similar sort of pattern to the previous year with the 1st XV playing exceptionally well in both defence and attack on occasion, but lacking consistency over the course of the whole campaign. Nevertheless, the overall record was the best in three years, and the points differential in all matches played was the club's best since the war.

The season got off to an encouraging start, with victories over London Scottish at Richmond (11-0) and over Bradford on the way back north (6-5). That form carried on into the regular season, and up to Christmas 1958 the Academicals were undefeated in 15 matches played, with 11 wins and four draws. Their first loss was to Boroughmuir FP on 27 December (6-5 at home) on an almost unplayable pitch, by which time the usual problem of players disappearing for district matches and international trials was beginning to take its toll and the prolonged period of frost which led to six successive matches between the start of January and the middle of February being cancelled was viewed as something of a mixed blessing. Unfortunately, when play resumed the team couldn't quite recover their earlier form and two defeats at Melrose (16-8 at the Greenyards on 21 March, when Stan Coughtrie was away playing for Scotland against England at Twickenham) and Edinburgh Wanderers (8-0 at Murrayfield a week later) saw the Academicals fall out of the championship race, ending up in fifth place behind Langholm, Melrose, Hawick and Wanderers.

Stan Coughtrie, who picked up the first four of his 11 caps for Scotland this season, and toured Australia, New Zealand and Canada with the Lions during that summer, was the Academicals' outstanding player; and it is worth noting that every time the team was beaten he was missing from the side. In addition to his long and accurate pass, he excelled in controlling the game tactically by accurate touch-kicking in both attack and defence. This season also saw future captain P.J. Burnet make his first few appearances for the club whilst on vacation from Oxford University. Burnet was capped once for Scotland in an 18-10 defeat in South Africa in 1960.

1958–59 2nd XV

Once again the 2nd XV had a good season, winning 15 and drawing one of their 19 matches. Meanwhile, the deep-rooted health of the club enabled it to field a 5th XV regularly for the first time since before the war, and largely thanks to the encouragement of club captain, J.A. Simson, the first 'junior tour' since 1939 was arranged for the Easter weekend, with 29 players from the 3rd, 4th and 5th XVs playing against Ross Sutherland in Invergordon on the Saturday (16-5 victory) and against a strong Perthshire Academicals XV on the Monday (3-16 loss).

While there were no notable successes in the Sevens, the record was better than it had been for a number of years, with the Academicals managing semi-final appearances at both Murrayfield and Melrose before losing narrowly to the eventual winners of those tournaments on each occasion.

1958–59 1st XV

Back: J.C. Walker, M.T.R. Marwick, W.D.C. More, J.C.N. Darling, G. McClung, I.M. Millar, C.F. Sleigh, M.J. Sands

Middle: S. Coughtrie, J.K. Millar, D.J. Marshall, J.A. Simson (*Captain*), T. McClung, A.F. Gardiner, J.H. Marshall

Front: J.B. Neil, T.L.B. Adam

With T. McClung as captain, the Academicals finished the 1959–60 season with a record which was second only to Jack Hegarty's great Hawick team. However, *The Chronicle* (July 1960) states that 'the season was rather less successful than the statistics would seem to indicate':

Victories have often been narrow and life has been led somewhat danger- ously. The forwards' chief weakness was a certain lack of mobility and a failure to get on the loose ball. For the big occasion, however, the pack could produce a great effort and there is no doubt that the XV has been a very difficult team to beat. The backs have shown very good form on occasion and a persistent belief in hard running and passing as the fundamentals of the game.

The outstanding player of the season was undoubtedly the captain T. McClung. His long and accurate kicking was invaluable, while his powerful bursts tested every defence. Indeed, such was his stature as a player that without him the XV's very good record in Scottish games would have been but an indifferent one, for he played a major part in turning several likely defeats into narrow victories. In J.H. Marshall as vice-captain and pack leader, the club was also very fortunate. He had the task of building up a pack that lacked the dominating physique, speed and authority of those in recent years, and he succeeded in producing a very serviceable unit. Marshall's club loyalty was demonstrated when he declined a place in the Edinburgh XV on the day the Academicals were due to play a successful Gala side. His unselfishness and regard for the Club's interests were well rewarded by the inspired play of the pack in that match.

Special mention must also be made of K.W. Paterson-Brown, who retired at the end of the season. Though comparatively slight in physique, his speed off the mark, his untiring energy, and his ability to take advantage of opponents' mistakes have made him a very dangerous attacking wing forward and an invaluable member of Academical XVs during a very successful period in the Club's history.

There were three matches in particular which stood out – against Wasps, Hawick and Trinity College in Dublin.

On 14 November, Wasps played the Academicals during their first ever visit to Scotland. Despite the wind and rain both teams tried their best to play an open and entertaining game, but neither side could break the deadlock and the match finished as a 0-0 draw.

Accies v London Scottish, 1960

The Academicals versus Hawick match at Raeburn Place on 30 January was billed in the press as the 'game of the season'. At that stage the Academicals had won all of their 16 matches played while Hawick had lost only once in 19 outings. Straw had been laid on the pitch for a week before the match to guard against frost, but there was no way of counteracting the snow which started to fall on the morning of the game and continued all day – denying the Academicals backs the dry ball they had been hoping for. Hawick adapted better to the conditions and although they were perhaps fortunate to be 8-0 ahead at half-time, they were equally unfortunate not to add to that score in a ceaseless second-half siege of the Academical line. 'Two Academical handling movements in the first twenty minutes gave an indication of what we might have achieved on a fine day with a dry ball, but we have no hesitation in congratulating Hawick on their supremacy on the only day that mattered', was the gracious assessment of *The Chronicle* afterwards.

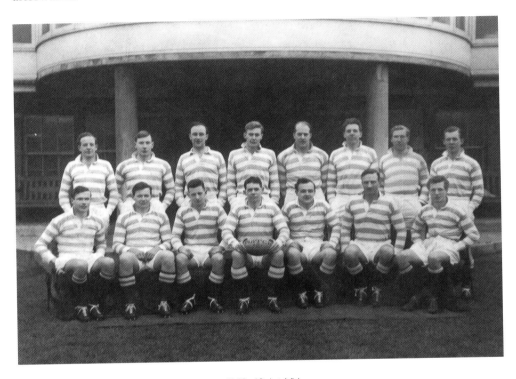

1959–60 1st XV

Back: W.M.C. Kennedy, J.A. Adam, W.D.C. More, I.M. Millar, R.W. Meikle, G. McClung, J.B. Neill, T.L.B. Adam

Front: J.C. Walker, M.T.R. Marwick, J.H. Marshall (*Vice-Captain*), T. McClung (*Captain*),

D.J. Marshall, K.W. Paterson Brown

On 27 February 1960 the world's two oldest rugby clubs met for the first time. The Academicals' first visit to College Park, Dublin, on the morning of the Scotland versus Ireland international match at Lansdowne Road, led to a close and exciting game against Trinity College, from which the visitors eventually emerged as 15-11 victors. According to *The Chronicle*: 'Handling errors could fairly be attributed to the truly magnificent hospitality lavished on the team at the Dinner in Trinity College on the previous evening, but the technical lapses merely added to the prevailing *joie de vivre* and contributed to a spectacular match'.

M.T.R. (Mike) Marwick was restored as captain for the 1960–61 season, and at the conclusion of that campaign the Academicals found themselves second in the championship table behind Hawick for the second consecutive year – this time they had the same number of defeats and draws as the Borderers but had played two games less, so missed out on sharing top spot by three percentage points. The outstanding performance of the season was undoubtedly the 14-0 victory over the champions-elect at Mansfield Park on 28 January. The Academical forwards gave nothing away in the scrums and as the game progressed D.J. Marshall, I.M. Millar and Marwick became increasingly dominant in the line-outs. The Academicals back-row harried Glen Turnbull, the Hawick scrum-half, relentlessly, while S. Coughtrie and T. McClung were in peerless form at half-back. Afterwards *The Scotsman* reported:

> Before an astonished crowd Hawick suffered their heaviest defeat for years at Mansfield Park, where the Academicals scored a strategical victory by one goal, two penalty goals, and one dropped goal to nothing.
>
> The Academical plan was apparent from the start – to thump the ball up the touch-line, via the powerful boots of their international half-backs, T. McClung and S. Coughtrie, and open out only in the opposing '25'.
>
> To do this the city pack had to achieve equality in the set-pieces, and this they achieved in their finest display of the season. In addition, the Academical back-row, with M.T.R. Marwick giving a captain's lead and J.A. Adam, a fast flanker, laid down such an iron curtain that the home half-backs, A.R. Broatch and R.G. Turnbull, were never able to develop their accustomed fluency.
>
> For once, too, the well-drilled Hawick were held in the loose, the efforts of D. Grant and A. Robson being matched by Marwick, Adam, I.M. Millar and D.J. Marshall.
>
> Once again in top kicking form, Coughtrie converted a try by G. McClung from near the touch-line and added two penalty goals after T.

McClung, the 'general' of the backs, had opened the scoring with a dropped goal. The most dangerous of the home backs, G.D. Stevenson, found himself with a tenacious opposite number in J.A. Simson, who was outstanding among the Academical three-quarters.

The Academicals team that day were: T.L.B. Adam; J.C. Walker, J.A. Simson, E.D. Saunders, G. McClung; T. McClung, S Coughtrie; G.W. Simpson, J.D.F. Miller, J.B. Neill, I.M. Miller, D.J. Marshall, J.H. Macfie, M.T.R. Marwick, J.A. Adam.

1960 2nd XV

In an overview of the whole season, *The Chronicle* (October 1961) stated:

Encouraged and led by Marwick, the XV trained strenuously and played with a tenacity of spirit that often disguised the fact that the team was still in the transitional from the greatness of a few years ago. The forwards, while always formidable and well drilled, were rarely 'terrifying' in the rampaging fashion of yester-year. The three-quarters' mode of attack had to be re-thought, for, with T. McClung seeming to lack a little of his ability to tear initial gaps that left a line with simple overlaps for the wings to exploit, three-quarters had to rely more on their own ingenuity to achieve breaks. There is no doubt, too, that the basic problems indicated were obscured, from a results point of view, by the all-round brilliance of Coughtrie. In length and accuracy of service, in individual break and dummy, and in mental grasp of the needful in any match, Coughtrie was outstanding.

The long kiss goodnight for the great Academical team of the mid-1950s carried on into the 1961–62 season, with the 1st XV finishing second in the championship for the third year running. The team also earned an international reputation with victories over Wasps, Cambridge University and Ebbw Vale at a time when each of these clubs were at the top of the tree in their own countries, prompting one English national newspaper to rate the Academicals as 'one of the six best sides in the British Isles'.

Some 35 years later, J.B. Neill, the captain this season, recalled that 'epic' match against Ebbw Vale:

We travelled to Wales and took away their unbeaten home record. We had three sources of inspiration that evening, our president, our touch judge and our full back. We were addressed at half time by our president who had found it necessary to have several small refreshments to keep out the cold. The same situation applied to our Welsh touch judge, who made inspired dashes up and down the line wondering how he would explain away his condition to his parents, who thought he was teetotal. However, as the Western Mail told us in banner headlines the next day, the real inspiration was our full back, Bruce Adam, who single-handedly kept the Welsh hordes away from our line. Bruce is known to still have dozens of faded copies available for sale.

1961–62 1st XV

Back: W.M.C. Kennedy, G. McClung, J.K. Millar, I.M. Millar, J. Macfie, G.W. Simpson, T.L.B. Adam

Middle: D.J. Marshall, J.A. Adam, S. Coughtie, J.B. Neill (*Captain*), J.H. Marshall, T. McClung, M.T.R. Marwick

Front: P.J. Burnet, D.J. Jardine

Under Neill's genial leadership the pack managed to punch well above its weight that season, with *The Chronicle* reporting:

In tight scrums the experienced legs of J.H. Marshall once more struck with success – even at Ebbw Vale, where front-row work is particularly formidable – and in line-out and general maul his brother D.J. proved a focal point of activity. The brothers Millar, neither of whom appeared to sartorial advantage in the new style woollen jersey which the XV used this season for the first time, nevertheless moved unobtrusively and to good effect in front and second row, while the masterly covering and general positional play of Mike Marwick has repeatedly tempted the thought that there can be few better players in this position. Wing-forwards J.A. Adam and Macfie, both possessed of fine bursts of acceleration, have excelled in cover defence.

Behind the scrum, the side has been fortunate in its personalities. The unique Coughtrie, talented in so many ways, received but his just reward when selected to play again for Scotland [he had not been capped since 1959]. T. McClung has still an authority in play that stamps him as no ordinary player, while his brother can demonstrate on occasion an electrifying burst of speed that leaves other three-quarters with a feeling that old age has for them suddenly arrived. P.J. Burnett has perhaps not quite played to form this season, but at Ebbw Vale he demonstrated the qualities at stand-off that earned him such a high reputation at Oxford. Jardine, one of the season's 'finds', has a remarkably fine defence and, though lacking the pace of many wings, is showing an increasing flair for making the most of scoring opportunities. On the other wing, Kennedy, also perhaps a little short of sheer pace, has compensated by the intelligence and variety of his play. Full-back Adam was undoubtedly the *enfant terrible* of the XV, being capable of both brilliant and execrable play.

This 1961–62 season was the last in which the brothers David and John Marshall appeared for the 1st XV, and by mid November of the next season T. McClung's name had also disappeared off the team sheet (although he was tempted back into 1st XV duty for the 1964–65 season after a couple of enjoyable seasons playing for an all-star 3rd XV featuring several other illustrious veterans). This meant that by the end of the 1962–63 campaign J.A. Simson, S. Coughtrie and M.T.R Marwick were the only players to have featured in the 1955–56 championship winning team still involved in the 1st XV. This might have been the beginning of the end of a golden era in the club's history, but the momentum built up during the previous decade carried on for a few more years and the club's record at the end of this season was pretty good. Arctic conditions turned Raeburn Place into an ice rink from early January to mid-March, and meant that only 18 games were played throughout the winter, of which the Academicals won 13, drew two, and lost three. In the championship they won 12, drew one and lost two out of 15 matches played, to finish fourth in the table. Accies also reached the final of the Sevens at Jed-Forest, before running out of steam against Watsonians and going down 18-0.

The side was bolstered by the arrival of two very good back-row players from the school in the shape of H.M. White and R.J. Arneil – with the latter, in particular, making an immediate impact with his 'skill, fitness and enthusiasm'. Having been moved forward from the back-row, Macfie was another valuable member of the pack at hooker.

Behind the scrum P.J. Burnet played well, before an injury sustained against Greenock Wanderers on 5th January kept him out for the rest of the season, and Coughtrie was his usual brilliant self at scrum-half (with G.S. Morrison a more than capable understudy when he was away playing representative rugby).

The relatively experienced duo of second-rower J.K. Millar and prop J.B. Neill were the backbone of the side, and they deservedly attracted the attention of district and national selectors – with Millar becoming an Edinburgh regular and Neill winning his first full international appearance against England on 16 March 1963, having missed out on a cap when touring South Africa with the Scots in 1960.

No sooner had Neill made it into the national team than his natural leadership skills caused him to be thrust into the captaincy role in only his second cap, against

J.B. Neill

France at Murrayfield at the start of the 1964 International Championship. Scotland won that match 10-0, and a fortnight later, on 18 January, Neill led Scotland to a remarkable 0-0 draw against Wilson Wineray's seemingly unstoppable All Blacks.

This was a remarkable result. The tourists had lost 3-0 to Newport in the third game of their four-month tour, but had since won 22 consecutive matches – taking the scalps of Ireland, Wales and England along the way – and they were hotly tipped to become the first New Zealand side ever to achieve a Grand Slam over the Home Unions. After drawing at Murrayfield, they won their ten remaining matches, which included a 12-3 victory over France in Paris.

That season Neill also led the national team to victories over Ireland and England for the first time in 14 years, in what was Scotland's most successful season since their 1938 Triple Crown success.

An intelligent and mobile prop forward who could hold his own in the scrum but had no interest in destroying his opposite number, Neill played in seven cap internationals in total, leading the side in six of those matches. After hanging up his boots he was a long-serving member of the EAFC general committee and was club president from 1980 to 1982.

Accies v Edinburgh University at Craiglockhart

While Neill was playing a key role in one of the most successful periods in the Scottish national team's history, things were not going quite as smoothly at club level, where the changing of the guard was beginning to take its toll – although the 1963–64 season was by no means a disastrous campaign. With M.T.R.

Marwick and S. Coughtrie also now gone (albeit Marwick came back into the team towards the end of the '60s and captained the side for the 1968–69 season, 13 years after leading the club to championship success in 1955–56), the team lacked the poise and self-confidence which had underpinned the club's success for most of the previous decade. This was particularly the case during the early part of the season, when the Academicals were victorious but unconvincing against Kelvin-side Academicals (20-16 away) and then slumped to three consecutive defeats against Bradford (0-3 at home), Wanderers (0-6 away) and Watsonians for the first time in ten years (6-8 away).

Accies v Edinburgh Wanderers at Raeburn Place. J.B. Neill gets his toe to the ball.

A brief revival brought six straight victories, including wins over West of Scotland (11-3 at home) and Wasps (8-3 at home), both of which were achieved despite four key players – J.B. Neill, J.K. Millar, P.J. Burnet and J.D. Jardine – being away on Edinburgh duty. However, this form could not be sustained and the calendar year finished in depressing fashion, with the Academicals playing out a 'pointless and dreary draw' against Royal High School FP at the start of December, and then losing to Cambridge University (3-17), London Scottish (0-9) and Boroughmuir FP (8-11). In fairness, the Academicals apparently 'acquitted themselves well' but did not have the necessary firepower against strong Cambridge and London Scottish teams, and against Boroughmuir the side was missing J.B. Neill, P.J. Burnet and J.D. Jardine – who were playing in the final international trial at Murrayfield.

Accies vs Hawick at Raeburn Place. J.B. Neill leads the race to the ball.

Things improved in the New Year, with the pack beginning to come into its own, but apart from some moments of magic from Burnet, Jardine and J.A. Simson, the backs struggled to show the sort of incision needed if the team was to get back to where it had been a few years previously.

While 1st XV performances might have often fallen short of the high standard of previous year, the team's record in Scottish matches was good enough to place the Academicals fifth in the table (P: 19, W: 15, L: 4, D: 1, Points: 249-173). And with youngsters such as full-back R. Kemp and winger J.N. Sands beginning to establish themselves as key players in the 1st XV, the general health of the club seemed to be assured for the foreseeable future.

R. Kemp lines up a conversion

The 2nd XV had a very good season under the outstanding captaincy of A.R. Watson, winning 22 of 25 games played, and broke new ground by travelling to Paris to play Vincennes 1st XV, narrowly losing 6-9. Also, for the first time since the war, the club was able to field a 6th XV on a regular basis.

The good times continued to roll into the 1964–65 season. With I.M. Millar captaining the side and T. McClung coming out of retirement to provide some invaluable experience, the 1st XV won 21 of the 25 matches played against all opposition, and 18 out of 22 Scottish matches played, to once again finish fifth in the championship.

Probably the best and almost certainly the most exciting match of the season was against Heriot's, when the Academicals found themselves trailing 6-12 with little more than five minutes to go. They were pressing hard but were unable to penetrate the hard-tackling Heriot's defence, until Tommy McClung converted a long-range penalty and then in the final minutes J.L.W. Shirlaw gained his reward for tireless chasing of the loose ball, when he took advantage of a crack under pressure by the Heriot's defence to score between the posts. McClung made no mistake with the kick to capture a 14-12 victory.

At the end of the campaign, *The Chronicle* (July 1965) reported:

Although the 1st XV results over the season are not the best we have ever recorded they cannot often have been bettered and they are even more creditable when considered in conjunction with the difficulties under which they were achieved. Hardly a week passed without at least two changes being forced upon us, making the build-up of team spirit throughout the Club very difficult. In all, thirty-five different players wore the numbered jerseys during the course of the season.

That good results were recorded by our first four teams says much for the ability of our reserves not only to rise to the occasion, but also to sustain their effort when becoming virtually 'permanent entrants' through the back door. Despite this turmoil, the team spirit was created to such an extent that for W.F. Davidson's farewell game for the 4th XV the Selection Committee were presented with fifteen names which they amended at their peril.

Unfortunately, the 1st XV's four defeats were all at the hands of Scottish Clubs, two of them the joint unofficial champions. More effort might well have turned these games in our favour, particularly the 11-12 defeat by West of Scotland and the games v Gala and Glasgow Accies, where our second half rally deserted us.

It is not easy to criticise a team which under I.M. Millar's spirited leadership has been reasonably successful, but had the forwards worked with greater effort and cohesion they could have given the backs rather more of the 'good ball' so necessary to turn pressure into the points which could have made it an outstanding year.

So unsettled a team gave many players the opportunity to show their paces who might otherwise have had to blossom unseen. The experienced gained by some of our younger members like A.D.W. Hamilton, I.J. Shaw and E.D Stewart, added to the tremendous enthusiasm shown by such as R.J.

Arneil, who increases in stature as he gains experience, and J.L.W. Shirlaw, who took his chances and held his place in the team with some fine performances, will ease Mike Kennedy's task in building next year's team.

We cannot complete a review of the season without mentioning the contribution by our elder statesmen, J.A. Adam, T. McClung and J.K. Millar, whose experience and refusal to accept defeat, a habit they have acquired in recent years, carried us out of many a tight corner.

Despite having to deal with the knock-on effect of constant call-ups to the 1st XV, the 2nd XV had another good season. And the constant stream of enthusiastic young players emerging from the school at this time meant that for the first time the club was able to field a 7th XV in four matches.

Having returned midway through the previous season from an 18-month stint working in London, W.M.C. Kennedy took over the captaincy for the 1965–66 season, and the 1st XV won 18 out of 24 matches played against all opposition, and 14 out 22 matches played in the championship, to finish sixth in the table. At the end of the season Kennedy, J.A. Adam and J.B. Neill retired from 1st XV rugby, and the loss of these three seasoned campaigners undoubtedly contributed to the problems encountered during the subsequent campaign. With 13 wins, five draws and six losses in matches, the 1966–67 season was the first time since 1954–55 that the Academicals had finished outside the top five in the championship – coming in eleventh. And with 16 wins, six draws and eight losses from all 30 matches played, it was the last time in 15 years that the 1st XV managed a better than 50 per cent return for a season. Probably the most convincing performance of the season was the 14-0 victory over Trinity College, Dublin, at Raeburn Place on 25 February.

At the end of the season *The Chronicle* surmised:

> Over all, the XV have not had as successful a season as in recent years. The pack and the backs seemed to lack the necessary ability to convert pressure into points. We were unfortunate to lose near the end of the season both J.D. Jardine and A. Lyell, the former playing on many occasions for Edinburgh and the latter for the North and Midlands. Both have left Edinburgh.

The frequent demand for players for the 1st XV made life difficult for the 2nd XV, and that team also lost more games than it won. There were, however, no such

Accies win the Edinburgh Borderers Sevens at Lomond Park, 1966

problems for the 3rd XV, which was in the privileged position of being led by J.B. Neill, only two years after he had been Scottish captain. Fielding such luminaries as Tommy and Gilbert McClung, John and Bruce Adam, and George Simpson, they swept to 23 victories in 24 games, scoring 378 points and conceding only 100. Their only defeat was to Corstorphine 2nd XV in the first match of the season. The 4th, 5th and 6th XVs had some good results but lost more games than they won. A junior tour to the North-west of England with matches versus Fylde and Penrith was considered a major success although both matches were lost.

With I.M. Millar carrying on as captain for a second year, the 1st XV won ten and drew two out of 24 matches played in the 1967–68 championship to finish 14 out of 31 teams. In all 27 matches played, the Academicals won 12, lost 13 and drew two.

Accies v London Scottish, Boxing Day 1968

It was another disappointing season for the club, although Rodger Arneil's selection for Tom Kiernan's Lions squad which toured South Africa during the summer of 1968 at least provided some cause for celebration.

Reading through old issues of *The Chronicle*, the emphasis on the social side of the club through the second half of the 1960s and into the 1970s is obvious. It seems to have been a general trend throughout British rugby at the time. Clem Thomas in *The History of the British & Irish Lions* states: 'A major criticism of the [1968] tour was that, in common with most Lions teams of the past, they did not take matters too seriously, and that enjoyment of the experience of touring was the primary consideration, with rugby of secondary importance. This is perhaps an over-simplification, but in essence it had an element of truth, for there can be no question that most British teams overseas did not have the same inner driving force and commitment which seems to impel and activate the psyche of the antipodeans or the South Africans'.

One player who could never be accused of taking the game lightly was Arneil. From an early age he had exhibited the sort of passion for the game which set him apart from most of his peers, as his friend and former team mate George Menzies explains:

> When Rodger was at school he used to sleepwalk a bit and on this occasion it was the night before a big game so he was dreaming about what he was going to do the following afternoon. He ended up hurling himself through the window on the first floor landing of the house he was in. He had dreamt that he was tackling somebody, but there was nobody there, of course, because he was asleep, and he went right through the window and ended up in the garden below. Fortunately he didn't hurt himself.
>
> The thing which was the absolute cornerstone for Rodger was his determination. I was actually faster over 100 yards than he was during the athletics season but I never got to the ball before him in a rugby match – he was just so determined – and he would tackle anything.
>
> There were players like Adam Robson who had tremendous skill and were very good all-round players. Rodger wasn't a play-maker like Adam, he was the man who knocked the opposition players down, took the ball on and got to everything first. He was an absolute action man.
>
> But he had a very good rugby brain as well. He would think about the game and how he wanted to play it.

Arneil played for the club for seven seasons, between leaving the Academy in 1962 and moving to England early in the 1969–70 season. He earned his first cap against Ireland in a 14-6 defeat at Lansdowne Road on 24 February 1968, and his second cap three weeks later in a 6-8 defeat at home against England. Towards the end of the season he scored three tries for the Barbarians against Cardiff. It might not have been a vintage season for Scotland, who lost all four matches in that year's Inter-

R.J. Arneil

national Championship, but Arneil had done enough to persuade the Lions selectors to give him a go when Englishman Bryan West withdrew from the squad on the eve of the tour with a leg injury.

Despite being a late call-up Arneil played in all four Test matches in what was ultimately a frustrating tour for the Lions. He also flew out to New Zealand for the 1971 Lions tour, making five appearances but joining the party too late to seriously challenge for a Test place. After moving south for business reasons, Arneil joined Leicester, where he played for two years, then moved to Northampton at the start of the 1971–72 season. He played 22 times for Scotland before eventually dropping out of top-flight rugby when business commitments took him to Germany in the winter of 1972.

Robbie 'Babe' Kemp, who had been vice-captain in 1967–68, was the players' choice to take over as captain for the 1968-9 season, but it was felt that a more experience individual was required, so, in an effort to stop the rot, Mike Marwick, who had recently come out of retirement, was given the job after a vote at the 1968 club AGM 13 years after leading the club to championship success in 1956.

Marwick might have brought authority and experience, but the problems facing the club were far more fundamental than a simple lack of leadership on the park, and the team finished 14th in the championship for the second year running – this time with 9 wins and a draw from 19 matches played.

It had been a glorious period in the club's history. But the game and the world were changing, and it was becoming painfully apparent that Britain's oldest club was in danger of being left behind. From the giddy heights of 11 consecutive top-five finishes in the championship, it was always going to be a painful descent – but nobody could have envisaged just how dramatic the collapse would be.

CHAPTER TWENTY-FIVE

I started playing rugby down at Raeburn Place in 1967 and it was a very different game to what it is now. The wingers used to throw the ball in at the line-outs but never used to bother to learn the codes. Some of us were still using leather studded boots and often these were worn through and would have nails sticking out which could give nasty cuts when rucking. The brown leather ball was still in use, which got very heavy and slippy in wet weather and difficult to see in failing light, you had to make your own tee in the ground to kick the ball — none of these plastic things they use now.

Of course the scoring was different as well — only three points for a try plus two for a goal — so high-scoring games were not common. There were no blood replacements or subs so you were just patched up and sent back on, or the team played with less players — and I was always surprised that this usually did not seem to affect the game very much.

At Accies the captain and the vice-captain took training on a Tuesday and Thursday nights from 6.00 pm to 8.00 pm, and we only had the old floodlights along the Comely Bank Road side. The changing rooms upstairs were used on training nights, but on Saturdays these became the 1st XV and the visitors' changing rooms. One of my abiding memories was of stud on stone as the teams came down the stairs and ran out on the park on Saturdays. Everybody wanted to be in the firsts . . . to have this privilege of coming down the stairs.

The 1st XV wore white shorts and all the other teams wore dark blue shorts . . . and obviously the white shorts became a mixture of grey to white after use. Clean and polished boots were expected when you were selected for the 1st XV. The jerseys were made of heavy material which became even heavier in wet weather. Little or no kit was supplied by the club and you were expected to wash your own jersey.

Euan Macfie

GEORGE MENZIES JOKES THAT he would like to meet the man who captained the 1st XV of Trinity College, Dublin (the world's oldest club), during their worst ever season, if for no other reason than because that is the only man in the world who can overshadow his own plight as club captain at Raeburn Place during the 1969–70 season. That year, Menzies led the world's second oldest club into 25 matches, of which 20 were lost, one was drawn and only four were won. In the championship, a record of three wins, a draw and 16 losses in 20 matches played left the club equal to Stewart's FP on 17 percentage points – ahead of Greenock Wanderers but nobody else.

It would, of course, be grossly unfair to take this throwaway line too literally, for Menzies was by all accounts a hard-working and popular leader, who performed minor miracles in keeping morale high amongst the players despite the problems being encountered on the park. The fact that the 1st XV still had the confidence to defeat Oxford University 9-0 at home and Jed-Forest 14-8 away towards the end of the season stands better testament to his leadership skills than the bare statistics.

Tellingly, Edinburgh Academicals were by this time the only senior club in Scotland without a dedicated coach. Jake Young, a former international referee and P.E. master at the Academy, was doing an invaluable job training the players at this point, and he would continue to do so when required right through until the late 1970s, but his input was restricted to fitness work.

On his appointment as club captain in May 1970, J.A. Crerar told the club's AGM that finding a coach should be a priority, but almost a decade had passed before this happened. John Huins, the coach of the school 1st XV and a great character who had scored an astonishing 85 first-class tries during the 1952–53 season (73 for St Luke's College and 12 for Neath and in Welsh trials) and was regular reserve in attendance numerous times for Wales, briefly filled the role of 'coaching adviser' at the start of the 1971–72 season; Malcolm Jack, a teacher at Loretto, fulfilled a similar role the following year; at various points during the early to mid '70s, John Douglas, the Edinburgh Wanderers player, helped out after doing his own training at Murrayfield on Thursday evenings; and John Frame leant his considerable experience and expertise from around 1976 onwards – but it wasn't until the start of the 1979–80 season that David Maxwell became the club's first official coach.

The SRU had set up a coaching advisory panel towards the end of the Sixties, but it wasn't until midway through the 1971 Five Nations campaign that Bill Dickinson was brought in to put the national team through its paces. This only happened after some serious hand-wringing by the notoriously conservative

Murrayfield hierarchy, and even then Dickinson was given the rather mealy-mouthed title of 'adviser to the captain' and told he would have no say in selection. So these were still the early days of rugby coaching, and there is no doubt that the club would have managed to stumble on had the far more serious issue of playing numbers not become a pressing concern.

By 1971, 91 per cent of British households had a television which allowed the likes of the great Welsh side of this era, and John Dawes' victorious 1971 Lions, to demystify the game for people who had not gone to rugby-playing schools. Full employment and increased mobility – there were five times as many cars on the road in 1970 than there were in 1950 – had helped drive a rapid grassroots expansion of the game, and the number of clubs affiliated to the SRU grew from 110 to 207 between 1965 and 1975, with the likes of Boroughmuir, Highland and Haddington emerging as genuine forces in the Scottish game. Edinburgh Academicals had once been the biggest fish in a very small pond, but with each passing year that pond was becoming more of a lake and the things which had previously helped Britain's oldest club to prosper were now holding it back.

The Robbins Report in 1963 had dramatically changed the education landscape in Britain by initiating a rapid increase in the number of school-leavers going on to university. With more and more universities being created all over Britain, many of which were providing specialised courses, the number of Academy boys going into further education outside Edinburgh increased from the mid 1960s onwards. Furthermore, cultural and economic changes meant that students were less likely to return to Edinburgh once they had finished their degree. All of this inevitably had an effect on a closed club like EAFC.

Another concern was that encouraging other sports and leisure activities at school meant rugby no longer had the grip on youngsters at the Academy it once had, which also affected the number of boys joining the club.

Only seven boys joined the club directly from school at the start of the 1969–70 season and only eight in the 1970–71 season. With 42 playing members retiring at the end of the 1969–70 season, the number of regular playing members in the club had dropped from 115 during the 1968–69 season to 67 for the 1970–71 season. Less than five years earlier, the club had been fielding seven teams on a fairly regular basis, but now getting four teams on the park had become a major struggle. The bottom line was that the club no longer had the strength in depth necessary to compete with the top teams in Scotland.

The gravity of the situation was being brought into sharp focus by the prospect of league rugby being introduced in Scotland in the near future. Norman Mair, the influential rugby journalist for *The Scotsman* and younger brother of former Academical captain Colin, was writing about the benefits which would come from introducing a more organised structure for rugby in Scotland, and at the Scottish Rugby Union's AGM, the general committee was authorised by the clubs to produce a scheme for 'competitive club rugby'. While the Academicals were in favour of this route forward in principle, the committee were not oblivious to the possibility that the club would be left behind in this new environment unless major steps were taken to revitalise the club's playing resources. Club and school loyalty would be tested to the limit if the Academicals ended up languishing outside the top flight of whatever structure ended up being introduced.

The issue of widening the club's player base was first raised at committee level on 25 March 1970, and at the next general committee meeting less than a month later a wide-ranging discussion took place, with the secretary recording:

> The idea of methods [of] increasing the Club membership with the object of increasing the depth of the playing membership and hence improving the chances of producing a really first class 1st XV was discussed. Other advantages would be more efficient use of club premises and, with more members and people using the bar, strengthening the club finances. The discussion was generally in favour of some expansion, possibly by opening the membership to those eligible to play for the Scottish Wayfarers. Full amalgamation with some club such as Edinburgh Wanderers was mentioned.

Then, on 21 October 1970, after another lengthy discussion, it was decided that the secretary should write to the central Academical Club detailing 'the concern over the falling membership and preparing them for any action which this committee might consider necessary'. The central club urged the football club not to be too hasty and asked to be given a full rationale of any decision made, accompanied with a list of alternative courses of action and the reasons why these proposals were discarded. In response to this a sub-committee – consisting of W.D. Hart (chairman), J.M. Martin, M.T.R. Marwick, G.M. Cormack and J.A. Crerar – was set up to decide on the best way forward.

That working group produced a confidential report in December 1970 which outlined four possible ways forward and explained the rationale behind recommending or rejecting each of those courses of action.

The possibility of carrying on as before was dismissed out of hand, as the sub-committee believed that the club needed 100 playing members to run the five teams it deemed necessary for the 1st XV to be competitive among the top teams in Scotland; and with fewer than ten players joining the club from the Academy in each of the last two years it was felt that the school was now, simply, too narrow a supply line if the club was to recover the ground that had been lost in recent seasons. 'If no change is made the club will probably grow weaker and with competitive league rugby on the horizon this could result in the end of the EAFC as a force in Scottish rugby', the sub-committee warned.

The paper then looked at the possibility of allowing restricted open membership, whereby all members of the Scottish Wayfarers Club – composed of former pupils from Fettes, Glenalmond, Loretto, Merchiston Castle as well as the Edinburgh Academy – would be allowed to join the club.

The attraction of this proposal was that it drew on a membership of 'similar character and background and would therefore not alter the nature of the club'. And as the Wayfarers played together at times in exhibition and friendly matches there was a degree of familiarity which might have eased the integration process. However, it was pointed out that the majority of Wayfarers in Edinburgh already played for either the University or Wanderers, and it was argued that there was no obvious reason why these players would choose to join the Academicals, especially if these clubs were already offering a higher standard of rugby, especially 'as the advantage of belonging to a club with a pavilion and a bar seems only a marginal attraction for a keen ambitious player'. Even if this option was to result in the desired increase in membership, the sub-committee felt that the recruitment of Wayfarers would be a slow process unsuited to the urgency of the problem. There was also concern about the impact this move would have on the future health of Wanderers, and the question of whether the name 'Edinburgh Academicals' could be retained in the title of such a club was also discussed.

Next, the possibility of the Academicals becoming a fully open club was considered. This would mean that any player who wished to join the club could do so, provided he was proposed and seconded by current members. In contrast to the Wayfarers proposal, the prospect of non-playing members was not even considered, and concerns were once again expressed about how easy it would be to retain the 'Edinburgh Academicals' name. It was pointed put that three clubs in Edinburgh – Boroughmuir, Trinity Academicals and Leith Academicals – had already gone open, and suggested that none of them had yet accrued any tangible benefit from doing so. When taking into account the rather mediocre playing record of recent seasons, it was felt that there was no reason why EAFC would be regarded as a more attractive proposition to prospective players than any of the other 'open' clubs available to them – 'although the club tradition and history might have some small pull'.

The sub-committee's final analysis of this option was:

> There are or will be too many Open Clubs and this will only result in too many clubs chasing too few players and hence the gain in playing membership from going Fully Open will be small and problematical.

The final option considered was that the club joined with another club in the Edinburgh area, and with the other former pupil clubs being ruled out because 'they have their own grounds and pavilions and the problems of union would probably be difficult', it was quickly made clear that Edinburgh Wanderers – ahead of up-and-coming junior clubs such as Dalkeith, Lasswade and Corstorphine – would be the ideal club to amalgamate with so far as the sub-committee was concerned.

It was pointed out that the two clubs played together during and for a short time after the Second World War, and that as Wanderers had a 'fair percentage' of Wayfarer members there should be no problem in integrating the two sets of players. With four senior teams as well as a colts XV, the Wanderers were in a strong position to help combat the recent drop in playing numbers at Raeburn Place.

There had already been unofficial contact with Wanderers and it was understood that 'they would like to obtain a more secure home with pavilion facilities', as opposed to the leased accommodation they were operating out of at Murrayfield. Wanderers also felt that their future as a combined club would be more secure if they had the Academy as a limited but continuous source of players.

This was clearly the preferred option:

The Committee definitely feel that in considering a combined club union with the Wanderers is definitely the first choice and only if this proposal was rejected should consideration be given to one of the Open Junior Clubs, or some other club.

The report concluded:

After consideration of the various options in going 'Open' the Committee are of unanimous opinion that the combined-club approach, i.e. joining with an existing club, is the only certain way to get the club back to a playing membership sufficient to make a strong and viable club, within the time available.

The Committee would therefore recommend that an approach be made to the Edinburgh Wanderers with the intention of creating an Edinburgh Academical-Wanderers (Rugby) Football Club.

A combined club with its considerably greater membership would be financially sounder and this is of considerable importance if Raeburn Place is to be maintained at its present level or made into a better and more active clubhouse.

If union with Wanderers was achieved the Committee see the development of a really strong club, which should certainly maintain a place in the 1st Division of any league. Also from the union a really good and attractive fixture list, outside of the league commitment, could be built up by using the best fixtures of each club.

Finally the Committee would point out that the pattern of rugby football in Scotland is on the change. The aim is to produce a higher standard of play and to achieve this the creation of fewer, larger and stronger clubs is one solution recommended by the SRU. The EAFC has always been one of the pioneer clubs in Scottish Rugby and in this changing situation we should be prepared to give a lead even if this action is created by necessity. It is better to do this than allow the proud name of the EAFC to sink into the obscurity of 2nd class rugby.

The general committee accepted the sub-committee's findings and a meeting between representatives of the two clubs was organised for 11 February 1971, at which a draft proposal for the formation of a new club was prepared. EAFC was represented by W.D. Hart, M. Martin, M. Marwick, M. Cormack, J. Crerar and T. Straton.

At the meeting it was explained that the Grange/Academical Trust had no problem with the proposal so long as the use of Raeburn Place remained the same. It was also explained that the Academy had no objection as long as the school's relationship with Raeburn Place wasn't altered and that boys leaving the school as Academicals had a rugby club available to them. It was accepted that the new club's representative on the Academicals Club Council must be an Academical, and as an ex-officio member of the Council it would be impossible for the field convener to be a non-Academical. A sub-committee was set up to draft a constitution for the new club and it was hoped that this document could be ratified by the membership of both clubs by July 1971, so that the fixture secretary of the new club could make arrangements for the 1972–73 season. It was envisaged that the new club would officially come into being on 30 April 1972.

It was also agreed that two or three pitches should be retained at Murrayfield for use by the new club; that Ray Tod would be asked to sound out the SRU about their view on the merger, and on the likelihood of the new club being admitted into the top division of any new league structure which might come into being during the next few years; and that the Academy art master should be asked about the design of a strip which would incorporate the colours of both clubs (ie. red, black, light blue and white), failing which it was agreed white shorts and a 'self-colour jersey' would be adopted as the club's colours.

There was a lengthy discussion about the name this new club should go by. Eventually it was decided that two suggestions should be put to the clubs, with the first being the recommendation of the joint committee:

1. East of Scotland FC (Incorporating EAFC and EWFC). [The statement in brackets was regarded as important because it acknowledged the origins of the club, and would prevent the formation of splinter clubs using these names.]
2. Edinburgh Academical/Wanderers FC

At the next EAFC general committee meeting (17 February 1971) it was decided to host an informal conference where the reasoning behind the proposed merger would be explained to club members. This took place on 10 March and afterwards it was estimated that a marginal majority of the 53 club members present were against the proposal. However, the committee remained confident that they could persuade a majority to vote in favour of their proposal and seemed fairly laid-back about the suggestion that a merger could lead to a high number of current members delivering a body blow by resigning from the club before this new venture had even got off the ground. It was decided that a notice calling a special general meeting should be drafted, which 'should explain clearly the situation leading to the proposals and should be based on the Report to the Committee of December 1970'.

The club voted on the merger at an SGM at Raeburn Place on the evening of 28 April 1971. The vote took place after a wide-ranging and occasionally heated discussion amongst the 89 members present.

After R. Tod had given a brief summary of the general committee's reasons for proposing the merger, A.D.W. Hamilton spoke about this being an opportunity to reinvigorate the playing membership of the club.

In response, B.A. Stenhouse argued that the committee's case had not really been made and expressed concern about the club no longer being a genuine 'old boys' institution for school-leavers. He believed more could be done to stimulate interest in the club and suggested that fuller reports of the club activities could be printed in *The Chronicle*. He finished by labelling the proposal a 'sell-out' to Wanderers. H.M.A. Rowan agreed, arguing that the position was not as desperate as was being suggested.

J.A. Crerar and J.G. Williamson then spoke in favour of the motion. Crerar said that a coaching committee had been considered, but no Academicals were available. He had spoken to the boys at school, but they just did not stay in Edinburgh to continue their education. The merger was necessary if the club were to be a force in the first division of the new league structure, he concluded. But A.M. Mowat countered that the junior teams were the backbone of the club and these teams did not play to be in the first division. He accepted that a larger player pool was required but preferred the idea of going 'open' to merging with another club.

G.W.S. Presslie spoke about the transformation which overtook the squash club when the squash league was introduced and said that he believed that the same could happen to the football club.

In supporting the motion, G.M. Menzies (senior) pointed out that in order to make up the numbers the 4th XV had been calling on non-Academical players. He stressed that members did leave Edinburgh for university and work and urged the club to act decisively in the face of this crisis.

C.J.R. Mair agreed with many of the points which had been made, but felt that the club was being railroaded into this action by a threat which had not yet materialised. He suspected that some of the trends might reverse themselves and that the league might not come into being. In any event, he would prefer the club to remain and fight for survival. If it had to die then it should do so with the flag flying. J.L. Paterson also spoke against the motion.

P.J. Wilmhurst said he was against the merger but might support going 'open', and he doubted that the FP clubs which had already gone 'open' were faring as badly as was being suggested. And Colonel Simson suggested that a 'public relations officer' be appointed to find out why the club was failing to recruit new members. In his view, the 1st XV had lots of potential and if money was a problem then he suggested that the Academical community would answer any appeal readily.

At this point the president decided that the debate had run its course and called for the ballot to take place.

The motion was:

In view of the recent decline in playing membership the Edinburgh Academical Football Club should merge its membership and assets with those of the Edinburgh Wanderers Football Club, should the latter club be in favour of so doing.

The general committee had previously decided on a 100-vote quorum for the ballot and that a majority of 75 per cent was needed to pass the motion.

The votes were as follows:

	For	Against	Abstain
Postal votes:	101	13	3
Ballot at the meeting:	36	53	0
Total:	137 (66.5%)	66 (32.04%)	3 (1.46%)

It had been a close-run thing; much closer than those opposed to the merger had anticipated, as John Paterson explains:

The committee had debated it and they saw it as the way forward, and having concluded that amongst themselves they looked to drive it through. But what they didn't appreciate was that the grassroots players were actually rather against it. It became a big conversation point in the bar and the feeling was definitely that we didn't want it.

Different people were against it for different reasons. My position was that we might have been reduced to four teams, but if we merged with Wanderers then we would only have two pitches, so more often than not teams would be playing at Murrayfield and the numbers would have dwindled very quickly. We just didn't have a big enough ground for it. I'd seen other mergers and while they were great for the first two years, with these new clubs able to run sometimes as many as thirteen teams, before long you were back to where you started from, if you were lucky. Whatever their reasons it seemed as if the vast majority of the membership were against the motion.

And because of that the *anti*'s were fairly relaxed under the assumption that it wasn't going to go through, so we maybe didn't work hard enough to mobilise members to vote against the motion. What we hadn't taken into account was that the Committee had written to all the club members and not surprisingly a huge postal vote came in favour of the merger – because when you elect your council you take their advice.

Immediately after the vote, the general committee held a meeting and decided to leave future discussions on the way forward to the incoming committee which would be elected at the next AGM in just under a month's time. It was suggested that the entire committee should resign, but this was considered neither justified nor practicable. It was also noted that several letters had been received from club members regarding the proposal, with one from Major N.G. Salvesen pledging to give the club £1,000 on condition that that the merger was cancelled.

At the club's AGM, on 26 May 1971, several leading members of the committee resigned their posts, including R. Todd after two years as president, A.P. Young as secretary, A.S. Watson as assistant secretary, W.M.C. Kennedy as lottery organiser, and G.M.H. Cormack, M.T.R. Marwick and J.B. Neill from the main committee.

At the same meeting, the outgoing president congratulated club captain

J.A. Crerar and vice-captain R.K. Sloan for their role in helping the club come through a difficult season with a fairly respectable record. The 1st XV had played 30 games, winning 15, losing 12 and drawing three. In the 'unofficial championship' the team had played 25 games, winning 14, losing nine and drawing two, to finish eleventh out of 33.

The president also spoke about the aborted scheme to join with Wanderers, pointing out that if the whole saga achieved nothing more than to stir up some enthusiasm and a few new ideas about how to move forward then it had been worthwhile. The threat of amalgamation had been staved off and for a while a feel-good factor permeated through the club. But the reality of the situation was that the problems the club had spent the last 14 months wrestling with were still there – and some sort of drastic action would have to be taken sooner rather than later if things were ever going to get any better.

CHAPTER TWENTY-SIX

A game for gentlemen in all classes, but never a bad sportsman in any class.
Bishop Carey, circa. 1890

THERE WAS CLEARLY A DESIRE within the club to harness some of the momentum and enthusiasm for the club which had been generated by the proposed merger, and the committee approached the 1971–72 season with admirable zeal.

Club captain John Crerar had a meeting with the boys from the top two teams at the Academy which he believed had been very positive; and he undertook to write to all playing members of the club, and boys leaving school, in an effort to encourage as many potential players as possible along to training. W.D. Hart, the new club president, said he would write to the non-playing members of the club before the start of the season, and in September 1971 an article appeared in *The Chronicle* urging the Accie community to get behind the club.

> . . . the need for recruits from the School [is] more urgent than ever before. It is not only the star performers that are required – the infusion of young players into lower teams is just as necessary.
>
> The Club facilities at Raeburn Place are first class. If, however, they are to be maintained or improved, the social side of the Football Club must become more vigorous and active. This can only be achieved if the non-playing members come to Raeburn Place on Saturdays to lend support on the touchline and then join their fellow members in the Pavilion after the game. The Club has recently appointed an Entertainments Convener to try to strengthen this side of the activities. This season the monthly informal dances have been a great success and for once have been profitable as well as enjoyable.
>
> The Special Meeting on 28 April resulted in a larger gathering of Football Club members at Raeburn Place than there had been for many a long day. If, as was apparent, the members wish to see the Academical Football Club continue as a leading force in Scottish Rugby, let them turn

their sentiments into actual and interested support, as only then will the future of the Club be assured.

Stirring words, but by the middle of August only three school-leavers had been to pre-season training, and a month later it was noted in the general committee's minute book that another three of last year's schoolboys were playing for Lismore.

It hadn't taken long for the old problem of player apathy to resurface. A number of players had been asked to captain the junior teams, but none were prepared to make that commitment, until mid September when Carfrae Paterson said he would lead the 2nd XV, and H.M.A. Rowan agreed to take charge of the 3rd XV on an informal basis. In October 1971 it was suggested that a club newsletter might be an effective way to raise morale within the club and encourage members to become more actively involved, but nothing more ever came of the idea.

On 24 November, John Crerar reported to the general committee that although five teams had been raised on a few occasions, the numbers at training had fallen away and the general attitude of some players, especially in matters like calling off, left a lot to be desired. He wondered if players were happy to play social rugby, and said that he felt the idea of merging with another club, or going open, should be looked into again. He added that he was not going to raise this issue officially yet because he was going to send a letter to the players and wanted to see if this would have any effect on the general attitude and numbers at training.

The season had got off to another inauspicious start with eight defeats, two draws and four wins from 14 matches played up to the end of November, including heavy losses away to Wanderers (29-6) on 2 October and at home to West of Scotland (40-0) on 23 October. In January 1972, *The Chronicle* was complaining that the most disappointing feature of the Academicals' 13-16 defeat to Leith Academicals earlier in the season was 'the almost total lack of supporters on the touchline'.

By the end of the season the 1st XV had played 31 matches, winning 11, losing 18 and drawing two, having scored 272 points against 437 conceded. In the unofficial championship the club finished 25th out of 33, with seven wins, two draws and 16 losses in 25 matches played. Injuries had been a factor, with the 1st XV finishing with 14 players in at least eight matches, but this could not excuse the all-round mediocrity which so often characterised the team's performances. The fact that the club was no longer being invited to Melrose and Hawick Sevens was indicative of the extent to which its standing in Scotland had plummeted. The 2nd XV had played 28 matches, winning ten and drawing three, while the 3rd and 4th XVs had never been able to field settled teams.

It had hardly been a vintage year, but the club member who reviewed the season in *The Chronicle* did his best to put a positive spin on the 1971–72 season:

The results this season have been disappointing, but there have been many satisfying moments.

The 1st XV generally defended well and, in losing eighteen games, they had only one really heavy defeat, 0-40, against West of Scotland. Compared with some other results throughout the country this score might almost be termed respectable. In speaking of defence, Norman Morrison and Mark Tulloch must be mentioned for their cover tackling, which had a touch of finality about it, and must have given great encouragement to other hard-pressed colleagues. In holding Hawick to 0-6 and beating Cambridge University – including thirteen 'blues' – 7-6, this side certainly showed great resilience and tenacity when faced with almost constant pressure.

It was unfortunate that few scoring chances went the way of wingers Duncan Mennie and Douglas Stephenson. Both showed that they have the speed to exploit reasonable openings and this was on no occasion more apparent than in the victory over Oxford University. Mennie showed his opportunism by chasing and gathering his own kick ahead before scoring, and Stephenson scored two memorable tries from his own half by out-running the Oxford cover defence in two touch-line dashes.

A late cancellation by Cambridge University of our return fixture did not prevent the 1st XV from travelling south. This caused considerable embarrassment to our hosts, for several college fields were found to be eminently playable. Eventually a game of 'coarse soccer' was arranged, and the whole weekend turned out to be an unqualified success. Sadly, the Irish trip was cancelled, but a 'social visit' was made to the Inverness area by an 'A' XV and a Junior XV. The rugger was not greatly enjoyed, the Juniors being mis-matched, but once again, as far as social activity was concerned, this tour certainly did not fail to get off the ground.

Speaking at the AGM on 14 June 1972, W.D. Hart acknowledged that the social side of the club was going well, with the dances at Raeburn Place being 'almost too well supported'. However, this made it all the more frustrating that non-playing members were so reluctant to get behind the team on Saturday afternoons.

> Support of the XV has again been lamentable. After last year's decision to go it alone it had been hoped that some improvement in support would have occurred, but this hasn't been the case. Thank you to the loyal few who have turned up regularly to provide support both on the touchline and in the pavilion – I hope they would be joined by more club members during the coming season.

It wasn't to be. The 1972–73 season started off in a depressingly familiar vein, both on and off the field. With Tony Hamilton as captain, and Malcolm Jack, a teacher at Loretto, helping coach the side, the 1st XV lost 20 out of the 26 games played by the end of January, which included heavy defeats to Boroughmuir (41-7 away), Gala (52-8 away), Wasps (42-0 away) and Hawick (56-9 away).

On 31 January, a special committee meeting was called by Hamilton, at which he outlined a bleak future for the club unless radical action was taken soon. He explained that recent results had been very poor and that there was now a considerable gulf between the Academicals and the leading clubs in the country. While injuries to senior players had not helped the situation, the lack of strength in depth within the player pool at the club meant that the absence of the likes of John Crerar, Duncan Mennie, Mike Cochran and Derek Emslie had been far more damaging than should have been the case.

He pointed out that the club's recent record meant that there was a good chance that the Academicals would end up in division three when the new league structure was introduced for the 1973–74 season, and that would have serious ramifications on the ability to recruit the best players from the school. Three senior players had already indicated to him that they were probably going to play elsewhere next season. Competitive rugby was going to make the strong stronger and the weak weaker.

Three possible routes forward were suggested:

1. Opt-out and become social first and rugby second.
2. Go open.
3. Merge with Edinburgh Wanderers.

Having already spoken unofficially to representatives from Wanderers, Hamilton had ascertained that they were still interested in joining forces, leading him to propose that 'the committee make official contact with Edinburgh Wanderers with a view to merging subject to players and members' approval'. This was seconded by J.A. Crerar.

G.M. Menzies said he would like the club to explore the possibility of merging with another club. J.L. Paterson, J.N. Kennedy, D.B.S. Stephenson and G.J.M. Graham said they were against the merger but liked the idea of going open. And W. Menzies, who had recently joined the committee as assistant honorary match secretary, said that he was against the merger but wasn't totally opposed to the idea of going open if something had to be done. The remainder of the committee – W.D. Hart, G.M.H. Cormack, A.F. Gardiner, H.M. Inglis, M.T.R. Marwick, T. McClung and G.W.S. Presslie – all said that they were interested in hearing what the players thought.

It was decided that there should be a meeting of the players after training on Tuesday, 13 February, where Tony Hamilton would propose the merger, John Paterson would propose going open and George Menzies would propose the possibility of merging with another club. Nobody was prepared to argue for the status quo. Of the 62 players at this meeting, eight voted for the merger with Edinburgh Wanderers, five voted for no change, five abstained, six left before the vote and 38 voted for limited associate membership whilst retaining the name of the club.

In view of this the proposal to merge with Wanderers was withdrawn, and it was agreed to pursue the 'limited open' route as a matter of urgency. Letters were sent to the president of the Board of Directors of the Academy and to the president and secretary of the Academical Club, advising them of the club's new position and asking about the viability of the scheme, with particular regard to the use of Raeburn Place and the use of the Academical name and colours. It was decided not to write to the non-playing membership just yet so as to avoid press coverage until a definite plan had been formulated.

The proposal did not meet with any immediate opposition from either the

Academy or the Academical Club, although the latter made it clear that their support would be dependent on four key conditions:

1. There needed to be a definite percentage limit to the number of associate members allowed to join the club.
2. A constitution was needed.
3. There should be a limited percentage of associate members allowed to serve on the committee.
4. The school's access to Raeburn Place should not be altered.

A sub-committee was set up to draft the new constitution for the club which needed to be ready in time for the club's AGM at the end of May. The key points in this document were:

I. The name of the Club shall be [remain] the Edinburgh Academical Football Club.

II. The Club shall consist of Honorary Members, Ordinary Members and Associate Members.

III. Honorary Members shall be such persons as shall be elected by the Club in General Meeting. Honorary Members shall be entitled to all the privileges of Membership without being liable to make any contribution therefor to the Funds of the Club.

IV. Ordinary Members who may be playing or non-playing Members shall be Members of The Edinburgh Academical Club duly qualified by payment of an Annual Subscription as defined in Article VII.

V. Associate Members who may be playing or non-playing Members shall be such other persons duly qualified by payment of Annual Subscription as defined in Article VII and who have, in the form required by the General Committee of the Club, been proposed and seconded by Ordinary Members of the Club and elected by the General Committee of the Club subject to the following conditions:

(i) The names of the persons proposed as Associate Members shall be displayed in a conspicuous place in the Pavilion at Raeburn Place for at least four weeks prior to their election. An interval of not less than four weeks shall elapse between the nomination and the election of such Associate Member. In the event of any Ordinary Member having objection to the election of a proposed Associate Member, he may state in writing his objection to the Secretary of the Club within three weeks of the display of the proposal of such a prospective Associate Member. In the event of there being ten such written objections by Ordinary playing Members to the proposal of an Associate playing Member, such proposed Associate playing Member shall not be elected. In the event of there being ten such written objections by Ordinary Members, playing or non-playing, to the proposal of an Associate non-playing Member, such proposed Associate non-playing Member shall not be elected.

(ii) The numbers of Associate playing Members elected to Associate playing Membership in accordance with the foregoing provisions of this article shall not exceed 30% of the Ordinary Playing Members for the time being. If and so long as the number of Associate playing Members shall be or shall exceed 30% of the Ordinary playing Members, no further Associate playing Members shall be elected.

(iii) The number of Associate non-playing Members elected in accordance with the foregoing provisions of this article shall not exceed 30 per cent of the Ordinary non-playing members for the time being. If and so long as the number of Associate non-playing Members shall be or shall exceed 30 per cent of the Ordinary non-playing Members, no further Associate playing Members shall be elected.

VI. Any member whose conduct is in the opinion of the General Committee calculated to injure the Club in any respect may be expelled from the Club provided that not less than three quarters of the General Committee are in favour of the expulsion.

VII. The Annual Subscription payable in advance by Members shall be decided by the Club at the Annual General Meeting or at an Extraordinary General Meeting called for the purpose. In addition to such Annual Subscription, Associate Members will pay annually such amount as at the material time forms the Subscription for Ordinary Members of The Edinburgh Academical Club. Such additional Subscription sums payable by Associate Members shall be collected by the Treasurer of the Club and remitted to the Treasurer of The Edinburgh Academical Club and used by him to offset The Academical Club's contribution to the running costs of Raeburn Place.

The season finished on a positive tenor, with the 1st XV winning seven out of their last eight fixtures, but this did not divert attention from the fundamental problems facing the club. League rugby was about to be launched at the SRU's AGM, so it was now or never for the club if it wanted to give itself any chance of having a future at the top end of the Scottish game.

The club was still managing to get four teams out on a regular basis, and that season five teams were fielded on eight occasions and a 6th XV once – but none of these sides managed to win more games than they lost. The thriving social scene at Raeburn Place was very helpful in attracting 'social' players, but the lack of genuine 1st XV contenders willing to train regularly meant that remaining competitive with the top clubs in Scotland was becoming an impossibility.

At the club's AGM, on 30 May 1973, there was, as expected, a wide-ranging discussion on the proposal to go 'open', with a number of older members of the club in particular seeking assurances that the interests of the school had been considered and that the traditions of the club had been safeguarded. However, when it came to the vote, the 46 members present were emphatically in favour of the committee's recommendation, that: 'The Football Club allows non Academicals to become Associate Members on the terms of the proposed constitution' – with 41 members voting for the motion, three voting against and two abstentions.

Pat Burnet then proposed an amendment to the new constitution, which was seconded by Bruce Adam, that ten players could veto a playing associate's application and ten non-playing members could veto a non-playing associate's application, provided they made this objection in writing to the secretary before the application has been approved by the committee.

Before the meeting ended at 9.42 p.m., Sandy Gardiner, the new president, reminded those present that the new football club constitution still had to be passed by the central Academical Club, and he urged all football club members to attend that organisation's AGM on 19 July, to help vote through the associate membership proposals. He needn't have worried: the parent club duly ratified the new constitution.

It was a seminal evening in the history of Britain's oldest rugby club, but if anyone at Raeburn Place believed that this was going to be an instant panacea to the problems of the last few years then they were sadly mistaken.

CHAPTER TWENTY-SEVEN

We used to go up to the Highland Sevens and that was always wild. I remember
going to put the ball in the scrum one year and the smell of alcohol was awful.
Our forwards were Doug Moffat, George Menzies and Mark Tulloch, and all of
a sudden this tremendous stramash erupted. I thought: 'What on earth have the
opposition done to our boys?' The scrum broke up and our three forwards were in
a full fist fight . . . with each other.

Rob Blair

ELGAR HOPKINS, ALONG WITH Stuart Jeffray, was one of the club's first associate
members at the start of the 1973–74 season, but it was some time later before he
realised that he was blazing a new trail:

> I was born and brought up in Wales, and I went to university in Birmingham.
> When I was there I played rugby with Geoff Ballantine, who had been at the
> Academy before finishing his schooling at Glenalmond. When I finished my
> degree his father offered me a job with Lizars optometrists – as it was then –
> which was great. When I got to Edinburgh I said that I needed to find some-
> where to play rugby and Geoff suggested Raeburn Place. The rest is history.
>
> I got a great welcome. I didn't even realise that I was the first 'open'
> member. I instantly made a lot of great friends – people like Mark Tulloch,
> Sandy Macrae, Gerry Sim – and the reason I stayed so long in Edinburgh, in
> fact the reason I am still here now, is largely because I instantly felt right at
> home at Raeburn Place.

The welcome might have been warm, but in these early days of being an 'open'
club, new members such as Hopkins were few and far between. There had already
been a number of non-Academicals – including Bill Bruce and Chris Woods –
turning out for teams lower down the club before it had officially gone 'open', and
for them the new constitution simply formalised their status at Raeburn Place. But
these players tended to fit into the 'social' category, and getting hold of individuals

with genuine 1st XV aspirations was a very different matter. With the general committee determined not to do anything which might be construed as 'poaching', the club was reliant on suitable individuals turning up at Raeburn Place off their own bat. In August 1974 the general committee noted that 'one or two prospective associates' were training at Raeburn Place, but rather than ask these players if they were interested in playing for the club during the forthcoming season it was decided to take a rather less direct tack and leave application forms lying around Raeburn Place in the hope that these individuals would fill one out.

The start of the 1973–74 season really was a foray into the unknown for the club. Not only were they taking their first tentative steps as an 'open' club, but they were doing so in the context of a brand new league structure, which had finally been introduced after several years of procrastination by the SRU. The club had been allocated a position in the second of seven National Divisions, each consisting of 12 teams.

This inaugural league campaign got off to a decent start, with the team winning four out of the seven games played by the start of December. The team's victories were over Aberdeen GS FP (19-12 away), RHS FP (18-7 at home), Ayr (14-6 at home) and Hutcheson's GS FP (9-4 at home); while the losses were to Dunfermline (10-21 at home), Stewart's Melville FP (15-0 away) and Kelso (3-12 away). The match against Jed-Forest match had been postponed.

There was then a three-month hiatus from league action, during which time the club was able to play some of the more attractive fixtures from the traditional fixture card – including Boroughmuir on 22 December (6-3 win at home), London Scottish on Boxing Day (39-0 defeat at home), Hawick on 12 January (37-9 defeat at home), Cambridge University on 19 January (22-12 defeat away) and Gala on 2 February (56-6 defeat at home).

When league action resumed in mid February the promising form of the first half of the season could not be replicated, with only one more league point being collected in the four remaining fixtures – thanks to a 10-10 draw with Hillhead HS FP at Raeburn Place. The three defeats were against Selkirk (6-3 at home), Edinburgh University (6-3 away) and Jed-Forest (37-3 away). A seventh-place finish out of 12 teams in Division Two of the National League might not have felt like much to get excited about at the time, but given the trials and tribulations which were to follow it could be regarded, with the benefit of hindsight, as a major success.

'Original rules'
match played at
Murrayfield as part
of the SRU
Centenary Sevens
celebrations, 1973

An innovation introduced this year in an effort to increase competitiveness throughout the club was an 'Order of Merit' measuring the success of each team. The 4th XV, captained by the irrepressible Billy Menzies, raced into an early lead in this competition, and stayed there for the remainder of the season to win the much coveted barrel of beer.

The final placings were:

Place	Team	% of games won
1	4th XV	57.17
2	3rd XV	45.65
3	2nd XV	32.00
4	1st XV	24.07
5	5th XV	15.38

The 1974–75 season got off to an encouraging start with home wins over Trinity Academicals (39-4) and Kelvinside Academy (19-3) and a creditable performance in an away defeat against a strong Bradford side (18-0). A victory in the last few minutes over Glasgow Academicals (21-17 away) got the league campaign off to a perfect start, but those two league points were not added to until mid February. In the meantime there were losses to Kilmarnock (17-7 at home), Stewart's Melville (8-18 at home) and RHS FP (13-16 away), when the early loss of Tony Hamilton at full-back was crucial in a game in which the forwards dominated. A good crowd went through to Ayr and saw the Academicals outscore their hosts by three tries to one, but still end up losing 14-19 thanks to five Ayr penalties. The first half of the league programme ended with two hard-fought but ultimately fruitless games against Langholm (19-9 at home) and Jed-Forest (13-3 at home).

The Chronicle commentated:

It had become apparent that if we were to stay in Division II more points would have to be forthcoming from the amount of ball gained. Forward pressure and territorial advantage had not been turned into tries scored and too many games had been lost by the giving away of needless penalties.

A fine win against West of Scotland (29-14 at home) and a very good draw against Boroughmuir (8-8 away) got the mid-season 'friendly' schedule off to a good start. But with injuries depriving the team of as many as nine first-choice players on a number of occasions, Accies then slumped to eight straight losses between going down 56-6 to London Scottish on 26 December and 16-6 at Selkirk on 8 February.

It was, therefore, a big relief the following week when two unanswered penalties kicked by Tony Hamilton were enough to claim the points at Auldhouse versus Hutcheson's. The relief was short-lived, however. A 16-6 defeat in a vicious match at Selkirk and a 33-0 hammering at home to Gordonians meant that Accies would be relegated if they lost to Hillhead at Hughenden in the last league match of the season. Both clubs were sitting on four league points, but Hillhead had an inferior points differential, which meant that a draw would be enough to save Accies from dropping into Division III.

With all the clubs' junior games cancelled, a large and, for once, vociferous crowd travelled through to Glasgow to cheer the team on. It was a tense affair, with Hillhead dominating the first half and the Academicals defending doggedly to limit the score to 6-3 at half-time. After the break the pack began to assert itself and it wasn't long before Tony Hamilton levelled the match with his second penalty of the afternoon. With momentum on their side the Academicals continued to press but failed to make the most of three great scoring opportunities, and it looked as if this profligacy might come back to haunt them when Hillhead mounted one final onslaught during the last few minutes.

It seems that every Accies player involved in that match has a story to tell about their efforts to save the game, but the moment which has stuck in most supporters' minds was George Menzies' desperate last-gasp tackle which put the Hillhead winger into touch and goal just in time.

The season ended with two friendly matches – a defeat to Dunfermline (28-4 away) and a resounding victory over Edinburgh Wanderers (22-7 at home).

In April 1975 *The Chronicle* stated:

Although the results of the 1st XV have been disappointing they do not in many cases accurately reflect the performance of the team – particularly the forwards – and Walker Forsyth is to be congratulated on the manner in which he has captained the side in a season marred by a lot of injuries. Four associate members of the club have been regularly in the side and another four were called upon during the season.

The regular XV was usually drawn from: A.D.W. Hamilton; S. Jeffrey (Glenalmond), D.M. Mennie, C.S.G. Wallace, J.A. Crerar, A.L. Brownlee

(Fettes); D.F. Alexander, S.L. Symon, R.L.A. Blair; A.W. Forsyth (captain), D.W.J. Moffat, J.R. Walker, D.A. Gardiner, E. Hopkins (Birmingham University), C. Bouloux (Strathclyde University), G.M. Menzies, G.A. Blair (E.A. Staff), G.R. Ballantine, R.K. Sloan, M.P.N. Tulloch.

The spirit amongst the members of the 2nd, 3rd, 4th and 5th XVs is extremely high and the results obtained by these teams show a great improvement on last season. The 4th XV finished with the best record and W.G. Menzies once again captained them. The fact that he is also the Fixture Secretary and a member of the Selection Committee is considered by the other teams as a possible advantage.

Charlie Bouloux might have been breaking new ground when he was elected the club's first ever non-Academical captain for the 1975–76 season, and the number of associated playing members might have been getting close to 30 per cent of the overall playing membership, but many of the problems which had blighted the club before it had gone 'open' were clearly still there.

Pre-season training was very poorly attended, prompting the new captain to advise the general committee at the end of August, less than two weeks before the start of the season, that unless things improved there was not a 'cat in hell's chance' of the team retaining its place in Division II. By the start of October Bouloux was informing the committee that 'the sense of urgency was still not there and psychologically the side were not well equipped'. Injuries were also a problem, with vice-captain Elgar Hopkins out until Christmas and a number of other key players also being sidelined.

It was no major surprise, therefore, that the season started with six straight defeats, including four league losses to Highland (7-9 at home), Glasgow Academicals (3-26 at home), Dunfermline (7-32 away) and Stewart's Melville (3-42 away). Victories over Royal High (13-8 at home) and Ayr (24-3 at home) represented a mini-revival, but a comprehensive 32-9 defeat at Jed-Forest in the last game before the mid-season break was a sobering experience. At this stage another relegation battle seemed to be on the cards, but victory over Trinity Academicals (12-0 at home) provided some breathing space, and despite losing to Selkirk (16-9 at home) the team were in no real danger of being relegated even before they inflicted a first ever home league defeat upon Gordonians (16-9).

The momentum from this fine result was carried into the final match of season, when First Division side Edinburgh Wanderers were beaten 22-10 on their own patch. Despite Bouloux's early season concerns things had not gone too badly, and particularly pleasing was the fine form of the junior teams, with the 2nds, 3rds and 4ths all winning more games than they lost.

The Edinburgh Sevens were transferred this year from Murrayfield to Raeburn Place and, despite the atrocious weather and the lure of counter attractions, they were judged a success.

The players nominated Mark Tulloch as captain of the 1st XV for the 1976–77 season, but before his appointment could be ratified at the AGM a change in his business commitments dictated that he step aside. Rob Blair, who had come second in the players' vote, took on the role instead, and he proved to be a conscientious and hard-working leader.

1976–77 1st XV

Back: A.D.W. Hamilton, K.W. Paterson-Brown, D.A. Gardiner, M.M. Pringle, W.D.G. Loudon, G.M. Menzies, W.R.M. Henderson, R.A. Lutton, The Hon. J.S.W. Sempill

Middle: D.W.J. Moffat, E.J.E. Hopkins, R.K. Sloan, R.L.A. Blair (*Captain*), D.H.S. Maxwell, R.J. Sim, D.A.K. Watters

Front: D.A. Walker, W.G.R. Bain

Blair's enthusiasm and tireless encouragement meant that pre-season training numbers were good, and victories over Trinity Academicals, Kelvinside Academicals and Royal High augured well for the start of the league campaign – but it was not to be. Gordonians exacted their revenge for the home defeat that had been inflicted on them in the last match of the previous season (19-3 at Raeburn), then Melrose (30-12 at the Greenyards), Glasgow Academicals (13-3 at New Anniesland), Dunfermline (17-3 at Raeburn) and Stewart's Melville (29-9 at Raeburn) all piled on the misery, to leave the team pointless in the league as they approached the midway stage.

Eventually, however, the hard work which was being put in at training began to pay off, with the team claiming five of the six league points on offer before the mid-season break through a draw against Haddington (6-6 at Neilson Park) followed by victories over Ayr (7-3 at Millbrae) and Glasgow High (17-3 at Raeburn).

Poor weather during December and January led to a number of matches being called off, but two of the friendly games which did go ahead could not have provided more contrasting outcomes. On 18 December Accies were on the wrong end of a 38-8 score-line against Boroughmuir at Meggetland, then three days later John Frame made a one-off guest appearance in the 1st XV and inspired a hard-earned 11-9 victory over a London Scottish side containing internationalists Mike Biggar, Alastair McHarg and Ron Wilson – the first victory in this fixture in 18 years.

Blair was in excellent form, making a couple of telling blindside breaks from rucks: the second of which, with five minutes to go and London Scottish leading 9-7, set up Willie Bain's match-winning try. The other Academicals points came from an early Dave Loudon penalty and a well-worked Dougie Walker try. Ronnie Sloan was also a key performer, alongside David Maxwell and Ken Paterson-Brown in a back-row which smothered countless promising London Scottish attacks. The visitors' solitary try came from Charlie Bouloux, who had been called in as a late replacement for the visitors having not been selected for the Accies team.

When the league programme resumed in February, Accies were able to chalk up wins against Jed-Forest (12-6 at Raeburn Place) and Leith Accies (12-6 at Hawkhill) before finishing the league campaign with a draw against Kelso (12-12 at Poynder Park) to take their tally for the season up to ten league points – a total which had looked impossible at the beginning of November.

In April the Edinburgh Sevens were once again played at Raeburn Place. On a sunny afternoon a crowd in excess of 2,000 watched Edinburgh Wanderers win the tournament. A large marquee bar erected behind the 1st XV pitch was well used, and over 1,000 teas were served from the club kitchen, which had recently been refitted and enlarged.

If the 1975–76 season had been one of consolidation, then there was a definite sense that 1976–77 had witnessed the club begin to move forward after years of stagnation. In January 1977 *The Chronicle* had reported:

> There are at least five Club teams turning out every week and, in the main, their results are successful. The numbers at training have never been higher and those attending are showing the benefits from the interesting and varied sessions.

Rob Blair chases
down Roy Laidlaw's
pass to his fly-half.

Rob Blair looks to
move the ball away
from an attacking
line-out.

Perhaps the most encouraging feature of the season has been the welcome increase in the number of younger players at Raeburn Place. Last, but not least, mention should be made to the growing band of older supporters whose encouragement from the touchline has been much appreciated.

The message at the end of the season was broadly similar:

The 2nds, 3rds, 4ths juniors and 4ths seniors all improved on previous years, with the 3rds and 4ths in particular benefiting from the advice and guidance of John Crerar and John Frame.

The pressure exerted by the increased number of younger players at Raeburn showed itself in the fact that the 1st XV (with one or two honourable exceptions) was the youngest for many years.

Special mention must be made of the captain, Rob Blair, who refused to be deterred by early disappointments and produced not only a winning but an entertaining team.

However, Blair reckons that there was still a long way to go at this stage before Accies could regard themselves as ready for Division I rugby:

Some of us tried awfully hard but it was very much a rearguard action. The likes of Walker Forsyth and myself took it very seriously but there was too much of an amateur ethos throughout the club, and there wasn't a real hard-nut to knock heads together. We always left it late to get our act together, and we didn't have the strength in depth if we lost a few players to injury.

We had great trouble getting people down to train. That had been the great bugbear for some time – if you don't train you don't play was what we said, but that doesn't work if you don't have enough players – and we didn't have a coach. Douglas Elliot was the president in my first year as captain and he was always great with training tips and Jake Young did a lot of the fitness stuff, but the rest of it was left to the captain and there is only so much you can do if you are trying to concentrate on your own game as well.

With Blair carrying on as captain, the 1977–78 season followed a similar pattern to the previous campaign, being described in *The Chronicle* as somewhat hit and miss:

> When the team played well it was capable of beating anyone in the Second Division, and quite a few in the First. Unfortunately, that was not always the case, as the results show. The fact that we played two teams from Division Four and lost to them both [8-7 at Broughton on Hogmanay and 0-17 at Kelvinside Academicals in the penultimate game of the season] confirms this. Only when the team is capable of putting together a string of good results will the full potential of the side be realised.

After a home loss to Trinity Academicals (13-11), a stoppage-time victory at Glasgow Academicals courtesy of a late Gordon Wallace try (10-9) and a frustrating defeat to Bradford (19-12 at Raeburn) when the backs failed to capitalise on forward domination, the league campaign started brightly with a stirring second half fight-back bringing a 15-12 victory over Kelso at Raeburn Place, in what was the only defeat the eventual league winners suffered all season. But then three losses to Gordonians (6-15 at Seafield), Edinburgh Wanderers

(6-17 at Raeburn) and Clarkston FP (7-9 at Raeburn) pulled Accies back into more familiar territory close to the foot of the table. Two victories on the road, over Dunfermline (12-7) and Selkirk (also 12-7), would prove to be invaluable at the end of the season, before the winter break was ushered in with another two defeats, against Haddington (4-6 at home) and Ayr (15-24 away).

1977–78 1st XV

Back: P.C Thomas, J.H. White, A.D.W. Hamilton, E.J.E Hopkins, D. Lindsay, G.M. Menzies, M.M. Pringle, C.B.S. Richardson, K.W. Paterson-Brown, W.G.R. Bain

Middle: R.H. Monteith, W.R.M. Henderson, W.D.G. Louden, R.L.A. Blair (*Captain*), The Hon. J.S.W. Sempill, D.W. Pearson, R.A. Lutton

Front: C.S.G. Wallace, R.J. Sim

For a number of years London Scottish had been finding it increasingly difficult to organise a team to play the Academicals over the Christmas holiday, and when it became apparent that they would not be fulfilling this long-standing fixture this season, the committee agreed that 'it was of the utmost importance that a prestige game of some sort be staged at Raeburn Place on Boxing Day, both this year and in the future'.

It was decided that Douglas Elliot, in his capacity as president, should use his massive influence to pull together a select side to play against the Academicals instead. The London Scottish connection was not lost completely, with eight players from that club in the team. Against a team containing several present or future Internationalists, the Academicals held on grimly for the first 55 minutes, before a deluge of points for the select side during the last 25 minutes gave them a comfortable 32-8 victory.

The two teams that day were:

Edinburgh Academicals: W. Henderson; D. Lindsay, J. Sim, J. Frame, W. Bain; T. Cochrane, R. Blair; R. Lutton, R. Monteith, D. Pearson, D. Louden, M. Pringle, B. Crawford, G. Menzies, K. Paterson-Brown.

W.I.D. Elliot's XV: R. Grant; G. Kelly, D. Boyd (all London Scottish), B. Hay (Boroughmuir), T. McNab (London Scottish); D. Bell, G. Young (Watsonians); D. Fairbairn, R. Clark, T. Walker (all London Scottish), I. Barnes (Hawick), A. McHarg, C. Hook (both London Scottish), A. Brewster (Stewart's Melville FP), A. Caldwell (London Scottish).

The post-Christmas stretch of league games started with a 20-9 victory over Preston Lodge at Raeburn Place, followed by a 19-18 defeat to Jed-Forest at Riverside Park, and the season finished with a 7-7 draw against Glasgow High at Old Anniesland – leaving Accies in the bottom half of the table but safe from relegation.

This year's match against Preston Lodge seemed to pass without incident, which wasn't the case a few years later, when a mass brawl involving almost all the players and a few of the spectators erupted at Pennypit.

Elgar Hopkins recalls:

It was an evening match at Pennypit and there was this punch-up on the pitch which spilled over into the crowd. Somehow the referee managed to calm things down and we finished the game. The next Tuesday our team doctor – the great Clifford C. Lutton – who was involved in the ABA [Amateur Boxing Association] – turned up at training with a brown paper bag.

He said: 'I saw your match the other night and I thought I'd bring this along because none of you could punch your way out of it! If you want a lesson I'll show you how to punch!'

I'll always remember him saying: 'You're all a disgrace.' Not because we had been fighting, but because there had been players and supporters throwing haymakers and none of us had landed a decent punch.

Doc Lutton's son, Ralph, had captained the Scottish Schools side which had contained eight Academy schoolboys during the 1975–76 season, and when he joined the club at the start of 1976–77 Rob Blair had been quick to encourage the young prop to use his connections to tempt a few of his old classmates along to Raeburn Place. Within a couple of years the likes of Pete Drennan, Charlie Richardson, Alistair Brand, Rod Macrae and Peter Thomson were all playing for the club, and contemporaries from other schools such as Jamie Paton and Iain Wotherspoon from Loretto were also persuaded to join. These players would be important to the upturn in the club's fortunes during the next few years.

The build-up to the 1978–79 league campaign was reasonably promising, with a number of these young players showing up well in three convincing home victories over Penicuik (18-3), Glasgow Academicals (22-6) and Edinburgh University (25-12). But there were also two disappointing losses, against Trinity Academicals (16-6 at Bangholm) and Bradford (14-6 at Clayton Road), and when the league schedule started at the beginning of October it quickly became apparent that this inconsistency was more than just early season rust.

Defeat to newly promoted Madras (10-9 at Station Park), followed by a heavy loss at Melrose (29-10) and a similarly disappointing performance and score-line against Gordonians (22-15 at Raeburn Place) obliterated the optimism which had been built up during the previous month and a half.

At the end of October, a commanding forward performance paved the way for a morale-boosting victory over Edinburgh Wanderers (10-3), but then the lack of cutting edge meant that Accies were beaten by two late penalty goals against Clarkston, despite monopolising possession (9-6 at Braidholm). Accies were back to somewhere near their best against Leith Academicals, when an Alastair Dunlop try in the opening minutes set up a 17-13 win at Raeburn Place, which was achieved despite being reduced to 13 men for the last 15 minutes, after Pete Drennan and Jamie Paton were injured. Once again this form could not be sustained, and the first leg of the league season ended with defeats against Selkirk (29-10 at Raeburn Place) and Highland (14-3 in Inverness).

1978–79 1st XV

Back: R.H. Monteith, R.L.A. Blair, J.C. Russell, R.C.K. Douglas, D.A. Gardiner, P.N.M. Drennen,
K.W. Paterson-Brown, D. Black, W.G.R. Bain, P.C. Thomson

Middle: E.J. E. Hopkins, W.R.M. Henderson, R.A. Dunlop, The Hon. J.S.W. Sempill (*Captain*), M.M. Pringle,
D.W.J. Moffat, R.A. Lutton

Front: G.H Jackson, J.F. Paton

During December, Accies defeated Musselburgh (15-7 at Raeburn Place) and drew with Watsonians (9-9 also at Raeburn Place), then lost three games on the trot to, West of Scotland (3-0 at home), Royal High School FP (16-6 at Barnton) and a President's XV made up predominantly of London Scots on Boxing Day (35-10).

A cold and icy January meant there was no rugby for six weeks. Fortunately, this seemed to play into Accies' hands, with David Maxwell (assisted by Jake Young) proving his value as the club's first dedicated coach. Extra training sessions were organised on Wednesday nights in the Academy school gym and on Saturdays at various venues, including Gullane Sands and Meadowbank Stadium.

It was time and effort well spent. The remaining three league games were won without a single point being conceded – Ayr (8-0 at Millbrae), Glasgow Academicals (20-0 at Raeburn Place) and Jed-Forest (12-0 at Raeburn Place) – allowing Accies to climb to sixth place in the league table. It was a great way to end the season, but thoughts of what might have been achieved if the team had shown that sort of form from the start inevitably took some of the shine off what had been achieved.

Accies v Selkirk at
Raeburn Place

The general health of the club was encouraging. Training numbers had remained high throughout the season, and six teams were playing and winning on a regular basis. In order to encourage competition for places in the 1st and 2nd XVs, it was decided that there should be two 3rd XVs, one captained and coached by John Frame and the other by George Menzies, sporting a rather unusual training outfit.

> It was my business suit. It was a very good one from Forsyth's which had been worn thin at the knees and elbows so was no longer suitable for the office. I must have been about 33-years-old, and I thought that as I was nearing the end of my playing career there was no point of buying a new tracksuit or anything like that. Little did I know that I had another seven years to go. Luckily I had successive suits coming through.
>
> I remember David Johnston said that he had met Charlie Richardson, who had told him that he had just been down to Accies for the first time where there is this amazing old guy who just hangs up his jacket and starts playing. That wasn't quite the case – but I can see why he thought it was a bit strange.

For almost 15 years Menzies had been a great servant to the club, and his enthusiasm was clearly as strong as ever. At this time he was combining his many duties as field secretary at Raeburn Place with organising Wednesday night training sessions so that every player could train under the lights at Raeburn Place at least once a week, coaching and captaining the thirds, and, when required (which seemed to be more often than not), playing for the 1st XV.

He says:

I played my last game for the 1st XV at the start of the 1979–80 season, against Sunderland away. I was playing for the seconds and Alastair Dunlop couldn't make the trip so I was asked to go down as captain. I remember Ronnie Sloan and I having ice-cream on the pier on a lovely September day. We stayed in this hotel near the sea and on Saturday evening after the match we all decided to go for a swim in the sea. When we returned to the hotel with only our underpants on and our hotel towels wrapped around our shoulders, we discovered that there was a wedding reception taking place – with the bride and groom and their parents greeting their guests at the front door. So we joined the line for that, and I remember Brian Neill – who was vice-president at the time – wearing only a towel shaking hands with the bride. They took it in good heart.

A pre-tour tour. Club members on a guided tour of the Scottish and Newcastle brewery at Fountain Park, Edinburgh, before they caught a train from Waverly to London for the Calcutta Cup match at Twickenham.

CHAPTER TWENTY-EIGHT

Yes, it looks very nice but it used to be a lovely rugby club and you've turned it into a bordello.

George Menzies to his cousin Billy Menzies,
September 1975

WHILE THE PROGRESS OF THE 1st XV on the field had been of the slow and steady variety, the social side of the club and the club's infrastructure during this period were changing far more dynamically, with Billy Menzies the chief driving force.

Through the late 1960s and into the early 1970s dances at Raeburn Place had become an increasingly popular and fairly profitable feature of the club's social calendar, but apart from these infrequent big nights and the usual socialising on training evenings and after matches the clubhouse was scarcely used. This was something Menzies set about changing with untiring zeal and marvellous ingenuity.

After leaving the Academy in 1970, he had gone to Walsall to train in a steel foundry and learn the art of coarse rugby with Walsall RFC. A year later he returned to Edinburgh and took on the captaincy of the 4th XV, which soon became the team which every social player wanted to be selected for – some might even have called it 'a club within a club'.

He was co-opted onto the EAFC general committee as assistant match secretary in September 1972. 'I think my delightful school coach, John Huins, had told the club that when I came back from Walsall I would be a useful club man – no use at rugby but a good club man,' he explains. 'The number of teams we were turning out was down quite significantly – I think we were down to three or four – and Gordon Graham, the match secretary, was hell bent on trying to get things moving, as was I.'

By the end of the 1974–75 season the club was once again fielding six teams on a regular basis, and it was time for Menzies to move on to a new challenge. He became joint honorary secretary of the club, alongside his long-time friend, John

Paterson. This appointment gave him the scope to influence and radically change both the management structure and the culture of the club.

In 1963, while still at school, Menzies had formed Liberton Rovers Football Club, which became Edinburgh Academy's unofficial soccer team, playing at Liberton House, the Menzies family home, on Sunday afternoons. He had masterminded the construction of a small stand next to the pitch for seating players' girlfriends, and a social club with a slot racing track inside the house provided hours of fun (and gambling) on Friday evenings. The club carried on for eight years until the end of the 1973–74 season, when it was disbanded and reconstituted under the Edinburgh Academical banner at Raeburn Place, to be run in unison with the newly formed mixed hockey club.

The first committee meeting of the Edinburgh Academical Soccer and Hockey Club took place on 11 September 1974. It was made up primarily of rugby club members and their wives and girlfriends, looking to play sport socially during the week and at weekends, and for several years to come it filled an important role in helping increase the 'utilisation factor' of Raeburn Place.

Menzies says:

> During the winter we had the club opening for soccer on Sundays, and it wasn't long before you had other members of the rugby club coming down, and we were able to get a thriving social scene going. Then, during the summer we had the hockey during the week while cricket tended to take precedence at the weekend, and because we were letting the pitches out to various other hockey clubs, the place was actually busier during the summer than it was during the winter.
>
> The whole thing was about the utilisation factor. The more people we had playing sport at Raeburn Place the more value we would get from the clubhouse. But we also knew that if we wanted the girls in the hockey teams to come into the clubhouse then we were going to have to tart it up and make it a bit more attractive to the fairer sex – because, to be honest, the place was a bit tired and run-down.

In 1969 the rugby club had been behind the construction of the cocktail bar at the north end of the pavilion, but by 1972 it had become abundantly clear to most of the committee that a more comprehensive renovation was needed.

Unfortunately, problems in financing and co-ordinating such a major undertaking, especially given the uncertainty surrounding the future of the rugby club during the early 1970s, meant that it wasn't until early 1975 that any real progress was made. Things started to happen after Menzies, supported by the club house and entertainments convener Vic Murphy, came up with a scheme which would completely overhaul the crumbling edifice of Raeburn Place within four years.

The Ben Tod lounge is opened, 1977.

Phase one of this five-step plan involved refurbishing the main bar at Raeburn Place, which had previously been a fairly austere hall, minimally furnished with a few hard garden benches and wooden tables. Improvements included new curtains, carpets, wall seating, lighting and heating, along with the installation of an ice-machine, cash register, cooling shelf, music player and alarm system. The cost of all this was £6,000, which came from various sources – including a ten-year loan from Scottish & Newcastle Brewers, contributions from all the constituent clubs, and private donations from several club members who requested that the new bar be called the Carmichael Lounge in recognition of all the work that family had done to help improve Raeburn Place over the years.

The Carmichael Lounge, 1977

Work on the new bar was completed by mid September 1975, and at the same time the small room near the backdoor of the clubhouse was given a lick of paint and transformed into a committee room.

The groundsman, John Jackson, was relieved of his responsibility for operating the bar on Tuesday and Thursday nights, with Vic Murphy as house convener and Billy Menzies as bar convener heading a house committee which would run both the bar and club functions throughout the season. A new fruit machine was also installed, providing another regular source of income.

These changes and innovations immediately led to a growth in the use of Raeburn Place, which was a bonus financially, but necessitated an urgent revamp in the venue's management structure.

Historically, each constituent club paid an annual fee to the field committee to cover the running costs of Raeburn Place, while the bar was run by the rugby club during the winter and the cricket club during the summer, with the thriving squash club expected to leave a note of what they had spent in the bar when they used it – but stock control was a problem, as were disagreements over what each club should be contributing towards the overall running costs, and it was not unusual for a bar to be loss-making over the course of a single cricket or rugby season. Organising club members to staff the bars was also a struggle.

The Ben Tod Lounge, 1977

A debate over access rights to the newly renovated Carmichael Lounge was the catalyst to change. The rugby club might have been the driving force behind the project, but the other resident clubs had contributed as well, so it was important that all of these groups felt they were getting a fair deal. The solution, it was decided, was the formation of the Edinburgh Academical Sports Centre (EASC) which would bring together the rugby, cricket, squash, soccer and hockey clubs as one overall sports club, with members paying one overall subscription. The brainchild of rugby and cricket club stalwart Ian Stevenson, the EASC would be 'open' with a maximum of 30 per cent of the membership being 'associates'.

Enjoying the benefits of 'working' behind the new bar . . .

When the EASC was set up in September 1976, Menzies volunteered to run the bar:

My other main commitment was to establish a range of club social events for all members of the Sports Centre, with some suitable for children as well as adults. That took up about 50 per cent of my time. Originally we ran the place through a network of temporary bar stewards, who were treated to wild dinners in the clubhouse as pay for giving up their social lives to help us out, but the whole thing was geared towards generating enough income to get professional people in – which we eventually did with Jim Mancais (in 1978), followed by Mick Judge (in 1980) and then Frank Boyd (in 1988). We also wanted to get some money together so that we could continue improving the facilities.

No sooner had the refurbishment of the Carmichael Lounge been completed, than attention turned to improving the main function hall and re-equipping the kitchen, using a £5,000 loan from Scottish & Newcastle Breweries. This was completed by September 1976.

Within the space of two short years the 'utilisation factor' at Raeburn Place had increased exponentially. Between August 1975 and August 1976, bar turnover had gone from approximately £9,000 to around £22,000. In the year up to August 1975 there had been six disco dances and no private functions; during the next year there were 12 disco dances, two 'buffet members' dances', a Burns Supper and a Children's Christmas Party, and after the function hall was completed the clubhouse began to host around 25 private functions a year, including stag nights, 21st birthday parties and the wedding reception of Barbara Gibb and her new husband – a certain William G. Menzies.

Menzies explains:

> I thought that would give some credibility to what we were trying to do. I sold the idea to Barbara's mother, and astonishingly she jumped at it. It was a nightmare getting the renovations completed in time, the painters were in there the night before trying to get it finished off, but we got there in the end and it was a fantastic day.

Next on the agenda was some essential maintenance work during the summer of 1978 on the windows, inside and outside paintwork, electrical wiring and playing pitches, which would be looked after by the school after the departure of John Jackson from his position as groundsman in November 1978. A new fire exit to the rear of the building was also installed, while the stock room and beer cellar was enlarged.

Despite the discovery of damp rot in three of the club's six changing rooms in July 1978, which put an extra strain on the EASC's finances, the fifth and final stage of Menzies four-year development plan for Raeburn Place was completed in July 1979 – with the small cocktail bar enlarged and refurbished, the kitchen re-equipped and shifted into the area where the 1st XV changing rooms had traditionally been, and the downstairs changing rooms upgraded.

In August 1978, Jim Mancais and his wife Ellen were appointed full-time club-master and stewardess, and there was plenty going on to keep them busy. The bar now opened for lunches and evening drinks six days a week, a hectic social calendar was in operation, and there were typically between four and eight private functions being hosted at Raeburn Place every month. In April 1979, the Edinburgh Charity Sevens took place at Raeburn Place for the third consecutive year.

Barbara Menzies arrives at Raeburn Place for her wedding reception

In the days of ten o'clock closing times for pubs in Edinburgh, the city's rugby clubs used to take turn around hosting dances with a late licence, and Accies prided themselves on running the best disco in the city – with Raeburn Place invariably packed to the rafters. Peter Clark recalls one night during his spell as entertainments convener when the building was filled to capacity and all the doors had been bolted shut to prevent any more revellers from getting in. Yet, somehow, the place still seemed to be getting busier. After checking all the entrances for a third time, Clark wandered into the gents' toilets, where he discovered a chain of latecomers piling through an open window from the top of a ladder outside: 'like rats out of a drain pipe'.

The Accies Christmas Ball was a particularly popular addition to the social calendar, as Billy Menzies details:

> They used to have an Accie Ball at the Assembly Rooms on George Street but the numbers went down and it was not

Two Accie legends at one of the famous Christmas Balls. On the left, Pat Burnett, capped in 1960 against South Africa, and on the right, Bill Bruce, the much missed founder of the Edinburgh Athenian Touring Society (EATS).

organised for a few years, so we were casting around for something a bit different which might attract a few more people along to the club. Now, I'm a great lover of Christmas so I suggested a Christmas Ball and everyone seemed to agree that was a good idea. This was the Christmas of 1978.

We decorated the clubhouse and had a great time. It really took off and the next year it was oversubscribed. We couldn't afford a marquee at that time (although we did in later years with as many as 700 attending), so we had people on the balcony above the squash courts, people in the squash courts – people in every usable space we could find. It became a bun fight.

Jim Mancais had recently left and we had just appointed Mick Judge as the new club-master so he was invited down to this function as our guest . . . and it was an absolute nightmare.

The woman in charge of the catering turned up in a tight purple skirt and she had a lot of food for the buffet she was meant to be organising, but I wasn't sure that she had enough for the number of strapping rugby players she was meant to be feeding. We reminded her that these were big men who ate a lot, and she said she had plenty. But she stupidly went and laid it all out, which might have been okay if it had been 75 members of a local tennis club, but we at this stage were up to about 250, and that's a different sort of catering.

I remember her running up to me clearly in a state of distress, and saying, 'They're terrible. I can't cope.'

I said, 'What's wrong?'

'The food is virtually all gone.'

'How can it all be gone? You've only served about half of them!'

'They've taken far too much.'

So we went through to the kitchen and she was bending over to look in the oven to see how many hot potatoes she had left, just as a well-known club member was coming out of the wee office adjacent to the kitchen having just changed into his Father Christmas outfit. Now, there was a lot of stress in the room, but Santa was clearly unaware of this.

'Ho ho ho,' he said. 'Christmas has come early!' And she had this lovely petite bum which Ollie decided to pinch. She jumped up, screamed, and smacked him in the face. She then stormed out and that was the last I saw of my caterer.

So I went to the only reprobate I could think of who might be of any help to me, and that was Ken Gray. I said, 'Ken, we've got a serious problem here. All these people have paid good money for this, they have dressed up to the nines in their ball gowns and tuxedos, and there is no food.'

Ken said, 'Well it will have to be fish suppers.'

'I can't sell them fish suppers.'

Ken said, 'You're damn right, you'll have to give them away.'

So we ran a chain from the chip shop at the end of the road. I was the guy that had to take the orders – 'Salt and sauce, madam?'

Mick never let me forget that night.

The new clubmaster and his partner Janette Park were soon established as part of the fabric of Raeburn Place.

Jeremy Richardson:

If I think of the fun times we had at Raeburn Place, then they were crucial to that. They helped with fund-raising, allowed us to have lock-ins on Saturday nights, and if you were short of cash they would organise an IOU. They did a hell of a lot for the club and particularly the young players. Jeanette was like a mother figure to a lot of them.

Raeburn Place was buzzing. From a modest starting point, the clubhouse was beginning to realise its full potential. It was time for the rugby section to follow that lead.

CHAPTER TWENTY-NINE

When Barney took over as coach the whole ethos of the place instantly changed. I remember him saying he would put us in the 'shop windae' and he introduced this mindset that rugby was about more than fun, it was part of a day's work. There were a lot of guys in the pack – Charlie Richardson, Peter Thomson, Pete Drennan, myself – who were ready for this to happen. We didn't become a dirty team, but we got tough. We didn't let anyone take advantage of us, and that meant our backs were able to play rugby.

Elgar Hopkins

IAN BARNES WILL NEVER win prizes for diplomacy or tact, and when it comes to artistic merit the teams he coaches have more in common with Mike Tyson and Sonny Liston than Jayne Torvill and Christopher Dean – but as the 1970s gave way to the 1980s, and Accies found themselves still fighting relegation from Division II after six years of league rugby, rather than pushing for promotion to the top echelon of the Scottish game, he was exactly what was needed at a club which was becoming used to under-achieving.

An uncompromising second-row forward for Hawick when that club swept all before them during the previous decade, he had been capped seven times for Scotland between 1972 and 1977, and brought to Raeburn Place the sort of hard-nosed self-belief which had been conspicuously absent hitherto.

With Alastair Dunlop, a recent recruit from West of Scotland, captaining the side, and Ralph Lutton as vice-captain, the 1979–80 season got off to a highly promising start with Bradford being defeated for the first time in ten years, but the first league match of the season ended in disappointment at Riverside Park, when Jed-Forest squeezed out a 20-16 victory. A disappointing result but, as Hopkins recalls, a watershed moment in the development of the team:

The Borderers used to love playing against Accies because they knew they could kick the shit out of us and have it all their own way – but then, all of a sudden, we were going down there and giving them as good as we got. I remember going down to Jed at the start of the season, and Ralph must have been injured because I'm sure I was pack leader. Barney said before the match that if Jed started messing us about then I was to make the call and all the forwards were to pile in – a bit like the 99 call which the Lions had used in South Africa in 1974.

Jed had guys like Charlie Bird and Kevin Liddle playing for them and it wasn't long before they were trying it on. They were climbing all over us in the line-out so I decided it was time to fight back. I caught my opposite number, Bobby Lindores – the Jed captain – with an absolute beauty. It was probably the best punch I've ever thrown. He had to go off and when he came back on 20 minutes later with five stitches above his eye I thought there were going to be fireworks – but it was fine. All he said afterwards was: 'Look Elgar, I should have ducked. I know who your coach is so I should have known what was coming. We got what we deserved.'

The team then recorded two fairly comfortable home victories over Trinity Academicals and Langholm (18-0 and 19-6), but could not carry that momentum into their tricky expedition up to Aberdeen to face league leaders Gordonians. That game was lost (17-6). This seemed to dent the team's confidence, and what should have been a fairly easy match against struggling Edinburgh Wanderers at home ended up being a real struggle, before Accies eventually scraped a 10-6 win with less than 50 per cent possession from the set-piece.

Changes were made up front for the next game against second top of the table Clarkston with Dave Gardiner and Dave Loudon brought in to provide bulk and scrummaging power. That seemed to do the trick, with Accies monopolising possession to win 7-0. A scrappy match against Leith Academicals yielded a 7-6 victory, and in the last match before the mid-season break Haddington were beaten 19-8 at Neilson Park.

December and January were not particularly successful months for the club, with only two wins (over Musselburgh and Kilmarnock) and four losses (against West of Scotland, London Scottish, Broughton and Melrose). February began with the club's first trip to Ireland in several years for the International weekend. On the Friday, after various traumatic experiences with strike-bound airfields, the Accies took on Old Wesley, who eventually emerged victorious after a hard-fought match which could have gone either way right up to the very end.

1979–80 1st XV

Back: R.H. Monteith, P.N.M. Drennan, D. Lindsay, C.A. Gray, W.D.G. London, M.M. Pringle, W.R.M. Henderson, R.C.K. Douglas, E.J.E. Hopkins, D.A. Gardiner

Middle: J.F. Paton, D. Kerr, R.A. Lutton, R.A. Dunlop (*Captain*), R.L.A. Blair, P.C. Thomson, W.S.S. Howgate

Front: K.W. Paterson-Brown, D.J. Cartwright

The team had been distracted during the warm-up by a bunch of kilted Academical supporters wading across the River Dodder, which runs along the edge of Donnybrook, the Dublin ground where the team was playing. Disaster struck when Angus Todd's sporran caught in the water and upturned, emptying its contents into the freezing river – wallet, passport and most importantly match tickets. A strong man in adversity, he dived straight into the arctic water to retrieve them – and then stuck around long enough to watch the game and have a few pints in the bar afterwords.

After watching Scotland defeat Ireland 22-15 on the Saturday, Accies had been scheduled to play St Mary's on the Sunday, but a waterlogged pitch meant that the players had to endure a brutal training session instead.

Despite playing some of the best rugby of the season against Highland the following week, the match ended in disappointment (11-19), with the lack of a reliable goal-kicker proving decisive. The next match against Ayr was particularly frustrating. Dave Loudon picked up a knee injury after half an hour and could not return to the field, and with several other players going off the pitch to receive treatment at various points, Accies were up against it throughout – eventually losing 9-7 and forfeiting any lingering hopes of promotion. With the pressure off, the final game of the season against Royal High School FP was played with the sort of composure which might have been invaluable earlier in the campaign, to secure a comprehensive 15-6 victory. The season ended with heavy defeats in friendlies against Glasgow Academicals (26-7), who had been newly promoted to Division II, and against Hawick (31-7).

The performances of the junior teams continued to improve, with Tony Hamilton taking over from John Frame as captain of one of the 3rd XVs, a success rate of over 60 per cent in matches below 1st XV level provided reassurance that the club was definitely moving in the right direction.

The 1980–81 season began with a successful – if gruelling – pre-season tour to Germany, organised by David Kerr, an army officer who was playing in the centre for Accies whilst stationed in Edinburgh. Sleeping in army barracks, playing hard games against streetwise squaddies every day for a week, and drinking even harder in the NAAFI at night – the team returned to Britain ready for action.

Before they left for home the squad were invited by their hosts, the British Army of the Rhine, to an end of tour function. Tour manager Robert Millar stepped forward to pay his respects to the commanding officer and threw his cigarette stub out of an open window. 'Mr Millar,' the military man exclaimed, 'you do appreciate that we are sitting on top of the biggest armaments dump in Western Europe?'

The hard work put in on the German expedition looked like it was going to pay dividends when the team recorded two excellent victories over two Division One sides – Kelso and Melrose – but this pre-season form could not be carried into the league campaign, and two wins and two draws in eight matches left Accies languishing near the foot of the table over the Christmas break. The fact that four of the club's six league points had been picked up against the top three sides in the division from two home draws against Jed-Forest (13-13) and Selkirk (9-9) and an away victory over Jordanhill College (13-7) only added to the frustration that the progress of the previous season was not being built upon. The other league win before Christmas was over the soon to be relegated Edinburgh Wanderers (15-0 at Murrayfield).

Once again Accies entered the home straight of the league campaign with the prospect of relegation breathing down their necks. An emphatic 19-6 victory over Glasgow Academicals suggested that the team had managed to regain some of their early season confidence, but the lack of a consistent goal-kicker against fellow strugglers Highland in Inverness contributed to a depressing 6-0 defeat, and took the relegation battle to the wire. Accies played Ayr in the last game of the season, knowing that they had to avoid losing by 16 or more points to stay in Division II. A large crowd travelled through to Millbrae, and in a predictably fraught affair, Ayr emerged as 6-4 winners – meaning that Accies lived to fight another day in Division II.

At the end of the season *The Chronicle* noted:

One prime reason for the lack of success this season was the spate of injuries which hit us. Scarcely a week went by without injury of one sort or another, often keeping a player out of the game for a match or two. Our captain, Alastair Dunlop, suffered from continual ham-string trouble; and he showed fine spirit when playing at Ayr when obviously less than 100% fit. There were, too, many more younger players in the team this season, and they had their share of injuries as well; but we hope that they have gained experience from playing in a difficult season. Most of all we needed a steady, reliable place-kicker.

The 1981–82 season started with a friendly against Edinburgh Wanderers at Murrayfield on 5 September. The game was played in brilliant sunshine, but according to *The Scotsman*, the only bright feature of the game was the Accie linesman, John Paterson, parading the touchline in his Bermuda shorts.

That game was won 17-12, but in the next two friendlies the lack of experience in the Accies side was shown up, with a 15-9 defeat at home to Melrose and a 31-3 hammering at Kelso. But things picked up, and victories over Sunderland, Edinburgh University and Bradford gave rise to cautious optimism about the league campaign ahead. The team was undoubtedly assisted in the last of these matches by the presence within the Accie ranks of John Wright, a prop who had recently moved to Edinburgh from Bradford, where he

1981–82 1st XV

Back: W.SS. Howgate, J.D. Sutton, S. Munroe, C.A.Gray, A. Adamson, D. Young, J. Robertson, D.C. Hill, D. Miller

Front: K.W. Paterson-Brown, G. Henderson, P.N.M. Drennan, F. Paton (*Captain*), D.A. Gardiner

C.N.M. Campbell, N.P. Ireland

had been a regular in the 1st XV throughout the 1970s. Accies were dominating at the line-out, but half-time had already been and gone before the visiting team's captain put two and two together and realised 'that b*****d Wright knows our codes'.

The league season got off to a winning start against Haddington (18-7 at Raeburn Place), but the following week a horrific injury to Brian Crawford, who broke his leg in three places, clearly affected the team, and they lost 28-6 away to Royal High School FP, ending the match with only 13 men after Peter Ireland also picked up a leg injury.

Further injuries took their toll, with Jamie Paton and Dave Gardiner, the club captain and vice-captain respectively, missing large chunks of the season. But the club was fortunate to acquire the service of prop-cum-second-row Jim Barclay, formerly of Boroughmuir, who added some much needed stability to the scrum and plenty of vigour in the loose.

Accies won enough possession to beat Langholm at Milntown but couldn't convert pressure into points and ended up losing 13-7, and after a convincing 16-6 victory over Preston Lodge at Raeburn Place, it was a similar scenario against Jordanhill a fortnight later (15-0 defeat at Raeburn Place). The giving away of early points had proven costly, but there was no such laxity against Musselburgh and Clarkston in the final two league matches before the break, with Accies grinding out consecutive home victories (13-9 and 7-3 respectively).

The Musselburgh match was a particularly rugged affair, with *The Chronicle* noting:

> It would be best if we could draw a veil over the match against Mussel-burgh, always something of a local Derby, for it was marred by that 'unacceptable face of rugby' violence. Both sides were to blame; and while the referee had a very tough job, he should have been more forthright and applied the laws consistently and, in this case, stringently.

Despite the cancellation of eight games in a row from 12 December to 16 January, including a fixture against the Co-optimists on Boxing Day, three matches did go ahead before the league season restarted – with Accies claiming two comfortable wins over Kelvinside Academicals (47-0 at Raeburn Place) and Broughton (24-4 at Wardie), before putting in their 'best performance of the season' despite losing 16-14 to Stewart's Melville FP at Inverleith.

As *The Chronicle* explained:

> When it is known that the Accies played for three quarters of the game with only 13 men, and in the final stages a mere 12, and that the winning kick went over right on full time after hitting a post, the result is indeed an outstanding achievement, especially against 1st Division opposition.

Accies won the first of their three remaining league fixtures against Leith Academicals (20-6 at Hawkhill), lost the next one against Glasgow Academicals (28-22 at New Anniesland) and did not get round to playing Highland after that match was postponed due to bad weather. Because the result of that game would not have effected the final promotion or relegation placings, it was never rearranged.

The build-up to the 1982–83 league season did not go well, with five defeats during September to Edinburgh Wanderers (14-9 at Murrayfield), Selkirk (19-20 at Philliphaugh), Kelso (47-0 at Raeburn Place) Edinburgh University (11-15 at Raeburn Place) and Bradford (36-15 at Clayton Road), and only one win over Sunderland (20-7 at Raeburn Place). So it was not a great surprise that the league season also got off to an inauspicious start with a 19-25 reverse away to newly promoted Stirling County. But thereafter the team played very well, picking up five wins – over Glasgow Kelvinside (28-12 at home), Highland (17-12 at home), Jordanhill (12-10 away), Howe of Fife (19-3 away) and Clarkson (36-0 at home) – as well as a draw against Glasgow Academicals (12-12 away) – in the next seven league matches.

That put Accies on 11 points out of a possible 16. League sizes had been increased from 12 to 14 this year, meaning that Accies still had five games left, and with three of the top teams in the division – Haddington, Ayr and Langholm – still to play, promotion was on the cards.

On 7 December, Accies took on Heriot's at Goldenacre in what was supposed to be a friendly match, but the game was abandoned when all 30 players were sent-off for fighting. Trouble flared late on in the game and the referee, John Gunderson, a police detective, warned both captains. But at the next line-out punches started to fly again and the referee decided that he had seen enough. Particularly frustrating for Accies was the fact that they were winning 6-3 at the time. National notoriety ensued when Bill Beaumont was asked on *Question of Sport*: 'What was special about the Heriot's versus Edinburgh Academicals match on 7 December 1982?' He got the answer wrong.

Two heavy friendly defeats were suffered against the Co-optimists (68-12 at Raeburn Place) on Hogmanay and against Stewart's Melville FP (57-0 at Inverleith) on 3 January, before league action was resumed with comfortable home victories over Leith Academicals (44-0) and Musselburgh (23-12). There followed a month of poor weather which caused the Langholm game to be postponed until 26 March, and meant that the team took to the field against fellow promotion chasers Haddington having not played in four weeks. Despite this, a solid display from the pack laid the groundwork for a 20-6 victory at Neilson Park

Next up were highflying Ayr, who needed a win to lift the championship. Thanks to a never-say-die approach and some poor Ayr goal-kicking, Accies somehow won a match in which they had never been in front until the last few minutes. That result meant Accies travelled to Langholm knowing that a win would give them the championship ahead of Ayr on points difference, while defeat would leave them with nothing. Five coach-loads of EAFC players and supporters left Raeburn Place for Milntown that Saturday morning to watch a 'tense, nervy and sometimes brutal game'.

On the Monday after the match, *The Scotsman* reported:

There was a cup-tie atmosphere at Milntown on Saturday as hundreds of blue and white rosetted Academical supporters saw a thrill-a-minute encounter with the lead changing hands four times. There was never more then six points in it.

Accies made the better start and after eight minutes of pressure Johnny Sutton gave the visitors the lead with his second penalty attempt; but Langholm's powerful scrum soon started to make a difference, and with almost quarter of the match gone they took the lead when Kevin McConnel scored a pushover try, which Steven Little converted. An exchange of penalties between Kenny Hill and Little made it 9-6 to Langholm at the break; and another exchange of penalties after half-time, this time between Sutton and Little, moved the score to 12-9 in the home team's favour.

Deprived of first-phase ball, Accies had to rely on running any possession they could scavenge, but Langholm's first-up tackling kept them at bay until the hour mark, when Jamie Paton gathered a loose clearance and sent Stewart Howgate rushing back up-field on the counter-attack, to create the field position from which Ken Paterson-Brown squeezed over in the corner.

Accies were now 13-12 ahead, and the team could almost taste the success they had all worked so hard for. But, with play swinging from one end of the pitch to the other in a nerve-jangling finale, the game slipped away from them. Little landed two penalties to make it 18-13 to the Borderers at full-time – meaning that Ayr went up as champions and Haddington were promoted alongside them, finishing ahead of Langholm on points difference.

Melrose Centenary Sevens, 1983

Back: E. Drummond, J. Sutton, R. Young

Front: N. Campbell, K. Dodds, P. Drennan (*Captain*), B. Brown, J. Paton

That summer Hawick came calling for Barnes and he was never going to turn down the opportunity to coach his hometown club. Charlie Jackson (formerly of Ayr, Leith Academicals and Loughborough College) took over the reins, with David Bell (ex-Selkirk) taking charge of the forwards. Accies had come agonisingly close to promotion but had fallen at the final hurdle. Jackson said from the very beginning that he saw no reason why they could not go one better next season.

CHAPTER THIRTY

If you think you are beaten you are,
If you think you dare not, you don't,
If you like to win but think you can't,
It's almost certain you won't.

If you think you'll lose, you're lost,
For out of this would we find
Success begins with a fellow's will
It's all in the state of mind.

If you think you are outclassed, you are,
You've got to think high to rise,
You've got to be sure of yourself before
You can even win a prize.

Life's battles don't always go
To the stronger or faster man
But soon or late the man who wins
Is the man who thinks he can.

'A Message for Next Season'
– given to the players by Charlie Jackson ahead of the 1984–85 season

THE 1983–4 LEAGUE SEASON STARTED reasonably well, with the team picking up eight points by Christmas out of a possible 14 through victories over Stirling County (17-4 at Raeburn Place), Glasgow High/Kelvinside (14-9 at Old Anniesland), Glasgow Academicals (13-9 at New Anniesland) and Howe of Fife (10-6 at Raeburn Place). The Glasgow Academicals result was particularly impressive because it was the only match they lost on their way to the Division II championship that season. However, defeats to Royal High (12-9 at Raeburn Place), Highland (10-9 at Canal Park) and Clarkston (24-15 at Braidholm) meant that promotion was far from a foregone conclusion.

In October 1983 there was great excitement around the club when Peter Drennan was selected to play flanker for Edinburgh against Stu Wilson's 1983 All Blacks. The tourists won the match 22-6, but Drennan held his own against the terrifying Mark 'Cowboy' Shaw.

A 78-0 demolition at the hands of a strong Co-optimist team on Boxing Day was not great for morale and self-belief, but a promising win at the end of January in a friendly match against Stewart's Melville FP (22-9 at Inverleith) provided the momentum which took Accies on a run of five consecutive wins when the league programme restarted. Aberdeen Grammar School FP (7-6 at Rubislaw), Preston Lodge (22-6 at Raeburn Place), Langholm (18-0 at Raeburn Place), Gordonians (20-3 at Seafield) and Jordanhill (6-3 at Raeburn Place) were all taken care of, as the team marched towards yet another win-or-bust season finale.

Accies v Portobello at Cavalry Park, 1984

This time the opposition was Portobello, who were hoping to win promotion for the sixth consecutive time. Portobello needed a draw, while Accies knew that they had to win. The game would be played at Cavalry Park, where the home team had never lost a league match. Not surprisingly, it was an almost unbearably tense afternoon.

Charlie Jackson arranged for the team to stay in the Ellersley House Hotel in Murrayfield on the night before the game: he wanted his players to be focused; he didn't want them treating this match as just another game. The days of Accies playing just for fun were over. Success was no longer a bonus, it was expected.

On the following Monday, a report by Norman Mair appeared in *The Glasgow Herald* under the headline 'Academicals up for the first time':

Portobello 10, Edinburgh Academicals 12

THE EXCITED crowd at Cavalry Park broke ranks like undisciplined infantry and the closing yards of Steve McIntyre's try for Portobello were matters of mere hearsay to the engulfed press. But eye witnesses reported two or three tackles suddenly missed by the otherwise heroic Edinburgh Academical defence.

Graham Bruce's conversion, although across the slant of the following wind failed, but Portobello still had to come an invitingly kickable penalty awarded when Ewan Drummond's tackle on the lively Alan Halvorson was adjudged late.

Portobello, though, opted for what turned out to be an unrequited short-penalty routine. *C'est magnifique, mais ce n'est pas la guerre*, though that, frankly, is not how the home support put it.

There were many faces from the Academicals' illustrious past around the ropes. Even those which had worn well aged visibly in the long minutes until Ken McCartney's final whistle signalled that the Academicals, one of the eight original members of the Scottish Rugby Union, were at long last in the first division – at the expense, piquantly, of the most remarkable of Scottish rugby's emergent clubs.

It had not looked likely for most of the first half. The Academicals had that most helpful wind for the right-footed punter, following but right to left, yet Portobello had an ominous amount of the game.

They were much the quicker on to the second nibble at the line-out and they drove and rucked much better, with the back-row of Russell McIntyre, Steve Roy, and Gary Alexander going great guns.

However, the Portobello scrum was always under more pressure, and, in the second half, with the wind now tending to carry the ball to the Academical jumpers, the promising Jeremy Richardson and the experienced Kenny Dodds came tellingly into their own.

It was 12-6 at half-time; two penalty goals apiece by Drummond and Bruce, with Drummond, son of the inimitable Charlie, having converted a try by Jamie Paton. Picking up his scrum-half's pass on the bounce, Paton had ducked and weaved through a miscellany of wrong-footed tacklers, finally being driven over by Joe Munro for one of the most vital tries in the club's long story.

Accies on the attack against Portobello

Though young Graham Henry played a significant role at full-back in a famous victory, Paton was in a class of his own among the Academical backs. He is beautifully two-footed, an accomplishment he owes to some advice in his formative years from the headmaster at Loretto, Rab Bruce Lockhart.

The Portobello try was a fraternal affair, Russell McIntyre breaking clear to send his brother pounding past a momentarily tentative and shredded defence.

An enthralling game, in which Portobello surrendered their greatly cherished record of never having lost at home in the history of the league, was mostly clean as it was competitive.

By that tantalisingly narrow margin Portobello lost too what would have been the astonishing distinction of having climbed from the seventh division to the first in six successive seasons. And yet, as one left the clubhouse, one's thought was that no one would have known from the singing whether they had won or lost.

The two teams that day were:

Portobello: G. Bruce; M. Stewart, A Denham, I. Boyter, S. McIntyre; E. Henderson, A. Halvorson; M. Forrest, D. Muir, A. Wilson, D. Dickson, N. Ellis, S. McIntyre, S. Roy, G. Alexander.

Edinburgh Academicals: G. Henry; E. Drummond, J. Sutton, P. Heaney, S. Howgate; J. Paton, N. Campbell; J. Munro, B. Brown, R. Lutton, A. Adamson, J. Richardson, G. Richardson, K. Dodds, E Hopkins.

Accies celebrate their promotion to the first division

As far as Jackson is concerned, Jeremy Richardson, at the end of his first full season in senior rugby, was the key man for Accies:

> There was a strong wind right down the pitch. We played with it in the first half and when we turned round only 12-6 ahead we knew it was going to be tight, but Jeremy won the game for us – no doubt about that. Against the wind he won almost every single line-out in the second half – so they had no possession. And every time they established good field position we were able to relieve the pressure because on a windy day the ball invariably ends up in touch and they couldn't get it off Jeremy. That match is almost certainly my best memory in every rugby context.

For Elgar Hopkins, the sense of relief after all those seasons of struggling at the wrong end of the table was overwhelming, even if the match itself remains mostly a blur to him:

> It was very tense. All I really remember is getting to half-time, feeling really awful and going off behind a tree and howking up a plum tomato I must have eaten the night before, then running back onto the pitch and going like hell for the last 40 minutes. At the end all the guys in blue and white stripes were jumping up and down and waving their arms, so I started jumping up and down and waving my arms around too. But I had no idea what the score was, I hardly knew what was going on – I was so tired and it had been so tense.
>
> We got back to the changing room and the champagne came out. It was really emotional – I almost couldn't take it anymore.
>
> The Porty players were really good about it. They would have been promoted if they had won the match and they were very gracious in defeat. It was a real shame they didn't make it because it would have meant that they had been promoted from Division Seven to Division One in consecutive years, which would have been a great achievement – and they seemed to fall away a bit after missing out that year. I think they lost a bit of momentum after that game, I suspect it took the wind out of their sails a bit.
>
> We got the bus back to Raeburn Place and there was a guard of honour all the way from the gate to the door of the clubhouse, clapping us in. Needless

Changing-room celebrations

to say: we had a great night. We drank champagne into the early hours of the morning – it was just fantastic. And on the Sunday I had to play for a combined Accies-Heriot's team in an over 30s match at Goldenacre . . . which was tough going.

By happy coincidence, promotion for the first time to Division I coincided with the club celebrating its 125th anniversary, which meant that that season's dinner in the Adam Rooms at the George Hotel was to be the scene of a double celebration – but unfortunately things got a bit out of hand.

Jim Telfer, fresh from Scotland's 1984 Grand Slam success, was toasting the club, but by then the evening had descended into chaos and he could not be heard above the rabble. 'People were being sick in their soup . . . and that was before the piano was broken,' shrugs Rob Blair, with a weary smile.

Billy Menzies recalls:

We had got as many crammed into the George as we could – I think there were about 170 there – and some of the younger spirits got a bit carried away. Graeme Forbes was on my table and I remember him saying: 'That's enough', when an empty coffee pot just missed his head. So he picked up ours and launched it back in the direction it had come from. The whole thing just descended into a riot.

It was a nightmare experience. I had the joy of walking back in with the manager after the place had eventually been emptied, and the floor was completely covered with broken glass. It was crunching beneath our feet. Needless to say we were banned, and we've only just recently been allowed back in there again.

Lismore Sevens, 1984

Back: J. Scott, P. Drennan, B. Brown, D. Young

Front: J. Paton, K.P. Brown, R. Sloan

Nobody really knew how Accies would fare in their first season in Division I, but most impartial observers suspected that they would struggle. In the ten years of league rugby in Scotland, only three of the teams promoted as runners up in Division II had managed to avoid relegation the following season.

Certainly, Charlie Jackson was in no doubt that if Accies were to survive and prosper in the top flight then the squad would have to be bolstered.

We were the first team to bring a New Zealander over – Hamish Quinliven – a tight-head prop who gave the scrum stability and provided some toughness. We recruited him through a friend of Vic Murphy. He came over with his wife and we found him a job, somewhere to stay and made sure he had some cash in his pocket. His attitude towards training had a big impact on the rest of the squad. He used to stop and really let the guys hear about it if they were not giving 100 per cent.

We also managed to get hold of a young Irish flanker called Chris Pim, who had played against us for Old Wesley the previous year. He had a shock of red hair but it wasn't just that that made him stand out – he was a real all-action hero. So when I found out he was coming to Agricultural College in Edinburgh, I made sure he came to play at Raeburn.

And then there was the nucleus of good players and strong characters already there – like the Richardson brothers. Guy had gone off to Sandhurst, but Charlie was back in Edinburgh after serving in the Falklands and he led from the front as captain of the side. And Jeremy had a similar sort of attitude to Hamish. He doesn't suffer fools and as he got older and more sure of himself, his influence grew.

We had decided that we weren't going to play a standard game, we were going to have a go at people, we were going to run at teams from our own 22, and Sandy MacCrae at full-back (and later in the centre) was absolutely outstanding that season. We were beginning to get a core of guys who were determined to drag the standard up.

Accies had a golden opportunity to get their season off to a flyer, dominating their first league match against Heriot's at Raeburn Place, but somehow they lost the game 7-6. It was a bitter pill to swallow, but there was no time for self-pity. The following week they had to play defending champions Hawick at Mansfield

Park, and anything other than a top-class performance would inevitably spell disaster.

While the 23-6 score-line at the end of the match made painful reading, the game itself was described by Chris Rea in *The Scotsman* as 'thoroughly captivating':

> Edinburgh Accies, inexperienced in the ways of Division I and, despite the previous week's result against Heriot's, uncertain of their ability to keep afloat in the deepest waters, plunged in with such enterprise that they not only stayed the course but . . . cast off their inhibitions and surely played as positively as any side have dared to do at Mansfield Park in recent years.

After going behind in the second minute to a Keith Mitchell try, Accies found themselves 20-0 down at half-time and the writing appeared to be on the wall. However, aided by the departure of Mitchell with a rib injury, the visitors rallied well and spent most of the second half encamped in opposition territory. Eventually Chris Pim burrowed over after a number eight pick-up by Charlie Richardson, and Sandy Macrae kicked the conversion. If he had been successful with one or two of his six earlier attempts at goal the final outcome of the match might not have been altered, but the score line would certainly have been more respectable.

The team clearly drew confidence from their performance against Hawick, and a week later they got their first win of the season against previously undefeated Watsonians (18-12 at Myreside) – with silky smooth winger Dave Hutchison, in the side for the injured Stewart Howgate, scoring all Accies' points – four penalties, a try and a touchline conversion – on his Division I debut.

A 38-4 defeat to Kelso at Raeburn Place served as a timely reminder that giving an inch to one of the top club sides in Scotland is likely to result in the loss of a mile; but Accies then won four games on the trot – against Stewart's Melville FP (22-15 at Inverleith), Selkirk (21-6 at Raeburn Place), Boroughmuir (9-3 at Raeburn Place) and Jed-Forest (17-14 at Riverside Park) – to climb to fourth equal in the table at the mid-season break.

The new boys in Division I were confounding all expectations, and their success was being recognised with call-ups to representative rugby. Jeremy Richardson and Sandy Macrae made their Edinburgh debuts this season; while Charlie Richardson played his first game at that level in four years and went on to represent Scotland B against Ireland B. Hooker Barry Brown sat on the bench for Edinburgh.

The second half of the league campaign didn't quite live up to the standards set before Christmas, with representative commitments and an unusually high number of injuries meaning that the 1st XV was rarely at full strength.

Losses to Ayr (10-9 away) and Gala (28-15 away), a narrow win over relegation-bound Glasgow Academicals (9-6 at home), and another defeat to Melrose (12-4 at home), saw Accies begin to slip down the league table. But a victory over West of Scotland (13-7 away) in the last game of the season ensured a highly respectable seventh place finish in the table.

Despite having essentially the same squad in the 1985–86 season, Accies struggled to emulate the sort of form that had taken Scottish rugby by surprise during their debut year in Division I. The league programme started with a fine win over Gala (11-6 at Raeburn Place) but then losses to Heriot's (24-6 at Goldenacre), Hawick (24-6 at Raeburn Place), Watsonians (49-0 at Raeburn Place), Kelso (10-3 at Poynder Park), Stewart's Melville (22-6 at Raeburn Place), Selkirk (9-3 at Philliphaugh) and Boroughmuir (15-6 at Meggetland) saw Accies plummet to bottom of the table at the break.

In fairness, the team were not always the architects of their own downfall. Against Watsonians they had played a large chunk of the game with only 12 men on the park, and carrying the injured Jamie Paton on the wing for the last 20 minutes, thanks to the SRU's insistence that replacements should not be permitted at club level. Meanwhile, the Kelso, Selkirk and Boroughmuir games could all have been won with a bit more composure in the scoring zone, and a bit more luck in the goal-kicking department.

Despite this disappointing start to the season, the team were clearly gaining respect, as was reflected in the involvement of Joe Munro, Sandy Macrae and Charlie Richardson all with Scotland B this season (as well as Chris Gray, who had by now moved south to Nottingham) – although only Richardson made it into the side, as captain against Italy B. Macrae also trained with the full Scotland squad during the build-up to the Five Nations.

When the second half of the league campaign got under way, Accies played well to defeat Jed-Forest (12-11 at Raeburn Place) and then Preston Lodge (20-6 at Pennypit), but a lack of concentration against West of Scotland led to a 15-6 home defeat in a game which was there for the taking. Victory over Kilmarnock (32-6 at Raeburn Place) salvaged hope that Accies could avoid relegation under their own steam, but a desperately disappointing performance against Melrose (lost 16-4 at The Greenyards in a rearranged Thursday night fixture in mid April) created an end of season cliff-hanger, with everyone at Raeburn Place being forced into an anxious wait to find out if Preston Lodge would perform a miraculous escape act at Accies' expense the following week. It was unlikely, as they had to defeat West of Scotland by 46 points to leapfrog Accies – but stranger things have happened on a rugby pitch. In the event, Preston Lodge slumped to a 37-6 defeat and were relegated alongside Kilmarnock.

The 1986–87 season brought another close encounter with relegation. Victories over Kelso (24-13 away), Ayr (22-19 at home) and Bradford & Bingley (38-12 away) in friendly fixtures should have been an ideal springboard to the new season, but in the third of those matches two sending-offs would have serious ramifications on the first half of the club's league campaign.

Jeremy Richardson recalls:

I got sent off for over-vigorous rucking, so I was in the dressing room with my head in my hands when in walked Charlie. He'd been sent off too. He'd tackled someone on the touchline and followed through into the ground that was being built on next to the pitch. The unfortunate thing about that was that we both were banned by the SRU [Charlie for eight weeks and Jeremy for seven] and we missed most of the first half of the season. We had also both been selected to play in a brothers charity match the following week, with the Milnes from Heriot's, the Hastings and Kennedys from Watsonians, and the Calders, Scotts and Brewsters from Stewart's Melville, but we were unable to make it because we were immediately suspended.

I remember after the game, this chap came into the clubrooms with a tweed suit and wearing an Academical club tie. It transpired that he was a Yorkshire farmer who had been a boarder at the Academy in his youth. He said he had been coming to watch this fixture for nigh on 30 years and he had never been so embarrassed, and how disgraceful it was that Accies had had two players sent off. As far as he was concerned the club had been going to the dogs ever since it had gone open. He then said to Charlie Jackson, who was the coach and I think the only committee man with us at that time: 'Tell me, how many real Academicals were in that team?'

To which Charlie replied: 'We started with four and ended up with two.'

Despite the absence of the Richardson brothers, two home wins over Glasgow Academicals (31-13) and Heriot's (24-12) to one away defeat to Gala (13-20) in the first three league games, induced a quiet optimism to permeate around Raeburn Place. But morale and self-belief were affected more than they should have been by the loss of players through injury, work commitments, and various other non-rugby related reasons. This resulted in four straight defeats in the league – to Hawick (32-6 at Mansfield Park), Watsonians (13-7 at Myreside), Kelso (27-0 at Raeburn Place) and Stewart's Melville (9-7 at Inverleith) – and ensured that Accies would have to scrap it out in another relegation dogfight during the second half of the campaign. A 13-9 home victory over Selkirk in the last game before the mid-season recess would prove invaluable at the end of the season.

Losses to Jed-Forest (10-0 at home) and West of Scotland (29-7 away), a draw against Melrose (12-12 at home), and another loss to Ayr (9-6 away), would have been catastrophic to the team's chances of survival in almost any other season – but fortunately there was no shortage of other sides having equally poor campaigns, and Accies were only one of six clubs facing relegation on the Saturday morning of the final round of league matches. A 15-0 win over Boroughmuir at Raeburn Place, and defeats for Jed-Forest and Gala on that same afternoon, meant Accies stayed up. In only his second game for the club, Michael Walker, who was home on holiday from Bristol University, kicked 11 invaluable points in that vital game.

Ruminating in *The Chronicle* in May 1987, club president the Rev. Howard Haslett wrote:

> And so, brightly and confidently, we await next season. We look forward to a new fixture with CIYMS [Church of Ireland Young Men's Society] in Belfast, a revived one with London Scottish in London, and on old established one with Old Wesley in Dublin. And we have our dreams as well – international caps for two or three of the boys, a tour on foreign soil, and of being up there with the championship leaders when March comes around again.

It was going to take slightly longer than the good Reverend had hoped – but the club would take some major steps towards realising his vision during the next couple of years.

CHAPTER THIRTY-ONE

I always wanted to prove the point that if anyone thought that we were just easy doormat city boys then they would have another think coming – that was my attitude.

Jeremy Richardson

AT THE TAIL-END OF THE 1986–87 season Jeremy Richardson had been in the Edinburgh team which had defeated the South 21-18 on their own patch for the first time since 1979 to lift the District Championship. Richardson had looked good against Alan Tomes in that match, doing enough to earn selection as understudy to the Hawick, Scotland and Lions lock in the 26-man national squad for that summer's inaugural Rugby World Cup.

He did not play in any of Scotland's four matches that summer, so missed out on becoming the first member of the club to play international rugby since Rodger Arneil. By the time he picked up his long awaited cap against South Africa in 1994, the club had been represented by five other players at that level.

The first of these Internationalists was David Sole, who was already established in the Scotland team when he arrived at Raeburn Place at the start of the 1987–88 season. Sole's decision to join Accies in preference to some of the more glamorous sides in Scottish rugby was a major coup and a catalyst to the club's emergence as serious title contenders.

David Sole:

The choice of club came down to the fact that I didn't want to commute to the Borders and I had a number of pals playing at Accies. They were still in Division I after just managing to stay up at the end of the 1986–87. Also, when I looked around the other clubs in that part of Edinburgh weren't crying out for a loose-head prop – Heriot's had the Milnes, the Brewsters were at Stewart's Melville – and although I backed myself to get into any team, it made more sense for me to go to a club where they needed front-row, rather than have either myself or David Milne, for example, competing for the same jersey.

What I had enjoyed and really respected about Bath when I played there was the intensity of training. Because there was so much competition for places the Tuesday night sessions were really, really intense and edgy, with frequent punch-ups. I'm a great believer that you have to train the way you play, so bringing that sort of mentality was something I was keen to do at Accies.

The other thing was that the Rec had a very formidable reputation as a home ground, and although the numbers of supporters was never going to be quite the same as they were at Bath, I wanted Raeburn Place to be as impregnable as the likes of Mansfield Park in Hawick. I think we had that for a while – it was a tough place for sides to come and win – I remember beating Hawick there which was a huge result at the time.

The really frustrating thing was that we would beat the tough sides and then blow it against the weaker teams in the league.

Other important recruits to the club this season were Alec Moore, a powerful winger and a future Scotland Internationalist who arrived from Gala; Andy Blakeway from South Africa, who was the first in a succession of excellent players to arrive at the club as part of a highly rewarding relationship with Glenwood Old Boys rugby club in Durban; and Brian Hay-Smith, who had played infrequently for the club whilst studying in Aberdeen, was back in Edinburgh full-time and keen to make the number ten jersey his own. There were two notable departures in Charlie Richardson (who had moved to London) and Chris Pim (who had returned to Ireland after finishing his agriculture degree).

The pack, aided in training by the arrival of a new £2,500 scrummage machine donated by sponsors Fiat, won as much ball as any team in the league, but the lack of midfield thrust and a failure to bring the team's two most potent strike runners – Moore and Sandy Macrae – into the game enough meant that results were, on the whole, disappointing. The lack of a consistent goal-kicker was also still a problem.

Kelso issued a declaration of intent at the beginning of their successful league challenge when they dished out a humbling 37-9 thrashing at Raeburn Place. That was followed by a defeat at Hawick (19-8) a week later, before a 10-4 victory over

1988–89 1st XV

Glasgow Academicals brought the first league points of the season. Melrose made it a Border hat-trick (27-9 away), but Selkirk couldn't achieve the Grand Slam with Accies winning 14-12 at Raeburn Place. That victory was followed by a 12-6 success at Musselburgh thanks to two interception tries from Pete Drennan and Sandy Macrae, but the first part of the season ended as it had started, with defeats against Watsonians (16-3 at home) and West of Scotland (15-6 away).

Five tries in a 24-17 victory over Heriot's in a friendly at Raeburn Place on December 5 augured well for the second half of the season, and the resurrection of the London Scottish fixture at Richmond the following weekend (25-9 loss), as well as facing the Co-optimists on 28 December (28-4 loss) and Old Wesley in Dublin on the morning of the Scotland versus Ireland match (15-16 loss) ensured that the team were fully match-fit for the resumption of league rugby on 19 January.

Victory over Ayr with a last minute push-over try (16-15 at home) and a draw against Boroughmuir (9-9 away) eased Accies away from the relegation zone; but then losses to Kilmarnock (15-6 at home), Heriot's (18-12 away) and Stewart's Melville (12-18 away) would have put them back in Division II if Musselburgh had managed to beat Watsonians by 50 points in their last game of the season. Fortunately they did not – and the building programme which had brought the likes of Sole and Moore to Raeburn Place was able to continue.

In May 1988 Scotland went on a development tour to Zimbabwe, with five players connected to Accies on the trip – they were current players Jeremy Richardson, Alex Moore and Dave Leckie (who scored five tries in a midweek game against Zimbabwean invitation team, Goshawks), former player Chris Gray, and Damian Cronin, who planned to join the club in October 1988 and was listed as an Edinburgh Academical on that trip.

Cronin ended up staying with Bath after deciding that life as a hotelier in Dingwall was not for him, but there were several other new faces around Raeburn Place to provide strength and depth to the squad when pre-season training got under way ahead of the 1988–89 season. Dave McIvor had arrived from Glenrothes; Paul Hogarth had joined from Hawick (although a stress fracture in Hogarth's right foot meant that his appearances were few and far between); Simon Burns had moved across the city from Murrayfield Wanderers; Russell Adam had been recruited fresh from a Scottish Schools tour of New Zealand out of Dollar Academy; Calum Bannerman had signed up from Edinburgh University; and scrum-half Jock Dun returned to action after a year out with a knee injury. Rob Wainwright's name also started to appear on the team-sheet during the second half of the season, but injury and work commitments limited the army doctor's appearances until he became a regular in the team during the 1990–91 season.

With Jeremy Richardson installed as club captain, the season got under way with a disappointing defeat to a strong Bradford & Bingley side (31-12 at Clayton Road), but two wins over Ayr (18-13 at home) and C.I.Y.M.S. (63-15 at home) created some momentum for the start of the league campaign. In the CIYMS game, Simon Burns was successful with eight out of his eleven kicks at goal, raising hopes that a solution might at last have been found for Accies long-standing goal kicking problem. This proved to be wishful thinking.

After an emphatic 24-0 demolition of Stewart's Melville at Raeburn Place, a trip down to Poynder Park to face defending champions Kelso ended in frustration, when Andrew Ker orchestrated a narrow 12-11 victory for the home team.

Sketch of Raeburn Place in 1988 by Ian Lutton

1989–90 1st XV

Playing with a strong wind at their backs in the first half, Accies had muscled their way into an 11-3 half-time lead thanks to two early tries from David Sole and Rod Mitchell. But the advantage could, and probably should, have been much more, with Paul Hogarth crashing over for a third Accies try only for referee Ian Bullerwell to rule that the ball had not been properly grounded, and Simon Burns landing only one out of his six shots at goal. In the second half Ker kept Accies pinned back in their own 22, and then knocked over two drop-goals and a penalty to win the match. It was a disappointing result, particularly as Accies had outscored Kelso by two tries to nil, but the overall performance and closeness of the match were encouraging. Kelso had strolled to a 37-9 victory at Raeburn Place almost exactly a year earlier.

Jeremy Richardson wins a lineout v Jed-Forest, 1990

If that performance hinted that Accies had the potential to be genuine championship contenders, this was confirmed a week later when Hawick came to Raeburn Place. The Green Machine might not have been the all-conquering side they once were, but they still carried a formidable reputation, and they had not lost to Accies in 24 years. The visitors led 6-3 at half-time, but after the retiral of Tony Stanger with a leg injury after 20 minutes Hawick lacked a cutting edge behind the scrum, so they had to rely on the clever kicking of Greig Oliver and Colin Gass as they tried to keep their noses in front. After defending grimly for most of the first half, Accies began to gain the upper-hand at the pit-face with David Sole at his inspirational best, and this gave the half-backs room to start dictating the shape of the game. From deep inside his own half Jamie Paton sent a long miss-two pass to Simon Burns, who cut through the outside centre channel to feed Duncan Pearce. Russell Adam carried the move on and when he was stopped just short Paton was on hand to finish the move he had started – forcing his way over the Hawick line assisted by at least half of his pack. Burns kicked his second penalty to give Accies an 11-6 lead, but Hawick are never more dangerous than when the chips are down, and a late Gass penalty produced a furious five minute finale, with only a despairing dive from Dave McIvor preventing Gass from pinching the victory with a drop-goal at the death.

John Dun gets the ball away against Jed-Forest, 1990

Simon Burns reckons that match was probably his happiest memory of playing for the club:

> I remember speaking to some of the older members of the club afterwards, guys who had long since retired, and it clearly meant an awful lot to them. Hawick had been the top team for so long, and Accies had taken quite a few hammerings from them over the years, so I think that result showed that the days of Accies being just a mediocre side were over – because it might have been close, but it was no fluke. We thoroughly deserved that win. It meant so much to a lot of people, and looking back I think it was a key moment in that team's development.

The team that day was: S. Burns; A. Moore, R. Adam, A MacRae, D. Pearce; J. Paton, J. Dun; D Sole, W. Brand, J. Munro, J. Richardson, A. Adamson, D. McIvor, G. Richardson, I. Nicol.

Victory over Glasgow Academicals the following week (13-3 at New Anniesland) was followed by a home defeat against Melrose which can, with the benefit of hindsight, be regarded as a depressing portent of disappointments to come. Accies led 16-4 at half-time, but after taking several wrong options they eventually succumbed under an avalanche of Melrose pressure and went down 22-16. That result was a blow, but with Kelso, Boroughmuir and Hawick all dropping points it wasn't fatal to the team's title aspirations. Three straight wins for Accies over Selkirk (9-3 away) Jed-Forest (10-9 away) and Watsonians (50-15 away) put them second equal in the table at the mid-season break. They were still in with a shout – but there could be no more slip ups.

Unfortunately for Brian Hay-Smith, it was his spectacular blunder against Ayr in the first league game after the break which will forever, and rather unfairly, be remembered as the moment the team's championship challenge went up in flames.

As the man himself recalls:

> Our forwards were destroying their forwards, so we got a penalty try in the first half after they brought down the scrum when we were going for the pushover. I kicked the conversion, right in front of the posts – no problem. Then, in the second half we got another penalty try, which made it 10-10. The conditions weren't the best, it was wet under foot, and as I ran up to

Dave McIvor takes the ball on against Boroughmuir at Murrayfield with Jason Parrott and
Jeremy Richardson in close support

kick the conversion, my wrong foot slipped and I almost hit the corner flag.
It wasn't even close – I was miles away.

What everyone forgets is the fact that we then scored another try which
put us 14-10 ahead, so the game was still there for the taking. But we then
hoisted an up-and-under which Starky [Derek Stark] caught under his own
posts and then proceeded to run 95 metres to score the equaliser. That's
how it finished, 14-14.

A teenage Rowan Shepherd had come off the bench for the concussed Alec
Moore. It was only his third appearance for the 1st XV and his first league game.
He says:

I remember sitting in the changing room afterwards thinking this is great,
I've just played with all these guys who I used to read about in the paper. I

was disappointed that we'd not won but I was young and I thought there would be plenty more opportunities. Having said that, I also knew enough to keep my mouth shut, because everyone else was silent. Our coach, Charlie Jackson, didn't even know what to say.

Then Soley takes his boot off and as cool as ice he says: 'Well Brian, that's the league f****d then, isn't it?'

He got up, took his towel, and walked off to the showers. There was no fuss, he was completely calm. And it hit me, like a sledge-hammer, right between the eyes – I was playing with the big boys now. That was a big wake-up call for me.

Brian Hay-Smith:

Afterwards we had a few beers, and I wired into the port particularly quickly. On the bus back we stopped at Eaglesham for a pint and Soley said to me: 'You go get the beers and port because you blew the game.'

So off I went to get the drinks, and when I came out the bus was nowhere to be seen. So I'm sitting in the bus-stop on my two cases of beer holding two bottles of port and the supporters' bus drives past. It was literally like one of these comedy films: the breaks came on and it reversed back and picked me up. So we drank ourselves silly on the way home, and when we got to Raeburn I was three sheets to wind. Now, I've never been the bravest but I marched up to Soley and said: 'That was effin' ridiculous.' He looked at me and all he said was: 'You'll learn.'

Although it wasn't apparent at the time, the reality was that even after that draw the league title could still have been won. If Accies had won all of their remaining matches they would have finished a point clear at the top of the table. And even when the team drew with Boroughmuir a week later (16-16 at Raeburn Place) there was still an outside chance of clinching the championship on points difference. A sparkling seven try to nil victory over Heriot's (39-3 at Raeburn Place) and a solid if somewhat less spectacular win over Glasgow High Kelvinside (16-6 also at Raeburn Place) meant the team went into their final re-arranged fixture at the very end of the season chasing a highly unlikely 132 point home victory over West of Scotland – but they lost 15-14 and ended up fourth in the table. It was Accies best ever finish in the league but frustration at the number of games which had been allowed to slip away took quite a bit of the shine off their achievement.

During the autumn of 1988, Australia had toured Scotland and England, playing Edinburgh at Myreside on 9 November. David Sole and Jeremy Richardson were in the Edinburgh team, which lost 25-19. Three more Accies – Andy Adamson, Jamie Paton and Simon Burns – were on the bench, and Adamson came on in the back-row for Kevin Rafferty of Heriot's.

In the summer of 1989 Sole toured Australia with Finlay Calder's Lions squad, playing in all three Tests in the famous 2-1 series victory. At a less exalted level the club's Far Away Touring Society – comprising of such stalwarts of the clubs social scene as Tim Lees, BJ Boyd, Vincent O'Donoghue, the Gardiner brothers, 'Whispering' George Henderson, Allan Burns, Elgar Hopkins, Dave Hutchison, Ken Lauder and Magnus Moodie – embarked on a 17-day tour of Hong Kong and Thailand. It was a highly ambitious undertaking which had been two years in the funding and organising.

Vincent O'Donoghue:

> We had a great time, but we were perhaps too well organised for our own good. One of our fixtures was supposed to be against a local army side, but when Major Hontom, the army officer who had organised the fixture, saw our tour brochure he decided that we were a better team than we had led him to believe – so he scheduled us to play the New Zealand army team, which was stationed in Hong Kong at that time, instead.
>
> On the night we arrived we threw a party at the Excelsior Hotel where we were staying, for everyone we knew in Hong Kong. It goes without saying that we were all partaking in a few drinks, and that was when Major Hontom decided to tell Tim Lees, Ken Dodds and I that he had rearranged the fixture. We decided not to tell the rest of the squad until the day of the match.
>
> The next day we visited this magnificent aquarium which we travelled to by cable-car. As we looked out at the spectacular view we spotted this group of guys with back-packs running up and down the hills below. This was in temperatures approaching 40 degrees Celsius. It turned out that this was the New Zealand army boys warming up for the match.

On the afternoon of the game we were in the bar at the British Army base, where the game was going to be played, having a couple of beers while Ken Dodds ran around trying to organise a team. All of a sudden we heard this rumble outside – it was the sound of studs on the hard turf as our opponents charged onto the field – dressed all in black and looking pretty ferocious. It was amazing how many of our squad suddenly realised they were carrying injuries.

Believe it or not we were leading at half-time, curtsey of a penalty try, I think – but superior fitness, organisation and sobriety shone through in the end. We ended up losing fairly heavily.

Ahead of the 1989–90 season, Charlie Jackson repositioned himself as team manager and former Scotland A prop, Hugh Campbell, came in as head coach. The club was struck by tragedy on 7 September 1989, when David Pearson was killed in a car crash near the hamlet of Finaven, half way between Forfar and Brechin. He was a successful Edinburgh lawyer who hailed originally from Melrose, and had played prop for British universities. Pearson had joined the club as an Associate playing Member in July 1977, and played regularly for the 1st XV for the next few years. After hanging up his boots he served as Club Secretary between 1980 and 1984, and his influence was instrumental in the club gaining promotion from Division Two during this period. Thereafter, he continued to work tirelessly behind the scenes for the club as it consolidated the team's position in the top flight and they began to establish themselves as genuine championship contenders.

The loss of Pearson inevitably affected the mood of the club, and a 15-9 home defeat to Bradford & Bingley two days later was almost inevitable. Two victories over Ayr (26-10 at Millbrae) and CIYMS (20-13 in Ireland) during the next fortnight provided a more accurate indication of the team's potential.

The arrival of John Allan from Glenwood and Norrie Rowan from closer to home (Boroughmuir) had added experience and bulk to the Accie front-row. After a disappointing start to the campaign against Heriot's (25-7 defeat at Goldenacre), the team recovered well to win their next four matches against Stewart's Melville (34-6 at Inverleith), Kelso (16-3 at Raeburn Place), Hawick (16-9 at Mansfield Park) and Stirling County (23-15 at Raeburn Place). But two defeats against Border opposition delivered a body blow to the club's title aspirations.

Victory in the Heriot's U-21 Sevens

The first of these matches, against Jed-Forest at Riverside Park, was described in the *Scotland on Sunday* as 'an ugly affront to rugby, enough to make any traditionalist cringe'. This 15-4 victory for Jed-Forest put the Borderers top of the table, but it was overshadowed by two brawls right in front of the main stand. The lack of a reliable goal kicker once again cost Accies dearly – this time they missed half a dozen kicks at goal.

The next match, against Melrose at the Greenyards, could not have got off to a better start. The visitors dominated possession and territory during the first 15 minutes and eventually took the lead when Moore latched onto Burns' well-timed pass, cut inside his opposite number Angus Redburn, and then went outside home full-back Duncan Cameron, for a fine try. Against a young Melrose pack, Accies dominated up-front, but their backs failed to make the most of the wealth of possession they were provided with, and a masterful kicking display by Craig

Chalmers was the difference between the two sides. Not only did the Scotland stand-off send over five sweetly struck penalties, his kicking from hand was also devastating. 'As a full-back who was looking to attack from deep, the guy that gave you least opportunity to do that – by some distance – was Chalmers,' recalls Simon Burns. 'His tactical kicking was immense – he limited your opportunities so well.' Melrose won the match 15-9, which put them a point ahead of Jed-Forest at the top of the league.

Captain David Sole with the Barbarian team that played New Zealand at Twickenham in 1989.

During the second half of the season Accies defeated Gala (13-3 at Raeburn Place), West of Scotland (16-6 at Burnbrae), Ayr (22-3 at Raeburn Place) and Glasgow High Kelvinside (17-10 at Raeburn Place), but lost narrowly to Boroughmuir in the last game of the season (17-16 at Meggetland). Had the team won that match Accies would have finished second equal in the league, behind champions Melrose – but instead they finished fourth, just as they had the previous season.

During the summer of 1990, Scotland toured New Zealand with four Academicals in their squad. Sole captained the national team in both Test matches (a heavy 31-6 defeat in Dunedin and a narrow 21-18 loss in Auckland), while John Allan played in the first Test, and Alec Moore scored Scotland's second try in the second Test. Jeremy Richardson was also in the squad but did not make it into the Test side, although he did receive praise for his performances as captain of the midweek team, and particularly his display against Manawatu.

Richardson returned from New Zealand, changed his jumper and headed to North America on the Accies pre-season tour of Canada – visiting Montreal, Ottawa and Kingston, before spending a week in Toronto where they were warmly entertained by Toronto Scottish. While Sole, Allan and Moore decided that one rugby trip per summer was more than enough, Richardson had played a leading role in the fund-raising and organisation of this trip, and when Charlie Jackson dropped out he also took on the role of tour manager.

With a touring party of 25 first team squad members, Accies won all of the six games they played in two weeks. This included a victory over an Ontario Presidents XV which contained several Canadian internationalists.

Winners of 1989 Haddington Sevens, having beaten Trinity 20-14 in the final

Ronnie Sloan, the club's vice-president, played in a social match against an Ottawa Scottish XV, thus achieving the impressive feat of playing for the 1st XV at Accies in four different decades, having made his debut in 1965. His appearance in Canada wasn't the end of Sloan's rugby career: he continued to play intermittently for the club in social sides throughout the 1990s and into the new millennium.

Simon Burns took over the club captaincy for the 1990–91 season and led the team to three comfortable friendly victories over Bradford & Bingley (22-9 at Clayton Road), Ayr (30-3 at Raeburn Place) and C.I.Y.M.S. (56-3 at Raeburn Place), and a 27-3 victory at Glasgow High/Kelvinside in the first league game of the campaign. However, this form deserted the side against Heriot's and they went down 23-17 at home, in the only match Accies lost before Christmas. The next six league matches brought five wins – over Stewart's Melville (15-6 at Raeburn Place), Kelso (27-9 at Poynder Park), Hawick (29-12 at Raeburn Place), Melrose (8-4 at Raeburn Place) and Selkirk (36-3 at Philiphaugh) – and a draw against Stirling County (12-12 at Bridgehaugh).

Canada Tour 1990 – the squad enjoy a post-match beer in Toronto

Canada Tour 1990 – just after the Toronto Scottish Match. Jeremy Richardson, Remo Maciocia,
Dave McIvor, Kevin Wyness and Simon Burns

The victory over Melrose was achieved with the assistance of Jeremy Thomson, the club's most recent recruit from South Africa.

George Menzies:

Jeremy was a magnificent player. He was so fast, he read the game so well and he had wonderful hands. He was also a very nice guy. He arrived at Raeburn Place the week after playing in the Currie Cup Final for Natal in front of 55,000 people.

I said: 'We'll start you off in the seconds. We know you are a good player because you've just won the Currie Cup, but that's how we do it at this club. You have to show that you are better than the next person and then you'll get promoted.'

He said: 'I understand that exactly. Not a problem.' He'd just won the Currie Cup but was happy to prove himself for Accies seconds.

So we played Heriot's and both teams had a couple of their 1st XV players coming back from injury, there was something like seven district players on the field, and it was an absolutely wonderful game – it was far higher than the standard of the 1st XV game on the pitch next door. Jeremy played very well, as expected – I think he scored something like four tries – so the following week we were able to put him in the 1st team.

The second half of the season failed to live up to expectations. Accies defeated Jed-Forest (19-6 at Raeburn) in another bad tempered contest against those opponents, but were out-played by Gala (losing 17-12 at Netherdale). After hammering doomed Edinburgh Wanderers (55-3 at Murrayfield) to move within a point of top spot, the season ended in disappointment with two defeats against Champions elect Boroughmuir (7-6 at Raeburn Place) and Currie (24-7 at Raeburn Place).

Accies finished sixth in the championship table, but they did pick up some silverware when they defeated Stirling County 20-10 in front of 3,500 rugby fans at Meggetland to lift the Alloa Brewery Cup – making amends for their defeat to Heriot's in the final of the same competition the previous year. For once Accies benefited from accurate goal-kicking, with Brian Hay-Smith kicking two penalties and a drop goal, as well as scoring a try. Accies' other points came from a Graeme MacGregor touch down.

Twickenham
Sevens squad

Accies also enjoyed success in the Middlesex Sevens at Twickenham during the spring, reaching the semi-finals before going down to a red-hot Harlequins side.

Simon 'Billy' Burns remembers:

Their outside three was Will Carling, Everton Davies and Andy Harriman. The game had been nip-and-tuck when late on they gave the ball to Harriman with 90 yards to go.

I'll always remember the immortal cry of Stewart Howgate: 'Don't worry Billy, I've got him.'

Then: 'Oh no I've not. I've not got him at all, Billy . . . Billy . . .'

Writing in *The Chronicle* at the end of the season, club president George Menzies lamented that:

The slackening of interest throughout the Club during the wet, dark January and February nights may have played a role. Our performance against international opposition also suffered; and Pontypool, Gosforth, North of Ireland, Old Wesley and London Scottish were all comfortable winners. Hard though second and third choice players tried, there was simply not enough fire power to do justice to these fixtures. By contrast, in one of the vital games in the Championship a slightly weakened team just failed to beat Boroughmuir in a splendid game played in the most sporting spirit.

Unless all players make a more sustained commitment to the Club and their colleagues, the highest goals which we have the talent to attain, will continue to elude us. Victory in the Alloa Brewery Cup and the creditable display in reaching the semi-finals of the Twickenham Sevens should not be allowed to obscure the basic facts.

CHAPTER THIRTY-TWO

I used to love wandering down to Raeburn Place on a sunny September day when we were playing another one of the top sides. There was a real a buzz about the place. You were expecting a big crowd, we had a couple of Internationalists and maybe a British Lion playing for us and so did they. Rugby Special *were covering the game – and it was a really enjoyable time to be playing club rugby in Scotland.*

Simon Burns

IN SEPTEMBER 1990 THE CLUB announced that they had signed a lucrative sponsorship deal with Glenmorangie, worth £52,000 over three years. Some of that money was used to fund a trip to Montpellier in the south of France during the build-up to the 1991–92 season. While the game was still strictly amateur, players were becoming increasingly aware of their value, and Accies hoped that indulgences like this would help entice a few new faces to the club, as well as reward those who were already dedicating large chunks of their lives to training and playing at Raeburn Place.

It was also a great way of preparing for the season ahead. The team bonded over nights out on the tiles and afternoons lounging on the beach, but also trained hard and played an incredibly physical game against the locals.

Jeremy Richardson recalls:

Paddy Haslett was with us. A young hooker, just out of school, and in the first scrum he went for the strike against the head – which the gnarled Montpellier front-row didn't think much of. So the first scrum erupted and it was a running battle from then on.

One of my most embarrassing moments in rugby was in that match, when I tried to throw a left hook and the guy I was punching stepped back and I fell over on the ground. It was so undignified. And to rub salt in the wound I got booted by a spectator . . . right in the thigh . . . I got a massive haematoma. I really didn't want to show them I was injured, and thankfully the referee had decided he'd had enough and blew for full-time 20 minutes early.

Glenmorangie sponsorship deal

George Menzies, who had been instrumental in organising the trip, says:

In the 1980s Accies' 3rd XV had a regular home fixture against various French sides. These were the winners of the Coupe des Crus competition between local teams from various wine growing areas in Languedoc. Its organiser, Jean Fauré, Director of the Maison de la Culture et Jeunesse, realised that wine and rugby combined excellently to break down cultural barriers. Each French player brought the club three bottles of wine, often his own produce.

Jean Fauré told me that André Quilis, coach of Montpellier (and France A), wanted to play against a team with a Scottish style back row. McIvor, Leckie and Mitchell fitted the bill, so I organised a pre-season training camp ending with a match against Montpellier.

Their president Dr Daniel Donadio, who shared Jean Fauré's ideals, hoped for an annual fixture which would lead to lasting friendships between the players. Although Accies enjoyed the sunshine and warm

hospitality of their Mediterranean hosts, the fact that each of the four games played during the next four years ended early, amongst mass punch ups, meant that his broader aims were never quite achieved.

Jeremy Thompson had returned to Natal at the end of the previous season; and by the time the 1991–92 campaign had kicked off, Jeremy Richardson, who was now based in Glasgow, had joined GHK. Reinforcements arrived in the shape of Derek Ross (the latest import from Glenwood), David Jackson, who added strength and pace to the back-row, and former Hawick scrum-half Derrick Patterson. Bob Easson arrived back to help coach the backs.

Accies on tour again – Montpellier, 1991

The start of the season was disrupted by the World Cup with David Sole and new club captain John Allan away with the national squad. Alex Moore and Jeremy Richardson were both unlucky not to be selected; but at least they were able to get their point across to the selectors in the most satisfying way when they played in a hastily assembled Edinburgh Borderers team which defeated the full Scotland team (playing under the thin disguise of a Scottish Presidents XV) by 19 points to 13 at Murrayfield a week before the tournament began. Four other Academicals – Dave McIvor, Rob Wainwright, Rowan Shepherd and Derrick Patterson – were also in the Scottish Borderers side. Afterwards, Jack Adams insisted in the *Daily Record* that: 'Scottish rugby has had bad days – but I doubt if it has ever had such a humiliating one.'

The first league game was not played until 9 November, when Accies claimed a maiden league victory over Boroughmuir, the previous season's champions, at Meggetland. A week later Jeremy Richardson endured an unhappy home-coming when Accies defeated GHK (21-6 at Raeburn Place); and a week after that Brenton Catterall, who had played for Zimbabwe against Scotland during the World Cup, was unveiled as the club's ready-made replacement for Richardson in a disappointing defeat to Heriot's at Goldenacre (18-13).

Accies breezed through their next two league games, against Stewart's Melville (43-10 win at Inverleith) and Watsonians (33-7 win at Myreside), but then suffered another set-back when Hawick, who had lost four of their five league games so far that season, demonstrated that there was fight in the old dog yet – grinding out a 9-7 victory at Mansfield Park. The Accies pack had been unusually sluggish against Hawick, but with Rob Wainwright making his first appearance of the season against Stirling County a week later the forwards appeared re-energised – laying the groundwork for a comfortable victory (18-3 at Raeburn Place) which pushed the team up to third in the table at the mid-season break.

A win against Melrose at the Greenyards in the first match of the New Year would have really set the cat amongst the pigeons in the championship race – by reducing the gap between the two sides to just two points and cracking the aura of invincibility which had cushioned Melrose in their undefeated march through the league so far. Despite being without the influential Dave McIvor, who had decided to rest himself ahead of making his international debut against England the following week, the visiting pack was rampant as Accies scorched into a 15-3 lead at half-time. Behind the scrum, Derrick Patterson was orchestrating the game expertly at scrum-half, and Rowan Shepherd was in his element at stand-off – bagging four penalties and a sneaky drop-goal in that opening period. The other Accies points had come from an Alex Moore try.

A solitary Gary Parker penalty in the first half had been all Melrose had to show for their troubles, but after the break, when a scything run by Craig Chalmers set up a try for second-row Robbie Brown, the visiting team's self-belief seemed to waver; and two Parker penalties rescued a 15-15 draw. 'We should never have allowed them to come back from 12 points down,' insisted David Sole, afterwards. 'In the second half we took too many wrong options, wasted possession and kicked badly.'

Accies won their five remaining games – against Selkirk (16-13 at Raeburn Place), Jed-Forest (22-16 at Riverside Park), Gala (12-9 at Raeburn Place), Currie (18-0 at Malleny Park) and West of Scotland (27-9 at Raeburn Place) – but had to settle for second in the table, behind Melrose who didn't ever look like giving away their four point advantage at the top of the league.

1991–92 1st XV

That summer *The Chronicle* reported that:

This season saw the First XV reach it's highest-ever position in the national leagues. In doing so they at times played some of the most attractive rugby in the history of the Club. However, in the critical game against Melrose they allowed the eventual league victors to overhaul their lead and draw the game. Nevertheless, the team scored the most and conceded the fewest points in the competition, a fitting tribute to their tremendous talents.'

John Allan led from the front, and he along with David Sole, Dave McIvor and Rob Wainwright were all members of the Scotland team this year. Derrick Patterson and Alex Moore got B caps, while Russell Adam, Rowan Shepherd, Neil Renton, Malcolm McVie and David Jackson all played for the Scotland Under-21 side.

Two new recruits to the club, Brenton Catteral and Derek Ross, the former Zimbabwe's World Cup Vice-Captain, added a further dimension to the play as well as proving excellent club members. With Richard Moffit, Rod Mitchell and Simon Burns playing district rugby, it is clear why on its day the team could play devastating rugby.

Unfortunately, with so many representative commitments, the team suffered a string of defeats outwith the league, but the spirit displayed by the young reserve, most notably at Pontypool, gives encouragement for the future and hopefully a degree of confidence to the players themselves.

The 2nd XV still managed to play some good rugby, despite the constant call on players to fill gaps in the 1st XV.

Mention must be made of the 6th XV, whose playing experience and administrative expertise combined to win them the Glenmorangie Quaich for the most successful team of the year judged through the whole season.

David Sole retired from the game after touring Australia with Scotland during the summer of 1992. A testimonial dinner organised by Ronnie Sloan that October raised £20,000 which helped, along with a three-year extension of the Glenmorangie sponsorship deal worth £67,500, to pay for floodlights on the 2nd XV pitch at Raeburn Place. Meanwhile, John Allan returned home to Natal, and later that year would pick-up the first of three Currie Cup medals with the province. He would continue playing at that level for another five years, earning 13 Springbok caps. Brenton Catteral, Derek Ross and Russell Adam also moved on.

The loss of two bulwarks of the front-row such as Sole and Allan was a big blow, but the arrival of Martin Scott from Glenrothes and Duncan Wilson from Currie provided some new grunt at the pit-face, and Malcolm McVie began to establish himself in the second-row, despite the stiff competition for selection presented by the evergreen Andy Adamson and Jeremy Richardson, who was back from Glasgow. Chris Simmers would add some extra finesse behind the scrum, having played the previous season for the Racing Club of Paris.

The 1992–93 season was the first in which tries were worth five points as opposed to four. Accies league campaign got off to a promising start, with the team coming from behind to defeat Currie (18-14 at Raeburn Place), but thenMelrose showed their Championship pedigree by grinding out a hard-earned but ultimately convincing 14-0 victory in a cagey contest at The Greenyards. The team then squeezed past Watsonians, thanks to a late try by Richard Porter (16-12 at Raeburn Place) before really blossoming in a 33-20 victory over previously undefeated Gala in front of a large crowd at Raeburn Place – including a good number of people watching the game over the wall next to Inverleith Pond, who were shamed into making a donation by club president and indefatigable fundraiser Ronnie Sloan. By the end of the match there was more than £50 in his bucket. This victory was built upon with wins over Stirling County (16-3 at Bridgehaugh) and Hawick (46-12 at Raeburn Place) during the next fortnight.

Just when it looked as if Accies' inconsistency, which had so often undermined the team in recent seasons, might be a thing of the past, a trip to Poynder Park proved that old habits die hard. John Jeffrey, playing in the second row, inspired a ferocious performance from the home pack, paving the way for a 26-16 Kelso victory. A 43-12 victory over struggling Dundee HSFP was a satisfying way to end the first leg of the league season, but already Accies knew that they had to rely on Melrose and Gala slipping up if they were to improve on third place in the league.

A dour victory over Boroughmuir (10-7 at Meggetland) in the first league match after the Christmas break was pleasing in that it kept Accies' slim hopes of winning the Championship alive, but the performance level was well below the standard expected of genuine contenders, and the game left a lot to be desired as a spectacle of rugby.

After a six week break in competitive games brought about by bad weather and international matches, Accies kept the pressure on with a 22-13 victory over Glasgow High Kelvinside at Old Anniesland, but a 6-6 draw with Selkirk in their next match on a bleak and cold afternoon at Raeburn Place all but killed-off Accies' title challenge. Worse was to follow when a 10-0 half-time lead was squandered to Jed-Forest at Riverside (final score: 11-10 to the home team), on the same day as Melrose clinched the championship with 30-14 win over Gala at Netherdale.

During the run in, Gala had slipped up at Dundee HSFP, so Accies went into their last match, a re-arranged fixture against a depleted Heriot's XV at Raeburn Place, knowing that a win would secure second place in the league. They managed that with a 29-5 victory – showing the sort of enterprise and flair behind the scrum that had been so elusive at key moments during the season.

There was no shame in finishing runner-up in the league for the second consecutive year, but there was a fair degree of frustration around Raeburn Place, that once again matches which the team should have won were allowed to slip by. In fairness, the team was not helped by the constant absence of leading players because of injury and representative commitments. 'It's been a long and frustrating season for the Accies who have rarely, if ever, been able to field all (or even most) of the talent that is supposedly at their disposal,' surmised *The Herald* after the final league game.

The 1993–94 league campaign got under way with wins over Jed-Forest (17-3 at Raeburn Place) and Currie (33-13 at Malleny Park), before the fixture schedule sent Melrose to Raeburn Place for the first time in three years. It was a match which everyone knew beforehand would be pivotal to Accies' season.

The game started with fireworks, when a mass punch-up led to a penalty being awarded to Melrose. Gary Parker kicked the points but Melrose – who were without Craig Chalmers, their influential stand-off – were already struggling to live with the furious pace being set by the home team. With Dave Mitchell, Dave McIvor and Rob Wainwright dominating the battle of the back-rows, and Andy Adamson and Jeremy Richardson supreme in the line-outs, Accies unleashed wave upon wave of attack.

A dazzling break from Chris Simmers almost brought Accies their first try but he was clawed down just short. Instead it was Simon Burns who crossed the line, after Derrick Patterson and Dave McIvor combined to send him clear. The team's second score came right on half-time from a break by Ford Swanson, good link play by Burns, and a deft finish from Simmers. Accies led 13-3 at the break, and 16-3 immediately after the restart thanks to a Hay-Smith penalty.

But Melrose weren't beaten yet, and during the second half they started to crank up the intensity. Whereas their forwards had previously been ineffectual, suddenly Robbie Brown, Doddie Weir and Carl Hogg began blasting their way into every contact situation, and scrapping like wild dogs in the line-out. And where the backs had been sluggish, especially compared to Burns and Simmers, suddenly they were picking gaps and accelerating onto the ball at devastating angles.

It still took a moment of outrageous good fortune for Melrose to break Accies' strangle-hold on this match. Parker had kicked into the corner but Derrick Patterson appeared to beat him in the race to the ball, only for the referee to award Melrose the score – much to the chagrin of Patterson and every other Academical in the ground.

The passing of 15 years has not mellowed Hay-Smith. He is still furious and in no doubt that it was the turning point of the game:

> It was never, ever a try. Deek Patterson got there first, put the ball down and carried on over the dead-ball line. Then Gary Parker turns up, chances his arm and they get the try. He didn't even touch the ball. That was when the doubts started to creep in.

Writing in *The Scotsman* the following weekend, David Sole stated:

> If Edinburgh Academicals lose Division I by a point or two at the end of the season, they will be justified if they point an accusing finger at the referee for their match against Melrose, David Leslie. In making one decision, he determined the course of their fixture against the defending champions, so that from that point in the game onwards there was only going to be one winner.
>
> The decision? Gary Parker's try in the corner, not long into the second half. Admittedly, the referee was not in the best position to award the try as he was following the play. From behind, it may well have appeared that Parker was, in fact, first to the touchdown. But from in front, it was apparent

that Parker did not even touch the ball, let alone exert any downward pressure. Even the most partisan of Melrose supporters who surrounded me, not five yards from the incident, agreed that it was not a try.

The home side's heads went down and the Melrose pack was spurred into action for the remainder of the game – the rest, as they say, is history.

Parker's conversion attempt from the touchline appeared to dissect the posts, and after both touch judges raised their flags Leslie seemed to award the points, but as he made his way back to the halfway line he changed his mind – which was bizarre but hardly made amends for the injustice Accies felt they had suffered.

Two penalties from Parker cut the deficit to two points with just ten minutes to go. Accies had a chance to release some pressure when Melrose conceded a penalty in front of the posts – but Hay-Smith missed, badly. Then disaster struck. Accies winger Malcolm Changleng was penalised for obstructing Melrose centre Ross Browne, and Parker had the coolest head in the ground as he slotted the kick which put the visitors ahead for the first time since the opening minutes.

Accies piled on the pressure in a desperate attempt to rescue the match. Burns, Swanson and Patterson combined to breach the Melrose defence, only for Wainwright to drop the ball with the try-line beckoning. And in the dying minutes Accies were awarded another penalty in front of the posts. This time Rowan Shepherd, who had been excellent throughout, stepped forward – but his effort was even more wayward than Hay-Smith's earlier miss.

'Justice was done', said the Melrose coach Jim Telfer rather ungraciously after the final whistle. He was furious that referee David Leslie had not awarded Parker's conversion and he was also unconvinced about the validity of the last-minute penalty which had been awarded against his team. But there were plenty of dejected souls in the home camp who would have been more than willing to argue the case that Parker should never have been kicking a conversion in the first place, and that the penalty awarded against Melrose at the death was no more marginal than the one which they had successfully kicked to take the lead a few moments earlier.

Melrose had already lost at home to Gala in their first match, so Accies knew that if they kept plugging away then they were still in with a shout of winning the championship. Watsonians were beaten (31-21 at Myreside), but then Accies fell apart against a Gala side which managed to play an irresistible brand of open and expansive rugby despite the muddy conditions (30-3 at Netherdale); and a week later an opportunist try from Gordon Mackay, after a quick tap penalty from Kevin McKenzie, salvaged a 13-13 draw for Stirling County in the seventh minute of injury time at Raeburn Place.

The team recovered to register a comprehensive 22-3 win over Hawick. As always at Mansfield Park, it was a tough and sometimes brutal match, and afterwards the backs could not resist playing up to the glamour boy reputation with a pre-planned stunt.

Brian Hay-Smith:

We were in the changing rooms with the forwards sitting there totally spent – McIvor used to take all his kit off and sit in his jock-strap, cut and bleeding from all the effort he had put in – and on this occasion the backs went into their bags and pulled out bathrobes, cravats, and slippers. Off we went to the showers like the Racing Club of Paris, while the forwards spat and snarled in disgust. They loved it really – and they went straight into the clubhouse and told the Hawick boys about it, which got the banter going.

Rowan Shepherd:

The backs called themselves The Dream Team. Not because we thought we were great, but because it really annoyed the forwards. We'd put our arms round each other, wink at McIvor and give him the thumbs up. It would wind them up . . . so the whole thing grew arms and legs.

In the last game before the mid season break, Accies came from 14-0 down at half-time to beat Kelso (23-14 at Raeburn Place), but a defeat to Stewart's Melville in the first game after Christmas and another to West of Scotland (21-11 at Raeburn Place) in the penultimate game of the season, left the club languishing third in the league at its conclusion – seven points behind Melrose and one point behind Gala.

In November Rob Wainwright and Dave McIvor had both played in

Scotland's ill-fated match against the All Blacks, with the latter most unfortunate to be dropped after the 51-15 defeat at Murrayfield, despite being Scotland's most effective forward. Wainwright went on to score Scotland's only international try of the season, against England at Murrayfield – in a match the home team appeared to have won, only for a penalty to be awarded against the Scots for handling in a ruck in the final play of the game. Jonathon Callard made no mistake with the kick to give England a highly controversial 15-14 win. Television replays would show that it had in fact been an English hand on the ball.

Martin Scott, Dave Mitchell, Rowan Shepherd, Simon Burns and Ford Swanson, alongside Wainwright and McIvor, played for North and Midlands this season; Jeremy Richardson and Derrick Patterson represented Edinburgh; while Chris Simmers and Richard Porter turned out for Glasgow. Barry Stewart and Tam McVie – both of whom were new recruits from the school – were capped for the Scotland under-19 team.

Richardson, McIvor, Patterson and Shepherd toured Argentina with Scotland that summer, with Richardson captaining the midweek side to an impressive victory over Cordoba which almost led to a call-up to the full team. Wainwright was supposed to captain Scotland on that tour but picked up an injury the week before leaving and had to drop out.

Things might have been ticking over nicely at the top of the club, but problems were surfacing further down the ladder which would have ramifications in the near future. Six teams were still being fielded on a regular basis, however the strength in depth of previous seasons was clearly no longer there. The 2nd XV were relegated from the top flight of the inter-city 2nd XV leagues, and results were mixed right down the club. The 6th XV claiming the team of the year award for the second season running was not a good sign.

The 1994–95 season got off to a dreadful start, with the team losing four and drawing two out of its first eight league games. The defeats were to Jed-Forest (22-16 at Riverside Park), Melrose (20-10 at the Greenyards), Watsonians (26-25 at Myreside) and Stirling County (18-11 at Bridgehaugh). The draws were against newly promoted Dundee HSFP in the first match of the season (9-9 at Raeburn Place) and against Gala (0-0 at Netherdale), which was the first time since the inception of league rugby in 1973 that no points had been scored by either team in a top flight match. The victories were over Currie (14-8 at Raeburn Place) and Hawick in the last game before the mid season break (14-0 at Raeburn Place).

In his last outing as captain, Simon Burns led Accies to victory in the Madrid International
Sevens in June 1993, having overcome Harlequins in the quarter-finals and Cascais, the
Portuguese champions, in the semis before defeating Richmond 33-19 in the final.
Team: Ford Swanson, Simon Burns, Brian Hay Smith, Chris Simmers, Jason Parrott,
Adrian Fairbourn and David Jackson.

League restructuring meant that only the top eight teams in the league would
be playing in the new Premier Division One, and Accies' six league points put
them ahead of only Stewart's Melville and Currie with five games to go. A marked
improvement in both performance and results was required.

The team had suffered through the departure to West Hartlepool of Rob
Wainwright and Derrick Patterson, and the absence through injury for most of the
first half of the season of Jeremy Richardson. It had taken a while for some of the
youngsters who had joined the club during the summer of 1994 to bed in, but
during the second half of the season, the likes of lock Scott Murray, scrum-half

1994–95 1st XV

Back: A. Richardson, M. McCluskie, P. Haslett, B. Stewart, M. Waite, S. Murray, T. McVie, C. Newton, R. Hoole, E. Macdonald, K. Baillie

Middle: R. Moffitt, J. Richardson, S. Burns, R. Shepherd, D. McIvor (*Captain*), F. Swanson, B. Hay-Smith, C. Simmers, A. Adamson

Front: P. Simpson, K. Day, K. Troup, C. Murray

Phil Simpson and full-back Kenny Baillie began to come into their own as Accies finished the season in fine style.

Glasgow High Kelvinside were defeated (25-20 at Old Anniesland), Stewart's Melville were stuffed (30-0 at Raeburn Place), Boroughmuir shot themselves in the foot by trying to play expansively in treacherous conditions (9-8 at Megget-land), Heriot's were swatted aside (33-3 at Raeburn Place) and West of Scotland were eventually out-gunned (20-7 at Burnbrae) as Accies squeezed ahead of Hawick on points difference to finish third in the championship table behind Stirling County and Watsonians.

Eight years after being selected in Scotland's first World Cup squad, Jeremy

Richardson finally got his cap against South Africa in November 1995. He and Dave McIvor, who had last represented Scotland against New Zealand a year earlier, played pretty well in a 34-10 defeat – but both missed out on selection for that season's Five Nations campaign. In May, Richardson was included in the Scotland squad for the 1995 World Cup, but, as in 1987, he did not play any games. Neither player would be capped again.

Paddy Haslett, Barry Stewart and Tam McVie played for Scotland at under-21 level, Craig Murray and Kenny Day played for Scotland under-19s. Richardson captained the Edinburgh district side which also included Brian Hay-Smith and Haslett.

Accies had finished in the top three in each of the last four seasons, but they never quite managed to make it to the top of the pile. The reasons for this are varied and complex, and the assorted thoughts of five key players from this period makes interesting reading, although getting to the core of the question remains problematic.

Jason Parrott in action against the US Cougars at Melrose

Simon Burns:

We had a side that should have done better than it did. When you look back through old programmes and see some of the talent we had at our disposal, you can't help but shake your head and wonder.

There was that period of about five or six years when we were always there or thereabouts. During that time Boroughmuir won the league once, Stirling County won it once and Melrose won it a few times, and I think we were the sort of team that really should have won it once. I'm not sure if we deserved to win it terribly much more than that.

Brian Hay-Smith:

We trained as hard as any team. We were going down on our own on Monday nights to do sprint sessions with Alan Lorimer [the rugby journalist who had a background in athletics coaching], but at the same time we were never quite professional enough. One of the functions of the Accies club was always that we were one of the last vestiges of amateurism. We always wanted to really enjoy ourselves, so we gave it everything we had on the pitch and afterwards we switched off from rugby – whereas for the Melrose boys it was the be-all and end-all.

I remember speaking to Carl Hogg in the bar after that 17-16 game at Raeburn Place, and he said that even at 16-3 down they knew they would beat us. He said that he thought we probably had the better players, but they had the better team, and when they played us they always had this belief that they would beat us. It was a mentality thing.

But at the same time, although no-one would admit it, least of all the guys up-front, I think it got to the stage where we almost got ourselves too psyched up when we played Melrose. We were determined that they wouldn't have the *Indian Sign* over us – but they did and we froze two or three times against them. They were a difficult side to play and it was down to Chic Chalmers being at the top of his game, and with Graham Shiel and the Redpath brothers they had plenty of clever players. They were also hard up-front – like all Border teams.

Jeremy Richardson:

We had some skilful players, but we didn't quite have enough – and that's the reality of it. Anything else you come up with is, frankly, just an excuse – we weren't good enough in the final analysis. And you need that ability to perform under pressure, Melrose had it and as a team we didn't. It was probably more important to them collectively than it was to us.

David Sole:

There is something in the Border mentality which is slightly edgy, which was a characteristic we could really have done with at Raeburn Place, so that when the shit is about to hit the fan – in whatever way – there is that steeliness there which is going to carry you through. We had a bit of it, but not enough.

Rowan Shepherd:

It didn't all come down to the Melrose games. There were always other matches that we should have won but didn't. You win the league by winning the games you have to win. You'll always lose one or two, but we lost more than we should have in those days.

Simon Burns:

I used to wonder what I would be thinking if I was the opposition, and I always thought they would feel they had a chance against us. Accies are a good side, but you've always get a sniff against them.

Brian Hay-Smith:

Bob Easson used to say that he had never worked with such a talented bunch of complex characters. When it gelled it was great, but quite often we were all pulling in different directions.

Rowan Shepherd:

There was a massive amount of maturity in the Accies pack, with guys like Jeremy Richardson, David Sole, John Allan, Rob Wainwright and Dave McIvor – but we lacked a leader behind the scrum. When we first came in Garry Bowe was the guy who spoke and we listened, but he was at the tail-end of his career and I don't think he'll mind me saying that we soon overtook him in terms of where we were at physically and where we were going with the game. When he went we lost the boss figure. It was a funny time – we were just young and doing what came naturally, which wasn't necessarily what needed to be done to win the tight games.

Rugby-wise we were quite immature – we really didn't understand what our game was and how it worked. Melrose had a handful of leaders and Boroughmuir had Sean Lineen running the show in the midfield, but we had nobody with that maturity and steel which comes from playing international rugby. We could go down to Hawick and stuff them but the next week we'd blow it at home in a game everyone expected us to win.

When it came to the business end, we didn't have the game-plan to grind out that win. We really didn't understand what our game was and how it worked – we tended to fly by the seat of our pants. It may sound like an excuse, but there was this missing link between the guys who wanted to know why it wasn't working and the guys who just wanted to play rugby.

One of the highlights for me was playing Randwick at the Melrose Sevens in 1990. Their backline was David Campese, Lloyd Walker, Acura Niuqila and Mark Ella –all Australian internationalists – but we were leading at half-time after a glorious score under the sticks by yours truly. We were playing well and you could feel the crowd getting behind us, there was a sense that we were nearly there on all fronts, but we never quite made it.

Within the team we just wanted that credibility of being something more than a side with bags of potential – that could tear you apart on a good day but are likely to blow it if they don't get off to a good start. That went against everything that guys like Richardson, Sole and McIvor stood for . . . but there was something fallible about us.

Rowan Shepherd sweeps into attack while attempting to break the tackle of Ian Howden of Boroughmuir

CHAPTER THIRTY-THREE

The focus became increasingly on the 1st XV and we neglected the rest of the club. There was nobody coaching the seconds, let alone the thirds and fourths. There was no strong figure on the rugby side able and willing to push through a plan. When you are running a rugby club these days you are running a business and you need a three-four-five year plan – and you have to take care of all the different parts of the business, not just the shop window.

Jason Parrott

DURING THE SUMMER OF 1995, Rowan Shepherd had moved to Melrose in search of regular game time at full-back, where he felt his best chance of receiving an international call-up lay. His decision was almost instantly vindicated when he was selected to wear the number 15 Scotland jersey against Samoa in November of that year after the retiral from international rugby of the great Gavin Hastings. It also meant he finished the season playing for a club at the top of the league, instead of one in the relegation zone as would have been the case if he had stayed at Raeburn Place.

Hugh Campbell was by now heavily involved with coaching Glasgow, so he stepped down as forwards coach, and David Sole came in to do that job.

The new league structure meant that there were only eight teams in each of the four 'Premiership' divisions, and every team would play every other team in their league twice on a home and away basis. The league season would be wrapped up by Christmas, and the main focus of the second half of the year was to be the newly introduced Scottish Cup.

Over the last few years there had been a slow and steady migration away from the club, but Accies still had a pretty strong squad on paper, particularly in the back-row where they had four district back-row players at their disposal, with Dave McIvor, Rob Wainwright and Martin Waite representing the North and Midlands, and Rob Hoole playing for Edinburgh. Other district players included Malcolm McVie, Barry Stewart and Scott Murray for Edinburgh, and Simon Burns for the North and Midlands, and Chris Simmers for Glasgow.

The 1995–96 season started off pretty well, with two wins over Boroughmuir

(18-3 at Meggetland) and Heriot's (28-10 at Raeburn Place) sandwiching a draw against Gala (13-13 at Raeburn Place). But then a spate of injuries to key players – including Jeremy Richardson, Malcolm McVie, Chris Simmers, Brian Hay-Smith, who were all hurt in the fourth league game of the season (a 22-3 defeat at Melrose) – proved catastrophic and the team never recovered enough cohesion to avoid relegation.

The team only won two of their nine remaining league games that season, when they beat Watsonians 31-23 in an exciting match at Myreside, and a 35-14 victory over fellow relegation candidates Gala, which was Accies first win at Netherdale in 58 years.

But these highlights were mere punctuation marks in a season dominated by frustration and disappointment. Particularly tough to take was the team's 18-15 defeat to Melrose at Raeburn Place in the third last game of the season. Leading 15-11 going into the final four minutes, it looked as if Accies would get the win they needed to extricate themselves from the relegation battle. But then ten penalties were awarded against the home team in an astonishing finale, and from the last of them, which came five minutes into injury time, Bryan Redpath burrowed over and Craig Chalmers kicked the conversion to secure Melrose's victory. Players, coaches and spectators were all left devastated and furious – with David Sole telling the press that referee Colin Henderson's handling of those closing minutes had been 'tantamount to cheating'.

Despite this painful set-back, Accies went into their final league match knowing that a victory over Watsonians at Raeburn Place would save them, but after racing into a 15-0 half-time lead, thanks largely to two tries from Simon Burns, things went horribly wrong. Hooker Matt Day was sent off for stamping, and Gavin Hastings helped himself to 18 points as the visitors sent Accies packing out of the top flight with a 28-15 defeat.

A month later insult was added to injury when Sole was found guilty by the SRU of bringing the game into disrepute and banned him from all rugby for the next six months.

Famously, Sole had not been present at the hearing when this punishment was handed down:

The SRU told me to come in and explain myself, but I was really busy at the time so I said I was very happy to come in and talk to them on these dates –

and I gave them a list of dates I was available – but of course they wrote back saying they wanted me in on a completely different date. So I wrote back and said that I couldn't get a babysitter. That then became the issue.

You say things in the heat of battle, and I had been so cross at the time. Melrose were awarded a penalty five yards from their own line, so they took a quick one and although our guys were retiring and retiring the Kelso ref awarded penalty after penalty, literally walking us back ten yards at a time. Eventually they scored and won the match. There was also the fact that this was several minutes into injury time, and there hadn't been any injuries in the second half. So, of course, I was incandescent with rage and I said that I thought the referee's performance was 'tantamount to cheating', and that was the headline the next day.

Not only did the ban stop Sole from taking charge of the Accies forwards during the remainder of the season, it also meant that he could not continue to help coach the mini rugby section at Raeburn Place, where his sons were learning the game. This prompted Ollie Miller, who ran the mini section, to launch the SOS (which stood for both *Save our Sole* and *Sole on Sunday*) campaign, aimed at highlighting the absurdity of the SRU's decision. T-shirts and David Sole masks were produced for the kids to wear, and a letter was sent to Murrayfield suggesting that the club might change to soccer so that Sole could remain involved.

The mini section had been set up four years earlier by Miller, who had identified it as 'a good way for an older father to keep an active five-year-old entertained during the weekend'. It quickly took off and within a couple of years there were upwards of 100 kids learning the basics of rugby at Raeburn Place every Sunday. It is still going strong today and now feeds into the BATs set-up, so as to provide a continuous ladder for progress right through to the senior game.

Although Sole would come down to odd training nights at Raeburn Place to lend a hand after this ban was up, this was the last Scottish rugby saw of him as a dedicated coach. Andy Adamson succeeded him as forwards coach.

At first it seemed as if Accies' miserable season was going to carry on into their Cup campaign, when Watsonians dispatched them from the main tournament in the fourth round with a 33-6 score-line at Myreside. But this set-back ended up being a blessing in disguise, as it allowed Accies to enjoy some morale-boosting success in the Bowl instead.

SRU TENNENTS BOWL WINNER
SEASON 1995 – 1996 WINNER

Accies win the Bowl
final against Selkirk
at Murrayfield

Accies reached the final of this third tier competition with victories over Waysiders/Drumpellier (98-8 at Raeburn Place), Peebles (27-8 at The Gytes) and Hillhead Jordanhill (33-7 at Raeburn Place), before defeating Selkirk at Murrayfield, largely thanks to the accurate goal kicking of Ross Barber. The big centre converted his own and scrum-half Kevin Troup's first half tries, and kicked three penalties. Selkirk, meanwhile, were not as accurate with their shots at goal, and despite matching Accies' try count they paid the price for four missed penalties during the course of the match. Kenny Baillie secured the win when he was the first to react after Selkirk spilled the ball behind their own line as they tried to mount one final frantic attack.

The Accies team that day was: S. Burns; C. Allan, R. Barbour, G. Kiddie, C. Newton; K. Baillie, K. Troup; D. Graham, K. Day, J. Scott, A. Adamson, J. Richardson, D. McIvor, M. McVie, R. Hoole. Replacement: A. Dow for Newton.

It was a fitting end to Dave McIvor's time as an Accies player. He had decided long before the team were relegated that he would rejoin Glenrothes at

The win marked the final chapter in Dave McIvor's playing career at Accies. Before returning to his home club of Glenrothes, he was made an Honorary Life Member of the club

the end of the season. He had been an outstanding servant to the club for six years and this was recognised when he was made an Honorary Life Member.

Simon Burns:

> For pure class, Jeremy Thomson was the best player I saw play for Accies during my time in the team, but Dave McIvor was definitely the most influential.

Another silver lining to the season was the selection of Scott Murray and Barry Stewart to tour New Zealand in the summer of 1996. Stewart went on to make his international debut on the trip, as a late replacement for the injured Peter Wright, in the second of two Tests against the mighty All Blacks.

Two useful new recruits for the club for the 1996–97 season were centre Iain Leighton from Melrose, and reliable goal-kicker Bryan Easson from Stirling County, who was tempted along to Raeburn Place not long after the season had got under way by his father Bob, the Accies coach.

The team picked up five consecutive wins at the start of the 1996–97 league campaign, despite losing Scott Murray, who became one of the first big money players of the professional era, when he moved to Bedford on a part-time contract reputedly worth up to £150,000 a year after match fees and bonuses were factored in.

Although there were three slip-ups along the way – at home to West of Scotland, and away to Glasgow Accies and Dundee HSFP – promotion was secured with a handsome 39-12 victory over Gala at Netherdale, in Accies' last league match of the season. The championship was won by proxy three weeks later when West of Scotland beat Dundee High School FP 15-13 at Burnbrae with the last kick of the ball in the last rearranged game of the season.

The fight for promotion had been hard and, at times, brutal. Prop Jason Fayers was banned from rugby for four years after breaking a Kelso player's jaw with a punch in a bad-tempered match at Poynder Park. The SRU sanction pre-empted Jedburgh Sheriff Court's decision to convict Fayers of assault and order him to pay a £1,000 fine plus £500 compensation. David Sole and Jeremy Richardson were criticised at the time for writing letters to the court in support of Fayers, although their comments were generally taken out of context. The club's attitude was succinctly summed up by press officer Magnus Moodie, writing in that year's edition of *The Academical*:

> Whilst we are saddened that Jason Fayers, who is a pleasant young man to meet, should receive such a lengthy conviction, the Academical Football Club totally and unequivocally condemns illegal or unlawful violence on the field of play.

Some of the leading players affected by injuries this year included Paddy Haslett, Brian Hay-Smith, Ross Barbour, Craig Murray, Malcolm McVie and Jeremy Richardson. From the team selected for the first league match of the season, only three remained at the end. Haslett had been told that his career was almost certainly over, but after an operation to repair two slipped discs in his neck he returned to action, representing Edinburgh against Biarritz in the Heineken Cup at the start of the 1997–98 season, before eventually having to give up the game for good in October 1997.

Such was the carnage after a long, hard season that there was virtually nobody left to play Kilmarnock in the Cup, and the inevitability of the defeat in that match did not detract from the disappointment of ending the season on such a low note.

1996–97 1st XV

Back: K. Baillie, D. Wilson, P. Haslett, B. Stewart, S. Murray, J. Richardson, M. Waite, D. Bull, C. Allan, B. Brown

Front: N. Hannah, P. Simpson, R. Hoole (*Captain*), S. Burns, M. Duncan, K. Troop, I. Leighton

Jeremy Richardson had planned to retire at the end of the 1995–96 season, but had not been comfortable with leaving the club whilst it was on a downward trajectory, so had stayed on to help Accies regain their place in the top flight. With that task complete, he finally hung up his boots – fifteen years after first playing for the club

When Bob Easson was appointed full-time coach of the Edinburgh district team for the 1997–98 season, he was replaced at Accies by Roger Whittaker, a retired school teacher from the Midlands who had previously coached Leicester, Nottingham and the Scottish Exiles. Andy Adamson continued coaching the forwards, and Garry Bowe assisted with the backs.

The club had made it back in the top flight in time to celebrate their 140th anniversary – but it was to be an unhappy season. Writing in *The Academical* magazine at the end of the 1997–98 season, Magnus Moodie suggested that:

The makers of the film 'Groundhog Day', wherein a man wakes up every morning at the same boring time, in the same boring place, may have had the recent fortunes of the Academical Football Club in mind. The season past has been a truly awful one, reminiscent of two years ago, except, perhaps this time things were slightly worse.

It had all started so brightly. The pack had been bolstered by the arrival of prop J.J. Van Der Esch (who was born in New Zealand and would later play for Holland) from Dundee HSFP, and South Africa back-row Craig Harrison. A tremendous run in the League Trophy – competed for by Premier One and Premier Two teams while the countries' top players were away with their districts – teed up a pulsating play-off against Stirling County at Raeburn Place in early November. In a high scoring encounter, County squeezed home 41-37, but the fact that Accies had beaten Currie, Glasgow Hawks and Hawick on their way to the final raised hopes about the team's prospects for the league season proper.

But, as Moodie pointed out: 'At this point the Devil woke up and proceeded to throw ordure at us from all directions.'

Craig Murray had suffered a nasty broken nose, which required corrective surgery and 13 stitches, in an unprovoked attack during the League Trophy game against Glasgow Hawks. The club was left frustrated that the assailant, Allan Perrie, was only banned for six months – which did not seem to tally with the four-year ban handed down to Jason Fayers the previous year.

Melrose and Watsonians had finished first and second respectively in Division One the previous season, and both were expected to do well again, so the defeats suffered against those sides during the opening fortnight of the season were not entirely unexpected. But by the time Jed-Forest emerged from Raeburn Place with a 20-15 victory in the third league game of the season, panic had started to set in – and knives began to be sharpened.

A 23-9 victory over Stirling County at Raeburn Place raised spirits briefly, but with injuries beginning to pile up Accies were reduced to playing a number of 3rd XV players during a run of three crucial Edinburgh derby games in a week – against Boroughmuir, Currie and Heriot's – in early January. All three matches were lost by an average of well over 20 points per game

One other notable absentee during this period was Bryan Easson, who was sidelined after a training ground prank left him on crutches. Easson was sprint training with the Caledonia Reds when one of his team-mates decided it would be amusing to release the elastic rope he was attached to. The equipment sprung free and struck the stand-off in the hamstring, causing severe bruising. Barry Stewart,

Phil Simpson, Ross Barber, Kenny Baillie and Chris Black were other long-term absentees this season, while Paddy Haslett had been forced into retirement.

The on-going problem of finding a way for the country's leading players to be available for all club, district and country games meant that a rather peculiar league structure was put in place on a one-off basis for the 1997–98 season, whereby each of the three Premier divisions split into top and bottom halves after nine games, and then played four more games against the teams in their half of the league. After two more defeats to Hawick and West of Scotland, Accies were stranded at the bottom of the league at the split and Whittaker was informed by the club that his services were no longer required. A considerable degree of unrest had materialised about the lack of time he was spending at Raeburn Place. He had taken on a consultancy job in the Midlands and was unable to make Tuesday evening sessions. That, allied to a miserable run of eight defeats in nine league games, made his position untenable.

Club captain Simon Burns is ready for an off-load from Steven Reed against Boroughmuir during the ill-fated 1997–98 season. Despite this being one of the team's better performances that year, Accies lost 29–19, and were relegated at the end of the season.

Garry Bowe and Andy Adamson took over the reins, but there was no turn-around in the club's fortunes. In Accies' next match they were dumped out of the Cup by Watsonians, having fallen 24-0 behind within 20 minutes before steadying the ship slightly so that the final score-line was almost respectable at 55-22.

It seemed as if the pattern of depressing defeats and frustrating under performances was going to continue throughout the season, at least until the penultimate game of the league campaign when two late tries from Simon Light and John-Michael Howison secured a 33-6 bonus point victory at Raeburn Place – throwing open the possibility of salvation through a play-off against the second top side in Division Two.

But it all ended in Götterdämmerung at Goldenacre, with Heriot's simulta-neously securing their own survival in the top flight and sending Accies down with a 42-13 home victory.

One highlight in an otherwise thoroughly miserable season was a match between an Edinburgh Accies President's XV and a David Sole Invitational side (Sole's Slammers), played at Raeburn Place in November 1997 to celebrate the club's 140th birthday. In a free-flowing, high-scoring encounter, the veteran side showed that they could still turn on the style, running out winners by 60 points to 45.

The teams as listed in the programme that day were:

David Sole's XV: G. Hastings; I. Tukalo, D. Wyllie, S. Lineen, C. Allan; B. Hay-Smith, G. Oliver; D. Sole, K. Milne, D. Cockburn, J. Richardson, C. Gray, D. McIvor, D. White, F. Calder.
Replacements: I. Paxton, G. Corbett, G. Bank, G. Bowe, E. Saunders.

Accies President's XV: S. Burns; N. Hanna, M. Duncan, J. Howison, S. Howgate; I. Stent, L. Chalmers; J.J. Van der Esch, K. Day, D. Graham, M. McVie, T. Hughes, C. Harrison, E. McDonald, R. Dunlop.
Replacements: T. McBride, M. Russell, L. Andreou, J. Croall.

In an effort to pull the club back from the precipice, the EAFC committee put forward a dramatic proposal in April 1998 to join forces with Heriot's and Stewart's Melville in an effort to produce a north Edinburgh super-club in a similar mould to Glasgow Hawks – who had just marched to the Premier Two title and the Scottish Cup only one year after the amalgamation of Glasgow High

Kelvinside and Glasgow Academicals. Heriot's rejected the proposal almost immediately, and it never came to anything.

If Accies were to recreate former glories they would have to do so by themselves, but it was hard to see a way back for the club. By the end of the 1997–98 season they were already heavily reliant on a few senior players at the end of their careers and a group of youngsters who had been thrown in at the deep-end – and the player drain from Raeburn Place was set to continue. In the brave new world of professional rugby it was inevitable that ambitious

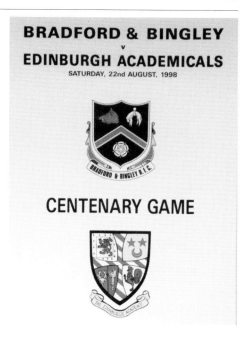

BRADFORD & BINGLEY
v
EDINBURGH ACADEMICALS
SATURDAY, 22nd AUGUST, 1998

CENTENARY GAME

Accies v Bradford & Bingley Centenary Match

players would look to go elsewhere after relegation. Barry Stewart's professional contract with Edinburgh Reivers excluded him from playing in Division Two while others chose to play Division One rugby elsewhere rather than stay on at Raeburn Place.

Attendances at pre-season training ahead of the 1998–99 season were depressingly low, and a lack of fitness and organisation led to the team-playing seven league games before they eventually managed to get a win on the board, against Kilmarnock Falcons (17-5 at Raeburn Place).

Performances and results did begin to improve during the second half of the season, and after a stunning exhibition of free-wheeling rugby in a 58-40 defeat to Musselburgh, the team recorded victories over high-flying Kelso, as well as Biggar, Dundee HSFP and Kirkcaldy – but this was all too little too late.

1998–99 1st XV

As in the previous season, Accies had actually accumulated more bonus points than any other team in the league, but a lack of killer instinct in this extremely youthful side – especially in the pack – meant relegation for the second successive year.

At least that momentum of the last few weeks of the previous campaign was carried into training ahead of the 1999–2000 season, with a hardcore of 40 players attending two or three times a week. The arrival of Lucian Colceriu (who played for Romania in the 1991 and 1995 World Cups) at the tail-end of the previous season had added some real menace to the back division, and Simon Burns and Brian Hay-Smith were persuaded by new coach Colin Mackay to stay on for one final season.

1999–2000 1st XV

Having won five of their first seven league games, Accies were sitting second in the table by mid November, and *The Academical* magazine was able to boast that:

> Spirit not seen for some years seems to have gripped the Club to the extent that whilst last year we struggled at times even to put out a third Fifteen there are now five teams playing regularly and an additional one getting out every so often to accommodate a new and enthusiastic membership.
>
> Great credit for this lies with many Academical players both young and old. Brian Hay-Smith, who delivered a rousing speech at the AGM when all around seemed plunged into despair; John-Michael Howison and Craig Murray for not only keeping the average age of a back division which is normally scrutinised by Age Concern for cruelty well below the 50 mark, but for a positive, enthusiastic approach that is rubbing off in an exemplary manner on some players younger than even they. Jason Parrott is his usual voluble but totally committed self and is playing some of the best rugby this writer has seen him do. But special mention must be made to some of our young players, particularly forwards, who seem determined to wipe out the bad last few years. Nathan Pike and Dave Rutledge, Andrew Boccoli, Rory Boyd, Danny and Shane Teague, Ben and Barney Brown and undoubted winner of anyone's most improved player award Stuart 'Stupat' Paterson who has come literally from nowhere to be a vital member of the 1st XV back row.

Four more victories on the trot took Accies to the top of the table by Christmas, and the return of Dave McIvor and Barry Stewart to their old Stockbridge stomping ground for the club's Boxing Day match against Edinburgh Borderers was another reason for plenty of festive cheer around Raeburn Place. Accies cruised to a 77-7 victory against a very similar guest team to the one which had proved a real handful the year before.

This feel good factor was sustained until the end of the season, and despite a surprising 43-8 away defeat to second placed Ayr at Millbrae in February, Accies held their nerve to clinch the Premier Three title with a thrilling 22-19 victory over Stewart's Melville at Raeburn Place.

Brian Hay-Smith:

We needed to score four tries to secure the championship, and in the last minute John-Michael Howison got the ball and ran the length to get the score we needed. I sort of jogged along to the halfway line before I gave up, and I stopped and watched as this whole team of young guys chased John all the way up the field. There wasn't a Stew Mel jersey in sight and they knew he was going to score. I remember just thinking: 'This is fantastic. What a way to finish. We're going to win the league. We've got all these great young guys, what a way to finish my career. Enough is enough.'

The turnaround that season from being absolutely crucified to where we ended up was astonishing. It was a lot to do with Colin MacKay as coach, and the older guys getting involved, and the young guys giving it everything. By that point it was back to the club mentality . . . to where it had been before. When we were going down we'd tried to buy our way out of it with a series of very poor southern hemisphere guys, who had no loyalty to the club whatsoever. Now we were back doing it with guys who wanted to be there . . . who weren't just chasing the easy bucks. It was a great way to finish.

In fact, there could have been a nasty sting in the tail for Accies. Stewart's Melville launched a final sortie in stoppage time, and an overlap was created for flying winger Gavin Sharp, who rounded his marker and sped for the corner. But he hadn't figured on the home team's cannonball Romanian centre, Lucian Colceriu.

Stuart Paterson:

I thought he was going to score – no doubt about it – then all of a sudden Luci, who was playing outside centre, appeared from nowhere. Gav Sharp went for the big hand-off, opened his ribs up, and Luci absolutely punished him. That was it, game over.

Gav Sharp subsequently came on tour with us to the Madrid Sevens and his call for the entire trip was: 'Ooooooh me ribs!' It was one of the most painful things I have ever witnessed.

The Accies team that day was: M. Blair; R. Porter, L. Colceriu, C. Murray, J. Howison; B. Hay-Smith, P. Simpson; D. Graham, D. Girdler, R. Spillsbury, R. Boyd, N. Pike, R. Dunlop, S. Paterson, C. Harrison.

Mike Blair makes a break during Accies' 2001 Shield run

Although there never looked like being any danger of Accies setting the heather alight on their return to Premier Two in 2000/2001, the early season results indicated that they had the ability to survive in that league. Having lost all their away games but won all their home games, the club was sitting comfortably in fourth place in the league at the halfway stage. But then a 29-5 defeat away to National League Division Three's Ardrossan Academicals in the Cup, followed by 42-6 loss to Ayr at Millbrae in the league, seemed to knock the self-belief out of the team. The young pack began to flounder on the heavy pitches during the winter months, and the absence through injury and work commitments of several key players was also a problem. The team did not win another league match until defeating Aberdeen GSFP in a rearranged fixture at the beginning of April – which was too late to avoid relegation. Selkirk's victory over Biggar in their re-arranged fixture two weeks later sealed Accies' fate.

Duncan Harrison halts a Haddington attack at Murrayfield as Rory Boyd looks on

Craig Murray scythes through the Haddington defence

The team did manage to string together a run of results against lower league opponents – Strathendrick, Hamilton, Dalziel and Livingston – to reach the final of the Shield, where they met Haddington, who had just been promoted into the same league that Accies had recently been relegated into.

With club captain Craig Murray starting the match on the bench, having only recently returned from injury, Haddington enjoyed the better of the first half but tries from flanker Mike McLennan and scrum-half Phil Simpson kept Accies in the hunt and they only trailed 16-12 at the break. Then a five try burst sank the East Lothian side without trace. Luci Colceriu put Accies ahead with the first of these scores, then Tom Hopper raced 80 yards for the try which swung the game out of Haddington's grasp. Craig Olsen jigged his way through an open gap in Haddington's defensive line to make it 31-16, Hopper grabbed his second score, and as a final flourish the outstanding Mike Blair took the ball on the full from Phil Smith's clever cross kick to score the try of the day. Haddington grabbed a late consolation score, but by then it was all over, bar the shouting. Not for the first time, Accies won silverware at Murrayfield in the same season as being relegated.

Stuart Paterson:

> That match was Mike Blair's springboard to stardom. He was playing full-back that day and just dominated, then at the end of the game he scored this ridiculously good try from a cross-field kick by Phil Smith – there won't have been many better tries scored at Murrayfield.

The Edinburgh Accies team that day was: M. Blair; T. Hopper, L. Colceriu, C. Olsen, C. Williams; P. Smith, P. Simpson; D. Harrison, M. Eadie, D. Graham, R. Boyd, J. Parratt, S. Paterson, J. Parrott, M. McLennan. Subs: C. Murray for Colceriu (49), N. Pike for Boyd (59), A. Desson for Graham (59), C. Elliot-Lockhart for Paterson (71), P. Burns for Harrison (76), M. Paterson for Olsen (78), S. Thyne for Williams (78).

The Sevens season continued brought heartening victories at Musselburgh and Strathspey, and a final appearance at the Goldenacre U21s' tournament and Whitecraigs. These successes, and the ability to field three competitive Sevens throughout the spring, owed much to Fijian recruits who brought a unique exuberance to the tournaments in which they participated.

Craig Murray lifts the
Shield following Accies'
comprehensive victory
over Haddington

That summer Colin Mackay decided that travelling to and from Dollar for training was becoming too time-consuming and stepped down as head coach. Less than a year later, in April 2002, he was tragically killed at the age of 43 when he was struck by a car on the first day of a golfing holiday in Spain. He had been a successful and popular coach for the club, and his loss was a major blow to everyone who had worked with him at Raeburn Place.

Ahead of the 2001–02 season, Jim Hay, the former Hawick and Scotland hooker, who had previously coached at Preston Lodge and Gala, was appointed head coach. Phil Smith was asked to continue combining playing with coaching the backs.

Mike Blair and Nathan Pike had moved on to Boroughmuir, and would soon be awarded professional contracts with Edinburgh. Within a year Blair was being capped for Scotland on their summer tour to Canada and the USA.

The team celebrate their Shield victory at the home of Scottish rugby

Meanwhile, powerful winger Charlie Williams had finished his degree at Edinburgh University and joined the army. In November 2004 he was skydiving in Africa when his feet got entangled in his parachute's rigging and he dropped 3,500ft into a Kenyan shanty town. Astonishingly he lived to tell the tale, having been saved by the corrugated iron roof he had smashed through at 120mph, which apparently broke his fall. He woke up dazed in the living room of a shack, surrounded by wreckage and the astonished locals, having suffered just three cracked vertebrae and a dislocated finger.

The Madrid Sevens squad, 2000: Paul Godman, Dan Teague, Mike Blair, John-Michael Howison, Jason Parrott, Craig Murray, Stuart Paterson, Mike MacLennan, Gav Sharp, Nathan Pike

Two years previously, when Accies had found themselves in the third division for the first time in 26 years of league rugby in Scotland, they had been able to bounce straight back. They could not repeat that feat this time around. Accies never looked like being relegated, but neither was there ever any real prospect of their going back up. They finished fifth in the table, were knocked out of the Cup in the third round by National One side Ross High, and then dispatched just as quickly from the Shield by Duns.

Jim Hay's job as a match summariser for Scottish Television meant that he was rarely around on Saturday's, and it was decided that someone who was able to commit fully to the club was required if a return to former glory were to be achieved.

CHAPTER THIRTY-FOUR

You cannae shoot a cannon out a canoe.

Ian Barnes

THE EAFC COMMITTEE TURNED once again to Ian Barnes, who had been head coach at the club between 1979 and 1983, and had more recently guided Hawick to the 2000–01 Premier One title for the first time in 14 years – before walking away from Mansfield Park when a disagreement over player incentives escalated into a bitter dispute about the direction in which the club was moving.

Before long three more Hawick men, each with impeccable rugby credentials, had joined the Accies coaching team. Scotland and Lions legend Jim Renwick took charge of the backs, assisted by former Hawick winger and international referee Kenny McCartney, while Terence Froud, the larger-than-life erstwhile Hawick prop, agreed to manage the side.

By the end of August, Finlay Calder, another Scotland and Lions legend, was also on board. The former Stewart's Melville stalwart started off coaching the 2nd XV (with Dave Parker as team manager), but before long his remit widened to mentoring youngsters, spotting opposition teams, helping coach at all levels throughout the club and anything else which was asked of him. Six years later his contribution recognised when he became an Honorary Life Member of the club.

Ian Barnes returns to Accies

Terence Froud

Jim Renwick   Finlay Calder

Barnes was in typically brash form as he looked ahead to the 2002–03 season. At his first meeting with the players he told them that:

Four years ago, when we went back to Hawick, the club was in a mess – senior players with a bad attitude and young players who did not know the score. We set ourselves a target – to win both the league and the cup within five years – and we did it. We have set ourselves the same target here.

He had perhaps underestimated the size of the task ahead. Years of bouncing around in the second and third divisions had taken its toll, and the 1st XV squad lacked experience and depth – a situation compounded by the recent departure of Nick De Luca and David Linton to Heriot's, Dave Callam to Hawick, and Peter Burns, who had decided to play at Kirkcaldy during his final year at St Andrews University.

There was, however, a hardcore of players still at the club – who were determined to play a role in resurrecting this ailing institution.

Jason Parrott, with whom Barnes quickly developed a love-hate relationship, was still playing – 15 years after his first appearance for the club. His in-your-face style might not have been to everyone's liking, but no-one doubted his commitment to the cause, and his desire to see his beloved Accies succeed.

Stuart Paterson had played stand-off for the 2nd and 3rd XVs at the Academy, but kept growing and moved to the back-row during a year out in South Africa between 1997 and 1998. He was now in his third season as a regular in the 1st XV and a focal point in the club's vibrant social scene.

Greg Campbell was a coltish Aberdonian in his second year at Edinburgh University. He was raw, but tough and brave – and he worked hard. During the next few seasons he switched from lock to the back-row, and emerged as the spirit of the Accies pack.

Tearaway open-side flanker Jamie Boyd was the team's outstanding player – when fit. And his brother, Rory, provided the pack with a solid core.

Ed Stott was a no-nonsense hooker; while Duncan Graham and Andrew Desson were gentlemen of the front-row – apart from one unfortunate incident when the latter was yellow-carded for spitting at an opponent.

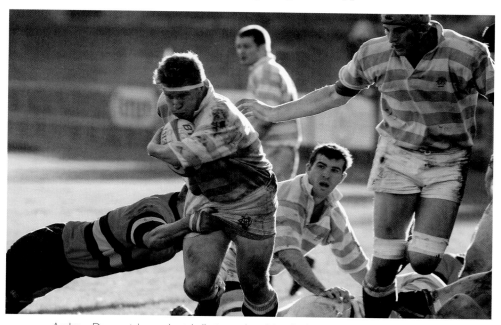

Andrew Desson takes a short ball at a ruck as Matt Rodgers and Alistair Dale look on

The well-spoken Canadian-Scot had got between two scuffling players during an Accies home match against Corstorphine. After calming the situation down, he removed his gum-shield and realised that his mouth was full of saliva. Unfortunately he forgot to turn away from Corstorphine's balding and rather bad-tempered lock before emptying his mouth, and despite the profuse apologies starting before the slimy deposit had even landed, the referee had no choice but to yellow card the mortified prop. The fact that his parents were at the match during a rare visit from Canada inevitably added to Desson's embarrassment.

In the backs, Luci Colceriu was still playing; while Stewart Little and John-Michael Howison had the potential to be a formidable partnership in the centre if they could both stay fit.

The side was captained by Malcy McVie, who had first played for Accies 3rd XV whilst still at school on the morning of Scotland's Grand Slam winning Calcutta Cup match at Murrayfield in 1990. He had moved to Watsonians in 1997 and by 2002 was contemplating retirement, but Barnes had persuaded him to return to Raeburn Place for one more season (and it ended up being three).

A handful of fringe players had arrived from Hawick – including Alistair Marsh, who quickly established himself as the foundation stone of the pack at tight-head prop; Richard Wire, a flying winger; and Jonathon Else, who only played one full season at scrum half before a knee injury pushed him prematurely into coaching.

Other new faces were back-row forward Matt Rodgers from Australia, the talented but eccentric stand-off Rory Grant, classy centre Jimmy Oliphant, hooker Richard Wood and a young scrum-half called Matthew Coupar from Blairgowrie – who immediately made his mark with some electrifying breaks and a couple of huge tackles in that year's Mansell Cup pre-season tournament at Goldenacre.

An 80-point defeat against a Bradford & Bingley side fielding two Tongan internationalists was of little rugby value in terms of preparation for the start of the 2002–03 season, but as a bonding exercise the trip to West Yorkshire helped pull the squad together.

Unfortunately, league points are not awarded for camaraderie; after defeat to Haddington (17-15 at Neilson Park) and a draw against Musselburgh (12-12 at Raeburn Place) in the first two league matches of the season, Barnes was in a more reflective mood. 'Maybe we should be looking for steady progress rather than a transformation', he wrote in his programme notes the following week.

Big wins over Corstorphine (33-0 at Raeburn Place) and Ross High (38-14 away) raised morale, but those two teams were out of their depth in Premier Three, and losses to Dunfermline (17-12 at McKane Park), Stewart's Melville (10-7 at Raeburn Place), West of Scotland (31-14 at Burnbrae) and Dundee HSFP (19-16 at Raeburn Place) left Accies floundering in the race for one of the four promotion slots up for grabs that year due to further league reconstruction. The last of these losses was a particularly bitter pill to swallow given that Accies were leading with only a few minutes to go, but scrum-half Ralph Mercer missed touch with a clearance kick and Dundee scored on the counter-attack.

David Barnes wins a close lineout ball against Stewart's Melville

A comprehensive 27-3 defeat at home to Haddington did not bode well for the second half of the league campaign, but by then Gareth Brown and the genial but volatile Maori centre P.J. Solomon had arrived from Gala, and a 33-15 victory at Musselburgh in Accies' next match was a turning point in terms of the team's morale and self-belief.

After two comprehensive victories over Corstorphine (43-13 at Union Park) and Dunfermline (41-5 at Raeburn Place) there was a disappointing defeat to East Kilbride (19-10 at Torrance House), which meant that some of the momentum manufactured during the previous three weeks was lost for the Scottish Cup fourth round tie against Heriot's at Raeburn Place on 14 December 2002.

This would have been a big match in any era, but given the recent contrasting fortunes of these two great rivals the game took on an extra dimension – especially for the home team. Heriot's had been one of Scotland's most successful teams during the professional era, having won the championship in 1999 and 2000, and at that time they were stalking Boroughmuir at the top of Division One – so for Accies this was a chance to prove that they were down but not out.

Andrew Desson, Rory Boyd and Greg Campbell scramble for the ball against Heriot's as
Jonathan Else and Richard Wood arrive in support

That was the plan – but on the day the gulf in class between the two sides was painfully exposed. Heriot's had already raced into a 24-7 lead by the time Solomon (Accies' best player up to that point) was shown a straight red-card for punching Heriot's' hooker (and ex-Academical) David Linton in an off-the ball incident just before half-time. The home team defended manfully in the second half, and managed to keep Heriot's at bay until they scored their fifth try in the 66th minute, but that score opened the floodgates and three more tries before the end gave Heriot's a 50-7 victory. The last of these tries was scored by former Accies 1st XV captain Craig Harrison. Solomon was duly banned from any involvement in rugby union for 21 weeks by the SRU, but by then he had already gone south to play rugby league for Gateshead Thunder.

In the four league games after Christmas, Accies defeated West of Scotland (28-10 at Raeburn Place) with probably the team's best performance of the season, lost to Dundee HSFP (40-25 at Mayfield), lost heavily to Stewart's Melville FP when the squad was so depleted by injuries that the starting backline contained six genuine wingers (53-7 at Inverleith), then vanquished Ross High (25-0 at Raeburn Place) – to finish fifth in the table, eleven points behind the fourth promotion spot.

The Accies Kinsale Sevens squad with the some of the South Sea Drifters – including Waisale Serevi, one of the greatest exponents of the abbreviated game – who had just won the Heineken Senior Men's Competition Cup. Accies, under the guise of the 'Ben Tod Loungers', had reached the quarter-final of the Junior Men's Competition Cup.

The 2002–03 season witnessed the birth of the club's relationship with Biella in the north of Italy. Finlay Macpherson was involved from the start:

It all started when Vittorio Musso, president of Italian club Biella, met an old Accie at Shanghai Airport. Vittorio asked him if it would be possible to organise a game for Biella if they came to Edinburgh for the 2003 Scotland versus Italy game, and Accies were more than happy to oblige.

In March 2003, on the Italian Six Nations weekend, we welcomed Biella to Raeburn Place for the first time, and in an exciting match the combined Accies 2nd and 3rd XV coached by Finlay Calder beat their guests, after which both teams had a great night in the clubhouse.

In 2004 Accies reciprocated the arrangement and a squad of 25 players – made up of members of the 1st XV team through to the 4th XV and led by the 1st XV captain Malcy McVie – plus eight social members, travelled to the north of Italy. Initially all 1st XV squad members had been made unavailable for the match in case of injuries, but this was to be disregarded within 30 minutes of arriving in Italy when Malcy reminded us that Scottish teams did not lose in Italy. Unfortunately Matt Williams, the Scotland coach at the time, had not been informed of this rule!

The hospitality we received whilst over there was phenomenal, with Accies once again winning the big match. The tour has now become a regular fixture on the club's social calendar. It is expected that this tradition will continue after a very successful 2008 trip, with Jimmy Tyrrell remaining the only player to have played in every game since the initiation.

Lock Alastair Dale had arrived at the club midway through the previous season, and was a regular in the 1st XV by the start of the 2003–04 season. Veteran stand-off Alec Guest had joined the club to play social rugby, but the competitive instinct could not be tamed, and he played most of the season inside Australian centre Adam Stafford, who gave the club two years sterling service both on the pitch and in the bar with his cohort Matt Rodgers. Chris Dickie, straight from school, quickly established himself on the wing and Morris Dillon from Highland via Hawick was a class act at this level.

Accies were determined to go one better than they had managed the year before, and although there were slip-ups along the way – against Cambuslang (34-22 at Coates Park), Musselburgh (23-6 at Raeburn Place) and East Kilbride (11-6 at Torrance House) – the team was always well positioned in the Premier Three Championship race. The title was eventually secured with a 37-7 victory over Berwick at Raeburn Place in the last game of the season

The match was effectively over by the interval, as Accies harnessed the breeze to apply relentless pressure on the visitors' line and took the lead within a minute after Alex Guest and Stuart Little combined for Richie Wire to score. Guest converted before slotting a drop goal to keep the scoreboard ticking over. Another successful penalty from Guest seemed scant reward for the territorial supremacy Accies had enjoyed, but when a mazy run by Morris Dillon was thwarted just short, Wire was once again on hand to complete the move.

Guest's conversion and another penalty gave Accies a 23-0 lead as they turned to face the elements and a Berwick onslaught that saw Jorin Grimsdale recalled twice for forward passes and Rodney King unable to hold a final pass.

2003–04 1st XV. *PhotoEvent*

With the third quarter safely negotiated without loss, Accies resumed control and any doubts over the outcome were dispelled when John-Michael Howison sent Matt Coupar through a gaping hole in the Berwick defence for a try converted by Wire. With the official party already heading off to prepare for the presentation, Howison dived over for a bonus point try, converted by Wire.

Premier Three Champions, 2004

Liam Cox belatedly unlocked the Accies defence for an injury time score converted by Matt McCreath. But by then the home team were already celebrating. They were going up – and they were on their way back.

The hard grounds took their toll on the squad during the build-up to the 2004–05 season, and the injury situation had reached such epidemic proportions during a pre-season match at Livingston that Jim Renwick was tempted out of retirement for a one-off appearance in the blue and white hoops of Edinburgh Academicals. It was a sunny day and Renwick was in shorts and t-shirt. The pitch was rock-solid and a succession of injuries reduced Accies to thirteen men at one point, so Renwick volunteered to come on at stand-off – much to the delight of the Livingston number ten. 'Are you not a little bit old to be playing this game you little fat b*****d?' taunted the young up-start. A few moments later the same player tried to step inside the only Internationalist on the pitch and was flattened by a forearm smash. His legs were still going as his body hit the ground.

2004–05 1st XV. *PhotoEvent*

Back: O.G. Downes (*Physiotherapist*), M.L.T. O'Hagan, P.E. Burns, A.R. Beasley, G.R. Ferris, S.J. Paterson, G.D. Campbell, A.J. Dale, M.C. Rodgers, M.J. Dillon, A.J. Marsh, E.C.L. Stott, R.I. Browne, A.J. Norrie, J-M. Howison, N. Mackenzie (*Fitness Coach*)

Middle: H.C.M. Mitchell (*President*), G.J. Douglas, M.P. Best, A.G. Brown, Prof D. Graham, M.J. McVie (*Captain*), R.J. Parrott, A.L. Desson, J.P.L. Boyd, W.M. Coupar

Front: P.J. Arnold, R.A. Wood, J.P.O. Forbes, J.M. Henderson

The injury crisis stretched into the regular season, and by the following May a total of 61 different players had been involved in league or cup matches for the 1st XV. Fortunately, the squad had been augmented by the arrival of the likes of Gavin Douglas, an elegant utility-back who had kicked the winning drop-goal for Hawick in the 2002 Scottish Cup Final; Euan McConnell, a technically out-standing old-style loose-head prop from Australia; Paul Arnold, a useful stand-off from Grangemouth; and the return of Peter Burns to the club following his graduation from university.

Trinity Academical players Stewart Murray, Robert Ritchie, Simon Ford and Keith Bobby all answered SOS calls during the course of the season. Their own club was trying desperately to steady itself in National League Division Two having been relegated the previous season, and its ability to field competitive teams was heavily reliant on the three-way association it had entered into with Broughton and Edinburgh Accies during the summer. It was important for the future health of the association that they were able to send a few players in the opposite direction (along to Raeburn Place or Wardie) on the few occasions they were required to do so.

The season got off to a bumpy start, with the 1st XV winning their first four home games, against Murrayfield Wanderers (32-12), Dundee (28-24), Peebles (23-11) and Selkirk (27-17); but losing their first four away matches to Stewart's Melville (23-5), Haddington (34-8), Jed-Forest (21-13) and Stirling County (52-0). The pattern was broken with a 22-7 win at Kirkcaldy and an away win against Perthshire in the Cup (16-12) in a match which pitted the brothers Matthew and Patrick Coupar against one another. The following season Patrick moved south to Edinburgh and joined forces with his older sibling at Raeburn Place.

After a disappointing loss to Berwick (13-8 at Scremerston) and a satisfying win over Kelso thanks to an injury-time penalty from Myles O'Hagan (26-25 at Raeburn Place), revenge was reaped against Haddington in the Cup after their league victory earlier in the season (21-17 at Raeburn Place).

Frustration ruled the day after Stewart's Melville's 25-16 victory at Raeburn Place. Having dominated possession, two soft tries were surrendered. Then, with Accies pressing hard, visiting prop Paul Wharakura was sin-binned and Stewart's Melville claimed they didn't have front-row cover on the bench so the scrums went uncontested, thus neutering an area of Accie domination at a crucial point in the match. 'We were effectively punished for them having a player sin-binned,' protested Barnes afterwards.

The team made heavy weather of beating Murrayfield Wanderers (20-19 at Murrayfield), lost to Haddington (17-9 at Raeburn Place) and Dundee HSFP (56-12 at Mayfield), beat Peebles (25-2 at the Gytes), lost to Selkirk (26-13 at Philiphaugh) and then beat Kirkcaldy (33-9 at Raeburn Place).

At the end of February, Accies played Selkirk at Raeburn Place in the fifth round of the Cup. On a gloriously sunny Sunday afternoon in Stockbridge this thrilling match was the perfect antidote to the non-spectacle of the previous day, when Scotland had kicked six penalties to grind out a dull 18-10 victory over Italy at Murrayfield.

Both teams set off at a frantic pace . . . and then accelerated. Accies had the better of the first half, but trailed 23-18 at the break thanks to three long-range tries from the visitor – and it took a 40-yard penalty from Gavin Douglas on the stroke of full-time to tie that match 34-34. Simon Murdoch gave Selkirk the lead in the first period of extra-time, but this was soon cancelled out by a Gavin Douglas try after a scything break from Matt Coupar. The match ended as a 41-41 draw, but Selkirk progressed to the quarter-finals by virtue of having scored five tries to Accies' four.

The league season ended with three wins over Berwick (45-12 at Raeburn Place), Stirling County (24-17 also at Raeburn Place) and Kelso (5-3 at Poynder Park), followed by a loss to Jed-Forest (22-12 at Raeburn Place). Accies finished sixth in Premier Division Two – safe from relegation but not challenging for promotion as might have been the case had they shown a bit more tactical maturity at critical moments in key games.

During the summer of 2005, the association between Broughton, Edinburgh Academicals and Trinity Academicals and was taken to a new level – when the three clubs came together to set up a new rugby club called the BATs, which aimed to harness the rugby potential of the established rugby playing schools in north Edinburgh and develop the game in schools where football is still king.

The BATs project was the brainchild of Ian Barnes and Accies secretary, John Wright. They have been enthusiastically supported by a committed band of hard-working volunteers, including Andrew Walker (who is Director of Rugby) and Vincent O'Donoghue from Accies; Graham Bonner, Martin Scott, Richard Chalmers, Gerry Love, Colin Devine and Andy Turtle from Broughton; and Allan Spencer and David Gibb from Trinity. This initiative has led the charge in developing rugby at grass roots level in Scotland. Between September 2006 and

Mike Blair, Ross Rennie and Simon Webster take a break from Edinburgh training to run a session
with the BATs at Raeburn Place

March 2007, the BATs 500 organised training sessions in 25 different schools, reaching over 12,000 pupils. They regularly field five teams for kids of secondary school age, as well as an under-18s side and a development team aimed at providing youngsters with that first important step into senior rugby.

The club's first Development Officer was Joe Edwards, a former New Zealand Maori player, who was in the Hawick team which won the league in

Mike Blair and Simon Taylor with one of the mini rugby squads

2001 and the league and cup double a year later. He played eight league games for each of the constituent clubs that season (2005–06).

Malcolm McVie had finally decided to hang up his boots, and Andrew Desson initially took over as captain but when injury brought a premature end to his playing career the club was extremely fortunate that a ready-made leader was available in Dan Teague, who had returned to Accies after four years of studying in Aberdeen and playing for Aberdeen Grammar – bringing with him Australian centre Luke McCann. Another recruit, David Rattray, added some serious pace on the wing.

2005–06 1st XV. *PhotoEvent*

Back: P.E. Burns, G.R. Ferris, R.J. Parrott, S.J. Paterson, M.C. Rodgers, P.M. Coupar, L.A. McCann, M.P. Best

Front: R.H. Miller (*President*), R. Browne, P.J. Arnold, D.J. Teague, A.L. Desson (*Captain*), Dr J. Oliphant, O. Downes (*Physiotherapist*)

In absentia: J.P.L. Boyd, A.J. Broatch, A.G. Brown, G.D. Campbell, W.M. Coupar, A.J. Dale, G.J. Douglas, J. Edwards, A.P. Fenton (*Manager*), Prof D. Graham, J-M. Howison, N. Mackenzie (*Fitness Coach*), A.J. Marsh, M. O'Hagan, S. Patience, D. Rattray, E.C.L. Stott

Jim Renwick had decided that he could no longer commit to travelling up and down the road from Hawick three times a week, so former Musselburgh stand-off and Haddington coach Cliff Livingston took charge of the backs. Renwick and McCartney were still going to help out, and as the season heated up their commitment intensified – meaning that the backs had more than enough experience and expertise to draw from.

With only one team being promoted from Premier Division Two, there was no room for slip-ups during the 2005–06 season. The league campaign got off to a flying start, with Accies winning their first six games – against Dundee HSFP (28-27 at Mayfield), Cartha Queens Park (38-19 at Raeburn Place), Hillhead-Jordanhill (32-13 at Hughenden), Kelso (24-10 at Raeburn Place), Selkirk (22-17 at Philiphaugh) and Murrayfield Wanderers (35-0 at Raeburn Place). But this momentum could not be sustained and three defeats in the next four matches – to Jed-Forest (27-16 at Riverside Park), Berwick (25-17 at Scremerston) and Gala (26-16 at Netherdale) – put a serious dent in the club's championship aspirations. The one win during this period was over GHA (41-18 at Raeburn Place).

The team recovered enough to post two more league victories over Haddington (19-10 at Neilson Park) and Dundee HSFP (26-17 at Raeburn Place), plus a Cup victory over Glasgow High Kelvinside (29-8 at New Annies-land); but then an infuriating home defeat to Hillhead-Jordanhill (49-30), when a nineteen-point half-time lead was thrown away, highlighted once again the fallibility within the team.

Scrappy victories over Selkirk (24-13 at Raeburn Place), Murrayfield Wanderers (20-10 at Murrayfield) and Jed-Forest (23-17 at Raeburn Place) kept the prospect of promotion alive, before GHA delivered a fatal blow with a 20-18 victory on a cold, wet and muddy afternoon at Braidholm.

By this point Accies had also been knocked out of the Cup by Berwick (16-7 at Scremerston), which meant that there was very little for the team to play for during the remainder of the 15-a-side season. So it is to their credit that they won their next four league matches – against Cartha Queens Park (22-19 at Drum-breck), Berwick (31-10 at Raeburn Place), Gala (32-18 at Netherdale) and Haddington (35-24 at Raeburn Place) – before losing the last match of the season, a rearranged fixture on a Tuesday night in mid-April, against Kelso at Poynder Park (30-14).

2006–07 1st XV. *PhotoEvent*

Back: G. Reid, J. Henderson, S. Patience, C. Kinloch, A. Broatch, E. Stewart, N. Pike, R. Lovat, S. Paterson, J. Parker, G. Douglas, D. Rattray

Front: S. Walker, P. Arnold, M. Campbell, P. Burns, G. Campbell, D. Teague (*Captain*), O. Miller (*President*), P. Coupar, R. Browne, L. McCann, R. Bonner

The 2006–07 4th XV celebrate becoming the unbeaten champions of the East of Scotland 3rd XV League

Accies finished third in the league, which was bitterly disappointing given the promising start, and the fact that they had beaten the top two teams – Dundee HSFP and Cartha Queens Park – both home and away, but blew it against teams further down the table.

With the Accies' second string winning promotion into the top flight of the 2nd XV league, and the 3rd XV coached by Finlay Macpherson and managed by George Menzies also going strong, the general health of the club was encouraging.

According to Ian Barnes' five-year plan, the 2006–07 season should have seen Accies winning both Premier One and the Scottish Cup, but having missed out on

Jamie Parker fends away the tackle of Steve Gordon of Glasgow Hawks. *Scotsman*

promotion from Premier Two the previous season that became a non-starter. However, although the timescale had changed, the intent remained.

Three new forwards would play leading roles this season. Backrower Jamie Parker was the most recent recruit from Hawick. Nathan Pike had returned to his roots, bringing with him a wealth of professional experience from his time with Edinburgh and then Rotherham; and he was joined in the boiler-house by Ed Stuart, brother of James, who had played for Accies during the 1999–2000 season, before returning to South America and representing Argentina against Mike Blair's Scotland in the summer of 2008.

The ageless Joe Edwards played all 28 competitive matches this season, and at the other end of the spectrum, several exciting youngsters had arrived at the club – Paul Loudon and James Murray from Edinburgh Academy, Lewis Niven and Ruaridh Bonner from Trinity Academy and Chris Kinloch from Fettes. Stuart Walker also played a handful of games for the 1st XV, though still only 17, having come through from the Accies mini and midi-rugby sections and then the BATs under-18 team.

Another youngster – 19-year-old Kiwi utility back Quentin Gardiner – also played this season. He had played the previous year in Dubai and Pretoria with

Joe Edwards makes a charge against his former club, Hawick. *Scotsman*

the New Zealand Sevens team, and had been persuaded to spend a season in Scotland by Joe Edwards.

Work commitments had taken Alastair Dale back to his native Ayrshire, and he had joined Glasgow Hawks; Gareth Brown had decided to spend his last few years as a player with Gala; and Matt Coupar had got restless waiting for a chance to play in Premier One and jumped ship to Watsonians.

The league season started with three victories over Kelso (27-19 at Poynder Park), Hillhead-Jordanhill (22-0 at Raeburn Place) and Selkirk (14-11 at Philiphaugh); a defeat against Stirling County (24-29 at home) when the scrum struggled and easy tries were surrendered; and then two more wins against Cartha Queens Park (22-14 at Drumbreck) and Jed-Forest (23-10 at Raeburn Place) in Matt Rogers' last game before returning to Australia. With six games played, Accies were joint top of the table.

But things went horribly wrong in the next match against old rivals Stewart's Melville at Inverleith. The team had started well playing into the wind, and with the forwards bullying the scrum and dominating the breakdown they turned around 10-0 up. More of the same would have been enough to close out the game, but instead the discipline disappeared and silly points were conceded. Stewart's

Melville ended up running away with a 24-17 victory. Worse was to come the following week when Hamilton Accies raced into a 21-0 half-time lead at Raeburn Place, and then held on for a 21-17 victory.

The collapse against Stewart's Melville seemed to have dented the team's self-belief, and although Gala were beaten at Netherdale – that result owed more to lady luck than anything else. Trailing 19-14 at half-time, Greg Campbell scored a disputed try in the corner leaving Gavin Douglas a conversion from the touchline on his wrong side. His effort hit the post and then bounced off the cross-bar before toppling over – for a 21-19 victory. It was an almost identical story against Biggar the following week, except this time Tom Stuart got the all important try and Douglas didn't need the assistance of the woodwork.

Gavin Douglas aims another successful kick at goal with the assistance of Alistair Marsh. *Scotsman*

Having sailed perilously close to the wind during the previous fortnight, the fickle hand of fate evened things up the following week with a real sucker punch. Leading 17-16 against GHA at Braidholm, Dan Teague rumbled over from a close range ruck for what seemed to be a perfectly good try. The referee awarded the score but then one of the touch-judges intervened and it was chalked off. A scrum was awarded to GHA for an Accies knock-on – much to the chagrin of Teague (who insisted that the ball had squirted forward after he had exerted downward pressure), his team-mates, the coaching staff and the visiting supporters. GHA worked their way back up-field and scored an unconverted try to claim a 23-17 victory. Accies frustration was multiplied by the fact that flying winger David Rattray appeared to have scored in the corner at the end of the first half, but the referee ruled that he had been held up.

That result left Accies sitting in the third promotion place, trailing GHA by six points and one point ahead of Hamilton, at the half-way stage in the league campaign. Stirling County were streaking clear at the top of the table.

A comfortable 45-10 win over Kelso at Raeburn Place, a less convincing 12-10 victory at Hughenden versus Hillhead-Jordanhill and a 22-17 win over Selkirk at Raeburn Place elevated Accies up to second place in the league, and they carried that momentum on into the top of the table clash against Stirling County at Bridgehaugh. The team's 26-22 win in this match narrowed the gap at the top of the table to six points.

Ross Browne looks to exploit space from full-back. *FotoSport*

After beating Cartha Queens Park (21-12 at Raeburn Place) in the last game of 2006, the New Year got off to an inauspicious start with a 26-19 defeat at Jed-Forest. That match was attended by a number of members of the 1957 Accie team which had shared the old unofficial championship with Jed-Forest – who had been invited to a pre-match lunch at Riverside Park to celebrate the 50th anniversary of that season.

A 22-7 victory over Stewart's Melville at Raeburn Place got things back on track, and then Accies started their exciting Cup run of this season in the least glamorous of circumstances – defeating National League Division Three side Newton Stewart 5-0 in one of only four games to take place on a miserable Scottish winter weekend. The weather was so bad that at one stage the referee took the players off the pitch to allow a hailstorm to pass – and in places the mud was over the players' boots.

Jamie Parker found the conditions particularly tough and he was replaced by Stuart Paterson just after half-time. He was standing under the hot showers in the changing rooms, with all his kit still on, when word arrived that Greg Campbell had broken his thumb so he would have to go back on for the last ten minutes.

An 11-10 victory over Hamilton the following week guaranteed Accies Premier One rugby for the following season, with three league games to go. All of those matches were won – 42-10 against Gala at Raeburn Place, 22-21 against Biggar at Hartreemill and 22-10 against GHA at Raeburn Place – but by now all eyes were on Accies' exciting Cup run.

The Malleny Park clash was dominated by attritional forward play. Ed Stuart, Jamie Parker and Joe Edwards take a breather as Greg Campbell receives treatment. *Scotsman*

Nobody gave Accies a chance against Premier One Champions Currie at Malleny Park on the Friday night before Scotland's Six Nations clash with Italy at Murrayfield – and, sure enough, they looked dead and buried after only ten minutes.

By that point Currie had scored two un-answered tries and flanker Patrick Coupar had sprained his ankle, meaning that Greg Campbell was going to have to play virtually the whole game in his first match back since breaking his thumb just over a month earlier. A Gavin Douglas drop-goal at least got Accies off the mark, but that was soon cancelled out by an Ally Warnock penalty.

Things went from bad to worse when Sinclair Patience dislocated his shoulder and Alistair Marsh was taken off with a calf injury – resulting in a major reshuffle in the front-row. Peter Burns came off the bench, Joe Edwards moved from hooker to tight-head prop, and the diminutive Gordi Reid came on at hooker and proved that rugby is not always about the size of the dog in the fight.

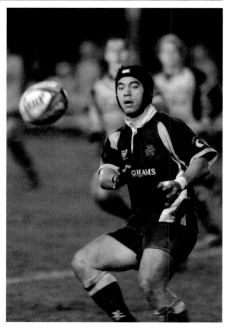

Quentin Gardiner moves the ball wide against Currie at Malleny Park. *Scotsman*

Currie extended their lead to seventeen points with a second MacMahon try on the half hour mark, but just before the break Accies drove Campbell over from a close range line-out and Gavin Douglas kicked the conversion – and all of a sudden, it was game on.

Within five minutes of the restart Nathan Pike had scored Accies, second try, Douglas added a penalty five minutes later to tie the match, and with five minutes to go David Rattray clinched the match after a mazy run through Currie's frantic cover defence (final score: 25-20).

In the next round Accies made a slow start at Murrayfield Wanderers but eventually ran out 78-12 winners against the Premier Three side. That gave them a juicy quarter-final draw against Hawick at Raeburn Place.

There was no shortage of intrigue in this match. Four of the Accies starting team were ex-Hawick players – Douglas, Marsh, Edwards and Parker – and, of course, Renwick and Barnes had played all their serious club rugby for their home-town club.

Injuries were beginning to take their toll and the shortage of front-row cover

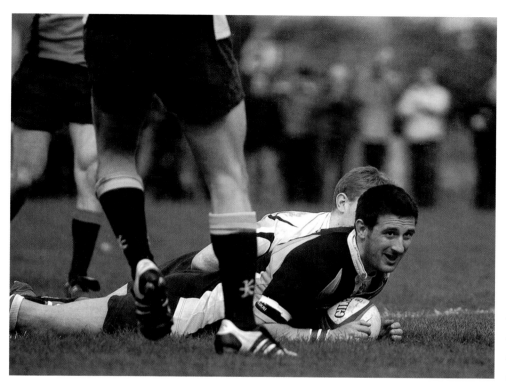

Gavin Douglas pounces on a charged-down clearance to score against Boroughmuir at Raeburn Place. *Scotsman*

Luke McCann looks to offload as he breaks the Hawick cover defence. *Scotsman*

was of particular concern; so Ed Stott – who had moved to Barcelona in April 2006 – was persuaded to fly back to Edinburgh to sit on the bench. He would make two more return trips before the season was out.

Accies gifted Hawick the perfect start, when a clumsy Ross Browne clearance kick was charged down by Kevin Reid and Wullie Blacklock was on hand to tumble over the line with only two minutes played. Barry Sutherland missed the conversion and two long-range penalties from Gavin Douglas gave Accies a solitary point lead with a quarter of the game gone. Then a catch-and-drive yielded a try for Jamie Parker to give Accies an eight-point cushion at the break.

Hawick kicked a penalty at the start of the second half, but could not establish parity up-front, and with 11 minutes to go some good scavenging work by John-Michael Howison allowed Michael Campbell to break down the tight touchline for Accies second try. Five minutes later Sutherland kicked a penalty, which meant Hawick only needed a converted try to get a draw, but that was as close as they came.

Two weeks later Accies booked their place in the Cup Final with an emphatic victory over a lacklustre Boroughmuir side at Raeburn Place. Tries for Paul Loudon, Ross Browne and Mike Campbell, plus a drop-goal, penalty and conversion for Douglas, gave Accies a 23-0 half-time lead. An Angus Martyn try handed Boroughmuir a life-line, and for a while Accies looked slightly flustered – but when Campbell charged down Scott Hadden's clearance and Douglas flopped on the ball for try number four with 20 minutes to go, the game was over as a contest. Neil Malloy got a consolation try for Boroughmuir, but Accies finished the day as they had started it – well and truly on top – when a driven line-out propelled Pike over the line to make it 38-14.

Accies were in the Cup Final for the first time in the

Mike Campbell makes a searing break up the blind-side to score Accies' second try against Hawick. *FotoSport*

tournament's twelve years history. They had won both the Bowl and the Shield – now they had the chance of becoming the first club to collect the full set. This time the opponents would be Glasgow Hawks. It was a day of celebration at Raeburn Place, but for Alistair Marsh the final whistle at the end of the semi-final was a bitter-sweet moment.

Alistair Marsh hands off Rory Couper of Boroughmuir. *Scotsman*

Two years previously he had booked his wedding to Lorraine McColm at Mansfield House in Hawick. At that point he thought it was unlikely that he would be playing in the Scottish Cup Final in the summer of 2007, but just to be on the safe side he had made sure that the big day was booked for 5 May – which was a week after the usual end of April date for the showcase event. Unfortunately, the date was pushed back for the 2006–07 season, and it looked as if Marsh – who along with John-Michael Howison, Greg Campbell and Stuart Paterson, was one of the only four players in the semi-final squad to have played for the club throughout Barnes' tenure as coach – was going to miss out.

Fortunately for Marsh, his remarkably patient and understanding fiancé suggested the wedding be moved forward to 11 a.m., and with the aid of a helicopter and police escort the groom was at Murrayfield in plenty of time for kick-off. Meanwhile his bride and guests listened to the action on BBC Radio Scotland in the bar of the Mansfield House.

Ed Stuart rises high to win the ball at a lineout in the Cup Final at Murrayfield

Ed Stuart takes an offload from Gavin Douglas and charges forward with Duncan Macleod, Ed Stott, Nathan Pike, Lewis Niven, Greg Campbell and Mike Campbell in support. *Scotsman*

Marsh's journey to Murrayfield might have been epic, but the match itself fell some way short of being a classic. Accies made the brighter start and soon took the lead with an Ed Stewart try from a driven line-out. Gavin Douglas missed the conversion and an earlier penalty, but he made some amends when he sent over a sweetly struck drop-goal to extend his side's advantage.

Slowly but surely Hawks began to get the measure of Accies, much vaunted pack, and a couple of Mike Adamson penalties closed the gap to just two points. The second of those penalties came after Ed Stuart was sin-binned for killing the ball in his own 22, and during his absence Hawks were able to grapple a strangle-hold on the match. First a loose pass from Ross Browne gifted John Fitzpatrick a clear run at the Accies line, then Ally Maclay touched down after a cool off-load out of contact by Murray Strang. By the time Stuart returned Hawks were ten points to the good.

Peter Burns slips through the Hawks defence and looks to offload. *Scotsman*

Mike Campbell snipes up the touchline, rounding the Hawks defence. *Scotsman*

The agony of defeat. Ed Stuart contemplates what might have been following the final whistle. *Scotsman*

Ed Stott looks ruefully at the celebrating Hawks team. *Scotsman*

Accies rallied briefly, and Dan Teague was shunted over the line after an irresistible forward drive, but Hawks were playing in their fifth final and their experience began to show in the final quarter, when they looked fairly comfortable as they kept Accies at bay. Two more Adamson penalties sealed the match for the Glasgow side.

The spirit which had carried the team back into Premier One and to the Cup Final remains as strong as ever despite defeat at the final hurdle. *Scotsman*

The team that day was: R. Browne; J. Howison, L. McCann, P. Loudon, D. Rattray; G. Douglas, M. Campbell; P. Burns, J. Edwards, A. Marsh, N. Pike, E. Stuart, D. Teague, G. Campbell, J. Parker. Replacements: S. Walker, D. Macleod, E. Stott, L. Niven, C. Kinloch, S. Paterson.

Accies had failed to play with the same sort of intensity which had over-whelmed Currie, Hawick and Boroughmuir in previous rounds. It was a disappointing end to the season, but the main aim had always been promotion and that target had been achieved several weeks earlier.

CHAPTER THIRTY-FIVE

You did that trot from the changing rooms to the pitch, and this sounds pathetic
but you liked it because it was part of the tradition. You knew that club members
had been doing this for more than a hundred years. The other team must have
hated that little jog over the 2nd XV pitch – but it was our thing.

It was never a great pitch, but it had something to it that I'll never be able to
properly put my finger on –something to do with the history of the place. It's hard
to create an atmosphere when all you've got is an old cow shed and an open field,
but it was just a fantastic place to play rugby . . . and I'm sure it still is.

Rowan Shepherd

THE RENOVATION WORK CARRIED out during the 1970s had prompted a decade of
growth in the use of Raeburn Place as both a sporting and social venue. The
upturn in the fortunes of the rugby club during this period was both a cause and
effect of this process. However, by the late 1980s things were beginning to stagnate
again. While the fortunes of the 1st XV were not immediately affected, there
were problems beneath the surface that needed to be addressed as a matter of
urgency.

Club membership had reached a peak of 764 in 1986, but by March 1989 it
had dropped to 660 and this trend was expected to continue. This was at least
partly related to the fact that after ten years of constant use but very little upkeep
the facilities had fallen behind alternative venues in the city. The pavilion might
have possessed a certain sort of rustic charm to the hardcore of regular users, such
as Simon Burns, who says:

A lot of people over a lot of generations have stood there having a great time
on a Saturday night. It has probably been just about my favourite place in
the world to go and have a beer, just because of all the great times we've had
there. If you took Raeburn and dumped it anywhere else in the world, they
would have smashed it up and used it for fire kindling. It was shoddy, tatty,
all of that . . . but it was great.

However, to the outside eye it was tired and out-of-date. Serious expenditure was required just to make the building wind-proof and water-tight.

Raising the required capital was not going to be easy. Money was tight – not helped by the recent loss of the club's late licence and the extension of opening times across the city – and there was also a growing unease about the Academical Club's liability for the Sports Centre's debts, especially after the Council had reluctantly agreed to allow the Sports Centre and its constituent clubs to go fully 'open' in 1985. Around this time the Accie Council approved the following resolution:

> The Club does not have the necessary resources to continue supporting the Centre and cannot call upon its wider membership to provide new resources for a facility in which the Academical interest is clearly diminishing.

A Joint Working Party, set up by the Accie Council and the Edinburgh Academy school directors, recommended selling off a chunk of the ground to raise capital – but this inevitably met with strong opposition. In May 1989, Billy Menzies produced a paper entitled 'The Future Viable Strategy for The Edinburgh Academical Sport Club', in which he warned that:

> The option of selling part of Raeburn Place for development . . . would improve the capital position in the short-term, but would further weaken several areas which the centre depends on for income. This action would effectively end the possibilities of increasing facilities. It would also result in a serious split within the membership and resignations of important Academicals, some of whom are the main activists within the present Sport Centre.
>
> The Sports Centre must provide a wider range of facilities to standards which are now provided elsewhere in the City. This would allow membership of the Sports Centre to be attractive to a much larger market.

Menzies suggested selling off the whole of Raeburn Place and purchasing extra land at Newfield, on which a 'multi-purpose Sports Centre' could be developed, to be used by the school and the Academical clubs. It soon became apparent, however, that the school was not keen on this proposal.

Within a year Menzies was involved in a new scheme, in which a private company made up of five directors with strong Academical ties, would take on a 125-year lease of the whole of Raeburn Place. By investing £1 million in renovating the pavilion, upgrading the existing sporting facilities and installing some new facilities such as a health suite, skittle alley and a floodlit all-weather training pitch, it was hoped that Raeburn Place could be transformed into a profitable sporting complex in the heart of the city. The lease would safeguard access to the improved facilities for existing user groups, and membership would be guaranteed to all Academicals – but, ultimately, the plan was just too radical at the time to get off the ground.

In the end, a far more pragmatic approach to dealing with the immediate problem was adopted. The Raeburn Place Appeal was launched in September 1991 by Ronnie Sloan, the rugby club's vice-president.

Ronnie Sloan recalls:

> They were going to sell the training pitch along Raeburn Place because they needed to raise £100,000 to pay off debts and do some essential maintenance work. But a group of guys such as Tommy McClung went round and got 100 people to give loans of £1,000 each, and within a few weeks they were able to go to the Accie Council and say: 'There's £100,000, don't sell the land.'
>
> That bought us time but didn't solve the problem. So I got roped in to raising money and one day I was at Goldenacre, it must have been an Accies-Heriot's match, and I noticed the wall they have in their clubroom with the names of people who have donated money to the club engraved into each brick. So I adapted that idea for our purposes and I had this big graphic in the clubhouse where people could buy bricks, plates, panels and windows for different amounts of money.
>
> We raised enough cash to pay off the debt, upgrade the showers and changing rooms, and get the upstairs wind and water-tight. Within a couple of years we had collected nearly £200,000, and that kept the clubhouse going for another decade or so.

In the aftermath of the International Rugby Board's watershed decision in August 1995 to remove all restrictions on payments or benefits to those connected with the game, the EAFC set-up a sub-committee charged with bringing forward proposals for the development of Raeburn Place so that it met the standards expected of a professional sport. After months of negotiation and planning, a scheme championed by Vincent O'Donoghue and John White was eventually pulled together, which would have involved turning approximately 0.4 acres of land along the northern edge of the ground into retail, office and residential premises on the Comely Bank frontage, and concealing a 3,000-seat stand facing northwards to Inverleith Pond. This would obviously have required the 1st XV pitch to be relocated. The proceeds from the land development were to be used to renovate the inside of the clubhouse and facelift the outside, while the squash courts were to be made into a rugby museum.

Provisional talks with the City of Edinburgh Planning Department had been encouraging, and the Academical Council seemed to be open to the idea – but when push came to shove they were not quite ready to commit. 'It just seemed to drift away,' recalls O'Donoghue.

Every cloud has a silver lining, and at least the failure of this initiative highlighted the problems in communication which existed between the three organisations responsible for the management of Raeburn Place. For any proposal to move forward it was vital that all three stakeholders were singing from the same hymn sheet – but while the Academy and the Academical Club Council had a pretty close relationship, the Sports Centre was out on a limb at this point. During the next few years a number of active football club members were elected to the Council and this helped foster greater links between the three bodies, which was essential to the survival of Raeburn Place during this difficult period.

During the next four years several options were looked into, including the possibility of joining forces with the Grange Club, and building a two-way stand straddling Portgower Place with a walkway running underneath it from Comely Bank to Inverleith Park. Another idea involved taking over Portgower Place (unofficial talks with the Council indicated that this would not be major sticking point) and knocking down the Academical clubhouse, which would create room for an all-weather pitch for the Grange's thriving hockey section, while the Grange's pavilion would be enlarged and improved to make it suitable for hosting the memberships of both clubs. However, the Grange committee were hostile to both ideas (which was a complete turnaround from the situation in the mid-1980s, when the Academical Club Council had declined an approach from the Grange about the possibility of joining forces).

The possibility of selling Raeburn Place and relocating to the Newfield extension site was revisited, and discussions also took place on the viability of moving to a greenfield site on the outskirts of Edinburgh – but neither of these options was seen as being particularly desirable. The National Lottery Fund and the Sports Ground Initiative were approached for funding, but to no avail. And a deal which would have involved the Academicals getting a new pavilion built for them free of charge by Cannon Health & Fitness Clubs, in return for that company being granted the right to develop a base in this prime location close to Edinburgh's city centre, was also considered.

But it wasn't until the end of the decade that a plan which would eventually give Raeburn Place a sustainable future finally started to be pulled together.

Tony Hamilton recalls:

I was asked if I was interested in being elected president of the Academical Club and at my first meeting of the Accie Council I literally walked into a discussion about shutting down Raeburn Place. It was losing money and they didn't really see that it was benefiting enough Academicals to justify the continuing cost. I said straight away that they couldn't possibly do that, but if I was going to take that line then I knew I had to get involved.

This was in 1999, at which point the football club was struggling in the third division and the cricket club's fortunes were down as well. We needed to generate some money, so I picked up a contact the club had made with the local hotelier – Festival Inns – to ask if they wanted to get involved with some sponsorship. That got through to their big boss, Kenny Waugh, and he suggested a meeting at which he said he could do a bit more than just a straight sponsorship, and he outlined his vision for a hotel on the site of the old Raeburn House Hotel and our pavilion.

It seemed to me like a bloody good idea. I said we couldn't sell him the land but we probably could arrange a long-term lease of the ground if he could build and run a new clubhouse for us. Within a couple of months of that first meeting we had reached pretty much the same arrangement as we have in place now. The plans for the hotel were drawn up by a guy called David Cochrane – who was, funnily enough, an old Academical as well – and we really didn't think anyone would object. We thought it would go through the planning process and in eight weeks' time we would be moving forward again. But then it all went sour.

We are very lucky that Kenny Waugh has remained very enthusiastic about the whole thing, despite all the hassle and the spiralling costs. Despite everything, he has always been as good as his word.

An Extraordinary General Meeting to amend the Academical Club Constitution took place on 27 April 2000, and the changes required to allow the proposed development of the pavilion area to begin were passed by 575 to 3, including proxy votes.

That summer Tony Hamilton, as Chairman of the Sports Centre, outlined in *The Academical* magazine, the situation at that time:

All initial discussions and outline agreements with Festival Inns Ltd are now satisfactorily concluded to enable the submission of the formal planning application. It is anticipated that this will now be lodged during October [2000]. The developers are very hopeful that the plans will be acceptable to the Planning Department and will gain approval from the Planning Committee. If all goes well it may indeed be possible to begin work in the summer of next year [2001]. To date we have letters of support for the plans from the SRU, the Scottish Cricket Union, the School together with six residents of North Park Terrace.

Festival Inns Ltd will be granted a lease over the land currently occupied by the Squash Courts and the present pavilion on which they will build an extension to the Raeburn House Hotel. Prior to this they will build a completely new pavilion, to a high specification, immediately to the north of the existing building which will be the property of the Club. This building will incorporate all the modern facilities for the sports played at Raeburn together with the latest in medical and fitness requirements. Even the referees will have grade one changing facilities.

There will be full kitchen and bar facilities within the pavilion. In addition to a main bar/social/dining area, which will run the length of the building, there will be a separate Members Bar.

The potential benefits to the club are fourfold. We will not lose any of the principal playing area retaining the full cricket ground and rugby pitches.

We will have first class changing facilities. The pavilion will be run professionally and the maintenance and running costs will be taken care of by Festival Inns. We will have an annual rental income, to rise with RPI, to meet our field costs and subsidise the various sports sections.

We have held an informative meeting with our immediate residents and suggestions raised there have, where practical, been incorporated into the plans and the development procedures.

It all seemed so promising . . . but a year later, Hamilton (who was by now the Academical Club president) wrote in the same publication that:

While it appears that little has happened since the report in *The Academical* last year, there has been considerable activity. This has revolved around the planning process together with a genuine desire to lessen the impact of the development on our neighbours.

The result of this was that the formal planning application was put forward in May this year – 2001. The planners came back with a number of recommendations which they thought were appropriate in the light of their own planning requirements and suggestions, which would answer some of the points raised by local residents.

It appeared from the attitude of the Planning Department, who share our desire to retain Raeburn Place as a green open space, that we should attempt to satisfy the points raised. This has resulted in a complete revision of the Hotel building and the entrance thereto, and these new plans will be placed before the Planning department in September. It is hoped to have copies posted in the clubhouse shortly.

Further consultation will then take place with our immediate neighbours and we would hope to have a decision from the Planning Department by Christmas.

In 2002 he wrote that:

On the face of it, little has changed from the position we were in last October! Many people now stop me in the street to ask what is going on. My hairdresser, who works in Comely Bank, advised me some time ago that Planning Consent had been obtained. Alas, not yet.

A great deal has, in fact, been going on. The third and hopefully final re-design of the hotel building, endless meetings with the Planning Department, consultations with Historic Scotland, and an in-depth discussion and correspondence concerning the recently re-drawn flood plain of the Water of Leith. Our man in the Planning Department is now on long-term sick leave, and the cudgels have been taken up by another and so it goes on.

There is, I believe, light at the end of the tunnel. I am advised that as there have been many objectors to the proposed changes, the Planning Department have to be very sure of their ground before they are in a position not only to recommend the proposal to the Planning Committee, but also to defend that recommendation vigorously when the time comes.

I am advised that we have now reached that position and before you read this article the Application will have been before the internal planning management committee, and, hopefully, a date will be known for the formal Planning Meeting some time in October. I, for one, certainly hope so!

It was a similar story in 2003:

Those of you who are close to Edinburgh will have read in last December's papers that the proposed development at Raeburn having been passed by the City Planners was turned down by the Councillors on the Planning Committee. This after three years in drafting and redrafting the plans to finally satisfy the Planning Department.

While our partners in the development, Festival Inns Ltd, advised us immediately that they would appeal against the decision of the Planning Committee, it took until the end of May to put in place the team of experts required to handle the appeal. An impressive team led by Gordon Steel QC has now been assembled and the formal appeal to the Scottish Executive was lodged in June. That appeal process has now advanced and the date for the Appeal is set for the end of January 2004.

As part of the process in putting together our case for the Appeal the support of independent architectural opinion was sought. While our overall scheme was fully supported there were a number of issues raised which, in the opinion of the independent architects, would further enhance the planned building. This view was taken on by the developers and new plans incorporating the suggested changes have now been produced with a view to submitting a further planning application which will run in parallel with the ongoing appeal. While all this has an untidy look to it we are advised that if we are to proceed to a satisfactory outcome then this is the most expeditious way forward.

Festival Inns continue to foot the bill for the development and have now extended their support in taking on the running of the food and bar side of the pavilion together with meeting our manager's wage and a contribution to overhead costs. This has been gratefully received.

This protracted process was beginning to take its toll, and on the same page of *The Academical* as Tony Hamilton's most recent update, a report from Gordon Wallace (who had jumped out of the frying pan and into the fire by taking over as Chairman of the Sports Centre Committee immediately after his term as president of the Academical Club had finished) outlined the financial strain caused by these past three years of uncertainty. He wrote:

This is such an ideal solution to the problems of providing sports facilities at Raeburn Place in the modern day that it is worth giving the project every chance to succeed.

However, what has happened over the last 3 years, or so, is that deficit budgeting has been taking place on the basis that the go ahead for the development was just around the corner and that it was vital to keep the Sports Centre and Clubs going in the interim. The alternative would have been to close down Raeburn Place.

During the summer of 2003 this accumulated deficit had reached about £120,000 – £30,000 of loans from individual members, the central Academical Club, and a £90,000 overdraft. It was decided by the Council we could no longer count our chickens before they hatched and the combined Sports Centre and Rugby Clubs were instructed by the Council to run at break-even or better from now on. The Bank of Scotland also advised they were not prepared to increase our current overdraft on its current unsecured basis past £90,000. With the very real threat of the Academical Sports dying out at R.P. a number of Accies, who have happy memories of Raeburn Place and also experience of running it in the past, have faced up to this challenge.

Many of you will have already received Bill Menzies' invitation to join the 'Silverbacks' sponsorship scheme and this has had a good response. Ralph Lutton has revived the Lunch Club, Willie Liston the 100 Club. Despite being the age of professional sport, where some players expect payment, we are ensuring that playing subscriptions and 'match fees' are collected.

We are in sight of reaching our break-even target for the coming season despite falls in sponsorship and contributions from the SRU. But due to a hang over of creditors from last season we face a much more difficult problem in working within our overdraft.

One of the problems is due to a decline in Sports Centre/Football Club membership over the past three years, perhaps as much due to disenchant-ment with Scottish Rugby in general than the Edinburgh Accies in particular. We are not holding out the begging bowl but asking you to become involved in reviving the fortunes of arguably the most famous Rugby & Cricket Clubs in Scotland. If, though, you think Accie Rugby and Cricket have no place in the present open/'professional' set up, and Raeburn Place should be going in a different direction please let us know.

For the next four years, Gordon and Dottie Wallace gave generously of their time and money helping the football club stabilise its financial position. It was an unenviable and often unpopular job, but someone had to do it. Other club members who were working hard behind the scenes to help dig the club out of this hole included: Dave Parker, John Wright, Olly Miller, Frank Spratt, Bill Kemp, Vincent O'Donoghue, George Menzies, Walker Forsyth and Jason Parrott.

The message from Tony Hamilton in the autumn 2004 edition of *The Academical* was depressingly familiar:

While it appears that little has happened since the report in *The Academical* last year there has been considerable activity. This has revolved around the planning process together with a genuine desire to lessen the impact of the development on our neighbours.

The initial Planning Application, put forward in December 2002, for the new pavilion and extended hotel was passed by the Planning Authorities only to be turned down by the Councillors. It was decided that this decision

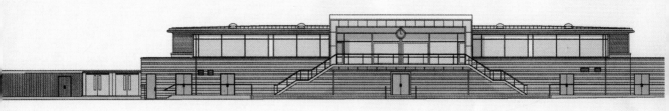

should be appealed. In preparing the appeal it became clear that there were The club house plan a number of genuine concerns expressed and in addressing these concerns our plans were basically redrawn.

In December 2003 the original scheme was put on hold and the new plans were submitted. Again the Planning professionals passed the scheme which was now supported by Historic Scotland and the Royal Fine Arts Commission.

Despite this, the members of the Planning Committee again turned down the scheme on a split vote of 6 to 5 at their meeting in June this year. It is interesting to note that the Labour vote on committee was substantially in favour with both Conservative and Lib Dems against.

We have now decided to formally appeal against this second decision and it appears likely that the appeal will be heard in January or February 2005.

In autumn 2005 Hamilton wrote:

Looking back through my papers I note that the initial correspondence regarding the development at Raeburn Place started in 1999. It seems we have not travelled far since then as there are, as yet, no new facilities in place. Our crumbling facilities are still standing (just) and we are indebted to the financial assistance of Festival Inns and the Herculean efforts of our Honorary Sports Centre Manager Gordon Wallace in keeping the place going.

Despite the snail's pace I think we are now winning. We were successful with our appeal against the City Fathers' turning down our second planning application. A full public enquiry was held in January though we had to wait until May for the result. We are indebted to Festival Inns and the impressive team assembled to explain the detail of the scheme to the reporter. I note particularly the contribution of James Simpson of Simpson & Brown Architects, who has been largely responsible for the redesign of the hotel, supporting the aims of the project and on a fine delivery at the enquiry.

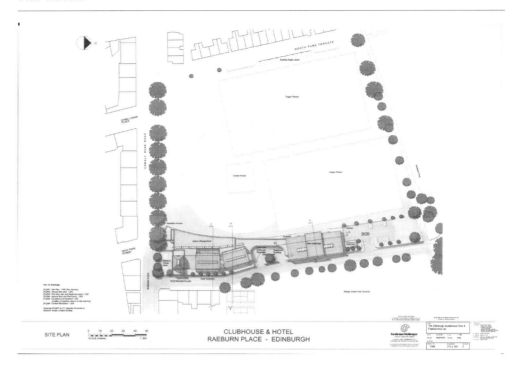

Site plan

Festival Inns then applied for a license to run the expanded hotel and the new clubhouse at the Licensing Board at the end of June. The license went through unchallenged.

During July and August we have been working through the detail of the various legal agreements which will have to be put in place to enable Festival Inns to formalise their funding proposals.

We have established three main committees to finalise the structure of the deal with Festival Inns and the leases required, detail the specification of the new pavilion and formalise the management agreement under which Festival Inns will manage the facility. All three committees have concluded their deliberations and our solicitors are drawing up the documentation. It is hoped to have the legals agreed in early October.

If this is on time then Festival Inns will conclude the work required to apply for the Building Warrant, probably a three month exercise, and with a fair wind work could begin in the early New Year.

With the 150th anniversary of the Football Club in season 2007–08, what better time to have new accommodation at Raeburn Place. Perhaps it will have all been worthwhile after all!

Progress at last, or so it seemed. In the autumn of 2006, Hamilton informed the readership of *The Academical* that:

After another year of considerable effort for all concerned, we are now in the position that a final agreement has been reached with the planners regarding the extension of the Raeburn House Hotel and the construction of our new pavilion with all the accompanying facilities. The Hotel Group have had their application for a new license approved, including the ability to run the bars and catering services in the new pavilion for the Club. The building warrant for the new works has been obtained. Of the three contractors interested in the development, one has been selected and the final stage of the contract process, the final agreement of the sub-contracted work, is now well advanced. The various legal agreements between the Club and Festival Inns have now been agreed. The proposed start date is early November [2006].

Rather than build the pavilion for the Club first, it has been decided that we must go for the savings which tackling the whole exercise at one time will provide. This has involved Festival Inns installing the provision of temporary changing and social facilities for the club for the 45 weeks which the construction of the new pavilion will take. The accommodation units have been sourced and we hope the utility companies will be able to connect up the power supplies in time for us to move operations into them before the proposed contracts start.

You never know but next year I may be writing my report for *The Academical* from the new club office in the new pavilion!

He should be so lucky! Perhaps Hamilton found it too painful to write the next update, which would explain why Academical Club president, Bill Menzies, was given that responsibility in the autumn 2007 edition of *The Academical*:

It is hard to believe that another year has come and gone, and sadly we still have to report that the building of the new clubhouse and hotel at Raeburn

Place sports ground has not yet materialised. Festival Inns, our development partners, have to date had considerable difficulties in negotiating suitable terms with a contractor to undertake the project. Considerable credit must still go again to members of our development team, and, in particular, Tony Hamilton, Frank Spratt, Roy Dury, John McLaren and Ewan Alexander for their continued perseverance to deliver this type of development, which is so important to securing the long term future of Raeburn Place and create a modern headquarters for the Academical Club.

The vision had been to have Britain's oldest rugby club ensconced in the plush surrounding of their brand new clubhouse in time for their sesquicentenary celebrations, but hold-ups caused by a combination of legal wrangling, political manoeuvring and the need for some financial juggling had made this an impossibility. The club would spend its 150th year lodged in the unfamiliar surroundings of the temporary clubhouse, which had been generously installed by Festival Inns at the southern end of the 1st XV pitch. It wasn't an ideal start to such a momentous season – but before long everyone involved in the club would have far more pressing concerns to occupy their minds.

A graphic of how the new club house and hotel extension will sit at Raeburn Place

CHAPTER THIRTY-SIX

What we are looking to build here is a club that will last another 150 years.
Ian Barnes

HAVING BEATEN THREE Premier One sides, including champions Currie, on the way to the previous season's Cup Final, there was a degree of confidence around Raeburn Place ahead of the 2007–08 season that Accies were ready for life in the top flight. There was no major recruitment drive during the summer, although the squad was strengthened for the coming season in a few key areas.

David Blair in action for Accies following his return from Sale Sharks. *Dave Patterson*

Winger Matt Coupar had returned from Watsonians. Stand-off David Blair – younger brother of Mike and third son of former club captain Robert – had come back north from Sale Sharks and originally split his time between training and playing with Accies and working with the SRU National Academy, before being offered a full-time contract with the Edinburgh professional team at the start of December. And Greig Laidlaw, another Edinburgh professional, played eight games at scrum-half and stand-off.

Joe Edwards – the father figure of the pack – had returned to New Zealand after the Cup Final. He was replaced as BATs development officer by Iain Berthinussen, former Scotland under-21 cap and Border Reivers professional. The Gala-born centre brought a wealth of experience and enthusiasm to his day job, and added class to the 1st XV back division. Unfortunately a knee injury meant that his involvement was limited to the two games at the beginning and three games at the end of the league season, plus two cup games.

A major blow two weeks before the start of the league season was the news that

Matt Coupar sprints in to score against Heriot's. *Dave Patterson*

Jamie Parker had defected to Goldenacre. As it happened, Accies played Heriot's at Raeburn Place in the first round of league matches, and this inevitably added extra spice to an already keenly anticipated encounter. The match ended in a 10-10 stalemate, with two Matt Coupar tries being cancelled out by a Marc Teague double. 'It was the right result, but we were the better team,' insisted Barnes afterwards. 'At half-time, we were looking good, but we let them off the hook in the second half. We over-cooked the goose up-front. Matt Coupar was a threat every time he got the ball, but we didn't get him into the game enough. For us it was definitely a case of two points lost rather than two points gained.'

If Barnes felt frustrated at drawing that match, it was a very different story a week later when Accies were trampled over by Melrose at the Greenyards in a 40-6 defeat.

Kiwi hooker Mark Price arrived in the

Ruaridh Bonner kicks for touch as Stuart Paterson looks on. *Dave Patterson*

Mark Price makes a break for the line to score against Hawick at Raeburn Place. *Dave Patterson*

week leading up to the next match against Hawick at Raeburn Place. He made an immediate impact in that game, scoring a try in a narrow 13-12 defeat. But at the following Tuesday training session he broke his ankle in the warm up and did not play again until the end of January.

This was fairly typical of Accies' season. By the time the team lost 27-7 to Glasgow Hawks at Old Anniesland in the fourth match of the league campaign, there were 21 members of the 1st XV squad out with medium or long-term injuries – including Sinclair Patience (broken hand), Iain Berthinussen (knee), John Berthinussen (torn tendon in foot), Greg Campbell (broken thumb), John-Michael Howison (knee cartilage damage), David Rattray (torn tendon in foot) and Paul Loudon (rib injury) – making Laura Calder the busiest physio in Scottish rugby. During the course of the season 52 different players represented the 1st XV in league matches.

Ed Stuart takes the ball into the heart of the Hawick defence as Alistair Marsh and
Nathan Pike follow in support

The situation was such that Barnes found it necessary to go overseas twice to bolster the squad. In early October, flanker Tom Stuart – younger brother of James and Ed – was lured back to Scotland from Argentina; and at the start of November, South African front-row forward Gavin Edwards was brought in to add some meat where it was most needed.

South African Gavin Edwards playing against Glasgow Hawks
during his second stint at Accies. *FotoSport*

Despite the injury crisis, the team rallied briefly with wins over GHA (16-12 at Raeburn Place) and Dundee HSFP (20-19 at Mayfield), but any hopes of escaping the relegation dog-fight were immediately put out to pasture by three painfully narrow defeats to Ayr (21-20 at Raeburn Place), Stirling County (23-21 at Bridgehaugh) and Currie (27-26 at Raeburn Place).

A 38-22 defeat to Watsonians at Myreside followed by a heartbreaking 14-12 loss to league leaders Boroughmuir at Raeburn Place left Accies equal bottom in Premier One at the half-way stage in the campaign.

Chris Dove, playing for the 2nd XV, makes a break through the Stewart's Melville defence followed by Gordi
Reid, Euan Milne, Jonathan Got and P.J. Solomon, while Phil Trodden lurks out wide. *Dave Patterson*

Greg Campbell receives an elbow in the face from Angus Martin at a lineout. *Scotsman*

Fired up as usual, Greg Campbell bulldozes his way over Olo Brown. *Scotsman*

Ed Stuart wins the ball at a lineout assisted by
Nathan Pike and Peter Burns. *Scotsman*

Tom Philip was now coaching the Accies backs, but had always insisted that he would be back playing before the season was out. After three-and-a-half years of struggling with chronic hip, back and groin pain the former Scotland centre eventually realised that goal against Melrose as Accies got the second half of their league season off to a winning start at Raeburn Place.

As Iain Morrison later explained in the *Scotland on Sunday*:

Off the pitch Philip is quiet, almost shy, but he is a different animal once the whistle blows. Against Melrose he stared Stewart [his opposite number] down at

Tom Philip in his role as coach. When he took to the field, however, he was Accies'
most destructive and penetrative player. *FotoSport*

every opportunity, repeatedly broke the line, made one try and he flew into every contact as though this match was his last. Where Philip is concerned every match could be. The man known as 'Tank' helped his club record a vital 16-8 victory that has helped them climb out of the Premier One relegation zone. Melrose coach Craig Chalmers admitted he was probably the difference between the two sides.

Dan Teague adds:

Tom's a really good technical coach. He's good at motivating guys as well because he's so emotional about how much he'd love to be playing, and it makes you think. It works well with Barney, because he's quite old school and Tom brings his expertise of playing modern professional rugby – so it gives us a bit more of a balance than we maybe had before.

Paul Arnold orchestrating play against Hawick from full-back. *FotoSport*

Nathan Pike rises against Ayr assisted by Ed Stuart and Patrick Coupar. *Dave Patterson*

This victory represented a 42-point swing from the last result between the two clubs. But this was not, as hoped at the time, a turning point in the season. A week later Accies lost 20-12 to Hawick at Mansfield Park, and after beating Glasgow Hawks (18-15 at Raeburn Place) they lost again to fellow relegation strugglers GHA (17-15 at Braidholm). Philip played in only the last of these three matches, as he was still struggling with a hamstring injury, which continued to limit his playing involvement throughout the remainder of the season. A 30-6 victory over Dundee HSFP at Raeburn Place in the last league game before Christmas put some daylight between Accies and the relegation zone – but there was still a long way to go before safety was assured.

Two games were played during the week between Christmas and New Year as part of the club's sesquicentenary celebrations. On 29 December, Accies took on a Co-optimists side containing several professionals and a clutch of players looking towards selection for the upcoming Club International matches against Ireland and Wales.

It was a close game, with the Accies leading into the final quarter, until late touchdowns from Charlie Keenan, Andrew Maxwell and Craig Wilson gave the Co-optimists a 45-31 win, which they probably deserved. Jamie Millar, Trinity's teenage scrum-half, scored the try of the match, when he came on as a replacement winger, promptly collected Ruaridh Bonner's quick line-out throw, and darted home from 30 yards along the left touchline.

Chris Kinloch on the counter-attack, supported by David Blair and Stuart Walker. *Dave Patterson*

On Hogmanay, the first recorded rugby match in Scotland was commemorated when an Academical select took on an Edinburgh University team, dressed in period outfits and playing under the original rules of the game as brought to Edinburgh by the Crombie brothers 150 years earlier. The match was split into three periods of 25 minutes, and although modern rugby instincts inevitably showed from time to tome, the afternoon was a huge success. In the end the University team won by four tries to two, despite the presence in the home ranks of such experienced campaigners as Ronnie Sloan and Ralph Lutton. Back in 1857, the team captains were solely responsible for negotiating the rules of the game before and during matches, but for the purposes of this match Malcolm Duck – Academical, restaurateur and erstwhile referee – controlled the game sympathetically and with appropriate good humour.

The Accies and Edinburgh University squads pose before the 'original rules' match. *Dave Patterson*

The 'original rules' match in full swing. *Dave Patterson*

Edinburgh University on the attack. *Dave Patterson*

With the festive fun and games out of the way, it was soon back to the far more serious task of avoiding relegation. First up was a trip west to play Ayr in appalling conditions at Millbrae. Playing with the wind and sleet at their backs during the first half, Accies took an early lead through a Greig Laidlaw penalty, but Ayr muscled their way back into the game, and after Alistair Marsh was sin-binned the home team took immediate advantage, with their scrum-half, Cameron Taylor, nipping over from the base of a dominant scrum. Good running from Tom Philip and Chris Dickie made a Greg Campbell try in the 34th minute, and Laidlaw's conversion made it 10-5 for Accies at the break – which is how it stayed until home winger Ryan Holland scored in injury time to rescue a 10-10 draw for his team. Not for the first time, Accies had dropped valuable league points right at the very end of the game. But a draw at Ayr was not to be sniffed at, and a 23-16 victory over Currie at Malleny Park a week later was even more encouraging.

Jim Oliphant spots a gap against Dundee High. Chris Dickie lies in wait on the wing.
Dave Patterson

2nd XV flanker Adam Booker makes a surge for the Dundee High line, supported by Jamie Henderson, Phil Jenkinson, Rory Ward and James Gilbert.
Dave Patterson

A heavy defeat to Watsonians (31-6 at Raeburn Place) brought Accies back down to earth with a bump, and turned the next league match against fellow strugglers Stirling County at Raeburn Place into a huge match.

Before then Accies defeated Howe of Fife 30-12 at Duffus Park in the fourth round of the Scottish Cup, but then lost 38-8 in the fifth round to new league champions Boroughmuir at Meggetland.

The Berthinussen brothers had made their long-awaited comebacks in the first of those cup games, and were both in the team for the Stirling County match two weeks later – but this could not prevent a desperately disappointing 26-21 defeat. Salvaging a bonus point from another match which should have been won was of little comfort.

A game of inches. Stuart Walker comes agonisingly close to scoring – typical of Accies' season that year. *Herald*

The misery kept on coming. Next up, in the penultimate league match of the season, were Boroughmuir – again – at Meggetland. Accies appeared to have this game won when Iain Berthinussen sprinted home from 40 metres to give the visitors a 14-13 lead with ten minutes to go – but in the 79th minute, Boroughmuir number eight Ben Fisher popped up on the left wing to score the game's decisive try (final score: 18-14).

To make matters worse, mercurial prop Peter Burns was taken out by a flying fist during a driving maul, suffering a fractured eye-socket and sinus, and a torn and detached retina – which required multiple laser surgery to save his sight and ruled him out of rugby for the next six months.

With GHA getting a bonus-point victory over Dundee HSFP at Braidholm on the same afternoon, Accies' future was no longer in their own hands. They were a point behind the Glasgow side with each team going into their last game. All they could do was beat Heriot's at Goldenacre, and hope that Stirling County – who had not yet fully extricated themselves from the relegation dog-fight – would do them a favour against GHA at Bridgehaugh.

The week leading up to the Heriot's game was tense for everyone involved at Raeburn Place, and this was reflected in a twitchy start to the match, as poor discipline threatened to derail Accies' fight for survival. The loss of Chris Kinloch with a dislocated knee after only ten minutes did not help settle nerves. At one point Heriot's stand-off Murray Strang hoisted a cross-kick rightwards, towards Marc Teague, the home team's prolific winger. His cousin, the visiting captain Dan Teague, was lying in wait:

I nailed him. The high ball was coming over and he went up for it. I was the only man within 15 yards of him and I knew I couldn't let him land because if he got his feet back on the ground he was going to score. So I took him high and early. It was a horrible challenge. I thought I was definitely off. But Marc was alright about it and the referee knew we were cousins so he let it slide. In any other game it would have been at least a sin-binning.

To make matters worse, he was injured for four weeks afterwards – he jarred his shoulder when he hit the ground – he was raging about that.

With 35 minutes played Accies were trailing 12-3, but then David Blair collected the ball on the halfway line, went outside his man and fed Paul Loudon who raced home. That reduced the gap to just two points, and a couple of minutes later Blair sent over a penalty to give his team the lead for the first time – but just when it looked like Accies were beginning to get a grip of this mach a needless penalty was conceded in front of the posts, and Heriot's scrum-half Graham Wilson sent over the easy three-pointer to restore a narrow lead at half-time.

David Blair slices through the Heriot's defence at Goldenacre. *FotoSport*

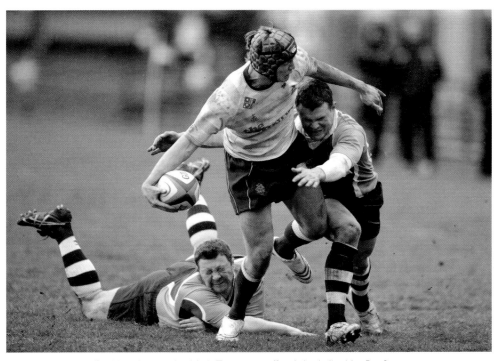

Paul Loudon evades Mark Teague to offload the ball wide. *FotoSport*

Some stern words were delivered to the team by Finlay Calder during the break, and with the wind at their backs in the second half Accies began to play with the sort of purpose required to get the win they needed. Dan Teague was immense, driving his team forward by sheer force of will. In the midfield, Paul Loudon oozed class, but even he was outshone by his centre partner Iain Berthinussen, who seemed to conjure space every time he touched the ball.

Iain Berthinussen breaks through the central midfield on his way to scoring under the posts. *FotoSport*

Three Blair penalties versus one from Wilson edged Accies into a precarious 22-18 lead – an advantage which was far too slender for comfort, especially given the team's propensity to grasp defeat from the jaws of victory. It wasn't until the 75th minute, when Iain Berthinussen skipped clear from 35 yards out and motored to a touchdown between the posts, that victory was assured.

Tom Philip congratulates David Blair upon hearing that Accies had secured their place in Premier One the following season (with a little help from Stirling County). *FotoSport*

As the game moved into injury time, David Rattray crossed for the team's third try, which immediately raised faint hopes of a four-try bonus point. With news filtering through that Stirling County were leading GHA 6-0 at Bridge-haugh, that would surely have been enough to preserve Accies' Premier One status. But despite a final flurry of desperate attacks, Heriot's held strong, and time ran out.

The team and supporters endured several nerve jangling minutes in the drizzling rain in front of the stand at Goldenacre, waiting for news from Stirling. Eventually the call arrived from Lewis Stuart, rugby correspondent for *The Times*, who was reporting on that match. Final score: Stirling County 6, GHA 0.

Accies were staying up. They had escaped relegation by the skin of their teeth – but that didn't matter a jot. There had been plenty of things wrong with Accies' season, but at the moment of truth the team had stood up and got the result they needed. The club's revival could continue.

Captain Dan Teague takes the game to the Barbarians at Raeburn Place. *Dave Patterson*

Dan Teague sums it up:

Some of the young guys came of age in that game. To be put under that sort of pressure and play your best game, rather than just playing well when no one is expecting anything more from you: that takes balls. People might say that the Heriot's boys' hearts weren't in it because they had nothing to lose

433

or gain from that match, but they definitely wanted to put us down – and I don't blame them. If the roles were reversed and that game had been to put Heriot's down, I know we would all have been gunning for it. How much would we enjoy that – it would be a cracking night out. So we had to scrap for everything we got.

That win against Heriot's was better than the Currie game the previous year. There was so much more pressure on us. No one gave us a chance of beating Currie so all we were doing was going out there and playing – but in this game we knew we had to win or everything was going to go to pot.

If we'd gone down to Premier Two it was game over. We'd have lost all the young players we had coming through, because the SRU Academy – despite what they say – do tell these guys that they have to be playing Premier One rugby, and you can bet that Heriot's and the other Edinburgh clubs would have been on the phone to all of them within 48 hours of us being relegated. All the hard work that had been put in to building up the squad would have been wiped out in one fell swoop.

It would have been really hard to come back from that. We'd have lost all the momentum that had been built up during the previous couple of seasons, we'd have struggled to retain guys, and we'd have lost a lot of money as well . . . it would have been back to square one.

With teams like Jed-Forest, Aberdeen Grammar, Stew-Mel, Haddington, Gala and Dundee High in that league, you wouldn't fancy your chances of getting out of there straight away.

Eleven days later, on Wednesday 10 April, Accies brought the curtain down on their 150th season with a match against the famous Barbarians. Stage managed with military precision by Jeremy Richardson, it was a terrific occasion, with a sell-out crowd of 3,000 cramming into Raeburn Place to watch the world's greatest invitational side take on Britain's oldest club.

Sadly for the home team, they did not quite have the experience or the class to live with a Barbarians side which might have been lacking star names but was still stuffed full of seasoned professionals, including the Edinburgh Academical international full-back, Stuart Moffat. Having said that, the home team did a lot better than the 43-0 score-line suggests.

The double-crest, specially designed for the celebration game.

The match-day ticket.

When the Barbarians cut loose they had too much pace and power for an Accies side which soldiered on manfully throughout, but it was not all one way traffic, and if the Accies boys had been able to demonstrate a little bit more composure at key moments then they could, and probably should, have got themselves on the score sheet.

The Accies and Barbarians squads. *FotoSport*

This was demonstrated with around ten minutes to go, when the Academicals launched several phases of ambitious attacks but then succumbed to a sucker punch when the Barbarians stole the ball in contact and winger Lee Best ran from his own 22 to score a try in the corner.

The teams that day were:

Edinburgh Academicals: M. Coupar; C. Dickie, P. Loudon, I. Berthinussen, D. Rattray; R. Bonner, M. Campbell; L. Niven, M. Price, A. Marsh, N. Pike, E. Stuart, J. Berthinussen, D. Teague, T. Drennan.
Replacements used: G. Edwards, J. Henderson, R. Lovett, S. Walker, P. Arnold, R. Browne, V. Satala, S. Willet, G. Laidlaw.

Barbarians: S. Moffat (Viadana and Scotland); L. Best (Worcester), M. Allen (Bedford), N. Macleod (Cardiff), C. Moragn (Bristol and Wales); R. Miller (Newcastle), N. Runciman (Worcester); D. Williams (London Welsh), G. Bulloch (West of Scotland, Scotland and Lions), Ngalu Tau (Doncaster and Tonga), J. Phillips (Bedford), P. Sidoli (Newport Gwent Dragons), T. McVie (Heriot's), G. Fessia (Sale and Argentina), G. Quinnel (Worcester).
Replacements used: A. Moretti (Viadana and Italy), B. Evans (Sale), C. Hammond (Nottingham), Ledua Jope (Army and Fiji), R. Samson (New-castle), R. Blake (Cambridge Uni.), T. Howe (Banbridge, Ireland and Lions).

Referee: M. Changleng (Gala)

Winger Dave Rattray races past former Accie Stuart Moffat

Greig Laidlaw makes a break with Lewis Niven and Nathan Pike on hand in support

Gavin Edwards finds space, supported by Alistair Marsh, John Berthinussen and Greig Laidlaw

Mac Henderson, the oldest living international player, with the Calcutta Cup (won earlier in the year by Mike Blair's Scotland team at Murrayfield) at the post-match dinner

That evening, a celebratory dinner attended by 600 club members and guests took place in a specially constructed marquee at Raeburn Place. In proposing the toast to the Edinburgh Academicals Football Club, Finlay Calder said:

When J. Montgomerie Bell, R. Craigie Bell, William Blackwood, Alex. Dunlop, D. Dunlop, W.S. Fraser, D.R. Lyall, J.H.A. Macdonald, J. Mackenzie, Duncan McNeill, Tom Patterson and J. Tod met in the offices of Robert Balfour in St Andrew Square in January 1858, I wonder if they had any idea just what impact their meeting would have on countless generations of young men – for it was they who set up the Edinburgh Academical Football Club, which has played such a key role in establishing the game throughout Scotland.

There will be some amongst you tonight wondering why I have been asked to propose this toast to the club. I must confess, when Jeremy told me there were 600 coming, those self-same thoughts went through my own mind. Why have I been sucked into this place . . . this Raeburn Place?

Well, I suppose I like the fact that the club caters for all levels of ability — from the David Blairs and Tom Philips of this world to the children of a slightly lesser rugby god, playing manfully for Adam Beasley's BATs development team, or George Menzies and Finlay Macpherson's 3rd XV. This is a club that proffers the hand of friendship no matter the background or ability.

A friend of mine far more erudite than I has summed it up. His name is Richard Escot, and he is the chief rugby writer for *L'Equipe* in Paris. Every two years, when France come to play Scotland in the Six Nations, he makes a pilgrimage down to Raeburn Place and stands at the wall next to Inverleith Pond to look across the park. I once asked him why he does this, and he said that he tries to imagine what it must have been like at that first international between Scotland and England in 1871, and imagine too all the great players who have graced this ground since 1858; and then he said: 'This is where the soul of Scottish rugby is kept.'

Ladies and Gentlemen, this soul that Richard talks about was set down by those men in Robert Balfour's office back in January 1858. Be proud of it. Cherish it. And isn't it nice to think that 150 years from now rugby will still be being played in this wonderful corner of Stockbridge?

LIST OF INTERNATIONALISTS

1871	BENJAMIN BURNS	1897	ALFRED BUCHER	1939	IAN HENDERSON
1871	JAMES FINLAY	1897	ALEXANDER ROBERTSON-	1947	DOUGLAS ELLIOT
1871	ROBERT IRVINE		DURHAM	1947	ALEXANDER WATT
1871	WILLIAM LYALL	1898	JAMES REID	1949	JOHN MACPHAIL
1871	THOMAS MARSHALL	1898	THOMAS NELSON	1950	DONALD SLOAN
1871	JAMES MEIN	1899	JOHN GILLESPIE	1951	HAMISH INGLIS
1871	FRANCIS MONCREIFF	1900	JOHN CRABBIE	1951	NORMAN MAIR
1871	GEORGE RITCHIE	1900	LEWIS BELL	1951	KENNETH DALGLEISH
1871	ALEXANDER ROBERTSON	1900	WILLIAM MORRISON	1956	TOMMY MCCLUNG
1872	LESLIE BALFOUR-	1900	PHIPPS TURNBULL	1959	STAN COUGHTRIE
	MELVILLE	1901	FRANCIS DODS	1960	PAT BURNET
1872	EDWARD BANNERMAN	1901	ROBERT NEILL	1963	BRIAN NEILL
1872	WILLIAM MARSHALL	1904	GEORGE CRABBIE	1968	RODGER ARNEIL
1873	JAMES SANDERSON	1907	JOHN SCOTT	1986	DAVID SOLE
1874	ARTHUR YOUNG	1908	HUGH MARTIN	1989	CHRIS GRAY
1875	ALEXANDER FINLAY	1911	DAVID BAIN	1989	ADAM BUCHANAN-
1875	NINIAN FINLAY	1911	RONALD SIMSON		SMITH
1875	JAMES GORDON	1911	STEPHEN STEYN	1990	JOHN ALLAN
1875	ARTHUR MARSHALL	1913	GEORGIUS MAXWELL	1990	ALEX MOORE
1875	DUNCAN ROBERTSON	1913	WILLIAM WALLACE	1992	DAVID MCIVOR
1876	JAMES GRAHAM	1914	JAMES WATSON	1992	ROB WAINWRIGHT
1876	GEORGE PATERSON	1914	ALLEN SLOAN	1992	MARTIN SCOTT
1877	THOMAS TORRIE	1914	ARCHIBALD STEWART	1994	MARGARET MCHARI
1878	GEORGE MCLEOD	1920	GERARD CROLE	1994	JEREMY RICHARDSO
1878	DUNCAN IRVINE	1921	JAMES SHAW	1994	DEREK PATTERSON
1878	WILLIAM MACLAGAN	1921	JOHN MCCROW	1995	ROWAN SHEPHERD
1879	ERROL SMITH	1921	JOHN STEWART	1996	BARRY STEWART
1880	JOHN TAIT	1922	GEORGE MACPHERSON	1997	SCOTT MURRAY
1881	CHARLES REID	1924	ROBERT MILLAR	2002	MIKE BLAIR
1881	PATRICK SMEATON	1927	WILLIAM ROUGHEAD	2002	DONNIE MACFADYEN
1881	FRANK WRIGHT	1932	FRANCIS WRIGHT	2002	STUART MOFFAT
1884	EDMUND STRONG	1933	JAMES HENDERSON	2004	TOM PHILIP
1884	CHARLES SAMPLE	1934	KENNETH MARSHALL	2005	PHIL GODMAN
1885	THOMAS IRVINE	1934	JACK WATHERSTON	2005	JAMES STUART
1886	MATTHEW MCEWAN	1936	HARVEY DRUITT	2006	DAVID CALLAM
1886	THOMSON CLAY	1936	HUGH MURRAY	2008	NICK DE LUCA
1888	HENRY STEVENSON	1937	DUNCAN MACRAE	2008	ROSS RENNIE
1888	THOMAS WHITE	1937	RAB BRUCE LOCKHART		
1894	WILLIAM MCEWAN	1939	GEORGE GALLIE		
1895	JOHN DODS	1939	IAN GRAHAM		